Crises of Political Development in Europe and the United States

STUDIES IN
POLITICAL DEVELOPMENT

1. *Communications and Political Development*
Edited by Lucian W. Pye

2. *Bureaucracy and Political Development*
Edited by Joseph LaPalombara

3. *Political Modernization in Japan and Turkey*
Edited by Robert E. Ward and Dankwart A. Rustow

4. *Education and Political Development*
Edited by James S. Coleman

5. *Political Culture and Political Development*
Edited by Lucian W. Pye and Sidney Verba

6. *Political Parties and Political Development*
Edited by Joseph LaPalombara and Myron Weiner

7. *Crises and Sequences in Political Development*
by Leonard Binder, James S. Coleman, Joseph LaPalombara, Lucian W. Pye, Sidney Verba, Myron Weiner

8. *The Formation of National States in Western Europe*
Edited by Charles Tilly

9. *Crises of Political Development in Europe and the United States*
Edited by Raymond Grew

Crises of Political Development in Europe and the United States

Edited by Raymond Grew

CONTRIBUTORS

DAVID D. BIEN
FOLKE DOVRING
JOHN R. GILLIS
RAYMOND GREW
J. ROGERS HOLLINGSWORTH
STANLEY G. PAYNE
WALTER M. PINTNER
ROMAN SZPORLUK
KEITH THOMAS
ARISTIDE R. ZOLBERG

PRINCETON, NEW JERSEY
PRINCETON UNIVERSITY PRESS

Published by Princeton University Press, Princeton, New Jersey
In the United Kingdom: Princeton University Press, Guildford, Surrey

Library of Congress Cataloging in Publication Data will be found on the last printed page of this book

This book has been composed in Linotype Caslon Old Face
Clothbound editions of Princeton University Press books are printed on acid-free paper, and binding materials are chosen for strength and durability.

Printed in the United States of America by Princeton University Press, Princeton, New Jersey

FOREWORD

THIS IS a unique book in that for the first time a group of distinguished historians have analyzed the evolution of the countries of their specialization according to a common framework of concepts developed by political scientists. The authors of this ninth and final volume of Studies in Political Development were persuaded to review the experiences of sixteen Western countries in terms of certain theoretical formulations proposed by the Committee on Comparative Politics of the Social Science Research Council in *Crises and Sequences in Political Development*, the seventh volume of this series.

The collaboration was not easy, but the results are instructive for both historians and political scientists. There is an inherent tension between the historian's sensitivity to the unique, which rests upon an abiding respect for the particulars in any situation, and the commitment of political science theorists to seek universal patterns that can only be found at a level of abstraction at which the particular is no longer sovereign. Historians are usually comfortable with generalizable concepts only if they seem to emerge as by-products of reverent treatment of the particular; at best they should be merely unexceptionable expressions of the facts themselves, or mere after-thoughts.

At the outset of this experiment in collaboration those involved knew of the vivid difference between the historian's respect for the particular and the theorist's awe of abstract ideas. Yet the problem was discounted. It seemed at first to be little different from the universal problem of science—that of testing general hypotheses against data or evidence. Indeed, it was assumed by some of the political scientists that the historians should be able to work with ease with the theoretical concepts proposed because they seem to be close to the kind of general themes which historians have long employed as they have skillfully practiced their art of "periodizing" history. It was reasoned that since historians are accomplished at identifying the essential character of historical periods and at dating their beginnings and endings, they should find it congenial to identify when particular countries might have experienced the several "crises" that the political

Crises of Political Development in Europe and the United States
0-691-07598-0/78/00000v-04$00.50/1 (cloth)
0-691-02183-X/78/00000v-04$00.50/1 (paperback)
For copying information, see copyright page

theorists had suggested as probably critical in determining the course of political development.

As Raymond Grew, who managed this endeavor with great patience and wisdom, makes clear in his introductory chapter, the historians approached their tasks with profound misgivings, wanting ever more precise definitions of the abstract concepts and advice as to how the "exceptional" events of their countries could be reconciled with abstract theories about common experiences of "ordinary" countries. There was resistance to the very idea that any form of meaningful change had or was occurring in Western societies—only ethnocentric social scientists could believe that there could be such a difference as "traditional" and "modern" societies—and to the extent that any degree of change had to be acknowledged, it was best to declare it to be idiosyncratic and certainly devoid of any overtones of being "developmental" or in any plausible way constructive. None of the historians wanted to write anything which could be construed as implying that they might believe in anything so naive as Progress. Better to remain agnostic as to whether all the examples during the last two centuries of economic growth, scientific and technological revolutions, and the development of complex human organizations from universities to health delivery systems should in any way be seen as suggesting "development" or "modernization."

It soon became apparent that the only possible bridge between respect for the reality of the particular and concern for the relevance of disciplined abstractions would have to be that most elusive of human capabilities, good judgment. Judgment is an evaluative act; it proceeds from competent understanding of the particular facts to a careful balancing of both general concepts and common sense. Those who have good judgment are neither mesmerized by facts nor intimidated by abstract concepts, and while they may play at possessing mere common sense, they in fact must have a degree of un-common sense.

Fortunately Raymond Grew selected for this enterprise historians of good judgment, who in the end rose above their distrust of abstractions. Out of their travails they contributed, as the reader will shortly discover, to an enriching of the original concepts that they were given as their tools of analysis. Indeed, each of the authors has something new and significant to say about each of the five concepts that presumably constitute the major "crises" in political development—the crises of "identity," "legitimacy," "participation," "penetration," and "distribution." As each author wrestles with all the arguments that can be marshaled as to why his country is unique with respect to each "crisis," we are, almost inadvertently, enlightened about new dimensions of essentially common human experiences. The English sense of national identity is, for example, not only obviously different from the German and the Italian, but more interestingly different from the Scandinavian and the Polish. The evolution of legitimacy in Belgium was a significantly different matter from the realization of legitimacy in Spain. By juxtaposing France's problem with legitimacy against those of most European countries and the United States, it becomes obvious why even one of the great revolutions of history was inadequate for resolving the issue of legitimacy for the French. The problems of "participation" in country after country have such interesting differences that one is left wondering why anyone could have seriously believed that participation could ever be merely a function of social class. And so it goes with each of the "crises." None was a routine matter in any country, yet all countries in varying degrees experienced each of them, and some repeatedly had the same "crisis."

The experiment of looking at Western nation building in terms of the five crises was not only enlightening for understanding Western developments, but it is also informative for appreciating what is taking place in the non-Western world. Grew observes in his introduction that the authors wavered between two versions of the identity crisis: Identity 1, a territorial concept of nationhood, and Identity 2, an ideological expression of national uniqueness; yet these are the two poles (which minimize ethnic and linguistic differences) that are the essence of nationalism in most African and Asian states of today. Nearly all of the authors describe legitimacy as being derived from a profound sense of deference to Christian religious authorities; a situation in sharp contrast to that found in present-day developing countries, where few or no prior authorities existed who had comparable claims of legitimacy. On the crisis of "penetration," the authors generally point to the path-breaking role of the church in the West, an institution with no counterpart in Asia or Africa, and where greater reliance therefore had to be placed upon the second best Western institution, the army, to achieve the functions of penetration.

Grew correctly notes that the authors generally have more difficulties in establishing significant "sequences" of the "crises" in the different national experiences. In part the problem arises because the same crisis can repeatedly return. (Even this complaint, however, is qualified by the acknowledgment that there is a "ratchet effect," that is, societies cannot go back and pretend that changes have not taken place: restored monarchies are not the same as original ones, and once "participation" engulfs the working class the power of trade unions does not easily wither.) Yet in spite of the tentativeness of the historians, it is obvious that the Western countries followed in two general "sequences": one in which legitimacy and participation were resolved early (England, Scandinavia, Belgium, and the United States) and the others in which penetration came early (Germany, Poland, and Russia).

Thanks to our authors we now have a much clearer understanding of the consequences of having experienced spontaneously the sequences of crises, as did the early developing states, or of having to self-consciously struggle with them, as have the leaders of the late developing states. Readers may, for example, come to different conclusions as to whether the British were or were not more fortunate than the people of other countries by the challenges of their various crises, but unquestionably the study of the sequences helps to explain why the British, in spite of their early mastery of the other crises, should in the end have such great difficulty with the problems of "distribution."

Each reader of this work will find in this book new insights as well as the pleasure of agreeing or disagreeing with more authorities about the histories of more countries than in any other recent work on European and American societies. The Committee is pleased that its theoretical concepts were in no case automatically and unthinkingly applied, but that they challenged the authors and led to new creative formulations about the histories of the countries we all thought we knew the best.

In the end this exercise has demonstrated that scholarship is not neatly divided between theorists and empiricists, between generalizers and specialists of the particular; but rather, that in that sizeable chasm between abstract formulation and particular cases there is room for much creative work, which demands above all the art of judgment. The Committee congratulates Raymond Grew and all of the authors of this work for exhibiting both competence within their specializations and good judgment in their combining of facts and concepts.

LUCIAN W. PYE

ACKNOWLEDGMENTS

The Authors wish to thank all the members of the Committee on Comparative Politics for their stimulus, confidence, patience, and quite extraordinary tolerance of differing views and methods. All of us owe particular gratitude to Lucian W. Pye, who worked with us most closely; but the editor's debt is much the heaviest and extends from Lucian Pye to Joseph LaPalombara, Robert E. Ward, and Bryce Wood, who helped at many stages; to Gabriel A. Almond, Leonard Binder, Samuel P. Huntington, Sidney Verba, and Myron Weiner, who gave needed support; to S. N. Eisenstadt and Stein Rokkan, who shared ideas and manuscripts, and to John A. Armstrong, who provided the kind of criticism that makes any scholarship cooperative. It is important to add that none of these people is responsible for the use we made of their advice and encouragement.

CONTENTS

Crises of Political Development in Europe and the United States

CHAPTER 1

The Crises and Their Sequences

RAYMOND GREW

Each of the following essays is an independent study of the political development of a Western nation or nations. Each was written to stand on its own as analysis and, along with a brief bibliography emphasizing works in English, as an introduction to current interpretations of each country's political history. The several authors have thus maintained a sovereignty as indominatable as that of the nations they study. At the same time, the chapters of this book employ common categories of analysis and an essentially parallel organization. Conceived comparatively, they are intended to be read together, each in the context of the others. The categories used, though not always the ways of using them, are taken from the work of the Committee on Comparative Politics of the Social Science Research Council; and this volume —the ninth in the series, *Studies in Political Development*—is also an experiment in the application of some of the Committee's ideas.

These ten studies treat the national political history of Belgium, France, Germany, the United Kingdom, Italy, Poland, Russia, the Scandinavian countries, Spain and Portugal, and the United States. Since each case has its special interest, the omissions of chapters on other important Western examples is regrettable, particularly on Austria and the Balkan countries, with their historical conflicts over nationality; on Switzerland, with its federal system, tradition of neutrality, and high standard of living; and on the Netherlands, with its early commercial and urban development and long history of representative institutions. The countries considered, however, include some whose modernization came early and some where that process has been relatively late, some that have been nations for only a century, some whose national frontiers roughly correspond with cultural and linguistic boundaries, and others where they do not; and they include the remarkable cases of Poland, which for a century and a half experienced political development not as a sovereign state but

Crises of Political Development in Europe and the United States
0-691-07598-0/78/000003-35$1.75/1 (cloth)
0-691-02183-X/78/000003-35$1.75/1 (paperback)
For copying information, see copyrgiht page

partitioned among its three powerful neighbors, and of the United States, a creation of European settlement. The states studied include examples of long-standing representative government and of durable autocracy, of nations torn by many revolutions, and of some always cited as examples of stability.

Important as this diversity is, the similarities may be more telling. All of the nations treated here have survived into the contemporary world (a very biased sample in the history of state building), meeting the needs of the present in large part with materials inherited from the past. Furthermore, the past for all of them held much in common. In close touch with each other, they shared European values, institutions, and traditions, used each other's ideas and technologies, traded and fought almost constantly. They have steadily imitated and learned from each other, and part of the interest of these essays is to see the policies, laws, parties, and administrative forms developed in one context adapted to another.

Essays in political history do not have to be essays in political development; but if the period they treat is longer than a generation, they usually are. In many respects social scientists preoccupied with modernization have not moved far from the eighteenth-century optimism of William Robertson:

> Having thus enumerated the principal causes and events, the influence of which extended to all the states in Europe, and contributed either to improve their internal government and police, or to enlarge the sphere of their activity, and to augment their national force; nothing remains . . . but to give some view of the particular constitution and form of civil government, in each of the nations which acted any considerable part during that period. While these institutions and occurrences, which I have mentioned, formed the people of Europe to resemble each other, and conducted them from barbarism to refinement, in the same path, and with almost equal steps, there were other circumstances which occasioned a difference in their political establishments, and gave rise to those peculiar modes of government, which have produced such variety in the character and genius of nations.[1]

Although confidence in progress has waxed and waned, ideas of progress have continued to underlie much of Western thought about

[1] William Robertson, *The Progress of Society in Europe*, edited and with an introduction by Felix Gilbert (Chicago, 1972), p. 97.

society. That tradition, always much attacked, is still vital enough to stir searing criticism as a centuries-old abuse of metaphor.[2] Yet liberal and Marxist ideas of how history moves, the apparent convergence of differing societies toward similar institutions and modes of production, the development of a world economy, and the actual history of European power and influence have all stimulated the extension to the rest of the world of what was once a specifically Western vision. Since World War II, the question of how societies become prosperous and politically independent, with literate populations, rational bureaucracies, and strong states, has seemed urgent. And it has been answered with scores of carefully elaborated models, theories, taxonomies, and descriptions written by analysts who, with the enthusiasm of prospectors, have sifted through the literature of political science, history, economics, sociology, and anthropology.

Often admirable and stimulating, the writings on modernization have in turn come under heavy attack. Definitions of the term are awesomely broad: "the ability to deal with continuous changes in political demands" and "a process of increasing complexity in human affairs" are among the more widely used.[3] Always there is an historian to counter that political demands are forever changing, an anthropologist to insist upon the complexity of the most "primitive" society. To argue that modernization is "a new type of 'Great Tradition' " pointing toward a worldwide civilization is at the same time to admit that the roots of the process lie in Western Europe.[4] Many reject such a view almost by definition as intolerably parochial or offensively imperialistic. Even if the term is admitted, serious conceptual and methodological problems remain. Theories of modernization tend to strain or misuse the Weberian ideal-types of traditional and modern society. As they become more sophisticated and broader, they encompass so many aspects of group living that no usable list of finite factors can be sorted out for systematic study. In most of the literature on modernization the favorite unit of analysis—the national state—is not that in which the subject of analysis, social change, occurs. And finally the very idea of modernization easily carries with it, poised to mislead or distort at every turning, a deterministic teleology that exaggerates change and attends only that part of it that points in the

[2] Robert A. Nisbet extends his criticism to contemporary developmentalism as well in *Social Change and History* (New York, 1969).

[3] S. N. Eisenstadt, *Tradition, Change, and Modernity* (New York, 1973), p. 79; David E. Apter, *The Politics of Modernization* (Chicago, 1965), p. 3.

[4] Eisenstadt, *Tradition*, pp. 203-11, 74.

right direction; theories of modernization can become relentlessly tautological. These are dangerous defects; and there are other charges to be made, nearly every one of which could be expanded into a separate study. They impose humility, induce fear, and invite a change of topic. Nevertheless, many of its most incisive critics conclude by salvaging something from the concept of modernization.[5]

The work of the Committee on Comparative Politics of the Social Science Research Council, and particularly their general statement, *Crises and Sequences in Political Development*,[6] falls within (and takes account of) the general literature on modernization, but has a more delimited focus. If it shares many of the defects and difficulties of that broader approach, it also offers some advantages. Building on the work of Almond and Powell,[7] who had extended structural-functional analysis to describe political development, members of the Committee achieved a kind of reductionist triumph: all the various functions ascribed to the modern polity by sociologists and political scientists could be reduced to just twelve. These in turn (with that somewhat suspect symmetry that seems to be part of the structural-functional aesthetic) were soon arranged into three groups. All the definitions of modernization could be taken to describe just three kinds of change: increased capacity, equality, and differentiation. The tendency toward greater political capacity, political equality, and political differentiation was the general direction of political development. In this way concepts of a political system and of political development could be integrated. Its historic functions were the system's "inputs"; development would be evidenced in general political "outputs" that could be carefully listed (procedural efficiency, universalistic

[5] Dean C. Tipps, "Modernization Theory and the Comparative Study of Societies: A Critical Perspective," *Comparative Studies in Society and History*, 15 (March 1973), pp. 199-226, in one of the ablest critiques makes most of these points and urges abandonment of the term. But note as examples of more latitudinarian approaches: Eisenstadt, *Tradition*, pp. 98-112; Samuel P. Huntington, *Political Order in Changing Societies* (New Haven, 1968), pp. 32-78, and "The Change to Change," *Comparative Politics*, 3 (April 1971), pp. 283-321; Joseph LaPalombara, ed., *Bureaucracy and Political Development* (Princeton, 1963), pp. 9-14; and Anthony D. Smith, *Theories of Nationalism* (New York, 1971), pp. 41-64, 109-50.

[6] Leonard Binder, James S. Coleman, Joseph LaPalombara, Lucian W. Pye, Sidney Verba, and Myron Weiner, *Crises and Sequences in Political Development* (Princeton, 1971).

[7] Gabriel A. Almond and G. Bingham Powell, Jr., *Comparative Politics: A Developmental Approach* (Boston, 1966).

laws, secularization, and so on) and that tended toward increased capacity, equality, and differentiation.[8]

Between these inputs and outputs lay a process of political transformation, complex in practice and often incomplete, involving conflict; this process, the committee hypothesized, could be understood in terms of certain crises or areas of critical change. After some refinement, these crises came to be considered five in number and to be labeled Identity, Legitimacy, Participation, Penetration, and Distribution.[9] Initially, each was seen primarily as a link connecting certain sets of political functions to enlarged capacity, equality, and differentiation; but these crises, once labeled, were also objects for study in themselves. If all modern polities dealt with change in the same critical areas, a basis for comparison among them might be established. Different political systems would, of course, have handled these crises in different ways and with different effects. It was not certain that all societies would necessarily have experienced all the kinds of crisis; none presumably, except in times of revolutionary change, would face crises in all areas at once. Perhaps, the Committee reasoned, the sequence in which a nation resolved these crises was related to the kind of political system with which it ended up and to the relative ease with which it became a "modern" polity. The concept of a sequence of crises might strengthen the dynamic element in an analysis that still bore some of the static qualities of the structural-functional categories from which it derived.

With these possibilities in mind, the Committee invited a group of historians to meet and discuss the application of these ideas not to current events in the Third World, their usual target, but to the record—both longer and better investigated—of Western modernization. Despite some mutual suspicion and disappointment, the two groups found their joint efforts stimulating; from that meeting developed the correspondence, planning, and subsequent conference that resulted (far more slowly than we had intended) in this book. Thanks to the SSRC, the authors were able in candid and critical discussions to go over each other's work, noting problems methodological and spe-

[8] This evolved into the "Paradigm of the Modernization Syndrome and the Crises of Political Development" presented in Binder *et al.*, *Crises and Sequences*, p. 65. For a quite different application of political function, see Robert T. Holt and John E. Turner, *The Political Basis of Economic Development* (Princeton, 1966), esp. pp. 50-51.

[9] They are conveniently described in Binder *et al.*, *Crises and Sequences*, p. 299.

cific, establishing with some excitement the common terms we could accept and the limits of our partnership.

Perhaps with some relief, the authors of these essays recognized that they were not dealing with anything so grand as an integrated social scientific theory, tightly woven with prescribed regularities and predicted causes. The Committee's schema uses a vocabulary common to the social sciences that draws with comfortable looseness upon the familiar, thus avoiding endless and artificial definition. It does point to some "central questions," and invites careful comparison in the sense that many have called for.[10] Better yet, it is historical, not only in the sense that interest in sequence emphasizes timing and historical context, but in the sense that "the outcome of a crisis can affect the system's capability for dealing with subsequent crises. Political experience is an integral part of political development."[11] Different outcomes and resolutions are permitted, and there is room after all for the "concrete particularity of history."[12] The five categories of crisis have the further advantage that they avoid, or allow the analyst to avoid, fashionable assumptions about the state as a cancer, or about any inevitable relations between the state and the people, an elite and the masses, or centers and peripheries. The crises are really five categories of crucial social and political relationships that invite discussion of who shares in what way in what aspects of politics at any given time. There is also reason to think that case studies such as we were invited to make offer a fruitful approach,[13] and there is at least some formal appropriateness in applying Western ideas of development to the Western experience. Finally, development is a gentler, more open term than modernization; and the focus on politics further reduces the temptation to claim too much. It turns from the implication of explaining the course of history and expounding theory to more modest concern with actual politics[14] and allows for the fact that, especially

[10] Semour M. Lipset and Stein Rokkan, eds., *Party Systems and Voter Alignments* (New York, 1967), pp. 1-2.

[11] The comment is from one of the most interesting applications of the Committee's concept of crises, Peter H. Smith, *Argentina and the Failure of Democracy: Conflict among Political Elites, 1904-1955* (Madison, 1974), p. 90. Note the earlier call for this sort of attention to history in Lucian W. Pye and Sidney Verba, *Political Culture and Political Development* (Princeton, 1965), pp. 554-55.

[12] Nisbet, *Social Change*, p. 263.

[13] Two of the best examples are Barrington Moore, Jr., *Social Origins of Dictatorship and Democracy* (Boston, 1966); and Robert E. Ward and Dankwart A. Rostow, *Political Modernization in Japan and Turkey* (Princeton, 1964).

[14] See Huntington, *Political Order*, p. 79, and the review of that book by Joseph LaPalombara in the *Yale Law Journal* (June 1969), pp. 1253-57.

in the West, political forms and demands and ideologies are often more similar than the social structure or economic conditions in which they operate. For the most part we have written as if the Committee's aim had been merely to provide a framework for comparative analysis of European political history.

Such flexibility is achieved at some cost. Eager to take advantage of the former, the authors of the essays in this volume may well have increased the latter. Explicit in the Committee's thought is the idea that political change has a direction—toward greater equality, capacity, and differentiation. In these essays those qualities, when mentioned at all, are usually attached either to very particular or very long-term changes. We, at least, have not found the empirical measures of them we once imagined.[15] Implicit in the Committee's thought is the suggestion that similar challenges may lead to different responses: but the essays that follow also allow for the reverse, for similar responses used to meet quite different challanges. The direction of historical development is further obscured.

We sought little uniformity as to the "stage" of development in each nation's history that should be treated, set no rules as to the chronological coverage to attempt. There is something suspect, after all, in the fact that the stage one studies almost always turns out to be "the transitional one," usually from "traditional" to "modern" society. We agreed to carry the discussion to the post-World War II period, and to try to avoid suggesting that present politics are history's goal. We could find little basis, however, for saying in advance how much history should be included. In Europe, at least, a truly traditional world is as hard to discover as society before the social contract. Medieval governments clearly possessed many of the attributes usually listed as modern,[16] and much critical development preceded the modern period. Most, but not all, of these essays emphasize the nineteenth century, the period in which the Western state, well established in its modern form, faced pressing problems of mobilization, participation, and stability in societies becoming more urban and industrial.[17] But each author chose the time span that seemed to him best for discussing

[15] Almond and Powell, *Comparative Politics*, pp. 190-94.

[16] Binder *et al.*, *Crises and Sequences*, pp. 64-65; Huntington, "The Change to Change," pp. 287-88.

[17] Robertson would have found that unhistorically narrow. He concedes that the state began to assume a new form in the age of Charles V, but later notes, "two great revolutions have happened in the political state, and in the manners of the European nations. The first was occasioned by the progress of the Roman power; the second by the subversion of the Roman Empire," *Progress of Society*, pp. 4, 7.

a particular country's pattern of political development. Analysis was thus allowed to build from the inside out, its scope determined by historiographic tradition and individual choice rather than imposed uniformity. The similarities that emerge therefore gain in significance, but this very flexibility threatens to erode further the sense of sequences among crises.

In some respects we did find the Committee's approach restrictive. Even within politics, the role of foreign relations is so central to national development that some contributors lamented the lack of a category that could be called crises of sovereignty. Survival, simply maintaining the state against its neighbor, can be a dominant function. Nor do the crises aid much in establishing the relation between politics and its environment—geography (if only Poland had had England's island!), economic and military competition with other nations, the effects of foreign influences, the role of ideas, social structure, economic organization, or culture. The historians in this project had been critical of the category of "integration" subsequently dropped by the Committee as too indistinct from the other crises, and they favored its being eliminated. But in their own essays they assess the relationship between state and society in a variety of ways. Nor are the instances studied always restricted to national states. It is not certain, after all, that the cases considered or the ways they are treated are entirely comparable, although our mutual influence on and criticism of each other's work may, more than method, have moved us closer to that goal.

Our greatest difficulty was with the concept of political crisis itself. The historian's tendency is to start with events as a kind of social sample to be analyzed, and the definition of a crisis as *any serious threat to the functioning of a political regime* has the breadth to encompass most of those "crises" traditionally included in the historical literature. It also allows stress on the element of conflict that is usually part of such crises, while inviting one to see events through the eyes of historical actors. One could imagine a very traditional seminar on Bismarck's policies comfortably conducted in these terms. But, by itself, even that definition of a crisis may be too narrow. The threats to a system as well as fundamental changes in it are often masked by custom, imperception, or political skill. Historical figures saw threats historians now discount, and overlooked some that later proved serious. If the emphasis on self-awareness in the process of political change seems valuable, the fact remains that the historian must not be dependent on the judgment of dead politicians. Furthermore, the idea of threat raises problems—how grave a threat over how long a period of time; politics, like life, is always dangerous—that are no easier to handle than the initial question: when is an apparent crisis critical to the process of development?[18] Nor should so important an historical process be assessed merely in terms of crisis management, whether it is "successful" or not. There is not necessarily much connection between the course of historical development and the dully instrumental issue of whether a government stays in office.

The first definition, then, though useful, was supplemented by a second: a "crisis" was also indicated by *an important change in the way politics worked*, by new institutions or changes in the political process; it does not matter whether these changes are "defensive" or "innovative," but they must now appear to have been *in some sense irreversible*. In many respects such a major institutional change in the various modes Binder elaborates[19] seems the best single sign of a crisis faced, but there can also be critical changes in a political system—changes of access or belief, for example—that use old institutions essentially unaltered. Changes in the political process, if not institutional, are likely to be so subtle a reflection of society that their very nature remains a subject of endless debate; and if it is established that a specific change has never been reversed, how do we determine whether the durability of the new direction was inherent in the change itself or the result of subsequent and perhaps unrelated changes? Broadened to include both institutional and processual change, the definition has the merit of shifting attention from events to the political system; but it encourages an exaggeration of discontinuity, tempts one toward the traditional-modern dichotomies we wanted to avoid, and still implies that critical changes in political development necessarily come in sharp, episodic bursts, although we know they need not.[20]

This is avoided by a third definition that considers the crises—identity, legitimacy, penetration, participation, and distribution—*a typology of the problems governments face*. In practice, the transmutation of "crises" into problems often permitted a far richer analysis of how politics operated in a particular society. That analysis had to consider slow or unnoticed change, to search for changes that might have occurred but did not, and for real threats that were not faced. The definitions of "problem-areas" proposed by Sidney Verba[21] were,

[18] See Verba in *Crises and Sequences*, p. 307n.
[19] *Ibid.*, p. 69; cf. *ibid.*, p. 300.
[20] *Ibid.*, p. 64.
[21] *Ibid.*, p. 298-99.

in fact, close to those our contributors employed (except in the case of identity, where his definition seemed unnecessarily restrictive). They may emerge from within the society, from government and politics, or from outside the nation. They may be so grave as to cause (or threaten) a breakdown in political function or of a whole regime; but they also may be ignored, yet pass away, or be adequately met, or fortuitously forfended (the response can precede the challenge —a dialectic is not required in the Committee's schema). To replace the concept of crises with the problems that governments face is to weaken the model of development in favor of a set of categories[22] descriptive of what governments do. That still permits significant comparison, and it allows for greater historical variety. Problems, however, may be harder to identify than crises in a way all analysts can accept; crises are likely to be manifest in those revolutions or breakdowns promoted to boldface in everyone's chronological chart. To ask scholars to consider the history of these problems, simply because it invites them to look at old questions in a new way, is likely to produce stimulating results. There is no firm assurance that they will all write about the same things.

We agreed in the interest of empiricism to use all three conceptions of a crisis—a serious threat, an irreversible change, a political problem. Crises such as the Dreyfus Affair, occasions when many forces of discontent suddenly come together, might or might not have a lasting effect. They could not be eliminated from consideration *a priori*. Similarly, changes in suffrage or administration might be fundamental even if no crucial threat seemed to have required them. An unresolved problem of inadequate taxes or ineffectual representation might drag on without resolution, to be affected less by political acts than by such social changes as increased wealth or literacy.

We needed all three definitions of crises, but none of them included very objective criteria for distinguishing major crises from minor. We considered an effort to establish more specific, possibly quantitative, indicators of critical change, and we yearned for a Richter scale of crisis intensity; but available data would not consistently support such precision, nor did this initial task require it. The quantitative indicators we do not have in forms that facilitate comparison will provide analytic power only when combined with theories not yet elaborated. In

[22] It seems better not to call them variables, reserving that term for the more carefully defined phenomena that fall within these categories and avoiding the implication that the crises are always either dependent or independent variables.

the meantime there is something to be said for making the most of the insights we already have rather than abandoning them in the name of an objectivity we cannot attain. It seemed to us wiser, for example, to assess penetration in terms of the range of activities governments attempted, the connections between administrators, local notables, and national interests, and the policies pursued rather than to work exclusively from harder (but scarce) data of uncertain implications on the organization of field administration and bureaucracy.

Identifying crises (and grandly labeling some as more important than others) remained an assessment at once highly subjective and yet fundamentally shaped by the enormous literature on the history of each country. Each author would deal with periods and events that literally hundreds of scholars have agreed were critical. When he went against common assessments, as we hoped he might, he would always have to make a special case. In short, we found the looseness (or flexibility), the subjectivity (or breadth) that the Committee on Comparative Politics noted in its own work essential to our efforts to apply the categories of crisis to the history we knew. We set out to see if it was true or useful that these five crises include most of what modern governments are required to do; that political changes and problems can be understood in terms of these five categories; that the questions, dissatisfactions, and conflicts centering in any one of these categories tend to rise or fall at different times; that as they rise in salience, there is likely to be significant stress within the political system; that responses to that stress tend to shape national politics; that the relationship of one problem (or crisis) to others through time casts light on or maybe even describes political development. The standard of a model, one expert has suggested, is that it should be low in rigor and high in "combinational richness."[23]

At first, the difficulties of putting complex events in any one of five pigeonholes (even when promisingly called crises) seemed more formidable than recognizing a crisis in the first place. These categories deal with quite diverse aspects of politics, and each—the social psychology of national identity, the traditions and values underlying legitimacy, the concrete institutional signs of participation, the more abstract problems of the relationship between society and government involved in penetration, and the connection to social structure implied by distribution—invites quite different measures. There were at least three obvious ways of sorting out crises. One was to establish conven-

[23] Karl W. Deutsch, *The Nerves of Government* (New York, 1963), pp. 16-18.

tional definitions: questions of voting are always matters of "participation," taxes belong to "distribution," and so on. Another was to assign the category in terms of how people agitated and governments responded: nationalist movements may have evoked aspects of all the crises, but the historical actors clearly considered problems of "identity" the central ones. A third approach would simply ask the historian to determine which of the five categories provides the best understanding of a set of events: a system of secular education, for example, might be by definition a matter of "distribution," have been handled by contemporaries as a test of "legitimacy," and yet justifiably be treated by historians as basically a matter of "penetration" or of "identity." Once again we sought to make a virtue of difficulty by trying in general to apply these tests simultaneously. When a crisis seems to fall in several categories, it is up to the historian to say whether this results from loose and overlapping definitions, is the sign of significant complexity, or indicates a particularly intractable crisis. A close reader of our volume will also note that different authors emphasize rather different aspects of a given category, particularly legitimacy. Although such variations may simply follow from vagueness, they may reflect reality; perhaps the roots of legitimacy (more, say, than of distribution) do vary from polity to polity.

This use of multiple definitions to recognize when crises occur and what kind they are has some merit besides candor. It asks the contributing historians to place their judgments in the context of what other scholars have written, and reduces the likelihood of overlooking points of major developmental change by providing several ways for recognizing crises and several tests for which of the five sorts of crisis was most significantly affected. The concept of "crises" being "resolved" has faded; one is merely looking at problems that at a given moment are (or seem) more or less pressing. For better or worse, most of the crises we emphasize have long held their place in historical tradition, and the sequences deduced from them are relative more than absolute, a chronology of salience more than clear sequence. None of our authors believes that all other historians would have to use these categories of analysis in precisely the same way or with identical results. Even so, some patterns of salience and sequence and change emerge with sufficient strength to be provocative.

The following ten chapters of this book are to be read, then, as brief discussions of the history of government in some sixteen Western nations. (Dovring writes about five Scandinavian states, Payne about

Spain and Portugal, Gillis and Szporluk give some attention to Austria.) Each chapter, including this one, is divided into four parts: introduction, the five crises, the sequence of crises, conclusion. These essays by no means limit themselves to establishing the sequence of crises,[24] and they generally take the crises to be less an explanation than a means of identifying aspects of political systems that particularly deserve explanation. They are historical not merely because most of the authors are historians, but because the subject requires them to be for the sorts of reasons Merle Fainsod has noted.[25] They do not assume that the process of political development has an end, and certainly not that it has been reached. Comparative in intent, they may be read in any order or, with caution, contrasted section by section; for the first point in making comparisons is the isolation of important analytic problems, and to that end the "differences arising from similarities" are often most fruitful.[26]

Crises

Despite their variety, these essays are part of a common enterprise, just as this volume itself is part of a series. To the approximations and suggestions of a score of scholars, ten more here add their judgments as to how the ideas of the larger undertaking apply to the political history of some European nations and of the United States. There should be some cumulative effect in so much effort, and that invites some general, even if personal, comment. In the course of our work we have further stretched the concept of crisis. Great crises, William James once wrote, show us how much greater our vital resources are than we had supposed. It would be nice to think that the five crises generously bequeathed us by the Committee on Comparative Politics had led to such a demonstration. But should the essays in this volume be thought to contain interesting or even important insights and interpretations, there is no way to tell what part of that is due to the skill of the player and what part to the cards he was dealt. Identity, legitimacy, participation, penetration, and distribution, however indeterminate, are categories for analysis; but crisis remains a metaphor. That is not all bad (Ortega y Gasset called the metaphor man's most

[24] Few authors, apparently, would be willing to; note Lipset and Rokkan, eds., *Party Systems*, p. 30.

[25] In LaPalombara, *Bureaucracy and Political Development*, p. 239.

[26] Aidan Southall's phrase, cited by Sylvia L. Thrupp, "Diachronic Methods in Comparative Politics," in Raymond Grew and Nicholas H. Steneck, eds., *Society and History: Essays by Sylvia L. Thrupp* (Ann Arbor, 1977), p. 315.

fertile power). Metaphors can inspire, but they cannot be tested. The term *crisis*, with its implications of pathological precision, is used in this book for the same reason an inheritance is still called an estate—a tradition is honored by extending its vocabulary to cover different circumstances. The five *categories* of crisis, on the other hand, hold up rather well; and the Western experience of them analyzed here suggests some points about each.

IDENTITY

On the whole, the extension from local loyalties to regional and national identity has been a relatively smooth, usually slow, development in the West, aided by cultural traditions as well as political and religious institutions rooted in the middle ages. Linguistic, cultural, and political boundaries have rarely coincided perfectly; but the resultant conflicts should not be confused with those of new nations seeking to establish the very possibility of a national identity.

Nationalism, too often treated as an autonomous force, is usually a response to other needs, a means of mobilizing support for such things as increased participation, social mobility, economic growth, or protection against threatening change. It follows that identity becomes a crisis when old political systems face challenges, internal or external, that require higher levels of public support. The identity crisis depicted in Russian novels of a nobility caught between two worlds proved politically important only as other crises placed new demands upon the system. Shared geography, language, culture, and historical experience do not of themselves produce political mobilization. For that, special institutions, benefits, and force appear to have been necessary; and a nation's subsequent political history, more than its cultural ties, seem to shape the form and level of mobilization.

The importance of identity does not mean that the political boundaries of national states are necessarily fixed or historically predetermined. Neither Portugal, long subject to Spain, nor Scotland, independent and then subject to England, lost its identity or found foreign rule intolerable. The present boundaries of the Scandinavian states (or of Belgium) could not have been predicted on the basis of geographic, linguistic, or ethnic factors, nor from earlier political arrangements. We have no laws to explain why the rule of Provence from the Ile de France came to seem less foreign than the rule of Wales from England or Catalonia from Castille. A dominant urban center that is an economic and cultural capital (London, Paris, Stockholm) appears to strengthen identity in comparison to nations in which the political capital (Madrid, Rome, Washington) is challenged for leadership in other spheres by other cities. And long traditions of political consciousness in the West make direct challenges to identity, such as those once attempted by the radical left in Europe, unlikely to succeed.[27] Because of the similarities and mutual familiarity of European cultures, even the most resented of foreign rule has rarely proved as disruptive of traditional identities within Europe as in Europe's colonies. Even in states long established (and contrary to most expectations), linguistic conflict appears to have increased in the twentieth century as social and economic demands are strengthened by evocations of regional identity.

Because national identity provides an effective basis for mobilizing increased support, national governments have sought to invoke it over a wide area, across social classes, and for an extended period of time. In the process political forms come to be related to social purposes, and identity to a political ideology. In Britain this occurred through the Reformation, civil war, and the constitutional arrangements of 1688; more intensely in France and the United States through their eighteenth-century revolutions. This second aspect of identity,[28] an ideological one, which deserves to be distinguished from the first, can be called Identity-2. It may be, as Payne implies, that Spain never fully developed an Identity-2, making the Spanish Civil War in part a battle in which political ideologies were confused with national identity. States formed in the nineteenth century (often with liberal values honored if compromised) generally developed a less intense Identity-2, which German governments tried to strengthen through secularist conservatism, and eventually with racial and totalitarian doctrines. Mussolini sought to remove the liberal component of Italian identity and to replace it with an ideology of his own manufacture that would allow increased mobilization. Belgium's relatively weak Identity-2 increased her vulnerability to linguistic challenge. The United States, on the other hand, is a rare example of a nation with a strong Identity-2 but weak traditional identity, or Identity-1 (marked by the erosion of WASP pretensions to represent an older, nonideological identity).

The boundaries of traditional identity are likely to be vaguely geo-

[27] Binder *et al.*, *Crises and Sequences*, p. 119.

[28] Many other distinctions can, of course, be made. See the multiple definitions in Smith, *Theories of Nationalism*, pp. 153-91.

graphic and ethnic; the boundaries of ideological identity, while building on the former, are primarily those of belief. Thus Identity-2 comes to be treated as if a matter of right choice (allowing for naturalized citizens), and may come to cut across Identity-1, dividing a nation or including as part of identity transnational ties of religion, race, class, or party membership. Democratic politics, by increasing the importance of broad political mobilization and by bringing to the fore interests and values little acknowledged in the older sense of identity, are likely to open up a crisis of cultural and then ideological identity in which competing factions seek, by redefining national identity, to exclude their opponents. In the late nineteenth century and early in the twentieth, conservative groups in particular tried in this way to assure their survival. Thus the propaganda leagues of Imperial Germany, anti-Dreyfusards in France, and anti-Semites everywhere sought to place liberals and socialists outside the nation, as liberals had threatened to do with aristocrats and Catholics.

Religion has been central in the development of identity in European states, part of the very conception of England, Ireland, Poland, Prussia, Russia, Spain, and the Scandinavian countries. And Christianity has remained tied to modernization and change as well as to tradition. But these relationships, so important in the formation of identity, often led to serious conflict as a more ideological identity developed, especially where the church was not Erastian and where the elites with whom it was closely associated came under attack. Thus the conflicts between church and state in the nineteenth century were—outside Great Britain, Russia, Sweden, and the United States—bitterly divisive, both threatening identity and placing new demands upon it.

The establishment of a national identity requires that the extremes of social conflict be overcome; only when the autonomy of the Polish aristocracy was reduced and modernization began under non-Polish rulers (after Poland was partitioned among her neighbors) did Polish identity become a political force. Similarly, social and political conflicts can reopen issues of identity seemingly resolved, as has happened in Belgium or Weimar Germany. Nearly everywhere the dominant national identity is subject to local challenge—in some Wales, Brittany, or Tyrol. When accompanied by the social tensions of modernization, these challenges may—in a Catalonia, Sicily, or Bavaria—lead to powerful movements rejecting identities apparently well established. There may, in fact, be a tendency when other elements of social integration are weak to increase the psychological satisfactions sought from identity, making it more critical in times of social change.[29] In Western history the meaning of political identity is at least as subject to rapid change as is any of the other categories of crisis.

At the same time, the potential for political mobilization that follows from a common identity often tempts political elites to provoke an identity crisis, or to meet conflicts first raised in other terms in the apparently more durable terms of identity. Once the polity is established, identity is the crisis preferred by those concerned to maintain their position—by conservatives since the mid-nineteenth century, by a Stalin, or by contemporary regionalists threatened by new waves of change.

LEGITIMACY

Of the five crises, legitimacy is the most general (and perhaps the most awkward to apply to non-Western cultures). The European concept of the state and its legitimacy is associated with traditions of religion, authority, law, social hierarchy, and community, and is analyzed in an extensive theoretical literature. Even in the most prolonged crises of legitimacy—in Poland or in Spain—the concept survived, much as the state itself has often survived violent changes of government. So strong is this sense, so strong are the practical reasons for acquiescing in the power of the Western state, that a kind of legitimacy can be acquired with the passing of a few years in which a government (such as Prussia or Austria in Poland) functions reasonably effectively. A government's claim to legitimacy is greatly strengthened by surviving through a great international challenge (military and/or political), as happened to Britain in the French Revolution, Britain and Belgium in 1848, the Third Republic in World War I, or the Soviet Union in World War II.

Since the French Revolution, Western governments have usually rested their legitimacy on a combination of custom, legal compacts, formal procedures, institutional expressions of public sentiment, and effective functioning. The political system's interest in keeping the sources of legitimacy diffuse reflects the fact that systematic, wide-

[29] This would fit with roots of the term that lie in Erik Erickson's theory of an adolescent crisis of identity. See Pye and Verba, *Political Culture*, pp. 529 ff. But note that the common estimates by political scientists of the strength of identity in Britain and Italy, for example, differ from those of Thomas and Grew in this volume.

spread attacks on a government's legitimacy have also long been a real possibility in Western political life. Each country has had its own experience of revolutionary doctrines, radical movements, and moments of broad political mobilization against dominant elites. A wide range of conflicts have proved capable—in the France of 1848, Italy of 1922, or more frequently in Spain—of producing that impotence of authority that becomes a crisis of legitimacy. Yet legitimacy, to be effective, need not be unanimously or wholeheartedly accepted, a comfort that no French regime has enjoyed in almost two centuries.

Modern governments have often sought to conflate legitimacy with their form of ideological identity (parliamentary procedure in liberal regimes, service to the goals of a single party in totalitarian ones), but the two are never identical. Legitimacy requires less of its subjects—acceptance of the right to rule—and in each society depends upon some restraint, even if vague and unstated, and some association of political power with the accepted social structure. From the Soviet Union to the United States, few governments could reverse their present religious policies without opening a serious crisis of legitimacy. The legitimacy sufficient to maintain a government's authority in quiet times may, of course, prove inadequate in times of crisis; but social change itself always threatens to widen the dangerous gap between real centers of social influence and established political institutions. As governments are expected to produce ever greater benefits, the risk increases that their legitimacy will be weakened by their failure to fulfill popular expectations—which, of course, is one basis for radical movements.

It may be, as Thomas points out, that what looks like legitimacy is simply the weakness of those who would overthrow the system; but it is also true that all political crises can end as crises of legitimacy.[30] Western states have attempted to forefend against this danger by treating challenges to their rule in other terms: by meeting challenges from the church in terms of penetration or participation, class conflicts with changes in participation and distribution. But failure to fulfill its assigned functions, especially military defeat, has proved increasingly fatal to the claims of legitimacy. Only victors escaped crises of legitimacy in 1918; and Italy, but barely a victor, suffered one soon after. Short of collapse, however, the emphasis upon legitimacy has been a powerful support of continuity in Western politics.

[30] Binder *et al.*, *Crises and Sequences*, pp. 135-37.

PARTICIPATION

The progressive broadening of suffrage in the nineteenth century gives the impression that participation crises have clear resolutions tending in the direction of steadily increased participation. Seen more broadly, however, the Western experience has been more cyclical and complex. Centralization, for example, which often reduces participation, has also been part of the effort to make society more democratic by reducing the dominance of local interests. Demands for participation may thus lead to centralization, followed by waves of decentralization in which some functions are reassigned to particular groups or regions. Classic issues of direct participation or representation thus recur in changed circumstances. Despite their similar participatory institutions, Western societies differ considerably as to what issues are properly matters for decision by the electorate, and those institutions function quite differently in states of different social structure, levels of communication and literacy, and political tradition—a point stressed in the discussion of Spain but valid everywhere. Even the trend to mass parties leaves significant diversity as to their roles.[31]

In fact, political parties are viewed with some ambivalence in most societies. Mediators between participants and the state, they tend to imitate the state's organization, while reflecting the social structure of society: bureaucratized and distant from the masses in Germany; fragmented and federal in the United States; clustered around the gentry and later the labor unions in Britain; instruments of clientelism in Italy; seemingly national and centralized in France, where in practice they are highly localized and individualistic. Internal divisions or poor leadership within political parties can, by depriving a large part of the electorate of an effective voice, in itself lead to a crisis of participation. And many a Western society has experienced these problems through the conflicts within governing parties or systematic exclusion of large socialist and communist parties.

Indeed, the exclusion from participation of important groups—debarred by standards of wealth, doctrine, or sex—has been an important element in Western political development, producing organized, nonparticipating oppositions whose existence threatened to make conflicts over participation into crises of legitimacy. In nineteenth-century Germany and Italy such exclusions reinforced class conflict and cynicism

[31] Huntington, "The Change to Change," p. 288.

about representative government, whereas in Great Britain early and strongly institutionalized participation led even extraparliamentary associations to look, at least initially, to Parliament. But everywhere shifts in social relations have proved likely to create pressure for parallel changes in effective participation,[32] and resistance to those changes has been a classic source of crisis.

In all societies some interests, regions, and classes tend to be better represented than others; but participation itself is not limited to political assemblies and voting. Other forms of influencing policy—from petitions and demonstrations to organized interest groups prepared to negotiate with those in authority—are important avenues of participation. Such activities can reinforce or undermine established institutions, provide flexibility, or provoke crises of participation. It may even be useful to distinguish societies in terms of the relative importance in political decisions of formal representative institutions as against more informal extraparliamentary participation. If one imagines a quotient based on the decision-making role:

$$\frac{\text{formal institutions of participation}}{\text{other institutions and interest groups}}$$

then different states might be grouped according to those with a high quotient (England, France?), one near unity (United States, Belgium?), and those with fractional quotients (Italy, Wilhelmine Germany?).

Although it has become commonplace to distinguish between limited suffrage—the nineteenth-century recognition that institutionalized if limited participation was both legitimate and useful to the state—and mass politics, the importance of increasing demands for participation in other institutions (unions, schools, businesses, professional associations, and so on) must not be overlooked. These later demands, as much as those aimed at representative government, have made crises of participation the most recurrent of political crises in Western society. The ideal of democracy continues to haunt institutionalized reality.

PENETRATION

The great model of institutional penetration in Western society was the church; and as states have sought to penetrate further, they have clashed with the church on matters of order and justice, civil records, regulation of marriage and the family, and provisions for education

[22] Binder *et al.*, pp. 168-69.

and public welfare. In the nineteenth and twentieth centuries conflicts on these matters were among the bitterest in society. Although the need to support large military establishments, the social effects of industrialization, and increased expectations of administrative efficiency and public welfare pushed the state to attempt ever greater penetration, each society developed its characteristic inhibitions of penetration through its social structure, liberal or traditional values, and the compromises of politics. Thus penetration in practice is rarely so complete or effective as the claims of the state make it seem.

For useful comparison between nations, it may be necessary to distinguish the various aspects of penetration: bureaucratic efficiency—the ability to have commands carried out; social extent—the geographical, social, or institutional boundaries beyond which the state has only restricted or indirect access; public purpose—the range of activities normally conducted by the state. Often one of these aspects may be so problematic as to seem in itself the effective measure of penetration, as in Scandinavian states extending into a sparsely settled frontier, or in Russia, challenged by vast territory and poor communication. Limited by class privileges and liberalism in Britain, where the state reached into society through the landed classes, penetration was differently limited (and therefore different in content) from Germany, where social fragmentation was the major constraint, or Italy, where client networks tied to local elites were the primary barrier. Yet the aspects of penetration are usually connected. Efficiency is likely to require a civil service, creation of which reduces the privileges of old elites. Shifts in public purpose may necessitate a specialized bureaucracy and the ability to intrude upon established civil or religious institutions. And strengths in one aspect—loyal cadres, few intervening institutions and easy communication, sharply defined responsibilities—can compensate for weaknesses in others, while changing the nature of politics.

European monarchies often rested their power of penetration as firmly on the military as on the bureaucracy, and in the early nineteenth century the army was often in the vanguard of reforms designed to increase penetration (in the 1820s in Spain, Italy, and Russia, through the period of unification in Germany). Everywhere, by the late nineteenth century serious conflicts and crises marked a general increase in effective penetration using subtler instruments. Seen over a longer period of time, however, the process of penetration may generally show the ebb and flow Thomas finds in the case of England. Domestic peace and political stability often require acquiescence in the special roles of groups such as French notables or German Junkers, of the church or corporations (as in France before the Revolution or in nineteenth-century Belgium or post-Bismarckian Germany), or even of a totalitarian party. In fact, effective penetration seems to require close alliance with the very groups that eventually delimit it.

Thus crises of penetration occur when the goals of the state are altered (as a result of political change or clear challenges such as those of war), or when political compromises have undermined effective rule or are exposed, in the light of social change, as service to narrow interests. Since representative politics and public policies lead to explicit statements of governmental goals, they make the limits of effective penetration more obvious and measurable, creating a pressure for penetration by fiat and force through a loyal bureaucracy rather than by private negotiation and compromise. As contemporary politics encourages the belief that policies should be determined at the center and then uniformly carried out, modern polities are liable to crises of penetration as the sphere of the state's activities expands and expectations for the state's capacity increase.[33] Pressures for greater uniformity (the result of improved communication, greater centralization, or changed political goals) are likely, however, to expose regional, ethnic, class, and religious differences previously obscured and to stimulate resistance. So long as some space is permitted between state and society there are problems of penetration.

DISTRIBUTION

Insofar as politics is about the allocation of power, it is also in some sense an extended crisis of distribution. The concept of a political system, on the other hand, accepts many basic elements of social structure as given, an attitude historically encouraged by the modern state from the time it first eliminated internal competition, and one that was later sustained by ideas of liberalism and evolutionary social change. In the West, at least, the greatest social inequities have usually been considered to rest outside the operative political system, much as the Constitution of the United States once attempted to exclude slavery from the sphere of political decision. The essays in this volume accept for their analyses that view of the political system from the inside, and they generally find crises of distribution the least common among the crises in Western history. When such crises have

[33] *Ibid.*, pp. 178, 216.

occurred, they have often led to changes in penetration or participation more than in distribution.

Short of revolution, the Western state has shown little willingness, perhaps little ability, to initiate major distributive changes; rarely until recently has it been compelled to do so. The direct resolution of distribution crises, on the other hand, is likely to be unusually clear cut. Alterations of land tenure (enclosures, confiscation of church lands, abolition of feudal dues and serfdom) intended to encourage individual dignity, scientific farming, and a market economy, have been dramatic events in the history of most Western nations, and should probably be distinguished—they could be called Distribution-1—from the crises of social welfare and demands for greater justice that follow industrialization (Distribution-2), despite the fact that the two sorts arrived close together and have been tightly connected in Russia and Eastern Europe since the Russian Revolution. Both the conflict involved and the nature of the economic system (including the extent of surpluses above subsistence) separate the two kinds of distribution crisis.

Issues of taxes, tariffs, and public works have also often led to intense conflict; yet the political process of every country is expected to encompass them and to produce precise policies. Broader issues of public welfare and social justice have proved, in contrast, to be both more difficult and more continuous. When they result from changes in economic organization and social expectations, clashes over distribution can rise quite independently of political programs. The very persistence of such issues, however, suggests that they do not often bring disabling crises until reinforced by crises in other sectors.

Clearly, the various sorts of crises are related to each other, and those relationships have some form and direction. A diagram can express part of this (Chart 1.1).

CHART 1.1: THE RELATIONSHIP OF THE CRISES TO EACH OTHER

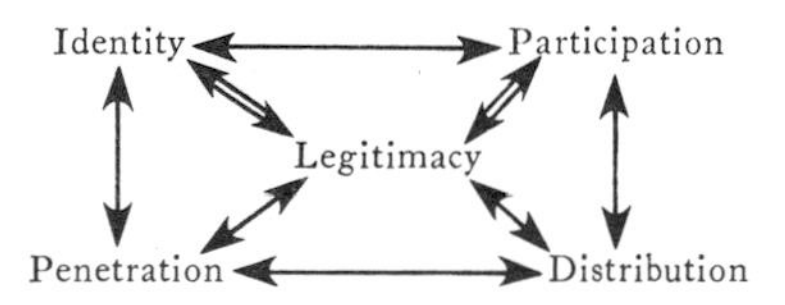

Legitimacy is likely to aid the resolution of any crisis; and a crisis of legitimacy is likely to be evoked by crises in any other category, though this connection is strongest between legitimacy and the crises of identity and participation. In the modern period crises of penetration are less clearly tied to participation than to the other categories. Before industrialization and democratic politics, however, when participation was more vigorous in a whole array of corporate bodies than in a single national assembly, penetration and participation were more closely, even reciprocally, related. The relationship between identity and distribution is similarly less direct, except in revolutionary or socialist regimes. But the relationships go well beyond what a diagram can show, and this may be indicated by considering two crises closely related (identity and legitimacy), and two less directly connected (penetration and participation).

Rapid social and political change, which strains all the functions of government, is likely to undermine legitimacy unless it, in turn, is reinforced by a strong Identity-2. If legitimacy remained unquestioned, it might obviate the need to mobilize society around identity (something of this sort occurred in tsarist Russia). The strength of identity and legitimacy in nineteenth-century Britain permitted limited penetration and high capacity; the desire to prevent challenges to identity and legitimacy in ninetenth-century Italy necessitated limited penetration at the expense of capacity. France used strong identity and penetration to compensate for problems of legitimacy, but efforts to reinforce legitimacy through reliance on identity brought a shift toward Identity-2 and competing ideological identities.

Participation and penetration, on the other hand, relate to each other less directly. Their increase is likely, as in the Habsburg Empire or Belgium, to expose unresolved issues of identity. Increased penetration without increased participation tends, as it did in Russia and Germany, to lead to an isolated elite and to institutional rigidity and inefficiency; for the state comes to depend upon a set of links with society that resists the formation of those new connections required as society changes. Strong participation and weaker penetration can lead to conservative policies and the strengthening of local interests and traditional privileges, as it seems to have in Poland, England, and the United States.[34]

When legitimacy and participation reinforce each other, as in Belgium and the United States, unresolved issues of identity that might be fatal elsewhere (for example in Germany, 1870-1914) are less

[34] *Ibid.*, pp. 96, 178.

serious. In Spain, however, increased participation without a well-developed Identity-2 failed to strengthen legitimacy. Since effective penetration requires legitimacy, it creates pressure for participation as a means of strengthening legitimacy. By making the state more visibly responsible for social conditions, penetration also raises issues of distribution. The nature of distributive demands and the policies chosen to resolve them depend in large part on the nature (and tradition) of political participation. Broad participation can nevertheless lead to a kind of abstention from demanding social policies (as in the United States and France), and narrow participation may emphasize social divisions or even undermine identity, as happened in much of central and Eastern Europe. Effective policies of participation, penetration, and distribution could go far, however, to resolve problems of identity and legitimacy.[35] Such fortuitous development—often expected of new nations—requires the stability of gradual change and an absence of foreign threat rare in modern history.

The relationship of the various crises to each other thus does seem to have something of the logical relationship suggested by Verba,[36] although the proposition is not subject to very precise tests. It follows also that political conflicts are more difficult to resolve when they simultaneously fall in more than one category of crisis or flow from one category to others—a tendency noted in many of the historical essays. Because these remain essentially functional categories, it is not surprising that ineffectiveness in one is likely to reduce effectiveness in others. It also follows that the response to a given problem is likely to prove most efficacious and less disruptive to the political system if that response falls in the "logical" category of the challenge—if, for example, the resolution of distributive issues is brought about through new taxes or welfare programs rather than through changes in the rules of participation or appeals to identity.

In practice, these are points of limited power. The relations among the five categories of crisis assume a kind of equilibrium (so that the changes possible in one category without effect on the others are restricted), and assume a tension between categories so that an innovative response in one may produce a crisis in another. These categories stem from an analysis that recognized inherent contradictions in trying to increase capacity, equality, and differentiation; ironically,

[35] *Ibid.*, pp. 74-75.

[36] *Ibid.*, p. 137.

there is a tendency to employ them as if political stability were common or always desirable.[37]

Sequence

Is there, then, for each nation a particular sequence of the five crises that can be said to describe its political development? The answer of the ten essays that follow is unanimous: there is not. Aside from the ambiguities of definition and complexities of interpretation discussed above, we find that the various kinds of crisis often recur, and that in many countries they are never clearly or finally resolved. Yet most of us find it important to determine whether different kinds of crises are met serially or simultaneously; the concept of cycles of crises appears in a number of essays; and many of us note, with Szporluk, that it does make a difference whether some crises precede or follow others (penetration before or after participation, for example).

If no full and precise sequence can be found, there may still be some descriptively useful patterns to be uncovered. Some polities, for instance, seem not really to have had a full-fledged political crisis in each of the categories. Those interesting omissions (no real crisis of participation in Russia, legitimacy in Germany, identity in Spain, or distribution in the United States) may imply a great deal about their respective political systems. However real the insight, it says little about the process of development as a whole, except that it seems not to have been uniform. No clear distinction emerges among countries here assigned incomplete, repetitive, or full cycles of crises, even when one courageously ignores the continuing absence of objective measures as to how high the tide of crisis must rise before it counts.

One can try another tack. Using the essays before us, it could be possible to compose a five-part table, listing by country those crises that were resolved early, late, or in between; those that either were never resolved or were recurrent; and those that never prominently challenged the system. Filling columns so crude would still sometimes strain intuitive daring; but if one persevered, for every country in this book some cells would remain empty (over one-third in all), and many would contain two or more of our familiar crises (in addition, nearly one-third of the entries would be labeled crises recurrent or unresolved). Sequence has been abandoned. Yet some pat-

[37] Pye and Verba, *Political Culture*, pp. 19-20, also note the tension between innovation and stability.

terns vaguely show, as in an underexposed negative subjected to forced developing. Only two cases, England and Scandinavia, would have all the same crises in all the same columns. The column of this imaginary table that could be filled most confidently would be the one headed "Crises Resolved Early" (the ambiguous meaning of that can be discussed later). When a political system can operate actively in some category of crisis as if its issues were resolved, the condition stands out; and it is noted with a conviction not present in discussions of sequences.

Our table would suggest two basic patterns of Western political development, one in which legitimacy and participation are resolved early (England, Scandinavia, Belgium, and the United States), and one in which penetration falls in that first column (Germany, Poland, Russia), the latter suggesting a kind of forced modernization. There are, of course, important differences within the groups; England and Scandinavia, for example, would also have a crisis of identity in that early column, whereas Belgium and the United States would not. Spain is close to the first group in that participation appears to be a leading category there. France and Italy stand between the two main groups, both with identity the crisis in the early category, closely tied to participation in Italy and old regime France, and to penetration in modern France. Perhaps our two tabular columns could provide the pedestal for some more theoretical structure.

Alas, the idea of an early crisis is a *double entendre*: early in a nation's cycle of crises and early in the history of European state building. For neither is there a fixed chronology. The farther back in time one goes, the more inappropriate the emphasis on nation and state; there is no natural beginning at which to start counting cycles of crisis. Most Western nations experienced the five crises in some form before the industrial and French Revolutions (even Belgium and the United States can be said to have done so, vicariously). All were greatly affected by the events of 1789-1815, and any study of European political crises is bound to focus on that period with gratitude for the analytic convenience it offers. The historian who pounces on the obvious, however, usually exaggerates discontinuity.

One merit of looking for patterns of crisis brought out in the following chapters is the degree of continuity within national political systems. That persistence of old patterns in new forms between 1815 and the 1880s helps to account for the diversity of crises and responses to them among Western states in that period—the one, it should be noted, in which the modern myths of English traditionalism, French instability, and German efficiency became dogma. Toward the end of the century, all Western nations experienced another round of crises that lasted through World War I, marking a period that equals the years of the French Revolution as a time of widespread and profound political change. Even then the response of political systems in large part followed from their previous experience of crisis. The point is simpler than it seems. Political systems respond to new challenges with the institutionalized patterns of behavior available to them. Broadly, those patterns were last reshaped during a previous crisis, and usually bear the imprint of their initial formation. This does not mean that one "successful" response (which presumably means a system-saving one) guarantees "successful" ones later.[38] Nevertheless, states with longer histories of modernization (or perhaps merely longer-lived patterns of response), like those of Scandinavia and the United Kingdom, continued to be more likely to meet their crises one at a time. Some continuity in national patterns of crisis is a finding to look for in these studies.

Attention to chronology underscores another simple point. The content and significance of the five categories of development changes with time. For much of modern history, England had the advantage of having no models of where change might lead; growing self-consciousness about development and the example of other nations has everywhere affected the crises themselves. So have current standards of technology, economic organization, social relations, and ideology. To forget that, an error the vocabulary of crisis can induce, would be to exaggerate continuity. Despite the historians' suspicions that some excessively simple ideal of progress underlay the Committee's work, they generally found a degree of irreversibility in the political process. Restored monarchies are different from those never shaken. Once established, institutions of participation tend to be maintained even when reduced to a mere facade. If there seemed a greater ebb and flow in matters of penetration and distribution, each flow was likely to rise higher than the last. Surprisingly, identity appeared more subject to reversal or at least to radical alteration, but such occurrences were hardly common. The sense that political change has some direction, with which the Committee for Comparative Politics began, is maintained.

[38] This point, noted in several of the essays here, is also made by Peter H. Smith, *Argentina and the Failure of Democracy*, p. 90.

For the Committee that direction lay in the three "goals" of capacity, equality, and differentiation more than in the five crises related to them. The political system that develops increased political capacity first (through legitimacy) is thus fundamentally distinguished from one that first achieves differentiation (through penetration) in modern forms.[39] Perhaps, then, the idea that some crises are resolved early, and that there may be continuity in the patterns of crisis within a political system, can be combined with a sense of chronology and direction to identify a developmental syndrome characteristic of each nation, one that leads to the repetition within that nation's history of a certain pattern.

In the logic of such a syndrome, if one of the crises receives little structural resolution, then other kinds of crises are likely to reinvoke the unresolved crisis. Thus new crises tend to occur in more than one category simultaneously, making their resolution more difficult and political instability more likely. Furthermore, recurrence of the same sort of crisis becomes more likely until a drastic change takes place in the entire system. The recurring crisis becomes the salient one of the political system, the one evoked by recurring needs, the one around which lines of opposition are firmest and compromise most essential to survival, and the one toward which opponents of the government seek to shift political conflict. Given the long and suspect tradition of writing about politics in physiological analogies, it should be harmless to add another: the recurrent crisis becomes, like the "target area" of pathology, an organic weakness, which quite different diseases are likely to attack.

On the other hand, in most political systems one or more kinds of crisis will have been resolved so effectively that they are unlikely to become crises again, short of revolution. These become categories of priority in the triple sense that they are likely to have been resolved early, that the political system is rather clearly based on their resolution, and that governing elites will try to have conflict shifted to these stablest and safest of political functions. Thus governments will often insist that conflict over issues of distribution is really a matter of legitimacy, or that conflicts over identity are really issues of participation. Finally, in some political systems certain crises (usually because of identifiable peculiarities in social structure or in the circumscription of politics) may never be evoked in severe form.

Thus a nation's pattern of political development could be described

[39] Binder *et al.*, *Crises and Sequences*, pp. 74-79, 293-95.

over a long period through emphasis on those crises given priority and those that are salient. It might even be that a shift in the crises given priority (from participation to penetration in eighteenth-century Poland, to identity after World War I) and salience (from identity to distribution in nineteenth-century Germany) may indicate a new "stage" or phase of development. Efforts to achieve increased equality, capacity, or differentiation—it can be argued—brought changes in one or more of the categories, thus relating the new "stage" to the direction of political development. The need for these increases in turn follows from new modes of production, external threats, and ideas. The syndrome, although only part of the whole political pattern, should therefore express, at least indirectly, the connection of a political tradition with exogenous forces and domestic society.

Because the syndrome is based on the concept of five crises, it ought more directly to take into account the relationships among these functions. The diagram is repeated (Chart 1.2), with the addition of

CHART 1.2: SOCIAL ATTRIBUTES AND THE RELATIONSHIP OF CRISES

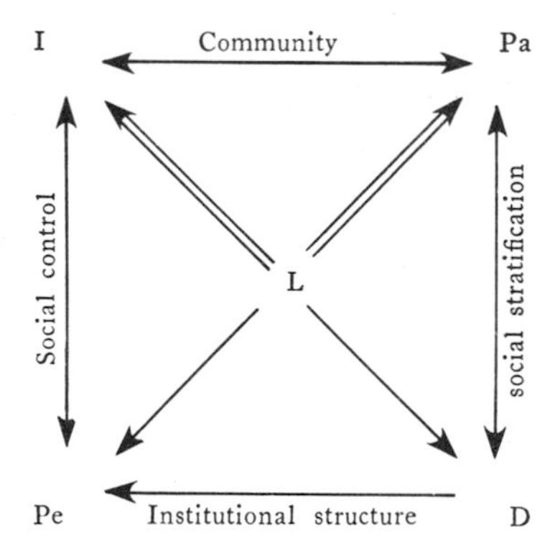

terms that evoke attributes of society most strongly involved in the relationship between crises. The relationship between legitimacy and the other crises may similarly be taken to evoke the practice of decision making (ideal, real, and customary) within a given political system. The two-headed arrow between a category of priority and a category of salience would represent the system's major axis of activity. One further extension of the syndrome is inviting. Political systems might be expected to seek to increase their effectiveness by building from their crisis of priority toward those adjacent, using instruments that worked well in one area on others. When the category of priority and the salient category (legitimacy and participation, for instance) reinforce each other, when compromises are effective, their political strength extends along the lines of the diagram to one or both of the most closely related crises (identity and distribution). Because of legitimacy's stronger links with identity and participation, reinforcement between these two categories will be especially likely to extend to the third. Crises in categories not on the active axis will, on the other hand, increase the strains on the salient category.

The essays that follow were not written with this syndrome in mind, and it is dangerous to use them as fodder for it. The effort below stands as a series of estimates, easily disputed (and one that begs the question of degree: penetration may be the category of priority in several countries yet be much stronger in one, giving its system a more effective base). But the temptation is irresistible. (Chart 1.3; the category of priority is underscored.)

One enigma is immediately illumined: the order of the chapters

CHART 1.3: SYNDROMES OF POLITICAL DEVELOPMENT

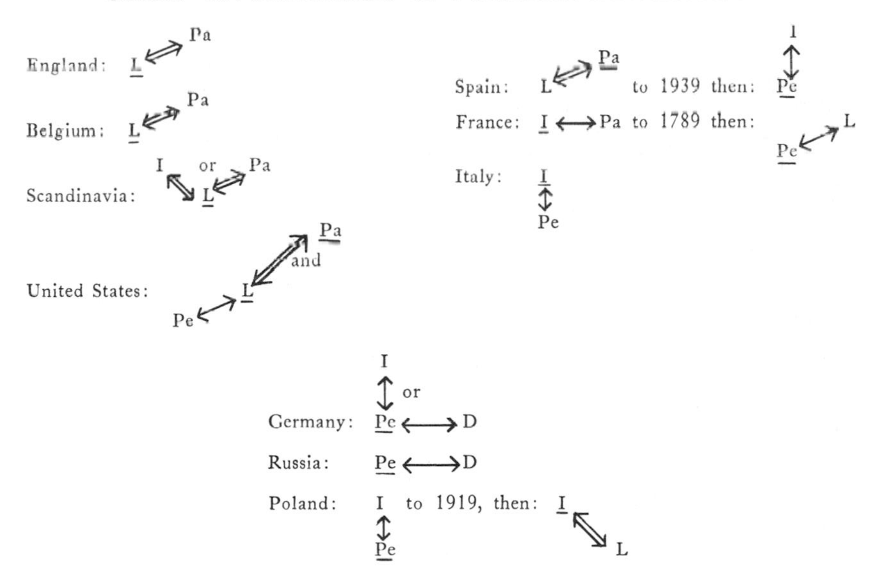

in this book.[40] Beyond that, the utility of these syndromes becomes less certain. It is either too early or too easy to make claims for the importance of whether a political system's syndrome builds from the "upper" (identity and participation) or the "lower" (penetration and distribution) crises, includes legitimacy or not, and so on. Even the fact that none of our cases builds from the possibilities of community $(\mathrm{I} \longleftrightarrow \mathrm{Pa})$ or social stratification $\begin{pmatrix} \mathrm{Pa} \\ \updownarrow \\ \mathrm{D} \end{pmatrix}$ may be a matter of definition. The attempt to construct from this a full theory (or description) of political development would be a *tour de faiblesse*.

Yet the effort to establish a mere syndrome can occasion interesting questions about single nations and about comparative political development. At this more modest level it can highlight the relatively limited demands made on the American federal government until recently; the impermanence of Bismarckian solutions despite public acceptance of the state and Germany's forced modernization; the deep divisions in France, where effective participation only slightly strengthened legitimacy despite impressive institutional continuity; the separation of Italy's political elite from the society they could not penetrate; Russia's distance from the Western political tradition. Such syndromes at least leave room for the point that England's development has been less smooth and Spain's more purposeful than the familiar lists of revolutions imply,[41] and they can illuminate the political tactics that led a Bismarck to challenge the legitimacy of socialists and Catholics, anti-Dreyfusards to fail in their challenge to the Third Republic, or Lenin to triumph. Some useful models might result if such analysis were refined and could be more firmly extended to include the relationship between a particular syndrome and class structure, the economy, political ideologies, and bureaucratic, corporate, and military institutions. Perhaps these syndromes can explain the peculiar forms and behavior of interest groups and parties. In any case, the concept of priority and salience can claim the virtue of acknowledging the role of political tradition while considering change the normal condition.

[40] Had the chapters been arranged according to the more chronological patterns defined by C. E. Black, *The Dynamics of Modernization* (New York, 1966), they would have fallen into four somewhat different groups: 1. Great Britain and France; 2. the United States; 3. Belgium, Germany, Italy, Scandinavia, Spain and Portugal, Poland; 4. (actually Black's fifth group) Russia.

[41] The interpretations of development in this volume tend quite consistently to view it as less purposeful, its changes less marked, its stabilities less certain than is usual in the literature on development. Cf. Almond and Powell, *Comparative Politics*, pp. 315-30.

Conclusion

This acceptance of change is in itself a Western characteristic, for each society has had time to make a kind of tradition of the political upheavals, waves of reform, or coups d'état that have become their accustomed mode of political change. In this, Western modernization may differ from that in other cultures where rapid change appears more deeply threatening, unusual, or externally induced. Much that is called modern elsewhere seems merely Western and natural here; rationalism, technological development, universalistic norms, the distinction between church and state are assumed to be part of the culture in these historical essays. State building is so old and self-conscious a theme in Western history that analysis in terms of development toward increased capacity seems fitting in a way it may not be for societies suddenly faced with the need to confront the West. Nevertheless, most of these authors find in Western experience a model that can be applied more broadly: most European nations thought of themselves as late developers; many felt they had too long been a cultural or economic colony of others (Italy, Germany, Poland); nearly all experienced the contradictions between efficiency and equality, change and stability. More than the older monarchies or pressured states to the east, the centralized republics of southern Europe, Payne argues, have had an experience comparable to that of the Third World.

But ideas of development, applied with such enthusiasm to the study of "backward" nations and much enriched by experience gained of non-Western societies, can now be fruitfully applied to their homeland. If development has in some sense been easier in the West (because rooted in Western values and experienced there more slowly), even so it has been disruptive and painful. In the West, too, tradition has shown its indispensability and tenacious strength. Western models suggest, in fact, that crises are not necessarily to be regretted—the stability of tsarist Russia, the skillful compromises of imperial Germany, or even the much-vaunted moderate evolution of England preserved problems that had to be met later in still more difficult circumstances. Neither must all crises be resolved. Much of the cultural vitality of the West and its very ability to adapt to change is related to enduring conflict and well-founded dissatisfaction. In writing about development, our essayists are inescapably moralists after all, never far from visions of a just democracy, attributing "successes" to the working of history and "failures" to the fallibility of statesmen. It is not surprising that many of us foresee (and welcome) a new wave of participation crises in the highly developed societies of the West. In all this we reflect the culture we mean to study.

All the participants are, I think, now more than at the beginning of this project convinced of the stimulus to be gained from interdisciplinary and comparative studies of Western development. Projects such as this raise problems of method, invite demands for models more refined, and press the need for better measures of social change based on more sophisticated social indicators and richer, more accessible data. Such efforts also underscore the parallel need for social theory in the style of the most advanced social science, and also for judgments in the manner of an older political philosophy that relates policies to values and social structure. Without both we are condemned to work in different ways when we study a process and when we try to see society whole, forced to seek through definition a precision we cannot obtain in research, led to the fading hope that investigation can resolve problems not yet formulated.

Even at this stage these essays point up a wide range of topics that to us now loom large but need further study: the problems of regions that develop their own defenses and adaptations as national political development pushes past them (or vice versa), the specific and often hidden connections among legal systems, interest groups, and bureaucracies. Institutional history, once so fashionable that it became pedestrian, deserves to be revived by new questions and methods. More easily appreciated in nonliterate society, the independent vitality of popular culture in the industrial West equally merits sympathetic attention. The list is easily extended, and it points to more investigation of the concrete interrelations among literacy, communication, social mobility, urban life, markets, customs, social values, and political organization. The analytic gains in treating political systems as autonomous are quickly limited by the artificial losses, and the concept of crises tends to be weak on factors external to the political system and to a given nation, particularly if those factors—international competition, the economic system, technology, and communication—steadily shape rather than sharply impinge on politics. Models of political development should not tempt us to explain too much, nor be allowed to stimulate too many ingenious answers before the questions are clear. Today's heuristic device must not become tomorrow's assumption. One of the strengths of these essays is that they do not attempt to create a closed system; another is their recognition of many paths to political survival—and of many higher goals. A next step should be the careful formulation of historical (and therefore not just developmental) problems, followed by the comparison of realities rather than abstractions. The Committee's broad categories of political development, like photographs of the earth taken from space, remind us that familiar terrain is part of a larger system, and urge us to compare diverse features that from a distance appear similar. They do not obviate the need for a closer look.

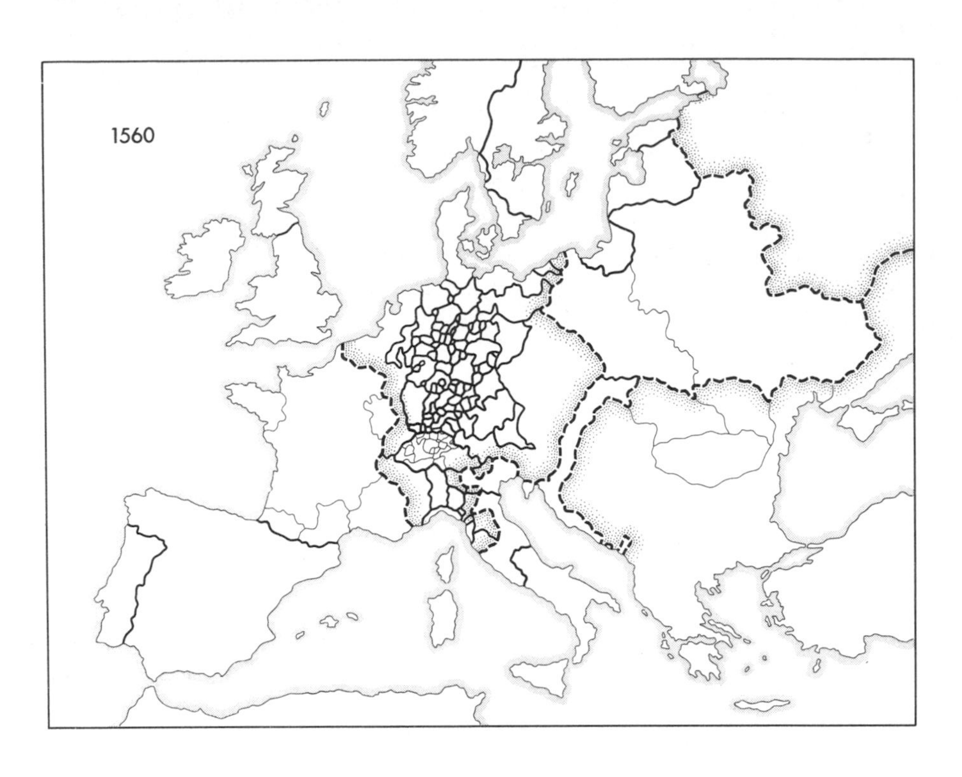
1560

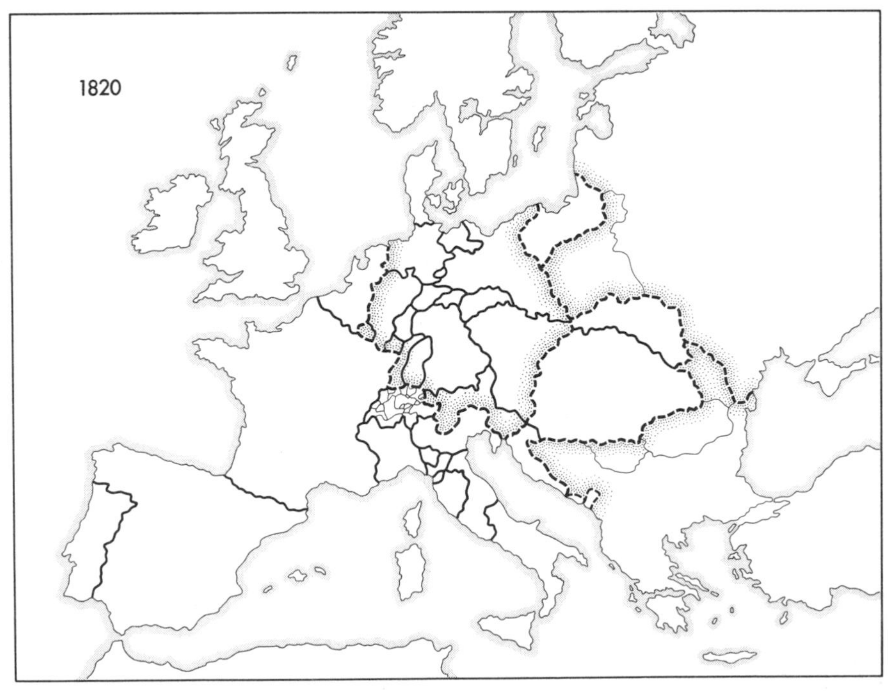
1820

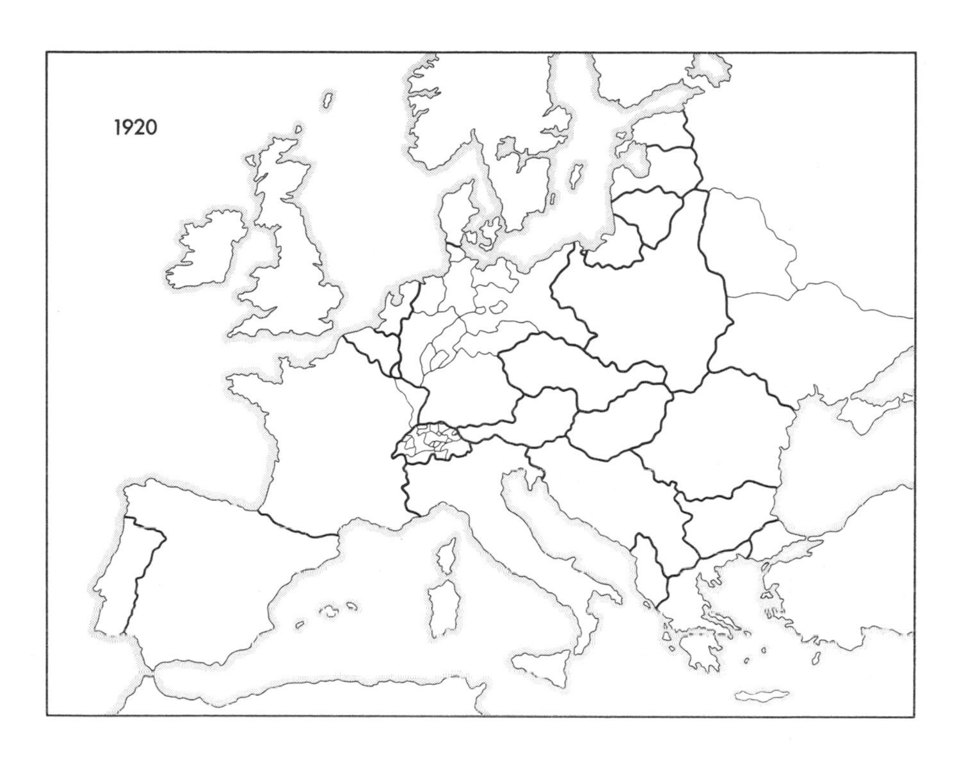
1920

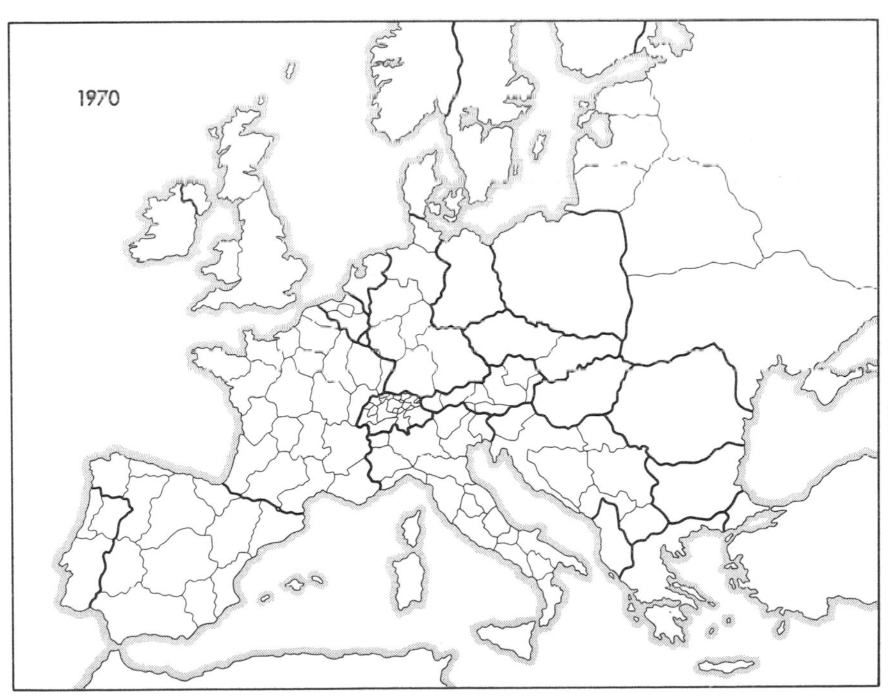
1970

CHAPTER 2

The United Kingdom

KEITH THOMAS

Analytic rigor in historical writing has always required the use of abstractions; and nothing is to be gained by resisting new concepts simply because they are unfamiliar. But the historian who is asked to employ the terminology of "political development" inevitably finds himself subject to certain inhibitions. For this new language seems to have a value-ridden quality. Beneath the talk of "modernization," "politically mature societies," "balanced growth," and "the successful resolution of crises," one can discern the assumption that the contemporary institutions of North America and parts of Western Europe represent a universal culmination of the political process, and that "stability" and "performance" are the ideal political goals for all societies. The political process, it appears, is to be studied from the point of view of the ruling group or "elite"; and the investigator's main problem is to classify the methods by which that elite manages to fend off or satisfy demands from below without involving "societal dissolution." The object of the enquiry thus bears a suspicious resemblance to that ancient ideal, the compilation of a handbook of political wisdom for rulers, teaching them in particular how to preserve political stability at moments when it is threatened. This objective—central to the preoccupations of both Aristotle and Machiavelli—seems to lie at the heart of modern "managerial politics."

It is not claimed that the authors of *Crises and Sequences in Political Development* would themselves subscribe to these ideological tenets; on the contrary they all adopt a posture of strict neutrality. But it is questionable whether their terminology makes such neutrality possible. What, for example, can they mean by "participation" if it is possible for an "elite" to continue to rule after "participation" has been conceded to the masses? And how can they recognize "successful performance" in, say, the field of distribution, unless they either have a prior idea of how much welfare or education is to be deemed ade-

Crises of Political Development in Europe and the United States
0-691-07598-0/78/000041-56$02.80/1 (cloth)
0-691-02183-X/78/000041-56$02.80/1 (paperback)
For copying information, see copyright page

quate, or assume, as they appear to do, that "success" means making the minimum concessions necessary to ensure the continued supremacy of the elite?

The language of "crises" reflects this same ideal of stability. For a "crisis" is a dangerous moment, which must be somehow or other averted. The medical origin of the term—as the crucial turning-point at which the patient gets either worse or better—implies that it is only the sick who have such experiences;[1] though it is conceded that, in the period of "modernization" at least, political systems are chronically subject to "inescapable tensions,"[2] and that, by implication, the process of growing up must inevitably involve passage through the usual childhood illnesses.

The historian's main difficulty, however, lies not in the ideological or evolutionary implications of this terminology, or even in a fastidious aversion to metaphors derived from managerial techniques ("conflict resolution"), electronics ("output" and "feedback"), or neo-Freudian psychology ("identity crisis"). Rather it is to be found in the elusiveness of the idea of "modernization" and in the imprecision of the five suggested "crises." So far as "modernization" is concerned, the three main ingredients—equality, capacity, and differentiation—though helpful initially, prove in the end to be difficult to identify. For, if we take the case of England, "capacity" was already being manifested by the reign of William the Conqueror, when the state was militarily effective and capable of producing so astonishingly thorough an administrative survey as Domesday Book; "differentiation" was to some extent attained by the development of political and administrative institutions in the twelfth and thirteenth centuries;[3] while "equality" in anything other than a formal sense is still a long way from being achieved. The identification of a "modernization threshold" in England is thus a subjective process. Some historians, emphasizing the decline of feudalism, the rise of a national church, and the growth of a strong central monarchy, might put it in the sixteenth century; others, focusing on the defeat of absolute monarchy

[1] For comment on the assumption that "a 'healthy' society is immune to revolution," see Barrington Moore, Jr., *Social Origins of Dictatorship and Democracy. Lord and Peasant in the Making of the Modern World* (London, 1967), p. 457n.

[2] Leonard Binder, James S. Coleman, Joseph LaPalombara, Lucian W. Pye, Sidney Verba, and Myron Weiner, *Crises and Sequences in Political Development* (Princeton, 1971), pp. vii-viii.

[3] Cf. F. W. Maitland, *The Constitutional History of England* (Cambridge, 1908), p. 105 ("Everywhere as we pass from the ancient to the modern we see what the fashionable philosophy calls differentiation").

and the consolidation of parliamentary government, would choose the seventeenth century; others, concentrating on the growth of the franchise, of mass-based political parties, and of a bureaucracy capable of dealing with the problems of industrialization, would pick the nineteenth century; others observe that it was only the twentieth century that saw universal adult suffrage and the welfare state; yet others, pointing to the survival of crucial educational and economic inequalities, and to an alleged tradition of "deference," would say that in England full "modernization" is yet to come. To take only historians who have written in recent years, the beginnings of the "modern" state and of "modern" British politics have been variously placed in the 1530s,[4] in the seventeenth century,[5] and in 1920.[6] Such discrepancies reflect a concern with different aspects of "modernization," but they also reveal the looseness of the term "modern": in Oxford University "modern" history begins with the fall of the Roman Empire, whereas the *Cambridge Modern History* starts nearly a thousand years later. A semantic study of the way in which historians have conceived of "modernity" might be more rewarding than yet another attempt to identify the English origins of this elusive quality. Political scientists also differ among themselves about the essential features of "modernization";[7] and as they find themselves forced to speak of "post-modernization," they are themselves recognizing that what is modern today is not necessarily modern tomorrow. To this extent we are deploying a term that has less intrinsic objectivity than does "capitalism," "industrialization," or the terminology of other rival evolutionary schemes.[8]

Difficulties also arise when one attempts to identify the five crises. "Crisis" is a much abused word in historical writing, and has acquired a number of different meanings.[9] Even in the terminology of political

[4] G. R. Elton, *England under the Tudors* (London, 1955), p. 184. Cf. Henri Hauser, *La Modernité du XVIe siècle* (Paris, 1930).

[5] Christopher Hill, *The Century of Revolution, 1603-1714* (Edinburgh, 1961), p. 1.

[6] Maurice Cowling, *The Impact of Labour, 1920-1924. The Beginning of Modern British Politics* (Cambridge, 1971).

[7] Cf. the description of participation as "the most fundamental aspect of political modernization" in Samuel P. Huntington, *Political Order in Changing Societies* (New Haven, 1968), p. 36.

[8] A useful demonstration of some of the weaknesses of the concept may be found in Dean C. Tipps, "Modernization Theory and the Comparative Study of Societies: A Critical Perspective," *Comparative Studies in Society and History*, 15 (1973), 199-226.

[9] As is well shown by Randolph Starn, "Historians and 'Crisis,'" *Past and Present*, 52 (1971), 3-22.

development it has three separate senses: 1) the existence of a political problem, whether or not perceived as such by the governing elite; 2) a problem so great as to constitute a threat to the whole political system unless it is solved by institutional innovation on a scale large enough to be regarded as something more than merely "routine"; 3) a critical turning point in the history of a political system. These phenomena are so different from each other as to make critical comparison difficult, if not impossible.

The situation is further complicated by the overlapping nature of the five crises themselves.[10] As one of the authors of *Crises and Sequences* concedes, "there are clearly many tasks to be accomplished before the present scheme can be a precise guide to research."[11]

In the following discussion the "crises" will be treated in their widest sense; that is to say, they will be regarded as five "critical problems" of a kind frequently encountered during a nation's political evolution. An attempt will be made to identify their occurrence in British history, and to indicate the points at which they produced either institutional change or the disruption of the political system. Such an approach inevitably leads to emphasis upon those aspects of the past that most closely foreshadow the future; it thus creates a "Whiggish" impression of irresistible evolution toward the British political system as we know it today. This, needless to say, is not the writer's intention. An inquiry into the origins of the present has its intellectual validity. But it is not the same thing as an attempt to recapture the texture of the past.[12]

The application of this new interpretative scheme to Britain has a particular interest. For Britain has long been regarded as a special case. The fact that she is an island and has successfully repelled so many attempts at foreign invasion appears to make her a unique case of spontaneous development, free from external influence. "What makes the history of England so eminently valuable," wrote H. T. Buckle, "is, that nowhere else has the national progress been so little interfered with, either for good or for evil."[13] Since the end

[10] See above, pp. 13-14.

[11] Sidney Verba, in Binder *et al.*, *Crises and Sequences*, p. 307.

[12] "History cannot be compared to a tunnel through which an express races until it brings its freight of passengers out into sunlit plains. Or if it can be, then generation upon generation of passengers are born, live in the dark, and die while the train is still within the tunnel." E. P. Thompson, "The Peculiarities of the English," *The Socialist Register* (1965), p. 358.

[13] Henry Thomas Buckle, *History of Civilization in England* (1857-61; World's Classics ed., London, 1903), I, 204.

of the seventeenth century, the development of the British political system has been remarkably peaceful. It was Britain's escape from the revolutions of 1789 and 1848 that most impressed nineteenth-century commentators. Yet Britain was the first country to undergo industrialization and has—until recently—proved herself capable of modernizing economically without imposing undue strains upon a political system inherited from a previous era. Foreign observers are struck by the apparent continuity of British institutions—the monarchy, the House of Lords, the common law, the ancient universities, and the public schools. This survival of traditional institutions in a modern society seems to make Britain the ideal example of step-by-step political development, in which change is accomplished by piecemeal empiricism, and where violent ideological confrontations are successfully avoided. It is presumably these features that lead one of the authors of *Crises and Sequences in Political Development* to speak of "the classic case of Great Britain."[14]

There are reasons for thinking that this conventional picture is misleading. Not only can the "traditional" and "deferential" elements in modern Britain be greatly exaggerated,[15] but a study of her past reveals the existence of sharp and sometimes violent discontinuities. Economically and socially Britain was the first country to modernize. By the early nineteenth century she had lost her peasantry and gained a large industrial proletariat. She acquired dense industrial cities and a huge overseas empire. Aristocrats participated in this triumph of capitalism, but its "traditional" aspects were a thin veneer.[16]

In politics, similarly, the impression of continuity is illusory. Until the eighteenth century England was notorious for her political instability. "It is well known how many civil wars the English have had," wrote Botero in 1589, "how many changes of regime and how many new kings."[17] The opinion of foreigners, wrote an English scholar in 1704, is "that there have been more shakes and convulsions in the government of England than in that of any other na-

[14] Joseph LaPalombara, in *Crises and Sequences in Political Development*, p. 211.

[15] See the remarks of Dennis Kavanagh, "The Deferential English: A Comparative Critique," *Government and Opposition*, 6 (1971), 333-60.

[16] Cf. E. J. Hobsbawm, *Industry and Empire. An Economic History of Britain since 1750* (London, 1968), pp. 3-7.

[17] Giovanni Botero, *The Reason of State*, translated by P. J. and D. P. Waley (London, 1956), p. 37.

tion."[18] It was only the relative immunity of Britain from internal violence during the French Revolutionary period that led subsequent historians to play down the discontinuities of English history and to portray the story as one of slow organic change.[19]

To understand the relative stability of the modern British political system, therefore, we have to go back to the period of violence that made it possible—to the seventeenth century, and even to the middle ages, when some crucial political institutions were forged.[20] The process of "political development" in England has been long-drawn-out; and we must be prepared to range over a very considerable period of time to find our five crises. Such a survey will necessarily be highly compressed and superficial, but it may at least serve to demonstrate that in order to understand the present it is still necessary to study the remote past.

Crises

IDENTITY

The present United Kingdom is a multi-racial state, comprising four separate units, each with a distinctive past history. Two of them, England and Scotland, existed as independent unified states for over five centuries before they were united under the same ruler in 1603 and integrated into a single political unit in 1701. The third, Wales, was never united under a single ruler until a few decades before its final conquest by the English in 1284; it was not fully assimilated into the English parliamentary and legal system until the early sixteenth century. The fourth element, Northern Ireland, was only created in 1920; it comprises six of the thirty-two counties of Ireland, and its boundaries remain highly controversial. Each of these component parts has its own social and cultural pecularities. Scotland has its own legal system and national church. A fifth of the population of Wales is Welsh speaking. Northern Ireland has its own regional parliament,[21] and a population that is fiercely polarized into Protestant majority and Catholic minority.

[18] White Kennett, *A Compassionate Enquiry into the Causes of the Civil War* (London, 1704), p. 17.

[19] Charles E. McClelland, *The German Historians and England* (Cambridge, 1971), p. 44.

[20] And not only in England. Cf. Yves Renouard, *Études d'histoire médiévale* (Paris, 1968), pp. 77-91. ("Comment les traits durables de l'Europe occidentale moderne se sont définis au début du xiiie siècle").

[21] Or did until 1972.

It is by no means clear that the inhabitants of the United Kingdom share a single sense of political identity. Asked their nationality, they are as likely to characterize themselves as English, Scottish, Welsh, or Northern Irish as to call themselves British. Indeed there is no term that accurately describes them all to the exclusion of others. For the word "British" refers to Great Britain, which, strictly speaking, excludes Northern Ireland; and if the term is used in a wider sense it includes all Commonwealth subjects of the queen. It is not surprising that history books frequently refer to "England," when their authors mean Great Britain or the United Kingdom.

It is therefore all the more remarkable that, Ireland apart, identity problems have seldom reached crisis proportions. One of the main reasons for this is that England (which now contains five-sixths of the United Kingdom's population) achieved national identity at a very early stage. The legacy of successive invasions had been a racial amalgam of Celtic, Roman, Anglo-Saxon, and Scandinavian elements, on top of which the Norman conquest imposed a new foreign aristocracy. But the invasions helped to eliminate provincial dynasties. Even before the coming of William I there existed a rudimentary territorial state with defined boundaries, a single ruling house, and a uniform system of ecclesiastical, judicial, and fiscal organization. The Normans and Angevins greatly extended the central government and legal system so as to consolidate a unitary state. No feudal monarchy went further in effecting the transition from feudal overlordship to centralized royal administration. The outlying areas were effectively linked to the center, both by the chains of dependence binding the population to its landed superiors (who in turn held their land of the king), and also by the activities of the sheriffs and itinerant justices who represented royal authority in the localities.

From the very start, therefore, England possessed a remarkable degree of uniformity in its institutional structure. Whereas the French kingdom was a mere combination of independent provinces, England was "more like a large French province than it was like a continental kingdom."[22] Its unity was cemented by the development of the common law (in the twelfth and thirteenth centuries) and the adoption (by the mid-fourteenth century) of English in

[22] Joseph R. Strayer, *On the Medieval Origins of the Modern State* (Princeton, 1970), p. 49.

place of French as the language of the court and aristocracy. The triumph of the vernacular was followed by the emergence in the sixteenth and seventeenth centuries of something approaching "standard" spoken English, leaving dialects and regional accents to become symbols of provincialism. Unity was also fostered by the imposition of a nationwide customs system with a marked absence of internal tolls, a unified coinage, and the early adoption of national weights and measures. It was further consolidated by the growth (from the thirteenth century) of a national representative institution, organized, not as a meeting of "estates," but on a territorial basis, so that from the beginning every blade of grass was "represented" in Parliament. After the unions with Wales and Scotland, parliamentary representation became a means of binding the newly acquired areas to the center. There were no provincial assemblies. Nor, after the loss of Calais in 1558, were there any continental possessions of the kind that had preoccupied the English Crown throughout the middle ages.

Since the Conqueror had ensured that local administration was conducted by men who depended directly on the Crown for their offices, it followed that the aristocratic leaders of the local communities tended naturally to look to the center. Few of the internal political upheavals of medieval England can be attributed to problems of identity. Regionalism played a relatively slight part in the numerous baronial revolts. Such movements were normally attempts to capture and control the central government rather than to dismantle it; the totally unrealistic Tripartite Indenture of 1405, by which the rebel leaders proposed to partition England and Wales into three separate blocs, is the exception that proves the rule. Regional sentiment was clearly apparent in three of the rebellions that disturbed the Tudor state—the northern-based Pilgrimage of Grace (1536), the Western (Prayer-Book) Rebellion (1549) and the Rising of the Northern Earls (1569)—but in none of them was it the main element, and in none did it generate a breakaway movement.

The sixteenth and seventeenth centuries saw the phenomenal growth of London, both as the economic capital and also as the home of Parliament, the Court, the central law courts, the Inns of Court and the fashionable world. This had the effect of drawing the political nation more tightly together. The regular visits of the provincial gentry to London for business and pleasure made them conscious of their membership in a national community,[23] while the steady flow of the lower classes in and out of the capital in search of employment had a similar effect; it has been calculated that by 1700 as much as a sixth of the population were spending at least part of their lives in the metropolis.[24]

This is not to say that regional differences were obliterated. On the contrary. For so small a country England has always displayed an astonishing range of cultural diversity. Inadequate communications hindered the formation of a national market and put limits to individual mobility. In the seventeenth century a man who spoke of his "country" still meant not his nation, but his county or locality; and the term "foreigner" was customarily applied to those who were not privileged local residents. Preindustrial England can be plausibly represented as essentially a federation of gentry-led county units—"a confederation of overlapping communities, politically united only on the unusual occasions when the representatives of these communities were summoned together in Parliament."[25] This sense of county identity may have been increased by the political conflicts of the Civil War era, when county communities often dissociated themselves from national trends, and when demands for decentralization were frequently voiced. But the essential fact was that the leaders of the county still looked to Westminster and the Court to fulfil their political aspirations. The county retained its vitality as a subordinate political unit, but it was never a threat to the central authority. When industrialization began after 1750, the differences between rural and industrial areas were greatly enhanced. Regionalism was an important element in the battles for parliamentary reform and the repeal of the Corn Laws. Indeed, in the nineteenth century the conflict between north and south was arguably "as much a leading theme of English as of American history."[26] Yet even then the sense of overriding national identity was great enough to sustain the unity of the political system. Parties and pressure groups cut across regional boundaries.

But though the identity of England as a political society has never

[23] Cf. A. F. Pollard, "The Reformation Parliament as a Matrimonial Agency and Its National Effects," *History*, 21 (1936), 219-29.

[24] E. A. Wrigley, "A Simple Model of London's Importance . . . 1650-1750," *Past and Present*, 37 (1967), 49.

[25] David Underdown, *Pride's Purge* (Oxford, 1971), p. 24.

[26] Asa Briggs, *The Age of Improvement* (London, 1959), p. 51.

been seriously in dispute, the subjective meaning of Englishness has undergone a number of changes. In the sixteenth century it seemed as if English identity was to be defined in essentially religious terms. The Reformation made the English church fully independent of Rome and generated a strong Protestant nationalism, reflected in the much-repeated sentiment that "God is English."[27] The myth that the English were God's peculiar people, specially chosen to carry out the divine plan for a pure religion and the destruction of Antichrist, was enshrined in John Foxe's *Acts and Monuments*, one of the most widely read books of the period; it played a dominant part in religious and political action for a century or more. The idiosyncrasies of the Anglican church and the military threat of the Counter-Reformation further enhanced the sense of isolation and separateness. A Protestant mythology was developed, teaching that England had been the home of a pure brand of Christianity brought by Joseph of Arimathea centuries before the Roman missions, and emphasizing the deliverances from the Spanish Armada and the Gunpowder Plot. Religious considerations underlay much contemporary pride in vernacular culture and native institutions.

The problem created by this habit of defining English identity in religious terms was, of course, that it left ambivalent the status of the various religious minorities attracted by continental models, whether of Geneva or Rome. In fact, most English Catholics remained loyal to the regime, despite the pope's attempt to depose Elizabeth I. But the mid-seventeenth century political crisis leading to the Civil War was exacerbated by the widespread feeling that Charles I, who had married a popish wife and supported the Arminian policies of Archbishop Laud, was jeopardizing the Protestant identity of the English nation. Similar antipopish feeling underlay the attempt to exclude James Duke of York from the throne (1679-1681) and the Revolution of 1688-1689, which replaced James by William III and decreed that the English throne should henceforth be occupied only by Protestants. Thereafter, with the concession of freedom of worship, English identity came to be defined in nonreligious terms. Despite their civil disabilities (which lasted until the nineteenth century), the minority religious groups, Catholic and Protestant, retained a strong sense of national identity. Exile on the Continent or

[27] John Aylmer, *An Harborowe for faithfull and trewe Subjects* (London, 1559), sig. P4. Cf. Hugh Latimer in 1537: "Verily He hath shown himself God of England, or rather an English God, if we consider and ponder well all His proceedings with us from time to time"; *State Papers of Henry VIII* (1830), I, 571.

emigration to the New World was the recourse of the recalcitrant minority.

Side by side with Protestantism in the definition of Englishness went the tradition of the "freeborn" Englishman, enjoying civil rights of a kind denied to most of the lower classes in European countries. By the sixteenth century villeinage in England was almost extinct. Civil liberties were widely extended and a strong legal consciousness was to be found, even at the humblest levels of society. "Every ploughswain with us may be a seneschal in a court baron," wrote a commentator in 1602. "He can talk of essoins, vouchers, withernams and recaptions; and if you control him, the book of the *Grounds of the Law* is his portesse, and ready at his girdle to confute you."[28] Everyone knew that the Englishman's home was his castle, and that on the Continent popery went with despotism and "wooden shoes." After the Revolution of 1688, legalism and individualism became essential elements in the English sense of identity: "We are at this day . . . the freest people in the world," declared a preacher in 1712.[29] It was felt that the Englishman was not only freer than his European counterpart but also better fed, dressed, and housed; in eighteenth-century cartoons John Bull was characteristically depicted as stuffing himself with roast beef.

This conviction that Britons never would be slaves underlay the popular radicalism of the late eighteenth and early nineteenth centuries. Despite its iconoclastic onslaught on Crown and church, the sturdy philosophy of Tom Paine was an unmistakably English product. It was to the English past that his supporters appealed. They resurrected the myth of the Norman Yoke, the free Anglo-Saxons, King Alfred, and a liberty-loving past. Although the argument involved repudiating the landed aristocracy as William the Conqueror's mercenaries, it was an appeal to a distinctively English heritage. In the 1790s the radicals saw the French Revolution less as an independent source of inspiration than as a demonstration of what English political ideas could accomplish when exported abroad.

International solidarity has never been a very marked feature of English radical movements. Any feelings of international brotherhood during the Civil War period were soon overcome by the realistic appraisal of the economic interests that divided England from

[28] William Fulbecke, *The Second Part of the Parallelle, or Conference of the Civil Law, the Canon Law, and the Common Law* (London, 1602), sig. B2.

[29] Josiah Woodward, *The Divine Right of Civil Government. A Sermon . . .* (London, 1712), p. 11.

her Dutch Protestant allies. Despite the protests of the Levellers, the New Model Army was fairly easily diverted into pursuing a war of colonial expropriation against the Catholic Irish; so that the English Revolution, as Marx observed, "met shipwreck in Ireland."[30] A sense of national differences continued to cut across class alignments in the industrial age. It is possible to compile a list of radicals who have actively pursued their cause across national boundaries; it would include the English "Jacobins," who sent addresses to revolutionary France and sympathized with the United Irishmen; the Fraternal Democrats (1845-1854), who admired Mazzini and Kossuth; and the Marxists and International Socialists of today. But the British Communist party (founded in 1920) has never been an effective force, while the Labour party has been doggedly insular, even jingoistic. When war broke out in 1914, the current wave of strikes abated and workingmen flocked to the recruiting offices; in 1939 the pacifist movement, so active between the wars, proved ineffective.

The final constituent in English identity has been imperialism; from their beginnings, colonization and overseas enterprise helped to create a sense of national self-consciousness.[31] By the nineteenth century most middle-class Englishmen felt a mission to export Protestantism and representative institutions to the benighted inhabitants of the colonial countries; and the working classes took a vicarious pleasure in the triumphs of empire. The flag, the queen, the national anthem have been potent symbols. Generations of schoolchildren brought up to contemplate a map of the world of which a third was colored red, felt a sense of complacent superiority that was only dissolved in the mid-twentieth century by the rapid demise of the British Empire. The United Kingdom's recent entry into the European Economic Community (1973) may ultimately call for further redefinition of English identity, but it has as yet had no discernible impact upon popular consciousness.

The consequences of the loss of empire can, however, be discerned in the Celtic areas, for it was principally by their common participation in imperial responsibilities that the Scots, Irish, and Welsh demonstrated their Britishness. It is no coincidence that the decades of

[30] Karl Marx and Frederick Engels, *Selected Correspondence, 1846-1895*, edited by Dona Torr (London, 1936), p. 279. Cf. Christopher Hill, "The English Revolution and the Brotherhood of Man," in his *Puritanism and Revolution* (London, 1958).

[31] Theodore K. Rabb, *Enterprise and Empire* (Cambridge, Mass., 1967), p. 101.

imperial decline have seen a recurrence of separatist feeling in Wales and Scotland. The association with England has become something less obviously to be treasured, while economic stagnation has intensified awareness of regional inequalities.

Wales, of course, has always had its own cultural traditions. After the Tudor Union the ruling gentry became substantially Anglicized, but the majority of the people remained Welsh speaking until the Industrial Revolution. The social gulf was symbolized by the development of Welsh Nonconformity and the culture of the chapel. In the nineteenth century the Welsh feeling of separateness expressed itself in successful agitations for the Sunday closing of Welsh public houses (1881) and the disestablishment of the Anglican Church in Wales (1914, though deferred until 1920). A short-lived Young Wales movement, launched in 1886, was followed in 1925 by the foundation of a Nationalist party. The appeal of the latter, however, has been cultural rather than political, and its disadvantage is that the culture invoked is that of Welsh-speaking, Nonconformist rural Wales, whereas the majority of the population of modern Wales lives in the industrial south and is neither Welsh speaking nor subject to much religious commitment. Welsh speakers declined from 60 percent in 1891 to just under 21 percent in 1971, while monoglot Welshmen have almost disappeared. At present, the Nationalist party, although polling over 10 percent of Welsh votes, holds only three of the thirty-six Welsh parliamentary seats. Government concessions, including the creation of a Welsh Office in 1964, have helped to keep feeling low. The essential fact is that most of Wales has been integrated into the British industrial economy. Since the nineteenth century the rebellion of the Welsh working classes against Anglicized gentlemen and employers has therefore taken the form, not of separatism, but of involvement in *English* politics and trade unionism. Welsh Chartism had no nationalist overtones, and modern Wales has been a bastion of the Labour party. Only continued economic recession can make Welsh separatism an effective force.

In Scotland, similar administrative concessions (a Scottish Secretary [1885], upgraded to Secretary of State [1926], and a number of government departments in Edinburgh) had until recently achieved a roughly similar result. There too, the industrial working classes felt more solidarity with their English counterparts than with the cultural nationalists; and it is only the recent sense of economic neglect by Westminster that has weakened this sentiment. But the new nationalism is also able to draw upon historical tradition. Scotland was a single kingdom for centuries before the personal union of the crowns,[32] by which James I became the first king of "Great Britain." Charles I's attempts to impose the Anglican Prayer Book upon the Scots provoked the nationalist Covenanting movement and the Scottish invasion of England (1639-1640), thus precipitating the meeting of the Long Parliament and assisting the outbreak of the Civil War. To this extent the breakdown of government in England in 1642 can be seen as the result of a Scottish identity crisis (and to some extent an Irish one as well, for it was the Ulster Rebellion of 1641 that forced Charles to call for an army, and thus brought relations with Parliament to a head). The subsequent breach between the Scots and their English parliamentary allies led to the Second Civil War and Cromwell's conquest of Scotland, resulting in the short-lived parliamentary union of 1653-1660. An enduring parliamentary and economic union was delayed until 1707, when the security of the Protestant succession seemed threatened by the possibility of an independent Scotland. Even then it was not the thoroughgoing "incorporating" union for which James I had hoped, but an economic and legislative union that enabled Scotland to preserve her Presbyterian church and her distinctive legal system. The last threat to the union came from the Jacobite risings of 1715 and 1745, but what they expressed was conflict within Scotland: hostility toward the Campbells and Highland resentment of the dominance of Edinburgh (Scotland has its "core" and "periphery" no less than the United Kingdom). Since the mid-nineteenth century, organized nationalist movements have called for various degrees of Home Rule and independence. But it is only recently that lagging economic development and the prospect of North Sea oil have given such claims effective support. The Scottish National party (founded 1934) has made striking advances in the last decade, polling 30 percent of Scottish votes in 1974 and gaining eleven MPs. The Kilbrandon Report (1973), which proposed legislative devolution for Scotland and Wales, was a response to this resurgence of nationalist sentiment, but its proposals are yet to be implemented.

Like the union with Wales, therefore, the link between England and Scotland was a case of political integration being achieved in

[32] On its formation, see G.W.S. Barrow, *The Kingdom of the Scots* (London, 1973).

advance of a single national identity. In both instances greater integration was subsequently achieved by economic unification and the assimilation of the regions concerned into a single class structure. Had Wales and Scotland remained predominantly peasant societies, such integration would have been much harder to achieve. As it is, the main threat to unity in modern times comes less from ethnic or cultural differences than from the relative economic underdevelopment of the Celtic areas.

The case of Ireland is much more complicated. It has never been effectively united. Its long history of semi-effective English overlordship lasted from the twelfth century until the mid-seventeenth, when Cromwell carried out the military subjugation of the island and bequeathed a class of absentee English landlords. James II's attempts to make Ireland his base in 1689 produced another war and further land redistribution. The attempt of the United Irishmen to join with Revolutionary France in the late 1790s led to the Parliamentary Union of 1801, which lasted, despite considerable religious and economic pressure, for a hundred and twenty years. A vigorous movement for Home Rule was ultimately converted into a bid for independence. This was achieved, after bitter fighting, in 1922, when the Irish Free State came into existence, leaving only the six counties in the Northeast to remain part of the United Kingdom.

The Belfast area had differed from the rest of Ireland in having a heavy concentration of Protestant settlers, and in being much more closely integrated with the English industrial economy. In 1914 the proposal to make Ulster part of a self-governing Ireland nearly wrecked the English political system. Had the Home Rule Bill, due to come into effect that year, not been shelved because of the outbreak of war, it is possible that Ulster would have forcibly resisted its incorporation in a self governing Ireland and would have done so with the support of a section of the British Conservative party. The Conservative Opposition canvassed the idea of refusing to pass the annual Army Act, thus depriving the government of military force at a time of mounting international crisis. At the Curragh a large group of British army officers declared they would resign rather than fight against Ulster. The outbreak of the 1914-1918 war averted the clash—a striking example of the way in which crises can be resolved by purely external events.

The establishment of a separate Northern Ireland, however, has proved to be a short-term solution. Because the Unionist party has been continuously in power at Stormont since 1921, the distinction between government and regime has been almost nonexistent. The Unionists have made little effort to secure the support of the Roman Catholics, two-thirds of whom remain an alienated minority,[33] though one deterred from breaking away altogether by the inferior economic and welfare arrangements offered by the Irish republic. In the late 1960s conflict between Protestant and Catholic in Northern Ireland led to prolonged violence and guerrilla war. The suspension of the Northern Ireland government in March 1972 made the issue one for the British government to resolve; and the outcome of this intense crisis—for the Northern Irish one of identity, for the British one of penetration—remains to be seen.

Finally, we must ponder the likely consequences of Commonwealth immigration into Britain since the second world war. The United Kingdom now contains over a million colored immigrants, mostly from India, Pakistan, and the West Indies, some unable to speak English and many attached to their own religious and cultural traditions. To some extent the British have always been ethnically heterogeneous. The ruling dynasties have been of foreign origin; and since the sixteenth century the country has absorbed successive waves of Dutch, French, Jewish, and Irish immigrants. They have done this by toleration and assimilation. But the assimilation of the latest batch of newcomers presents problems of a different order. Immigration has been restricted, while the inferior social and economic position of the colored immigrant communities increases the ultimate risk of serious racial tension. In the process the British sense of identity may have to undergo yet further redefinition.

LEGITIMACY

Nothing is more misleading to the student of English history than the apparent continuity of the country's main political institutions. Crown, Parliament, common law, shire, and borough: all were firmly established in the medieval period and their survival into the twentieth century has frequently been the subject of comment. But the functions of these institutions, and the criteria that have legitimized them in the eyes of the politically effective classes, have changed radically over the centuries.

[33] For the results of a survey of Catholic opinion carried out in the now obsolete conditions of 1968, see Richard Rose, *Governing without Consensus. An Irish Perspective* (London, 1971).

The medieval monarchy evolved from a feudal overlordship. To retain the support of the magnates, the king needed to demonstrate his dynastic legitimacy, his military capacity, his willingness to keep his coronation oath, and his respect for the rights of his chief followers. His failure to satisfy the magnates in any of these respects could precipitate a political crisis of a kind that might lead to a period of "anarchy" or disputed government, as in the reign of Stephen (1135-1153) or during the Wars of the Roses (1455-1485). It could engender demands for the redefinition of the king's powers, as in the conflict culminating in Magna Carta (1215) or the political crisis of Henry III's reign (1258-1267). It might even lead to the monarch's deposition and death, as in the cases of Edward II (1327) and Richard II (1399).

Although the coronation had long been a religious ceremony, it was only in the sixteenth century that the supposedly divine basis of the king's authority came to be particularly emphasized. This was partly because it was only then that the Crown asserted its headship of the English church and repudiated the authority of the pope. The Henrician Reformation precipitated a legitimacy crisis in the 1530s, when widespread support for papal authority was only quelled by a combination of new treason legislation and strenuous royal propaganda. For more than a century thereafter, the religious affiliations of the regime determined its legitimacy. The Civil War was provoked by the fear that Charles I proposed to betray the Protestant settlement; and later challenges to legitimacy were associated with the claims of an alternative religious allegiance, as in the case of Monmouth's rebellion against the Catholic James II (1685), the triumph of the Protestant William III in 1689, and the risings of the Jacobites.

In the seventeenth century there was a lack of clear agreement as to the source of royal authority. Broadly speaking, the period saw a shift from an appeal to divine right to more secular notions of utility and convenience. But the process is difficult to chart, since few political confrontations raised the issue explicitly. Politicians were concerned less with declaring the basis of royal authority than with prescribing the limits to be set to it. In order to secure greater penetration, the Tudor monarchy had developed new agencies of government and judicature that supplemented and, as some argued, threatened to supersede the ordinary processes of the common law. Yet even the ordinary law courts could be invoked to support the view that the royal prerogative entitled the king to act outside the ordinary course of law at times of emergency. This doctrine could justify arbitrary arrest and extraparliamentary taxation. The constitutional conflicts surrounding these issues culminated in the crisis of 1640-1641, when the Long Parliament dismantled the apparatus of conciliar government and set legal limits to the extent of royal authority. It took a civil war and interregnum to confirm this settlement; and another crisis in 1688-1689 to consolidate it.

The defeat of royal absolutism drove home the lesson that the king ruled for the convenience of the political nation rather than by divine authority. The execution of Charles I had been justified on the grounds that the king had committed treason by levying war against the Parliament and people of England; and though the makers of the 1689 Revolution did not endorse the view that James II had been deposed for breaking "the original contract between king and people," the ultimate effect of the revolution's settlement was to repudiate divine right and make it a constitutional doctrine that a king who ruled by a parliamentary title was *de jure* as well as *de facto*.[34]

Doctrines of divine right and patriarchalism did not die overnight, as is shown by the emergence of a clerical party of Non-Jurors who refused to swear allegiance to William and Mary. But after 1689 a ruler's legitimacy depended on a parliamentary title and a willingness to respect Protestantism, the common law, and the desires of the propertied classes. During the eighteenth and early nineteenth centuries the king's freedom to choose his ministers was eroded, not by legislation but by political pressure. As the monarch became merely the agent giving formal recognition to the political leaders commanding a majority in the House of Commons and constituting the Cabinet, the Crown retreated into ideological colorlessness, immune from political criticism. Today the continuing legitimacy of this attenuated monarchy requires its holders to take great pains about the conscientious discharge of their formal duties, to shun obvious political allegiances, and to avoid wounding the moral or religious susceptibilities of the bulk of the population. The abdication of Edward VIII in 1936 because of his desire to marry an Amer-

[34] Mark A. Thomson, *A Constitutional History of England, 1642 to 1801* (London, 1938), p. 178. For the difficulty that the Whigs had in popularizing a more radical view of 1688, see J. P. Kenyon, "The Revolution of 1688: Resistance and Contract," in Neil McKendrick, ed., *Historical Perspectives. Studies in English Thought and Society in Honour of J. H. Plumb* (London, 1974).

ican divorcée demonstrated the new requirement that the monarch should conform to the middle-class morality of the day, a limitation that many earlier rulers would have found intolerable.

The legitimacy of the English monarchy has thus survived without serious challenge, but only at the price of endless redefinition of its style and powers. What is remarkable, however, is the basic authority that the institution had attained before the period of obvious "modernization." The rebellions of the fifteenth and sixteenth centuries never threatened the monarchy as such. The Wars of the Roses, for example, enhanced the position of the Crown by the very fact of producing so many contenders for it. Tudor rebellions were not directly against the person of the king, but appealed to him against his supposedly "evil counsellors." Even the Civil War began in this traditional way. Parliamentarians claimed to be fighting *for* the king against his wicked advisors: Oliver Cromwell shocked many of his supporters when he declared that he would kill Charles I if he met him on the field of battle.[35] The lower-class tradition that the monarchy was illegitimate, being founded on conquest, had only a limited influence, while classical republicanism appealed to only a minority of intellectuals. The execution of the king in 1649 did not stem from ideological repudiation of the institution of monarchy so much as disillusion with the person of Charles I and the absence of any acceptable alternative. The republican government that followed failed to develop any distinct ideology of its own. It was acceptable because it worked—guaranteeing social order and carrying out a successful foreign policy. By 1657 Cromwell found himself under pressure to assume the kingship, and he probably would have done so had he lived longer. As it was, his death in 1658 and the collapse of public order after the military coup that overthrew his son ensured the restoration of the old order—not out of any dynastic commitment to the Stuarts, but, once again, because of the absence of any acceptable alternative. After the 1688 Revolution, the maxim that the king could do no wrong became the essential doctrine underpinning modern concepts of ministerial responsibility. As a symbol of national unity transcending the divisions of political faction, the monarchy remains the keystone of the British political system. It is an essentially conservative force, buttressing the established order and inhibiting the extreme expression of class antagonisms.

[35] Edward, Earl of Clarendon, *The History of the Rebellion*, edited by W. D. Macray (Oxford, 1888), IV, 305-306.

Like the Crown, Parliament has also undergone substantial shifts in the basis of its authority. It began as a semijudicial, semiconsultative body, and its two Houses had become firmly established by the time of Edward III. The omnicompetence of parliamentary statute was apparent by the 1530s, and the employment of acts of Parliament to consolidate the religious changes of the sixteenth century did much to establish the notion that the king in Parliament was a sovereign body capable of initiating fundamental political changes. Strict legal theory was, however, slow to recognize this development. Many of the most important statutory innovations of the Tudor and Stuart period had to be cast in fictitious declaratory form, as if they were mere restatements of existing law, rather than departures from it. Full recognition of the idea of sovereignty was not explicit until the mid-seventeenth century.

This intellectual lag, however, did not act as a very effective check upon Parliament's activities. Much more inhibiting was the prospect that the institution itself might not retain a place in the government of the land. In the sixteenth century, Parliament only met when it was needed by the government for the passing of legislation or the granting of money. If royal proclamation could supersede statute, and if royal finances could be otherwise secured, then Parliament would be unnecessary. During the first half of the seventeenth century, it looked as if the English monarchy might become an absolutism on the continental model and dispense with Parliament altogether. Charles I ruled without Parliament from 1629 to 1640. But his government collapsed in what might be called a crisis of legitimacy, penetration, and participation. Parliament assumed new powers during the Civil War and Interregnum, though the House of Lords was abolished as "useless and dangerous." Yet, even after the Restoration, Parliament was not yet firmly established as indispensable. Charles II ruled without it for the last four years of his reign, and his absolute methods of government commanded a good deal of support among the propertied classes. So, at first, did those of James II.[36] It was only the latter's mistakes (offending the church and alienating local oligarchs) that precipitated the foreign invasion of William of Orange; and it was only the ensuing failure of the politicians to provide William III with an automatic source of revenue that ensured the annual meeting of Parliament after 1689.

[36] As has been argued by J. R. Western, *Monarchy and Revolution. The English State in the 1680s* (London, 1972); and J. R. Jones, *The Revolution of 1688 in England* (London, 1972).

The legitimacy of the post-1689 political order remained uncertain, partly because of the Jacobite threat to the Hanoverian succession, partly because of bitter party conflicts in which the will to live and let live was singularly lacking. The Whig and Tory politicians were far from participating in the stylized ritual of modern party politics, where it is less important to win than to avoid spoiling the game. Political stability was only achieved in the 1720s with the growth of an oligarchical system in which government patronage was used to secure a ministerial majority in a House of Commons elected by a restricted electorate.[37] Until that point the use of state violence against political opponents had been as common as in any African state today. This can be seen in the executions of Strafford, Laud, Charles I, the regicides, Algernon Sidney, and Lord Russell, and in the political exile into which men like Shaftesbury and Bolingbroke were forced. Not until after 1715 did the practice of impeaching unsuccessful politicians fall into desuetude.

Between the Reformation and the Hanoverian succession there had thus occurred a series of legitimacy crises, during which the established order manifestly failed to command the support of all the political nation. These crises were resolved by the establishment of a Protestant limited monarchy, with effective power wielded by the leaders of a Parliament representing the propertied classes. The latter in turn exercised authority over their inferiors by a combination of economic power and social status. The system was further legitimized by a wide range of political and legal liberties—religious toleration for most Protestants, a free press, an independent judiciary and jury system, considerable freedom of public meeting, immunity from arbitrary arrest, freedom to petition and hold public meetings.

Even so, the conventions of the new system were slow to establish themselves. When Jacobinism raised its head in the 1790s, the old controls on free political expression were temporarily reimposed. Even within the oligarchy the expression of parliamentary opposition was regarded as factious. From the 1730s antiministerial MPs took their seat on the left of the speaker and were known as the Opposition, but the legitimacy of political party and "formed" Opposition remained controversial until the 1820s. The rules of two-party government were largely a nineteenth-century invention; and only in 1937 did the leader of His Majesty's Opposition begin to draw

[37] This is the theme of J. H. Plumb, *The Growth of Political Stability in England, 1675-1725* (London, 1967).

a public salary. The political neutrality of the civil service was also a nineteenth-century development. Paradoxically, it is to the very fact of being descended from the old "unreformed" civil service that the modern bureaucracy owes its independence; for it was the existence of freeholds and reversions that helped to prevent the growth of an American-style "spoils system" of public office.[38]

Although some of the features of British "consensus politics" are thus relatively recent, it is nonetheless important that the basic institutional structure of the system attained full legitimacy well before universal suffrage, and that a medieval Parliament, designed for quite different purposes, has managed to establish itself as the forum for the expression of modern party differences. The ancient principle of constituency-based representation, for example, has so far survived the demands of minority parties for the introduction of proportional representation. The very shape of the debating chamber, derived from the accidental fact that from 1547 to 1834 the Commons sat in St. Stephen's chapel, is now regarded as so fundamental that when the chamber was accidentally burned down it was deliberately rebuilt in the same style, with the house divided into two, and with the convention that members should speak from their seats rather than from a central rostrum. The legitimacy acquired by these trivial survivals has contributed immeasurably to the consolidation of the two-party system.

By the time of the Industrial Revolution, the legitimacy of Parliament was so well established that even the working classes, excluded from political participation, accepted it as the natural outlet for their grievances. In the late eighteenth century the great fear was that the numerous extraparliamentary associations for the promotion of franchise reform might constitute a sort of anti-Parliament. In fact all these external lobbies—such as the county association movement of the early 1780s—concentrated their energies on an appeal to Parliament rather than an attempt to supersede it. During the protracted participation crisis of the late eighteenth and early nineteenth centuries, there were few reformers, however alienated, who did not agree that it was a new form of parliamentary representation that they wished to secure; if, like the Chartists, they reengaged in massive public demonstrations, it was usually with the intention of presenting the House of Commons with a petition em-

[38] S. E. Finer, "Patronage and the Public Service. Jeffersonian Bureaucracy and the British Tradition," *Public Administration*, 30 (1952), 329-60.

bodying their grievances.[39] During the nineteenth and early twentieth centuries, the franchise was widened so as to embrace the whole adult population, but many of the conventions of political life remained those derived from an age when politicians were members of the same social class. "Our whole political machinery," as the Tory leader, A. J. Balfour remarked, "presupposes a people so fully at one that they can safely afford to bicker."[40] As a result of this institutional continuity, working-class politicians, far from challenging the institution of Parliament, have shown themselves zealous defenders of its traditions. The absence of a written constitution and of any defined political goals has given these inherited institutions the flexibility necessary for their survival. In modern times the legitimacy of the system remains secure. There is plenty of cynicism about politicians. But few deny their authority to rule.

Balfour's complacent view of a people fundamentally at one, however, can be overstated. It is true that monarchy, Parliament, peers, and common law have survived the period of political modernization. But all have been subjected to intense criticism. Monarchy has had to cede its powers. Parliament has had to open its doors. The House of Lords, by its diehard resistance to the Lloyd-George Budget of 1909, provoked a major legitimacy crisis, which was only resolved by the reduction of its powers in the Parliament Act of 1911. On the eve of the first world war the Tory leaders were encouraging the Ulstermen to repudiate the authority of Parliament itself. Even the common law was only saved from extensive remodeling during the Interregnum by the presence of lawyers in Parliament; and its workings in the eighteenth century did not command universal support. There was a distinction between the legal code and the unwritten popular code; certain crimes, such as poaching, tax evasion, and smuggling were widely condoned by the whole community,[41] just as motoring offences are today. In the 1790s Paine denounced the monarchy as descended from "a banditti of ruffians," and in the 1870s there were scores of republican clubs. At no time is it difficult to discern the existence of bitter alienated minorities re-

[39] For adherents to a more militant attitude, see T. M. Parssinen, "Association, Convention and Anti-Parliament in British Radical Politics, 1771-1848," *English Historical Review*, 88 (1973), 504-33.

[40] Introduction to Walter Bagehot, *The English Constitution* (World's Classics ed., London, 1928), p. xxiv.

[41] See Douglas Hay, Peter Linebaugh *et al.*, *Albion's Fatal Tree: Crime and Society in Eighteenth-Century England* (1975).

jecting all or part of the prevailing system: the "Jacobins" of the 1790s; the Luddites of 1811-1813; the revolutionary Spenceans of 1816-1820; the "physical force" Chartists; the syndicalists who, on the eve of the first world war, hoped to overthrow capitalism by industrial action; and in the 1960s the supporters of CND, Direct Action, and other extraparliamentary movements.

The existence of such minorities, however, is presumably irrelevant to the present inquiry, since the only "legitimacy" a political system need obtain is legitimacy in the eyes of those with power to overthrow it,[42] and this power these minorities never possessed. More recently, however, a powerful challenge has been mounted by the trade unions. In the early 1970s the unions successfully defied the authority of the Industrial Relations Act and resisted the jurisdiction of the Industrial Relations Court. Subsequently they overthrew by industrial action the government's policy of compulsory wage restraint. The claim of the unions to constitute a privileged enclave in society, exempt from external restraint, is the most obvious contemporary threat to the legitimacy of the political system since 1689.

Nevertheless, it is doubtful whether England has ever experienced a "pure" legitimacy crisis. Crises have only arisen when the regime fails to deliver other goods expected of it—law and order, religious toleration, political participation, or social justice. Even those minority groups who based their claims on legitimacy in the narrowest sense prove on closer examination to have had other objectives. The Fifth Monarchists of the mid-seventeenth century attempted armed insurrection as a means of inaugurating the rule of the saints, but they were also concerned to remedy the economic plight of the lower classes of London. The supporters of Charles II had not been prepared to act on behalf of their "legitimate" ruler so long as Cromwell was providing them with political stability and protection against the radical sects. There have been many political "crises" in modern British history, and all have inevitably raised the question of legitimacy. But those in which legitimacy has been the sole issue have been the least critical.

PARTICIPATION

Medieval government presupposed an ideal of harmonious cooperation between the king and the magnates. Periodically the barons

[42] See the incisive comments of Brian Barry, *Sociologists, Economists and Democracy* (London, 1970), pp. 66-67.

were forced into asserting their rights as the king's natural counsellors, by challenging the king's choice of advisers and the policies he pursued. Such confrontations as those of 1258 (Provisions of Oxford), 1311 (Ordinances), or 1318 (Treaty of Leak) can be regarded as miniature "crises of participation." They were, of course, conflicts *within* the governing elite rather than between the elite and the masses; and they came before the era of "modernization." Yet the nineteenth-century Whig myth of continuity between baronial leaders like Simon de Montfort and parliamentary magnates like the Marquis of Rockingham or Lord Grey of the Reform Bill was not entirely groundless. For the emergence in feudal times of a rough balance between Crown and magnates can be plausibly represented as a necessary precondition of the subsequent development of popular democracy.[43] Moreover, the appearance of Parliament as the king's Great Council gave these conflicts a new dimension. From time to time the king found it convenient to reinforce the magnates with representatives of the shires and the boroughs. As early as 1297 it was established that taxation could only be granted by the whole "community of the realm"; and by 1327 the Commons had secured the right to be present at every Parliament, though, of course, the Commons represented only the more substantial members of the community.

Parliament survived because it was convenient for the king's purposes; and it would be anachronistic to regard it as locked in conflict with the Crown. Even so, the reigns of Edward III, Richard II, and Henry IV saw many vigorous parliamentary challenges to royal authority. The Commons asserted their claims to criticise the king's finances, foreign policy, and even choice of ministers. Many of these conflicts (which it would be tedious to enumerate) could be plausibly identified as "crises of participation," though the Commons were usually as much a front for magnate intrigue as an independent political force. In the late fourteenth and early fifteenth centuries, baronial efforts were more directed to the alternative task of controlling the membership of the king's Council. Tudor government was also essentially carried on by the king and his Council, but the Crown had to turn to Parliament for money and for legislation. The use of statute for the implementation of the Henrician Reformation proved particularly important. Parliament's share in the formation of royal policy became a key issue in the constitutional conflicts of Elizabethan

[43] Moore, *Social Origins of Dictatorship and Democracy*, p. 417.

and early Stuart times; and it was central in the major crises of 1640-1649 and 1688-1689. After 1689, Parliament had to meet annually as the indispensable source of finance, legislation, and military discipline. Executive power gradually shifted from the king and his Council to a Cabinet reflecting the predominant political complexion of the Parliament of the day.

The seventeenth-century crisis had arisen essentially from the claims of the gentry and merchant classes to play a larger part in the making of government policy. But the Civil War led to the mobilization of lower social groups who had not previously manifested much political self-consciousness. The influence of the religious sects, some of whom were organized on democratic lines, the uprooting of men from their traditional milieux to serve in the parliamentary army, the effects of a century of increasing literacy and education, the stimulus of prolific pamphleteering and preaching made possible by the collapse of traditional controls—all these circumstances led to the formulation of reasoned demands for political participation of a kind unprecedented in England, or indeed anywhere else in the world. The most notable of these demands was the Leveller claim for householder suffrage, or on some interpretations universal manhood suffrage,[44] which was strenuously urged between 1647 and 1649 and as strenuously resisted. This protracted crisis of participation was "resolved," not by concession, but by military force directed against dissident radicals and the collapse of the participatory demands. Lower-class radicalism died almost overnight in 1660, and it remained virtually extinct until the later eighteenth century. The main reason for this otherwise baffling phenomenon appears to be that the dissenting sects, who had been in the van of the radical movement, were so busy struggling for toleration between 1662 and 1689, and for civil rights thereafter, that they had to abandon their claims to participation.

Yet despite the collapse of participatory demands, the parliamentary franchise was broadening. The changing value of money made the old 40/– freehold a less restrictive qualification than it once had been, while in the boroughs there was a marked tendency to move toward a wider franchise. By 1640 the electorate included yeomen,

[44] For a survey of the problems involved in interpreting the Leveller demands, see Keith Thomas, "The Levellers and the Franchise," in *The Interregnum: The Quest for Settlement*, edited by G. E. Aylmer (London, 1972).

craftsmen, and shopkeepers. Lord Maynard was disconcerted by the Essex election of that year—"popular assemblies where fellows without shirts challenge as good a voice as myself."[45]

Too much should not be made of this widely dispersed right to vote, for in the later seventeenth century both candidates and issues continued to reflect gentry preoccupations. But around 1700 the franchise was much more open than it was to be in the mid-eighteenth century, when contested elections became less frequent and the style of politics more oligarchic. Even after the Reform Act of 1832, the electorate was still proportionately smaller than it had been in 1722, when nearly a quarter of adult males may have had the vote.[46]

Despite its oligarchic structure, the unreformed political system did not lack some elements of wider participation. Most of the population were shut out of Parliament and parliamentary elections. But this did not mean that the excluded had no political power. The Elizabethan commentator, Sir Thomas Smith, wrote of the "day labourers, poor husbandmen, . . . merchants or retailers which have no free land, copyholders, and all artificers, as tailors, shoemakers, carpenters, brickmakers, bricklayers, masons, etc." that "these have no voice nor authority in our commonwealth, and no account is made of them but only to be ruled." But he added that "they be not altogether neglected. For in cities and corporate towns for default of yeomen, inquests and juries are impanelled of such manner of people. And in villages they be commonly made churchwardens, ale-conners, and many times constables, which office toucheth more the common wealth."[47] Since the middle ages England has possessed a bewildering mass of local institutions—parish vestries, courts baron, courts leet, village communities—each accustomed to making bylaws, appointing officers, and levying rates. They dealt with a variety of matters of local concern, and they were composed in many different ways. But they frequently afforded even the humblest members of the community some experience in self-government and the opportunity to participate in matters closest to their own interests. "Anyone who reads the manorial records,"

[45] J. H. Plumb, "The Growth of the Electorate in England from 1600 to 1715," *Past and Present*, 45 (1969), 107, 111; and see the excellent study by Derek Hirst, *The Representative of the People? Voters and Voting in England under the Early Stuarts* (Cambridge, 1975).

[46] Geoffrey Holmes, *The Electorate and the National Will in the First Age of Party* (Lancaster, 1976).

[47] Sir Thomas Smith, *De Republica Anglorum*, edited by L. Alston (Cambridge, 1906), p. 46.

writes a recent historian, "cannot fail to be astonished at the extensive participation of nearly every adult male in local affairs."[48]

In the eighteenth century the structure of local government grew more oligarchic, but in other ways political participation was widening. Britain had the largest and most sophisticated political press in Europe. Its citizens, with the exception of the religious dissenters, enjoyed civil rights, equality before the law, and personal independence. Public opinion could be freely expressed on any matter; and if the legislature or local magistrates proved unresponsive, then meetings and demonstrations could give way to riots. Eighteenth-century Britons rioted over an immense range of different issues. They did so with relative impunity, and the governing elite was sometimes sensitive to their protests.[49] To this extent "the growth of the political nation was always far faster than the spread of representative government."[50] The same was true in the nineteenth century, when the strike gradually replaced the riot as a means of obtaining the goals of the politically excluded.

Even the eighteenth-century Parliament was not utterly unresponsive to social change. Merchant MPs were scarcely more numerous at the accession of George III than they had been in the early fifteenth century, but a landed Parliament proved remarkably sensitive to the needs of trade and finance.[51] Nevertheless, many country gentry became alienated by the corruption and parasitism of the political system, particularly by its inefficiency in the conduct of the American war. It was their criticism, swollen by pressure from the new industrial classes, that created the demand for parliamentary reform. This demand was temporarily diminished by the administrative reforms of William Pitt, who attempted to prove that the old system could be made to work, and by the influence of the French Revolution, which by creating upper-class panic about "Jacobinism" led to a reactionary coalition of landed aristocracy and urban bourgeoisie, which was not dispelled until some years after the defeat of Napoleon.

[48] Carl Bridenbaugh, *Vexed and Troubled Englishmen, 1590-1642* (Oxford, 1968), p. 242.

[49] See George Rudé, *The Crowd in History, a Study of Popular Disturbances in France and England, 1730-1848* (London, 1964).

[50] J. H. Plumb, "Political Man," in James L. Clifford, ed., *Man versus Society in Eighteenth-Century Britain* (Cambridge, 1968), p. 16.

[51] Cf. Sir Lewis Namier, *England in the Age of the American Revolution* (2nd ed., London, 1961), pp. 5, 34. There were forty merchants in Parliament in 1422 (J. S. Roskell, *The Commons in the Parliament of 1422* [Manchester 1954], p. 125), and fifty in 1761 (Namier, *The Structure of Politics at the Accession of George III* [2nd ed., London, 1960], pp. 48-49).

In 1832, pressure culminated in the Reform Act. Further demands for the widening of the suffrage were conceded in the Acts of 1867, 1884, and 1918, which enfranchised, respectively, the town worker, the rural worker, and finally (for nearly half of those technically enfranchised had escaped registration on the electoral roll) all men over 21 and all women over 30. The "flapper" vote (for women over 21) came in 1928, and in 1970 the voting age was further lowered to 18. Other key changes included secret voting (1872), the restriction of corrupt practices (especially the Act of 1883), the construction of equal constituencies in place of the ancient units of shire and borough (1885), the payment of MPs (1911), the abolition of the House of Lords' veto (1911), the abolition of plural voting for university graduates and occupiers of business premises (1948), and the democratization of local government (municipalities, 1835; county councils, 1888; urban district and parish councils, 1894).

The skilful retreat of the oligarchy in the face of these successive demands has often been described; and it certainly helps to explain both the readiness with which the newly enfranchised elements accepted the old parliamentary framework and the extent to which the aristocracy and middle classes retained their grip upon the actual reins of political power. Nevertheless, England is not necessarily an exportable model of how to achieve mass political participation in a peaceful manner.

For the survival of English representative institutions, at a time when similar bodies were being eroded by royal absolutism elsewhere, had been the reflection of special conditions. Parliament was not organized in different estates that could be played off against each other, in the way that happened, for example, in Brandenburg-Prussia. Knights and burgesses sat together, and the Commons included younger brothers of the lords. Primogeniture and the early commercialization of English landownership meant that landed, moneyed, and trading interests were never distinct. Nor were peers formally exempt from taxation. There was thus a close community of interest between country and town. Moreover, from the Crown's point of view, Parliament was well organized for the conduct of business. It was genuinely representative of the propertied classes, and with 507 members by 1640 was the largest representative assembly in Europe.[52] The origins of wider participation thus lay in the

[52] As is pointed out by G. R. Elton, "*The Body of the Whole Realm.*" *Parliament and Representation in Medieval and Tudor England* (Charlottesville, Va., 1969), pp. 31-32.

inherited structure of society and its distinctive institutions, rather than in any special political wisdom on the part of the political elite.

Moreover, although the elite is usually congratulated in the textbooks for knowing when to give way, it was not always in command of the situation. Parliamentary government was only established after armed conflict. Charles I's mistakes prevented a peaceful settlement in 1642 and James II only obtained one in 1689 by abdicating altogether. It was because England had a bloody revolution in the seventeenth century that she escaped one in the nineteenth. It is true that in the nineteenth and twentieth centuries the classes in possession of political power always managed to yield before it was too late. But sometimes they cut it very fine. Much evidence can be accumulated to show the intensity of democratic agitation and revolutionary feeling in working-class England, especially between 1790 and 1822. These were years of underground conspiracy, harsh political repression, the suspension of many civil rights, and much popular demonstration. Although most working-class reformers saw themselves as reasserting traditional liberties in face of upper-class reaction, there was also a small nucleus of revolutionaries who hoped for a coup d'état and a proletarian insurrection. The years 1831-1832, when the Reform Bills were at stake, can be plausibly regarded as a revolutionary crisis, held in check by the "constitutional" element among the reformers and averted in the nick of time by the surrender of the king and lords to extraparliamentary pressure. "We were within a moment of general rebellion," wrote Francis Place, the organizer of reform.[53]

The crisis was resolved by the passage of the first Reform Act, which conciliated the middle classes but left the proletariat unenfranchised. From 1838 there was large-scale working-class agitation based on "the People's Charter," which demanded manhood suffrage, secret voting, the abolition of property qualifications for MPs, equal electoral districts, the payment of MPs, and annual Parliaments (that is, direct democracy). Although the Chartists had a "physical force" wing, their methods were essentially constitutional; and they proceeded by presenting giant petitions to Parliament. On the whole the government displayed restraint. It had little option anyway, since the apparatus of repression was weak; it was only under the pressure of Chartist agitation that the police force was extended to the coun-

[53] Quoted by Harold Perkin, *The Origins of Modern English Society, 1780-1880* (London, 1969), p. 368. For the threat of barricades in 1832, see J.R.M. Butler, *The Passing of the Great Reform Bill* (London, 1914), p. 411.

ties in 1839. But there was never any disposition to make concessions so as to avert revolution, and it was perhaps the demonstration of Chartism's nonrevolutionary character that led the politicians to revive the question of parliamentary reform after 1848. The Chartist movement subsided without any concessions being made. Divisions within the working class, increasing prosperity, the alternative route of trade union activity—all helped to take the steam out of the agitation.

Another participation crisis came in the 1860s, when there was talk of a People's Parliament and of a Grand National Holiday or general strike. The government's weakness was demonstrated by its failure to prevent a public meeting of the Reform League in Hyde Park on 6 May 1867; this may have converted some leading politicians into accepting the Reform Act of that year. If so, the government "allowed a reformist movement to score a revolutionary triumph."[54] The House of Lords lost its veto only in 1911, after another and even more serious political crisis. On the other hand, it is doubtful whether the cause of female suffrage was much advanced by those Suffragettes who from 1905 onwards adopted militant tactics, attacking and burning property, interrupting meetings, and engaging in hunger strikes. Such tactics drew attention to the issue, but it was parliamentary awareness of wider social change that brought women the vote in 1918.

The peaceful extension of participation was often as much a matter of luck as of judgment. The 1832 Act was intended by many of its supporters as a purification of the old electoral system rather than the beginning of a new one; it might never have got through if it had been recognized as the thin edge of the wedge. In 1867 the main participants were ill informed about the precise implications of the various reform proposals, and ended up by enfranchising more voters than they had intended; the act was meant to perpetuate the control of the propertied classes and form a "bulwark against democracy."[55]

It is, however, true that there was a relative absence of diehard opposition to parliamentary reform, at least among the party leaders. There were three main reasons for this. The first was that English landowners were economically secure enough to be able to make po-

[54] Royden Harrison, *Before the Socialists* (London, 1965), p. 136. But for a strenuous assertion of the view that the politicans went their own way, unaffected by outside pressure, see Maurice Cowling, *1867. Disraeli, Gladstone and Revolution. The Passing of the Second Reform Bill* (Cambridge, 1967).

[55] F. B. Smith, *The Making of the Second Reform Bill* (Cambridge, 1966), p. 233.

litical concessions; the second was that they lacked the means to resist demands by force; and the third was that the enfranchisement of new classes proved compatible with the retention of much political power in old hands. The first Reform Act had little immediately discernible influence upon the style or personnel of British politics. The effects of the Second Act were mitigated by the retention of the old constituency structure and by the growth of party organization; by controlling the process of electoral registration, it proved possible to enlist the support of new voters for the two old parties. In this way power was shared rather than transferred. As John Stuart Mill retorted when it was suggested that parliamentary reform would make workmen "masters of the situation": "They may be able to decide whether a Whig or a Tory shall be elected—they may be masters of so small a matter as that."[56] Aristocrats (defined as sons of holders of hereditary titles) formed a majority of British Cabinet ministers until 1906.[57] No son of a manual worker appeared in a British Cabinet until that year, and only one more before 1924. To some extent, of course, this impression of continuing aristocratic control is illusory. The personnel of nineteenth-century politics were frequently aristocratic, but the measures passed by governments after 1832 were overwhelmingly conceived in the interests of the middle classes. This was as much because of the moral and intellectual conversion of many landowners to bourgeois values as because of any fear of pressure from below. But to this extent power had shifted. On the other hand, the formation of a Labour party was delayed until 1900. When the working classes were fully enfranchised in 1918, Labour displaced the Liberals in the two-party system, but there was no Labour government until 1924, and no majority one until 1945. Such Labour ministries as have held office have not gone very far toward creating socialism. A two-party system inevitably reduces class conflict by forcing each side to moderate its demands in order to be able to pose as a "national" party.

In fact, as the suffrage has been extended, the importance of political participation by voting has diminished. The growth of monolithic party machines and the effective control of the House of Commons by the ministers of the reigning party[58] have combined to

[56] Quoted by Harrison, *Before the Socialists*, p. 123.

[57] Harold J. Laski, *Studies in Law and Politics* (London, 1932), chapter 8.

[58] For the development of this see Peter Fraser, "The Growth of Ministerial Control in the Nineteenth-Century House of Commons," *English Historical Review*, 75 (1960), 444-63; and Valerie Cromwell, "The Losing of the Initiative by the

reduce the range of choice open to the individual voter. Membership in a political party brings no extra influence, for today's parliamentary parties are virtually independent of their extraparliamentary organizations. Only at moments of internal disagreement among the party leaders, as in 1846, 1886, 1918, or 1931, has the party system threatened to disintegrate.[59] Postwar general elections have produced a high turnout at the polls, but all the surveys indicate underlying apathy and a weak sense of commitment to the parties, which are remote and inaccessible. The system of representation does not even ensure the rule of the party commanding the widest popular support; for example, in 1951 the Conservatives won more seats than Labour, and were thus able to form a government, although they actually polled fewer votes.

In any case, the complexity of government regulation in a large industrial state makes administrative action less and less controllable, even by Parliament. In the same way, foreign policy commitments are often secret or dimly understood, as became apparent in 1914. In such circumstances one can hardly speak of parliamentary sovereignty, let alone popular participation.

For the ordinary citizen the most important means of political participation has become access to one of the trade unions or pressure groups, who, by bargaining with the government and the bureaucracy, effectively determine the nature and outcome of most political decisions. Pressure groups have made themselves felt in Parliament since at least the early sixteenth century,[60] but extraparliamentary associations first became important in the later eighteenth century. Parliaments, however, though giving ample scope to the various interest groups among the MPs themselves, tended initially to be highly suspicious of pressure from outside the House; and the constitutional propriety of issuing instructions to MPs or petitioning Parliament was much debated. Nevertheless, it was the lobbying and petitioning of extraparliamentary associations that produced some of the most notable legislative achievements of the early nineteenth century: the abolition of slavery and the slave trade; Catholic emancipation; the first Reform Act; the repeal of the Corn Laws. "No important innovation, no decisive measure, has ever been carried out

House of Commons, 1780-1914," *Transactions of the Royal Historical Society*, 5th series, 18 (1968), 1-23.

59 Cowling, *The Impact of Labour, 1920-1924*, p. 8.

60 See, e.g., G. R. Elton, *Reform and Renewal. Thomas Cromwell and the Common Weal* (Cambridge, 1973), 77-78.

in this country without pressure from without," wrote Marx in 1862.[61] The extraparliamentary association, it has been justly remarked, "made possible the extension of the politically effective public."[62]

During the late nineteenth and early twentieth centuries, all sections of the community developed their associations—trade unions, business leagues, professional groups. As these associations came to enjoy closer relations with the government and the bureaucracy, the importance of votes and parties diminished. By 1920 the Webbs could write that "the real government of Great Britain is nowadays carried on not in the House of Commons at all, nor even in the Cabinet, but in private conferences between ministers with their principal officials and the representatives of persons specially affected by any proposed legislation or by action on the part of the administration."[63] In modern times the business of government is essentially that of negotiation between interest groups. They are consulted at all stages, from the formation of the party program to the implementation of legislation. The contacts between the bureaucracy and these outside groups are formalized by the admission of their representatives to standing advisory and consultative committees. The government's role is that of broker and coordinator. Pressure groups thus provide the citizen with an alternative means of influencing government policy. But membership in a large pressure group can be as frustrating as membership in a political party, for such a group will have its own hierarchy and bureaucracy, and may be equally inaccessible to the ordinary members. The "participation crises" of the future are thus more likely to be located within the organization of parties, trade unions, industrial firms, universities and pressure groups than in direct confrontations between government and people.

PENETRATION

By the thirteenth century the main functions of royal government were clearly defined. They comprised the administration of justice (though private jurisdictions still survived), the conduct of war,

[61] *Karl Marx and Frederick Engels on Britain* (2nd ed., Moscow, 1962), p. 478. For examples, see *Pressure from without in Early Victorian England*, edited by Patricia Hollis (London, 1974).

[62] Eugene Charlton Black, *The Association. British Extraparliamentary Political Organization, 1769-1793* (Cambridge, Mass., 1963), p. 279.

[63] Quoted by Samuel H. Beer, "The Representation of Interests in British Government: Historical Background," *American Political Science Review*, 51 (1957), 649.

the enforcement of military obligations, and the raising of taxation. In the fourteenth century the scope of government action was extended to the economic sphere; a more efficient system of taxation was developed, based on customs dues, clerical levies, and property taxes; successive Statutes of Labourers enforced compulsory labor and regulated wages. In the sixteenth century government penetrated yet further. Statutes, proclamations, and royal patents attempted to control virtually every area of national life: religion, agriculture, trade, industry, poor relief, book publication, movement in and out of the country—even sumptuary laws declaring how many courses an individual of any given social rank might eat at a meal or what clothes he might wear. The ecclesiastical courts regulated every detail of private morality. There never has been a time when the actions of the individual citizen were, theoretically, so circumscribed.

If it is an inescapable feature of "modernization" that the overlapping immunities, franchises, and jurisdictions characteristic of feudal society should give way to a more monolithic system of power and authority, then it can be said that by the mid-sixteenth century "modernization" had been substantially achieved. For by that time the state enjoyed a theoretical monopoly of legislation, jurisdiction, and the use of force; and most of the old immunities had been eliminated. What held the system together, however, was the way in which "natural" chains of authority were intertwined with those of central and local government. The MPs who formed the legislative body and the JPs who enforced the statutes were normally the leaders of their own communities by virtue of their landholding and their status as gentlemen. Their authority was thus simultaneously social and political.

So although England was "by medieval standards, an exceptionally powerful and effective monarchy,"[64] and by 1603 "the most centralised of states,"[65] the scope of government action was limited by the interests of the economically powerful classes. It was this limitation that produced the crisis of the mid-seventeenth century, when government regulation of social and economic life encountered mounting resistance, not from all the propertied classes, but from most of those who did not immediately benefit from royal privileges and monopolies. In 1641 the Long Parliament abolished the con-

[64] G. R. Elton in *The New Cambridge Modern History* (Cambridge, 1957-70), II, 441.

[65] D. H. Pennington, *Seventeenth-Century Europe* (London, 1970), p. 387.

ciliar courts that helped to make possible this exceptional degree of penetration. Insofar as the role of the state in economic and religious life was one of the major issues, the Civil War may be regarded as a major crisis of penetration. Paradoxically, however, the war itself led both sides to make more intensive demands upon the subject, both in taxation and conscription. The Parliamentarians mustered the first effective citizen army in English history; and the Interregnum witnessed the experiment of the major-generals, set up to curb royalist plotters and to stiffen local government by enforcing social and economic regulation.

The government's retreat from the sphere of local economic and social policy-making, though implicit in the legislation of 1641, only became apparent after the Restoration of 1660. Thereafter, the Privy Council ceased to intervene much in local affairs. The Poor Law, the regulation of ale-houses, and the repair of the highways remained objectives of public policy; but their administration was left to the largely unsupervised activities of the local gentry and clergy, meeting in Quarter Sessions as a sort of administrative, judicial, and even legislative assembly for each county. Foreign trade was tightly regulated on mercantilist principles, and there was a certain amount of intervention in domestic economic matters. But much parliamentary legislation, particularly after 1689, tended to be negative in character, as for example the numerous statutes creating new criminal offences against property. More constructive measures of economic improvement, like the acts setting up turnpike trusts or enclosure commissions, were left to the initiative of the private member, acting in response to outside pressure.

> Even such activities as police, fire protection, the conduct of the Mint, the postal service, the construction and maintenance of roads, canals, harbours, lighthouses, education, the provisioning of the army, the operation of jails, the servicing and accounting of the national debt, street-cleaning, garbage disposal, water-supply, street-lighting, regulation of domestic industry and trade were in large part or in entirety farmed out or abandoned to private-profit enterprise, to individual charitable initative, or to the ancient guilds. The government of British India was entrusted to a charter company operating for profit.[66]

[66] Jacob Viner in Clifford, ed., *Man versus Society in Eighteenth-Century Britain*, pp. 23-24.

That is to say, there was penetration of a sort, but most legislation was enforced by private agencies, not by the skeletal government bureaucracy.

The years 1714-1815 were thus the period in English history when local administrators were freest from national control and when regional distrust of the activities of the central government was at its height. At the beginning of the nineteenth century, taxation, justice, and defense still constituted the main business of public officials; and the repeal of the Elizabethan Statute of Artificers in 1814 symbolized the apparent readiness of the legislature to renounce what remained of its responsibility to regulate wages, apprenticeship, and the supply of food. It was the pressure of industrialism that provoked a spectacular reaction against this policy of internal laisser faire. How far the new policy should be regarded as an inevitable response to the urgent problems created by conditions in the industrial towns, how far it should be explained in terms of the influence of Benthamism or Evangelicalism upon the middle classes remains uncertain. But it is clear that from the 1830s the sphere of government was rapidly and substantially widened to include the oversight of public health, the provision of a police force, the regulation of hours of work and conditions of employment in factories and mines, the control of railway building, the supervision of prisons, and the rehousing of the working classes. It is true that until the 1870s the administration of these matters was largely left to specially created local authorities, with the government merely initiating and supervising; to this extent decentralization continued. But the important change was that these administrative changes were now initiated not by local members in private Acts of Parliament, but by the government in Public General Acts, though under pressure, of course, from individual bureaucrats and outside interest groups.

At the beginning of the twentieth century, government responsibilities widened further with the beginnings of a national system of social insurance. (This no doubt should be regarded as a change in "distribution," but the assumption of greater responsibilities for distribution is in itself "penetration.") The first world war produced an even greater advance in government penetration. War has always been a stimulus to increased government control. But there was no precedent for the manner in which between 1914 and 1918 the government achieved not only the successful mobilization of the armed forces (even before conscription was introduced), but also took over the rationing of food, the allocation of raw materials, the control of shipping and inland transport, and the supervision of the whole economy. After the war the apparatus of control was dismantled, only to be reconstructed on an even more intensive scale during the second world war. This time government controls were not so speedily discarded when the war was over. But the postwar Labour government effected a gradual shift from direct control by public planning to a new ideal of economic management. Governments now hold a general responsibility for the state of the economy, the volume of unemployment, the balance of payments, and the social and economic condition of the population. But they discharge it by acting as broker between the various interest groups, rather than by endeavoring to penetrate all aspects of the economy directly. Their recent inability to enforce a compulsory incomes policy suggests that governments are relatively helpless in face of pressure from major groups such as the trade unions.

So although the overall scope of state action has immensely widened in modern times, the story is not one of increasing penetration; on the contrary, government intervention has through the centuries advanced, retreated, and advanced again. Today such crucial institutions as the press or the universities enjoy a degree of independence that would have been thought intolerable by the government of Charles I.

But if by penetration is meant not the *area* of government intervention, but the *efficacy* of such intervention, the pattern is very different. For the reach of all pre-nineteenth-century governments greatly exceeded their grasp. England was early in developing a central administration, but slow in producing a corps of administrators. Medieval bureaucracy was an outgrowth of the royal household. First one branch, then the next, "went out of court," becoming a distinct department. In this way Exchequer, Common Pleas, Chancery, King's Bench, and Privy Seal successively evolved. In the late fifteenth and early sixteenth centuries there developed a new system of conciliar administration, with the central courts of Star Chamber and Requests, the regional councils of the North and the Marches, and new revenue courts like Augmentations and Wards. The whole structure was overseen by the Privy Council and the king's principal secretary of state. The cumulative effect of these innovations was to make the period c. 1470-c. 1560 one of strikingly new penetration, comparable to that of 1080-1230. It saw the erosion of aristocratic military power, the effective subjugation of the outlying regions, and the successful enforcement of the Reformation, and the dissolution of the monasteries. There were periodic revolts against the Crown's religious or fiscal policies, but each was suppressed by force, diplomacy, or a combination of the two.

Yet even at its most successful, the Tudor system suffered from fundamental defects. There was no standing army and, despite its attempt to enforce a universal obligation to military service, the Crown was dependent upon aid from the magnates when it came to suppressing revolts. There was no reliable source of information about the country that was being governed. The *Valor Ecclesiasticus* (1535) was a notable survey of ecclesiastical revenues, but Domesday Book (1086) remained an achievement unparalleled until the nineteenth century. Before 1696 there were no reliable statistics of foreign trade, and before 1801 no census of the population.

Most important of all, there was no adequate bureaucracy. Royal servants at the center were not professional administrators but *rentiers*, obtaining their posts by patronage, patrimony, or purchase, regarding their offices as private property, their duties as part time, and their income as derived not from regular salaries but from miscellaneous fees and perquisites. By the sixteenth century, ordinary law enforcement and local administration were carried out by that uniquely English functionary, the justice of the peace,[67] typically a country gentleman, firmly rooted in his community, unpaid, conscientious, but prepared to enforce only those aspects of royal policy of which he approved.

The Crown, in other words, accepted the basic pattern of local authority rather than attempting to penetrate it with its own bureaucracy. Government functions of justice, military organization, economic regulation, and taxation were exercized by local landowners in the king's name. Penetration thus depended less on the creation of a bureaucracy than on the attainment of harmonious relations between Crown and gentry. The story of the later sixteenth and early seventeenth centuries is of increasing conflict between the two. Statutes that blatantly conflicted with the interests of the landowners could be a dead letter from the start. Others were enforced only under constant pressure by the central government. In the 1630s this pressure increased, but so did the resistance to it. By 1640 ship money

[67] Whose origins, however, go back to the fourteenth century, not Saxon times, *pace Crises and Sequences in Political Development*, p. 230.

could no longer be collected, and the troops raised to repel the Scottish invasion mutinied and pillaged. As the contemporary commentator James Harrington remarked, it was not the Civil War that caused the dissolution of government, but the dissolution of government that caused the Civil War.[68] In this sense the war was the result of an unresolved crisis of penetration. Ironically, the short-lived English republic that followed was conspicuously successful in establishing an effective bureaucracy, capable of extracting huge sums in taxation, maintaining a large army, and building up a strikingly effective navy.[69]

After 1660 the central authorities achieved absolute penetration in some spheres, but only at the price of renouncing control over others. Local government was left to the gentry, who in return were prepared to help the state to discharge its minimal functions. Such economic regulation as was attempted only proved effective on a basis of local option.[70] Landowners voluntarily submitted to heavy direct taxation during the wars against Louis XIV, but showed a strong aversion to the growth of the executive. The later seventeenth century, however, was a period of administrative reform. It saw the rise of the Treasury and Board of Trade, the creation of many new revenue offices, the partial elimination of life tenures and reversionary interests, the end of tax farming, and the growing use of statistics. The long war against France led to an increase in the size of the executive, the mobilization of armed forces of unprecedented size, and a new system of public credit. But by European standards the bureaucracy of Hanoverian England was minimal. New laws were not thought to call for new means of law enforcement; instead they were left to JPs, common informers, and local interested parties.

When the reforming impetus began again after 1780, it was provoked by British failure in the American War of Independence and by the need to conciliate extraparliamentary reform movements. Later it was sustained by middle-class pressure. Its ultimate achievement was the creation of a salaried public service, rationally organized, appointed in open competition, promoted by merit, and disowning any

[68] *James Harrington's Oceana*, edited by S. B. Liljegren (Heidelberg, 1924), p. 50.

[69] See G. E. Aylmer, *The State's Servants. The Civil Service of the English Republic, 1649-1660* (London, 1973).

[70] See J. P. Cooper, "Economic Regulation and the Cloth Industry in Seventeenth-Century England," *Transactions of the Royal Historical Society*, 5th ser., 20 (1970), pp. 73-99.

political allegiance. Sinecures, reversions, fees, and patronage were swept away, and by 1870 the depoliticization of the bureaucracy had been achieved. This revolution in government made its impact upon the localities as well as on the center. From the 1830s, the JPs were forced to cede their administrative powers over alehouses, the poor law, prisons, highways, and county government to new authorities. The great Benthamite device was government by local elected boards, employing paid officials, and subject to the supervision of a central body, with an inspectorate to see that government regulations were enforced. There were inspectors of factories, of mines, of prisons, of emigrant ships, of health, of schools, of railways—indeed of every institution that was the object of legislative reform. These officials acquired wide discretionary powers and an accumulated expertise that generated a demand for further reform. They also assembled immense quantities of information in their reports and inquiries, making nineteenth-century Blue Books an unequaled repository of information about every branch of national life.

Penetration was not achieved at once. There were periods of reaction against the growing centralization, and in the mid-Victorian period the proliferating mass of specially created local authorities was very largely independent of Whitehall. Many matters—for example education, water supply, and the police—remained decentralized. Others, like the prohibition of cruelty to children or animals, were left primarily to enforcement by voluntary agencies with their own inspectors—"auxiliaries of the legislature." By continental standards the bureaucracy remained comparatively small. But as the central boards gradually turned into responsible ministries, answerable to Parliament for their activities, yet enjoying an increasing amount of delegated responsibility and administrative freedom, it was clear that a revolution in penetration had been accomplished. As a prominent civil servant remarked of the Public Health Act of 1866, "the grammar of common sanitary legislation acquired the novel virtue of an imperative mood."[71] One could demonstrate the penetrative powers of late Victorian government by pointing to the improvements in public health, the decline of smuggling, or the growth of public order. But for "a perfect marvel of successful administration," as one contemporary journalist called it, there was perhaps nothing to

[71] Sir John Simon, quoted by G. Kitson Clark, *An Expanding Society. Britain, 1830-1900* (Cambridge, 1967), p. 153.

surpass vaccination; for when the government decided to make vaccination compulsory, the authorities were able to account for over 95 percent of all children born between 1872 and 1883.[72]

In the twentieth century, penetration has been taken even further. Its extent is reflected not only in the welfare state and wartime controls, but also in the rapid growth in the number of government employees. In 1891 3.5 percent of the working population was employed by central or local government agencies. In 1974 the figure was 18.7 percent (or 26.2 percent, if the employees of nationalized industries are included).[73] In 1910, the share of the Gross National Product devoted to government expenditure was much the same as it had been in 1790—about 12 percent. But by 1975 it had risen to 53.1 percent.[74]

To represent all this as the triumph of an impersonal "state" or "bureaucracy" would be totally misleading. The extent of penetration has always depended upon the attitude of the politically influential classes. Until the nineteenth century, it was severely limited by the reluctance of the squirearchy to surrender their local autonomy. Thereafter, penetration depended upon the cooperation of interested pressure groups. The triumphant achievement of compulsory vaccination in the 1870s, for example, was only possible because the campaign had the backing of the medical profession. In modern times the scope and effectiveness of government policy continue to be largely determined by the relative strengths of the various interested groups.

DISTRIBUTION

It is often said that in England distribution came after participation.[75] This is true in the sense that it was only the twentieth century that saw the arrival of compulsory national insurance, a national health service, redistributive taxation, and the commitment of all political parties to the goal of full employment and a steady rate of economic growth. But the notion that the government has a duty to

[72] R. J. Lambert, "A Victorian National Health Service: State Vaccination, 1855-71," *Historical Journal*, 5 (1962), 13.

[73] Moses Abramovitz and Vera F. Eliasberg, *The Growth of Public Employment in Great Britain* (Princeton, 1957), pp. 8, 24-25; Great Britain, Department of Employment. *British Labour Statistics* (London, 1975).

[74] J. Veverka, "The Growth of Government Expenditure in the United Kingdom since 1790," *Scottish Journal of Political Economy*, 10 (1963), 114, table 1; Great Britain, Central Statistical Office. *National Income and Expenditure, 1965-75* (London, 1976).

[75] See, e.g., Binder *et al., Crises and Sequences*, p. 313.

intervene in order to secure minimal living standards is much older than that. It is true that the economic welfare of the nation was not uppermost among the objectives of medieval kings. But even they saw themselves as the dispensers of justice and material benefits. In the twelfth and thirteenth centuries there were the assizes of ale, bread, and wine, by which local authorities under central supervision endeavored to regulate the price and quality of foodstuffs. In the later middle ages there was government action to control wages and prices, to maintain a regular grain supply, and to regulate foreign trade, though the supervision of industry was normally left to such local agencies as town governments and guilds. Most important, the sixteenth century saw a series of statutes that developed and codified a national poor law, intended to secure basic subsistence for all "deserving" paupers and to coerce the undeserving into labor. It is true that responsibility for this system rested entirely upon the local authorities until 1834, when the poor law came under centralized control. It is also true that the system, which underwent many changes of character during its long history, was always intermittent and inefficient in its operation. Nevertheless, it had a continuous existence from the Tudor period until its conversion into the national assistance of modern times. England, indeed, is probably unique in having so unbroken a tradition of secular public relief; and the fact that "welfare" was—at least in principle—available long before participation (by contrast, for example, with the United States, where the two came in the reverse order) has made it appear more of a right and less of a concession.

Apart from the poor law, there were few attempts at any redistribution of national resources before modern times. In the reign of Edward VI, a "Commonweal man" such as Hugh Latimer could hold that the king should provide for the poor and "see victuals good cheap," and his colleagues talked even of public health and education. But the most massive act of redistribution—the dissolution of the monasteries, 1536-1540—benefited courtiers and landed classes only. Political power was employed to maintain society in its stratified form. Such concessions as were made were primarily intended to keep the lower classes from insurrection, an ever-constant danger in the eyes of the authorities. This was why the Elizabethan government established the poor law, tried to control the grain trade so as to ensure a constant food supply, and regulated industry in an attempt to maintain employment and industrial harmony. Legislation against enclosure was similarly motivated by fear of social disorder. When governments went further and tried to control market forces for fiscal reasons, or for the sake of medieval ideals of social justice, they risked direct confrontation with the propertied classes. To some extent this was what happened in 1640.

After 1660 the social policy of the Tudors and early Stuarts was largely abandoned. This was partly because of the destruction in 1641 of the conciliar government that had made it possible, partly because an improving economic situation caused the threat of insurrection to recede. Population pressure slackened off, the food supply increased, and openings for employment diversified. As a result, the main burden of checking profiteering and oppression fell upon the common people themselves. Food riots were frequent in the eighteenth century, and they had an avowed redistributive purpose; they were "legitimized by the assumptions of an older moral economy, which taught the immorality of any unfair method of forcing up the price of provisions by profiteering upon the necessities of the people."[76] These riots were directed against the profiteers themselves rather than against the government, though at times the distinction became a fine one. The Luddites of 1811-1812, who attacked machinery in order to coerce employers into making wage concessions, constituted a "quasi-insurrectionary movement,"[77] and they forced the government to deploy 12,000 troops against them.

Until the nineteenth century, therefore, the main distributive function of the state was to preserve the existing pattern of social stratification from violent attack from below. The allocation of material goods was left to the operation of the market, mitigated by the poor law and by government regulation of foreign trade. But some important kinds of distribution were effected by private philanthropy. Unusually favorable laws of charitable trust made possible an immense number of philanthropic foundations, which helped to compensate for the lack of state activity. This was particularly the case in the field of education. There was no state aid for education until the nineteenth century, and even then the state held back because of its reluctance to be embroiled in denominational disputes. Yet privately founded schools and universities helped to make the inhabitants of

[76] E. P. Thompson, *The Making of the English Working Class* (Harmondsworth, revised ed., 1968), pp. 67-68. See also the same author's article, "The Moral Economy of the English Crowd in the Eighteenth Century," *Past and Present*, 50 (1971), 73-136.

[77] Thompson, *The Making of the English Working Class*, p. 604.

mid-seventeenth century England better educated than those of almost any other European country. When England started on the road to industrialization she had a large reserve of literacy.[78]

During the early years of the industrial revolution, economic development was the task of the private entrepreneur. The state's role was confined to providing protection for foreign trade, naval and military support against commercial rivals, a legal system for the protection of property and enforcement of contracts, and a legislature that could be used by individual MPs and pressure groups to obtain statutory sanction for agricultural enclosure and the building of canals, roads, and railways. The government was not expected to ensure a constant rate of economic growth and was not forced to engage in overall planning. Industrialization, however, helped to precipitate the expansion in public services and government responsibilities that was such a feature of the nineteenth century. This was primarily a matter of creating a more effective legal and administrative framework for the new forms of economic activity, and thus belongs to the field of "penetration." But insofar as it was a response to new social problems, it had a distributive aspect.

Modern students of industrialization have not failed to point out that in Britain the state's resources did not have to be diverted to welfare at the critical time of economic growth, in the way that happens in the developing countries of today. "Prior to the nineteenth century," says one commentator, perhaps a little ingenuously, "economic growth in Britain was not encumbered by a labor movement."[79] It is true that the radical sects of the Civil War period had made sweeping demands for state provision of education and health and for extensive social and economic reform, extending in the case of the Diggers to agrarian communism. But the ideas of most of these reformers had a strong individualist tinge. The Levellers put political demands for participation above social ones, and were in any case fairly easily suppressed. Thereafter the radical tradition languished until the late eighteenth century. When it revived, its main concern was the reform of the political system, though the demand for participation cannot easily be distinguished from a concern to improve living standards; Tom Paine's program was social as well

[78] Carlo M. Cipolla, *Literacy and Development in the West* (Harmondsworth, 1969), p. 102. Cf. Lawrence Stone, "The Educational Revolution in England, 1560-1640," *Past and Present*, 28 (1964), 41-80.

[79] Karl de Schweinitz, Jr., *Industrialization and Democracy* (Glencoe, Ill., 1964), p. 112.

as political.[80] Chartism grew out of economic distress, and many of its adherents saw the vote as a means to an end; they wanted wage protection, factory laws, and the reform of the poor law.

The response of the governing classes to the demands of the industrial poor was ambiguous. On the other hand, they suggested that distribution should be regarded as a strict alternative to participation. The poor law had always had a penal element about it, and the workhouse system introduced in 1834 made the receipt of relief incompatible with ordinary citizenship. On the other hand, a combination of humanitarian sentiment and political prudence led to factory acts, truck acts, public health acts, and allied social reforms, which had the effect of damping down working-class pressure for political participation. The legislation of the 1840s in particular—the Factory Act (1844), the repeal of the Corn Laws (1846), and the Public Health Act (1848)—did much to diminish popular interest in the Chartist program. To this extent distribution was conceded in advance of popular demand.

It was, however, the increasing impact of organized labor that was primarily responsible for the social reforms of the later nineteenth and early twentieth centuries. The rise of the trade unions and the expansion of the franchise made political parties aware of the need to conciliate the working classes. Compulsory state education came in 1880 as a means of controlling the growing numbers of unemployed juveniles and ensuring the respectability of the newly enfranchised urban masses. After 1885 the deterrent principle on which poor relief was founded could not be expected to last indefinitely. Even so, social security came later in England than in Germany. Its real beginning dated from the 1906 Liberal government, which introduced the principle of old-age pensions, labor exchanges, school meals, school medical services, and compulsory health and unemployment insurance. "National Insurance," it has been said, "was the Liberal response to the threat of socialism."[81] For that reason it was not seriously opposed by the Conservatives, for "social legislation is the one form of legal enactment that an opposition responsible to a democratic electorate dare not fight."[82] The worker was protected against the full pressures of capitalism not by socialism, but by being com-

[80] Thompson, *The Making of the English Working Class*, pp. 101-102.

[81] Bentley B. Gilbert, *The Evolution of National Insurance in Great Britain* (London, 1966), p. 448. For a general discussion, see J. R. Hay, *The Origins of the Liberal Welfare Reforms, 1906-1914* (London, 1975).

[82] Gilbert, *The Evolution of National Insurance*, p. 451.

pelled to provide for himself and his family by national insurance. The *Beveridge Report* (1942) gave classic enunciation to the doctrine of a guaranteed minimum income and comprehensive insurance against unemployment, ill health, widowhood, large families, industrial accident, and old age. The further development of the welfare state was the work of the Labour government of 1945-1950. Today the social services account for nearly half of all government expenditure.

Meanwhile, the effect of two world wars and an intervening economic depression has been to establish the axiom that it is the government's duty to manage the economy in such a way as to secure high employment and a steady rate of growth. The impact of the two wars is hard to overestimate. They brought a variety of social tensions to the notice of the governing circles, and they demonstrated the enormous capacity of state regulation. The second world war, in particular, forced Britain, "in the interests of survival, into the most state-planned and state-managed economy ever introduced outside a frankly socialist country."[83] "The Government had, through the agency of newly established or existing services, assumed and developed a measure of direct concern for the health and well-being of the population which by contrast with the role of Government in the nineteen-thirties was little short of remarkable."[84] Today the government is held responsible not only for housing, wages, and the cost of living, but also for the physical environment and the quality of life. Yet economic rather than political reasons probably lie behind the rise in real wages and fall in hours of work during the past century.[85] As yet the government's impact upon the structure of society has been limited. Death duties have diminished the concentration of personal wealth by forcing the very rich to break up their estates in their lifetimes. But inequalities further down the scale have diminished only gradually.[86]

It is thus easier to trace the history of distribution in England than to isolate particular "crises," for although there has been much insti-

[83] Hobsbawm, *Industry and Empire*, p. 208.

[84] Richard M. Titmuss, *Problems of Social Policy* (London, 1950), p. 506.

[85] See E. H. Phelps Brown, with Margaret H. Browne, *A Century of Pay* (London, 1968).

[86] See Richard M. Titmuss, *Income Distribution and Social Change* (London, 1962); Jack Revell, "Changes in the Social Distribution of Property in Britain during the Twentieth Century," *Actes du Troisième Conférence Internationale d'Histoire Economique*, Munich, 1965, I (Paris, 1968), 367-84; *Royal Commission on the Distribution of Income and Wealth. Report No. 1* (London, 1975).

tutional innovation, it is hard to point to moments when the political structure would have been threatened had it not been undertaken. Yet crises involving distribution can be seen in 1640, with the breakdown of government after the reaction of the propertied classes against (*inter alia*) the social policy of the early Stuarts; in 1846, with the repeal of the Corn Laws, which, though ultimately accomplished by aristocratic leaders, appeared to many contemporaries as a direct challenge to the interests of the landed classes; in 1909, with the Lloyd George budget with its proposals for redistributive taxation, which incurred the resistance of the House of Lords and thus precipitated the political crisis resolved by the Parliament Act of 1911; and, more generally, the long series of welfare enactments that cumulatively helped to avert the violent expression of class conflict, while at the same time preserving the essentials of the class structure.

Timely concessions have thus taken the edge off the demand for more radical or socialist measures. Indeed, it may be said that effective distribution (in the form of consumer affluence) has usually proved an effective means of withstanding pressure for increased participation. Nowhere is this more apparent than in the history of the trade unions. The repeal of the Combination Laws in 1824 opened the way for peaceful union activity, although it was not until 1875 that the legal and political status of the unions was assured, and even after that date their evolution was temporarily interrupted when unfavorable legal judgments challenged their right to strike without incurring financial liability (Taff Vale judgment 1901—reversed 1906) and their right to make political levies on their members (Osborne case 1909—reversed 1913, reasserted 1927, and reversed again 1946). At present, the legal framework in which collective bargaining may be conducted is still a subject of dispute.

Up to a point, nineteenth-century unions proved themselves capable of effective industrial action, as in 1889, when the London dockers' strike secured a standard wage. But strikes were usually bids for sympathy rather than threats; and periods of genuine militancy have been infrequent. One such period was that immediately before the first world war—according to Ernest Bevin, "a period which, if the war had not broken out, would have, I believe, seen one of the greatest industrial revolts the world would ever have seen."[87] An-

[87] Quoted by W. G. Runciman, *Relative Deprivation and Social Justice* (London, 1966), p. 57. For a more cautious view of this episode, see Henry Pelling, *Popular Politics and Society in Late Victorian Society* (London, 1968), chapter 9.

other was that of the call of "Direct Action" to overthrow capitalism in the years immediately after the first world war. This received no support from official Labour party leaders and collapsed in 1921. When the General Strike came in 1926 over the issue of hours and wages in the coal industry, it was the law-abiding General Council of the TUC that gave way. Baldwin claimed that the country was "nearer to Civil War than we have been for centuries past." But the strike was not a challenge to Parliament, but only an attempt to mitigate economic hardship; indeed, it was the government rather than the unions that made it into a trial of strength.

In the mid-nineteenth century the main aim of the unions had been to improve the legal status of the industrial worker by abolishing the antiquated law of master and servant. The achievement of this goal was not followed by any revolutionary attack on the capitalist system itself. The early unions were dominated by skilled workers and were hostile to socialism. The Labour party became an effective parliamentary force in 1906; and the expansion of the franchise, combined with the enormous growth in union membership, gave it the electoral strength to replace the Liberals as one of the two major parties. But the Labour party aimed at a *modus vivendi* with capitalism, not at its overthrow; and the working classes did not show a conspicuous interest in social reform.[88] The first two Labour governments (1924 and 1929-1931) were minority administrations and therefore too weak to introduce any distinctively socialist measures; the third (1945-1951), though sponsoring nationalization and the welfare state, in effect retreated from the more sweeping socialism of the wartime period. Meanwhile, the economic deprivations of the years between the two wars had produced no effective communist or fascist parties. When in 1931 the financial crisis required a cut in unemployment benefit, the Labour Cabinet split on the issue; and the result was a long period of Conservative-based rule. The political system thus proved strong enough to withstand its failure to secure more distribution. So far it has even survived the inflation and unemployment of the 1970s.

Sequence

"When one proceeds . . . to compare societies on the basis of vaguely defined criteria," writes a recent authority on "moderniza-

[88] Pelling, *Popular Politics*, chapter 1.

tion," "the results are not likely to be fruitful."[89] Lack of precision certainly handicaps any attempt to identify the sequence of "crises" in British history; and it is doubtful whether any two historians, presented with the problem in its current state of formulation, would come up with the same solution. Nevertheless, it has proved possible to discern the five "critical problems" and to pick out the periods at which they were exceptionally acute. In general, the crises prove not to have been single events, resolved once and for all, but endlessly recurring problems. In medical terms they should be compared not to childhood illnesses like chicken-pox or measles, but to adult ailments like colds or influenza, which frequently recur and which through neglect or growing feebleness may at any point lead to bronchitis, pneumonia, or even death.

Nevertheless, something can be learned about the British political system from considering the sequence in which these problems have presented themselves at their most acute. The early attainment of national *identity* is one of England's most distinctive features. It has fostered the evolution of a remarkably homogeneous political culture in which differences of race, religion, and language have been of only intermittent political importance. The one acute identity problem still unsolved, that of Northern Ireland, continues to seem essentially peripheral to British politics (the spread of Irish terrorism to the United Kingdom notwithstanding); for all its horrors, it appears to offer no obvious threat to the system. Britain, as the authors of *Crises and Sequences* rightly say, achieved national integration before "modernization."[90]

Second came the achievement of substantial *legitimacy*. This meant that when universal suffrage was conceded it had to be tacked on to a form of government, a concept of constitutional liberty, and a style of political life that derived from an earlier era. Civil rights antedated political ones, and in a democratic age Parliament retained the gentlemanly conventions appropriate to a one-class legislature. These circumstances help to account for the survival of traditional elements in modern British life and the absence of "populist" democracy. For parliamentary institutions are older than popular sovereignty, and do not therefore derive their sole authority from it.

The history of *penetration* has been much more drawn out. It has

[89] C. E. Black, *The Dynamics of Modernization* (New York, 1966), p. 43.
[90] *Crises and Sequences in Political Development*, p. 87.

advanced in a series of spurts, followed by periods of relative withdrawal, and it is difficult to fit it into any clear place in the sequence. The extension of *participation* has also been a gradual matter, but the critical turning point can be recognized in the Reform Acts. It is less obvious as to which of them was the most "critical." Was it that of 1832, which showed that the old system could be changed? Was it that of 1867, which first enfranchised some of the working class? Or was it that of 1918, which brought about the largest single increase in the electorate by trebling the number of voters? What is fairly clear is that participation was well under way before the appearance of serious demands for *distribution*. The enfranchisement of the working classes did not immediately produce distributive claims; and such demands as were made were seldom so unmanageable as to constitute a serious threat to the system.

This rough sequence—identity, legitimacy, participation, distribution, with penetration developing in a parallel but uneven progression of its own—seems to bear some relation to the ideal type presupposed by the authors of *Crises and Sequences*, who remark that "crises of distribution *ideally* [!] occur at the end of a developmental sequence."[91] But the superficial impression of a well-spaced sequence, in which each problem is dealt with on its own, is rudely shattered when we recall the crisis of the mid-seventeenth century. For between 1640 and 1660 all the issues—identity, legitimacy, participation, penetration, and distribution—assumed crisis proportions. Several successive "elites" were overthrown, and the whole political system was at stake. This brief period of upheaval, when neofeudal magnates and neomodern radicals jostled together for political power, is reminiscent of the telescoping of stages of political development so characteristic of the developing countries. There is thus a sense in which the seventeenth-century crisis reflected the tensions of the "modernization syndrome." Its main effect was to establish after 1689 a form of political order capable of peaceful adaptation to new circumstances. The onset of industrialism generated new problems of participation, penetration, and distribution, but they were resolved within a framework inherited from earlier times. The partial revolution of the seventeenth century thus proved decisive, not least because the traumatic memory of the breakdown helped to make subsequent elites more responsive to demands from below.

[91] *Ibid.*, p. 282.

Conclusion

To this extent British political development may be plausibly regarded as the outcome of a series of particular historical situations, of the resolution of "crises" in a certain sequence. But how little in itself does this tell us! For the mere experience of these crises, even in an identical sequence, could be compatible with many different types of political order. "The greater the differences between two societies in technology, economy, social structure, legal system, constitution, religion, culture, and so on," writes one historian, "the more strained become analogies between their systems of government."[92] Even within one country it is important to know not just the sequence of crises, but their chronological relationship to other circumstances. We need, for example, to know not just whether participation came before or after distribution, but whether it came before or after literacy, or industrialization, or the decline of the peasantry. Similarly, it is important to know the technological context of penetration. "There is a significant element of 'investment' in altering old or in setting up new government," writes a recent administrative historian. "English local government might be very different today had not the first major reforms in that field been carried before a really effective system of national communications and transport had developed."[93]

If we are to understand the reasons for the peculiarities of the English political system, then we have to leave politics altogether and look at society, or rather look at politics as part of society. "We admire the stability of British government," wrote Taine, "but this stability is the final product, the fine flower at the extremity of an infinite number of living fibres firmly planted in the soil of the entire country."[94] The disintegrative (or integrative) effect of any particular crisis in English history has depended more upon the nature of the social structure than upon the sequence in which it has occurred. The ease with which the ruling elites have assimilated successive claimants to political power reflects the fluidity of that social structure—of primogeniture, of the early participation of the aristocracy in commercial land-management, of the constant symbiosis of aristocracy and bourgeoisie, and of the formation of the working class in a counter-revo-

[92] G. E. Aylmer, *The King's Servants* (London, 1961), p. 448.

[93] Oliver MacDonagh, *A Pattern of Government Growth, 1800-60* (London, 1961), p. 323.

[94] *Taine's Notes on England*, translated with an introduction by Edward Hyams (London, 1957), p. 162.

lutionary period (1790-1830), before any socialist ideology had yet developed. Around this social structure grew a religious code that was essentially apolitical in outlook (Puritanism having been tamed by 1660), and an educational system that fostered deference and social conformity (the alienated intellectual has been, at least until recently, a relatively uncommon figure on the English landscape). Most of these features were the result of the peculiar compromise implicit in the half-achieved revolution of the mid-seventeenth century.

A model of political development must also take account of the international situation. Quite apart from all the consequences that have flowed from Britain's imperial role (and they have been understated in this account), there is the fact of England's geographical insularity. It is this which, if we discount William III's arrival in 1688, has preserved her from successful foreign invasion for nine centuries. It freed Tudor and Stuart rulers from the need to develop large standing armies on the continental model, and it made possible the luxury of parliamentary resistance to royal absolutism. The absence of foreign intervention in the Civil War facilitated Parliamentary victory, just as its apparent possibility in 1660 speeded the Restoration. Military defeat in any one of the great wars of modern times might well have produced a major revolution. As Sir Lewis Namier wrote,

> The historical development of England is based upon the fact that her frontiers against Europe are drawn by Nature, and cannot be the subject of dispute; that she is a unit sufficiently small for coherent government to have been established and maintained even under very primitive conditions; that since 1066 she has never suffered serious invasion; that no big modern armies have succeeded her feudal levies; and that her senior service is the navy, with which foreign trade is closely connected. In short, a great deal of what is peculiar in English history is due to the obvious fact that Great Britain is an island.[95]

Hackneyed though they may have now become, these propositions are an essential reminder that the British sequence of political development has a unique pattern, only some of which can be conveyed by plotting the crises of identity, legitimacy, participation, penetra-

[95] Namier, *England in the Age of the American Revolution*, pp. 6-7.

tion, and distribution. For to trace the sequence in which crises have occurred, while regarding the reasons for the presence or absence of those crises as unimportant, is to analyze not causes but symptoms. It is as if we were to plot a man's medical history by recording the occasions on which his weight, temperature, or pulse rate had departed from the normal. For the possible reasons for such abnormalities are infinite; and even if two men had experienced these bodily changes in an identical sequence, it would not mean that their physique was necessarily the same.[96]

Some Related Readings

Most general assessments of the development of the British political system have been written by political scientists rather than historians. Good examples include Samuel H. Beer, *Modern British Politics. A Study of Parties and Pressure Groups* (2nd ed., London, 1969); Harry Eckstein, "The British Political System," in *Patterns of Government*, edited by Samuel H. Beer and Adam B. Ulam (2nd ed., New York, 1962); Richard Rose, "England: The Traditionally Modern Political Culture," in *Political Culture and Political Development*, edited by Lucian W. Pye and Sidney Verba (Princeton, 1965); and Stanley Rothman, "Modernity and Tradition in Britain," reprinted in *Studies in British Politics*, edited by Richard Rose (2nd ed., London, 1969). The latter volume also contains a succinct essay by W.J.M. Mackenzie on "Models of English Politics."

Two striking historical syntheses, both more or less Marxist in character, are Barrington Moore, Jr., *Social Origins of Dictatorship and Democracy. Lord and Peasant in the Making of the Modern World* (London, 1967), chapter 1; and E. P. Thompson, "The Peculiarities of the English," *The Socialist Register*, 1965 (being a reply to Perry Anderson, "Origins of the Present Crisis," *New Left Review*, 23 [1964]). In general, however, the best modern historical writing consists of detailed studies of individual periods and topics, and there is still no one-volume history of England that may be confidently recommended. A student who is previously unacquainted with British history might begin by reading the remarkable opening chapter of Sir Lewis Namier, *England in the Age of the American Revolution* (2nd ed., London, 1961), before turning to some of the following recent interpretations of key periods: Joseph R. Strayer,

[96] I am grateful to Dr. L. Hannah, Mr. J. A. Kay, and Dr. R. I. McKibbin for their advice on particular points.

On the Medieval Origins of the Modern State (Princeton, 1970), a useful corrective for anyone who thinks the middle ages irrelevant to "modernization"; G. R. Elton, *England under the Tudors* (London, 1955; 2nd ed., 1974); Lawrence Stone, *The Causes of the English Revolution, 1529-1642* (London, 1972); Christopher Hill, *The Century of Revolution, 1603-1714* (Edinburgh, 1961); J. H. Plumb, *The Growth of Political Stability in England, 1675-1725* (London, 1967); Asa Briggs, *The Age of Improvement* (London, 1959); G. Kitson Clark, *The Making of Victorian England* (London, 1962); Charles Loch Mowat, *Britain between the Wars, 1918-1940* (London, 1955). From such works he will be able to gain a fairly clear impression of what the main political "crises" of British history are normally taken to be. He can then move on to more detailed monographs illuminating some of the "key problems" identified by the authors of *Crises and Sequences in Political Development.*

On *identity* the most useful writing relates to the Celtic countries. Michael Hechter, *Internal Colonialism: the Celtic Fringe in British National Development, 1536-1966* (London, 1975) is a sociological work whose thesis is indicated by its title. On Scotland there is H. J. Hanham, *Scottish Nationalism* (London, 1969), and Sir Reginald Coupland, *Welsh and Scottish Nationalism. A Study* (London, 1954). On Wales, Glanmor Williams, "Language, Literacy and Nationality in Wales," *History*, 56 (1971); R. R. Davies, "Colonial Wales," *Past and Present*, 65 (1974); P. R. Roberts, "The Union with England and the Identity of 'Anglican' Wales," *Transactions of the Royal Historical Society*, 5th series, 22 (1972), Kenneth O. Morgan, *Wales in British Politics, 1868-1922* (revised ed., Cardiff, 1970); the same author's "Welsh Nationalism: The Historical Background," *Journal of Contemporary History*, 6 (1971); and Alan Butt Philip, *The Welsh Question. Nationalism in Welsh Politics, 1945-1970* (Cardiff, 1975). On Northern Ireland, see Richard Rose, *Governing without Consensus. An Irish Perspective* (London, 1971); and on recent immigrants, Ira Katznelson, *Black Men, White Cities. Race, Politics, and Migration in the United States, 1900-30, and Britain, 1948-68* (London, 1972). Some useful suggestions about English identity are made by Hans Kohn, "The Genesis and Character of English Nationalism," *Journal of the History of Ideas*, 1 (1940).

An important aspect of *legitimacy* is discussed by Archibald S. Foord, *His Majesty's Opposition, 1714-1830* (Oxford, 1964), and

Allen Potter, "Great Britain: Opposition with a Capital 'O,'" in *Political Oppositions in Western Democracies*, edited by Robert A. Dahl (New Haven, 1966).

For *participation* see J. H. Plumb, "The Growth of the Electorate in England from 1600 to 1715," *Past and Present*, 45 (1969); Derek Hirst, *The Representative of the People? Voters and Voting in England under the Early Stuarts* (Cambridge, 1975); John Cannon, *Parliamentary Reform, 1640-1832* (Cambridge, 1973); Geoffrey Holmes, *The Electorate and the National Will in the First Age of Party* (Lancaster, 1976); P. F. Clarke, "Electoral Sociology of Modern Britain," *History*, 57 (1972); Neal Blewett, "The Franchise in the United Kingdom, 1885-1918," *Past and Present*, 32 (1965); and H.C.G. Matthew, R. I. McKibbin, and J. A. Kay, "The Franchise Factor in the Rise of the Labour Party," *English Historical Review*, 261 (1976). Two important studies of the result of the enlargement of the franchise are Norman Gash, *Politics in the Age of Peel* (London, 1953), and H. J. Hanham, *Elections and Party Management. Politics in the Time of Disraeli and Gladstone* (London, 1959). On the modern parties R. T. McKenzie, *British Political Parties* (2nd ed., London, 1963), remains the standard authority. For other types of participation see George Rudé, *The Crowd in History . . . 1730-1848* (New York, 1964); E. P. Thompson, *The Making of the English Working Class* (revised ed., Harmondsworth, 1968); and *Department of Trade: Report of the Committee of Inquiry on Industrial Democracy* (London, 1977).

Penetration is discussed in many works on administrative history, of which the most notable include T. F. Tout, *Chapters in the Administrative History of Mediaeval England* (Manchester, 1920-1933); G. R. Elton, *The Tudor Revolution in Government* (Cambridge, 1953), in relation to which the criticisms of G. L. Harriss and Penry Williams in *Past and Present*, 25 (1963) should be noted; G. E. Aylmer, *The King's Servants, the Civil Service of Charles I, 1625-1642* (London, 1961); G. E. Aylmer, *The State's Servants. The Civil Service of the English Republic, 1649-1660* (London, 1973); Sidney and Beatrice Webb, *English Local Government* (London, 1924-1929); and Oliver MacDonagh, *A Pattern of Government Growth, 1800-60* (London, 1961). Henry Parris, *Constitutional Bureaucracy. The Development of British Central Administration since the Eighteenth Century* (London, 1969) is an unpretentious summary of much recent work.

Finally, on *distribution* there is Ernest Barker, *The Development of Public Services in Western Europe, 1660-1930* (Oxford, 1944); David Roberts, *Victorian Origins of the British Welfare State* (New Haven, 1960); Asa Briggs, "The Welfare State in Historical Perspective," *European Journal of Sociology*, 2 (1961); Bentley B. Gilbert, *The Evolution of National Insurance in Great Britain. The Origins of the Welfare State* (London, 1966); Bentley B. Gilbert, *British Social Policy, 1914-1939* (London, 1970); and W. G. Runciman, *Relative Deprivation and Social Justice. A Study of Attitudes to Social Inequality in Twentieth-Century England* (London, 1966).

CHAPTER 3

Belgium

ARISTIDE R. ZOLBERG

During the month that followed August 25, 1830, the Dutch government was faced with intermittent riots in Brussels and other southern cities. While the Dutch made half-hearted attempts to negotiate with southern representatives who desired administrative separation, and equally half-hearted attempts to subdue the rioters by force, a coalition intent on secession emerged. On October 4, a provisional government proclaimed the independence of the southern provinces under the name of Belgium. Following some territorial adjustments that gave the country approximately its present shape, the existence of the new state was guaranteed by the international community in 1839. Belgian society was among the most modern in the world. Its regime was strikingly liberal. But the surprisingly successful resolution of the crisis of legitimacy that distinguished Belgium from other Catholic countries in the first half of the nineteenth century, and which in turn greatly facilitated resolution of the crises of mass politics in the second half, can be understood only with reference to the outcome of earlier crises.

The central Low Countries was one of the European regions where, as a result of late medieval crises of distribution and of participation, secular constitutionalism vied with the feudal bond as the foundation of political legitimacy.[1] Medieval constitutionalism emerged from a specific social, cultural, and economic complex. The area comprising Flanders, Brabant, Holland, and Liège constituted a densely urbanized region with excellent physical communications, whose flourishing towns were founded on indigenous manufacture and on trade between the most active parts of the continent and England. Social life in these somewhat autonomous islands within a highly fragmented feudal society, ruled for the most part by nonindigenous overlords, was organized along occupational lines in the form of ex-

Crises of Political Development in Europe and the United States
0-691-07598-0/78/000099-39$01.95/1 (cloth)
0-691-02183-X/78/000099-39$01.95/1 (paperback)
For copying information, see copyright page

[1] "Low Countries" refers here to a geographical region that includes most of the contemporary Netherlands, Belgium, and parts of northern France.

clusive guilds. Functioning as the main institution of urban government, the guilds used their economic, political, and sometimes military power to enact, on behalf of the urban ruling classes, a complex system of charters of privilege from the various overlords. Within the towns, there were intermittent crises stemming from the emergence of new classes that sought to broaden participation further and to loosen the monopolistic hold of established patricians over economic activity. Although the guilds tended to become hereditary, and the patricians generally emerged victorious (except to a certain extent in Liège, where commoners gained early rights), class was irreversibly added to status as a relevant basis for participation and representation. Furthermore, people began to identify themselves as the inhabitants of municipalities rather than as subjects of particular lords. Amidst recurrent conflict between patricians and commoners, as well as between the towns and feudal lords, there emerged a new pattern of secular, quasi-republican authority, founded on the codification of privileges under the guardianship of councils representing estates. This pattern, legitimized by a new school of legal and political thought, had spread to the entire region by the early part of the fifteenth century.

From the fourteenth century on, the wealthy, strategic European middle ground became a major stake for state builders. For nearly a century, the Burgundian dukes used it as a staging ground to launch one of the first and most successful centralized states on the Continent, making considerable progress in transforming the nobility into a clientele dependent on the court and in creating a proto-bureaucracy of clerks. Competition between the dukes and active French and German dynasties for the support of local oligarchs led to the extension of the conciliar system from the municipal to the larger regional level centering on Brabant. After Burgundy was defeated by France on the eve of the fifteenth century, the Low Countries came under Habsburg rule. The Spaniards initially continued the political consolidation launched by the Burgundians over an area that now also included formerly French Flanders in the south, and that was extended northwards to include Gelderland in 1543.

The revolt of the Low Countries can be analyzed as an exacerbation of the crises of penetration and of participation triggered by incipient Spanish absolutism; of the crisis of legitimacy, since faith and political allegiance were intimately linked; and of a complex crisis of distribution that involved the emergence of capitalist manufacture, and was one of the sources of religious upheaval as well. We shall examine below whether it also entailed a crisis of identity, as has been claimed by many historians.

Catholic unity at the elite level was severely disrupted under the impact of Lutheranism and Calvinism. By mid-century, popular discontent related to the social dislocations stemming from nascent capitalist manufacture was expressed in Anabaptism and other millenarian movements. In the face of generalized unrest among all social strata, the emperor shifted to a policy of direct rule under a central administration loyal to Madrid, staffed by a Spanish bureaucracy and backed by the army. The church developed a parallel strategy. But the new policies necessitated the imposition of permanent taxes, in violation of the most cherished privileges guarded by the estates of the Seventeen Provinces. It was this conflict that brought about a full-scale uprising in the 1570s. After three decades of intermittent war, the Spaniards were in control of the south, but unable to subdue the north. Separation of the regions was sealed by the armistice of 1609, which entailed *de facto* recognition of Europe's first revolutionary republic, the independent United Netherlands, while the southern provinces (minus Liège, which was attached to the Holy Roman Empire) became a Spanish satellite. This arrangement was perpetuated by the Peace of Münster in 1648.

Paradoxically, although the revolt had failed in the south, active resistance to Spanish penetration, coupled with associated international events—the Armada was defeated in 1588—imposed severe limits on Spanish effectiveness in the seventeenth century. There was little resistance to Spanish rule because, like the Leviathan, it brought peace; economic tensions subsided because many capitalists emigrated and because the armistice settlement killed off commerce; and what Protestantism was not forcibly eliminated was expressed in Jansenism, a Catholicism with a Calvinist sensibility. Although the country was transformed into an orthodox garrison manned by the Spanish Army and by the Jesuits, the Spanish state, already in decline, was not even successful in raising the taxes necessary to implement its absolutist policies. Except for intermittent religious repression, Spanish absolutism in the southern Netherlands remained an intention rather than a reality, a thin veneer of imperial authority over an archaic land of small political communities ruled by their indigenous nobility, clergy, and patricians. The situation approximated the colonial system of indirect rule later found in India or northern Nigeria.

This is worth stressing because it prevailed during the very period when in France and elsewhere, state builders were reducing the remnants of medieval constitutionalism by imposing central bureaucracies on their subjects. Comparatively speaking, it was not so much the place of the crisis of penetration in a sequence that made the difference, but its absolute timing, its duration, and the capability of the center that initiated the effort. The situation might have been drastically altered had France retained the areas it conquered in the second half of the seventeenth century. As it was, the period of French control was too brief in the areas restored to the southern Netherlands to leave important traces except for the renewed ravages of war. A shift to the Austrian Habsburgs in 1713 initially meant little more than that within a somewhat diminished territory a Spanish court was replaced by an equally distant German court. It was only in the second half of the eighteenth century that attempts by a succession of dynamic centers to "modernize from above" precipitated a full-scale crisis of pentration. The ideological transformation associated with the Enlightenment, the activities of indigenous elites, and international events combined to expand it into a generalized crisis affecting all aspects of political development.

Around 1750, and especially after the accession of Joseph II in 1780, at a time when the region was experiencing the first spurts of an economic takeoff fostered by nearly a century of peace, the Austrian Habsburgs viewed their westernmost possession as a most suitable field for the experiment of enlightened despotism. Following a policy of deconcentration, they launched a most earnest attempt to establish a centralized "police and bureaucratic state" in Brussels, at the expense of the entrenched indigenous ruling strata in the many regional centers. Brussels, the capstone of a hierarchical system of territorial administration, became the seat of specialized ministries accountable to a governor; political control shifted from lawyers in parliaments to administrators in councils; taxation was modernized and increased. Albeit Catholic, the Austrians sought to rationalize church organization in a manner congruent with administrative needs. Jesuit primacy was undercut by the creation of a network of state-controlled secondary schools, using French rather than Latin as the medium of instruction, in which the authorities hoped to train children of the nobility and of the bourgeoisie as citizens useful to the Austrian state and to a modernized, state-oriented church. As in the sixteenth century, opposition among the upper strata probably helped generate, or at least gave form to, popular discontent, which was also a concomitant of the disruptions accompanying economic change. As in Paris, then a mere day away by post, and in America, whose situation many Belgians—as they now began to call themselves—viewed as being analogous to their own, a clash between central state authorities and the local political class over problems of taxation and representation triggered off a revolution.

For the established political class, known as "Statists" because of their defence of the traditional privileges of the estates, the uprising against Austria in 1789 was a war of independence against a centralizing metropole. Landed conservatives, they sought international support in order to establish an independent "Belgian Confederacy" within which they would play the dominant role through their control of the provincial estates. An alternative was voiced by new men, representing industrial and commercial rather than landed interests, and supported by middle-class townspeople outside the guilds. For these "Vonckists" (from the name of their leader), who came to be known as "Patriots" or "Democrats," the situation provided an opportunity to found a national state based on popular sovereignty. Conspiring to launch an indigenous armed uprising, they formed an alliance with like-minded triumphant revolutionaries in the Principality of Liège. The reentry of this territorial component (which had developed into an industrial quasi-democratic republic within the unique atmosphere of religious tolerance it had enjoyed since its separation from the Low Countries in the sixteenth century) added a substantial French-speaking, secular-minded, politically radical population to the Belgian political community. In the course of the revolutionary struggle, and partly in response to their persecutions as "heretics" by the Statists in alliance with the church, the Democrats —many of whom were Freemasons—developed a sharply anticlerical outlook. The division of the Belgian political class into two spiritual camps during this period left an enduring imprint on political alignments.

The fluctuating fortunes of Statists and Democrats were vastly overshadowed by the consequences of the decisive victory of the French revolutionary armies over the Austrians at Fleurus (June 1794). The Austrian Netherlands were formally annexed into the French Republic in October 1795. As integral parts of Europe's most active state for nearly twenty years, the nine Belgian departments experienced the full impact of the administrative, judicial, educational, and religious reorganizations associated with the various Revolutionary and Napoleonic regimes. The breakup and sale of land that belonged to abbeys and other ecclesiastical bodies, and which constituted approximately half the Belgian total, contributed to an even greater extent than in France to a fundamental transformation of the stratification system. The commercialization of land, together with access to the huge French market, fostered a second dramatic spurt of economic development. Belgium, which became Napoleon's arsenal, retained industrial primacy on the continent well into the nineteenth century.

In most respects, these trends were continued after 1815 when, as part of the European settlement, the Powers placed the Belgian departments of France under the authority of the Kingdom of the Netherlands. The inclusion of manufacturing Belgium into a leading trading and colonial economy provided further opportunities for the expansion of markets and for sustained economic growth. The constitution granted by William I to his Dutch subjects in 1814, revised to provide parity of representation for the south in 1815 (in spite of the fact that Belgium had a much larger population than the original kingdom), was far from liberal, but it did not entail a restoration of the *ancien régime*. The administrative institutions of the Napoleonic regime were generally maintained, often with the same men, but with their center in The Hague rather than in Paris, and with some pressure to replace French with Dutch as the language of public affairs.

Dutch rule was accepted without enthusiasm—in fact, a majority of Belgian representatives elected on the basis of extremely limited suffrage voted against the constitution or abstained—but without active resistance. Economic and religious interests shaped the initial orientation of the Belgian political class toward the trade-minded, Protestant House of Orange. Catholic opposition developed early on the issue of "freedom of education," that is, resistance to the development of a system of secondary and higher education controlled by a Protestant state, and was nearly unanimous. The Liberals were more divided. As Freemasons, many of them preferred a Protestant regime to the most likely alternative, a French-style restoration alliance of throne and altar; as industrialists, they feared isolation in a smaller country. It was only after the Dutch government adopted economic policies unfavorable to southern industrial development that some of them cooperated with a younger liberal opposition that demanded freedom of the press and ministerial accountability to a more representative parliament.

In the latter 1820s, the coming of age of a new political generation inspired by Benjamin Constant, Montalembert, and later Lammenais, as well as shared resentment of the government's renewed efforts to impose Dutch as the language of public affairs throughout the realm, and growing evidence of discrimination against the recruitment of southerners to civil and military offices, facilitated the organization of a Belgian Union of Oppositions. Campaigning against official candidates in 1828, the Union sought support among nonvoters who could be mobilized for street demonstrations, and by petitioning through intermediate elites such as the lower clergy, teachers, and petty government officials. The dislocating effects of continued industrialization, a temporary recession accompanied by inflation, and a bad crop, provided the conditions for wider politicization. By spring 1830, the Union had chosen a federalist solution, whereby the southern provinces would obtain cultural and economic autonomy within the Dutch kingdom. While the government vacillated, the July Revolution in Paris demonstrated that it was relatively easy to overthrow an unsatisfactory regime without bloodshed. On October 4, a provisional government declared Belgian independence.

The revolution resolved several aspects of various crises of development. It eliminated the irritant of authoritarian modernization from above under the aegis of a succession of states which, continuously for nearly a century, shared a specific strategy of penetration through a hierarchically organized field administration. This restored the possibility of establishing relationships between central authority and local communities that were more congruent with constitutional traditions, themselves founded on municipal interests. In relation to distribution, the revolution guaranteed that thenceforth the resources of industrial Belgium would no longer be reallocated to lesser developed areas within a larger political unit. The victorious alliance between Catholics and secularists provided the germ of a solution to the crisis of legitimacy that had afflicted all of Catholic Europe since 1815. As the struggle against the Dutch also entailed demands for more equitable representation on the basis of economic activity, the revolution also facilitated the further transition of Belgium from status to class as the foundation for political participation in representative government.

Crises

IDENTITY

To what extent did the inhabitants of Belgium, around the time of independence, share a common identity? In particular, what was the state of the linguistic attachments that became such a prominent feature of Belgian political life later on?

The starting point for the analysis of this complex question is a well established, but not fully accounted for, historical fact: ever since the early middle ages there has existed a line, running almost straight from Aachen to Calais, separating a northern zone of Germanic speech (closely related variations of Flemish and Dutch) from a southern zone of Romance speech (closely related varieties of Walloon with an eventual overlay of modern French). French-Walloon and Flemish-Dutch were used as the languages of business and public affairs at the local level in the appropriate regions until the nineteenth century; but French became the language of Court throughout the region during the Burgundian period, while Latin persisted as the language of learning until the sixteenth century, and in the south after the separation of the Low Countries.[2] That line of separation was drawn somewhat north of the linguistic line, so that the region under Spanish (and subsequently Austrian) rule straddled the linguistic frontier.

It is not clear to what extent, prior to the middle of the sixteenth century, the regions north and south of the linguistic frontier were differentiated in other cultural respects. Historians have debated the question ever since linguistic issues came to the fore in Belgium during the second half of the nineteenth century. Briefly stated, the traditional "Belgian" view is that prior to the middle of the sixteenth century, the southern provinces of the Netherlands, including areas of both Germanic and Romance speech (principally Flanders, Brabant, Hainaut, Artois and Liège) had more in common with one another than the Germanic areas of the south had with the homogeneously Germanic northern provinces (principally Holland and Zeeland). Hence, when the Reformation erupted, the south stirred, as did all

[2] To avoid confusion, we shall henceforth refer to the *languages* of Belgium as Dutch and French. It will be seen that the linguistic differentiation does not fully coincide with the ethnic differentiation between Flemings and Walloons. For a more detailed analysis, see the present author's works cited in the bibliography. We shall omit from this essay the very small group of German speakers.

of Western Europe, but remained true to its Gallic, Catholic sensibility. The austere north, under the same stimuli, more readily embraced Calvinism. From that point of view, Belgium resolved its crisis of identity very early. It was clearly one nation, unified by a common character, reinforced by a common religion, whose people happened to speak two different languages.

On the other side, it has been argued that Belgium is merely a state that contains parts of two nations. That case was stated more forcefully by the Dutch historian Pieter Geyl in explicit opposition to the work of Henri Pirenne, which provided the historiographic foundations for the traditional "Belgian" view.[3] It is founded on the notion that language was the main source of cultural differentiation in the Netherlands prior to the sixteenth century. Geyl argues that the regions of Germanic speech, grouped around the Flanders-Brabant-Holland core, responded positively to the Reformation; the French-speaking regions vacillated, but once Calvinism was stifled in France, they remained Catholic. Had history taken its natural course, there would have emerged a homogeneously Dutch-speaking, Protestant-dominated entity north of the linguistic line, leaving the remaining French-speaking provinces to be eventually absorbed by France. Instead, the actual line of separation was determined by the accidents of war. The Spaniards then re-Catholicized the south, thus separating the inhabitants of the southern areas of Germanic speech from the remainder of their "race" (*stam*).

From the point of view of an understanding of political development, both analyses are misleading, since for people of modest condition in the Low Countries, political identity in the sixteenth century was probably parochial, focused on municipalities and their hinterland, on villages and parishes; while for the nobility, lineage ties were more significant than any others. In the sixteenth century itself, identity probably focused on religion, but affiliations were unstable. In any case, although Belgian historians probably exaggerated the importance of a preexisting "Belgian" cultural character, Geyl's diatribe ignored a major point that Pirenne stated very clearly as early as 1893: what mattered most was that the line settled in 1609 determined separate

[3] Geyl's views are available in English in *The Revolt of the Netherlands, 1555-1609* (New York, 1966), as well as in *Debates with Historians* (New York, 1957). For Pirenne, see the discussion in Henri Pirenne, *Bibliographie de l'histoire de Belgique* (Gand, 1893), p. vii; and Volume VI of the *Histoire de Belgique* (Gand, 1926). For a less careful but more popular statement of the "Belgian view," see Frans Van Kalken, *La Belgique contemporaine, 1780-1930* (Paris, 1930).

development of north and south for over two centuries. We may therefore conclude that this separation contributed to the formation of Belgian identity by reinstating Catholicism as the religion of the entire population of the southern Netherlands, and by affirming its territorial definition while leaving, as a source of potential difficulty, the region divided into two linguistic zones. It is likely that in the seventeenth and eighteenth centuries a sense of territorial affinity grew slowly, primarily in reaction to the experience of being ruled by foreigners from afar. Although Catholic like their monarchs, the people and elites of the southern Low Countries knew that they were neither Spaniards nor Austrians.

Then, within a thirty-five-year period of intense political change, the Belgians were successively incorporated into two neighboring political communities, each of which was identified with one of the two dominant languages. French occupation intensified the trend, already launched during the Austrian period, toward the primacy of the French language among the growing bourgeoisie. The return of Liège to the Belgian political community more than compensated for the loss of French-speaking regions to France at the beginning of the century. Although the small-scale "Belgian Vendée" of 1798 may have reflected Flemish linguistic protest, among other things, it is most likely that in the long run the use of Dutch would have waned under the impact of a determined French commitment to cultural and linguistic homogeneity as the *sine qua non* of national unity, as occurred in many parts of France itself with reference to Dutch, Breton, or Provençal in the nineteenth century. The distinct "Belgianness" defined in opposition to some aspects of French rule would have become in time mere regionalism within a larger French political community.

Did the settlement of 1815, founded exclusively on balance-of-power considerations, reverse these trends? Among the popular strata there is no evidence that Dutch-speaking Belgians as a group were more favorably inclined toward the Dutch regime than the remainder of their countrymen. How could they have been, since the fundamentalist Catholicism of Flanders was sharply anti-Protestant? If anything, the local clergy that manned the schools stressed the *differences* between Flemish and Dutch language and culture in order to erect a barrier to assimilation. We have already referred to resistance by the political class as a whole to the imposition of Dutch as the language of public affairs. If the Liberals of Antwerp and Ghent, in particular, were known for their loyalism to the House of Orange, their preference (as that of some others for reunion with France) reflected economic interests and ideological considerations rather than discernible linguistic or cultural affinity. Finally, although Brussels and the Walloon provinces took the lead in the revolution, the Flemish provinces joined in after the Dutch attack on Brussels. On the whole, therefore, the Dutch experience probably contributed to the further development of a Belgian identity among the upper and lower strata.

It may have had a somewhat different impact on Dutch-speaking middle strata. Occurring after the most intensive period of French linguistic penetration, Dutch rule gave Flemish culture a new lease on life by revealing to secular-minded literate individuals of modest condition, including school teachers, local government officials, and other intermediate elites, the hitherto almost unsuspected—or repressed—existence of a modern literary and scientific culture in a standardized language almost identical to what was regarded as a mere "dialect" in Belgium. This exposure, together with such institutional innovations as the founding of a Dutch-language teacher-training school in Flanders and the inclusion of Dutch literature in the curricula of state universities, provided the conditions for the emergence of a small cohort of Flemish minded intellectuals, pejoratively known as *Flamingants*, shortly after Belgian independence.

In conclusion, although little can be said with assurance about the relationship between language and political behavior before the middle of the nineteenth century, the fact that language patterns did not coincide purely with regions, but were affected by class, accounts for the relative separateness of two components of the crisis of identity. Linguistic issues remained peripheral to Belgian political life so long as electoral participation was limited to a small percentage of the population. According to the first linguistic census (conducted in 1846), 57 percent of the population used Dutch as its ordinary language. Although that came as a shock to the French-speaking political class, it was probably an underestimation of the extent to which Dutch prevailed in Belgium. Brussels was itself largely a Dutch-speaking city at the popular level. But, regardless of region or even of the language in which they learned to speak, nearly all those who engaged in public affairs took French for granted. Hence, for all but a minority of political participants, the experiences culminating in the Revolution of 1830 confirmed, beyond the shadow of a doubt, their shared identity. They were not Dutch. On the other hand, when France became once again the home of liberty in July 1830, few wished to become French instead because, as a leading newspaper put it on August 10, "the Belgians have a nationality which one can ignore only by repudiating the extensive evidence of their history and by taking into account none of the numerous special characteristics they still display today."[4]

LEGITIMACY AND PARTICIPATION

Somehow, during the second third of the nineteenth century, a country whose political life initially resembled that of France came to look increasingly like Great Britain. Belgium, which had echoed the French Revolutions of 1789 and 1830, did not succumb to the upheaval generated by the collapse of the July Monarchy in 1848. How can the regime's resiliency, unmatched in continental Europe, be explained? Certainly not by the greater isolation of Belgium in 1848 than a few decades earlier since, if anything, the rapid growth of international communications increased the possibility of revolutionary contagion. For some contemporaneous observers, the answer was plain: Belgium had already experienced a revolution in 1847, when, after the Liberal party won a clear electoral victory, King Leopold reluctantly asked their leader to form a government. But to what did Belgium owe this precocious transition to party government?

The key lies in the contributions of Belgian elites to an early resolution of the crisis of legitimacy in comparison with the remainder of the Catholic world. Constrained by the consequences of earlier crises, they devised a political formula acceptable to the two major political camps. A congruent formula patterned the resolution of a crisis of penetration involving relations between central authority and the localities, the role of the state in education, and the establishment of armed forces. The Belgian political class was therefore able to resolve separately two phases of the crisis of participation and of distribution. In 1848, the middle class was coopted into the regime as an ally against the people, much as happened in Great Britain in 1832. The crises associated with mass politics, which arose in France in 1848, were postponed in Belgium, as in Great Britain, for about thirty years, a sufficient period for the stabilization of party government.

Before turning to an analysis of these processes, it is important to

[4] Quoted in Paul Harsin, *Essai sur l'opinion publique en Belgique de 1815 à 1830* (Charleroi, n.d.), p. 72. For a detailed analysis of national sentiment, see the articles by Stengers mentioned in the bibliography.

note that the parallel experiences of Belgium and Great Britain are attributable in part to two features that these otherwise very different societies shared in the nineteenth century. First, Belgium approached British levels of economic development. Around 1840, it ranked behind the United States and Great Britain, and about on a par with France, in agricultural productivity per capita; but in terms of industrial development, it was considerably ahead of France, and ranked second only to Great Britain as one of a group that also included the United States and Switzerland.[5] Within a short time, the country acquired the densest railroad network in the world. Second, just as England's insular location eased its crisis of penetration in comparison with continental Eurpean states, whose governments must exact from the population resources to build and maintain land armies, so Belgium's international situation as a neutral state under British protection eased the burdens of its government during the formative years. The price the Belgians had to pay for protection was the avoidance of republicanism; paradoxically, this eased resolution of the problem of legitimacy, since otherwise the Belgian political class might have been as sharply divided as was the French between monarchists and republicans.

Whereas in other Catholic countries the crisis of legitimacy, involving a struggle over the spiritual foundations of the state, and the crisis of participation, involving a struggle over representation on the basis of status or class, were inextricably linked to each other after 1815, in Belgium these crises could be settled in complementary fashion thanks to the circumstances of the Revolution of 1830. The Catholics—including church authorities—had participated wholeheartedly in the Revolution. Unlike many of their French counterparts who "emigrated inside" after July, they had a stake in the search for a constitutional compromise that would make the new state viable. If anything, in Belgium it was a segment of the anticlerical camp, loyal to the House of Orange, that withdrew from the political arena as long as a restoration of Dutch rule remained possible. Severely weakened, the "patriotic" liberals could hardly be adamant on spiritual issues. Having founded their Union of Oppositions on the question of broadened representation, ministerial accountability, and civil liberties more generally, the revolutionary leaders naturally expanded participation somewhat after their victory. Finally, since there was no in-

[5] For detailed data, see P. Bairoch, "Niveaux de développement économique de 1810 à 1910," *Annales: Economies, Sociétés, Civilisations*, 20 (1965), 1091-1117.

digenous noble lineage with a clear claim to the throne, the selection of a monarch itself provided an opportunity for a binding compromise between the two spiritual camps.

Reviving the American precedent, which had become naturalized in 1790, the provisional government called for the election of a constitutional congress. It had a Unionist majority, with French- and Dutch-minded minorities; but the majority included men leaning fairly clearly toward one or the other of the established spiritual camps. Legitimacy was thus founded neither on traditional dynastic right nor on an exclusive set of spiritual values, but on a constitution that itself rested on a political compact among ideological groups who were viewed as representative of the population. Although medieval traditions of "Belgian democracy" contributed little to the institutional aspects of the constitutional settlement, these traditions constituted a national myth that did contribute to legitimacy by demonstrating continuity between what was being advocated in the present and what had existed in the past.

The congress agreed on a "republican monarchy" inspired both by the new French charter and by the British model of parliamentary government, but with features going beyond both in a liberal direction. It was headed by a "King of the Belgians" with no prerogatives except as granted by the constitution and the laws of the kingdom. His only remaining area of personal authority was command of the armed forces. Diplomatic considerations weighed heavily toward the choice of Leopold of Saxe-Coburg. As Victoria's early tutor, mentor, uncle, and later uncle-in-law, he was a guarantor of Belgium's continued national existence, as well as, from the point of view of the Powers, a reliable watchman over the potentially disturbing fountainhead of liberalism. To cap his diplomatic usefulness to the new state, he married Louis-Philippe's daughter a year after his inaugural. Having learned his role at the English court, he was likely to respect the constitution. Finally, as a Protestant, he was likely to remain above the spiritual battle. Although the new monarch reluctantly accepted the severe limitations on executive authority imposed by the constitution, the problem of ministerial accountability was not yet settled.

Constitutional provisions for political participation were strikingly extensive for the world of the 1830s, not so much in the proportion of the population qualified to vote, but in the character of the institutions for which they voted. Although the constitution makers insured the dominance of their own class by limiting the franchise on the basis of taxation, their desire to produce a balance between the two ideological camps led to the cooptation of new strata of electors. Initially, about the same proportion of the population voted as in the July Monarchy; but by 1840, Belgium had 1 elector for 95 persons as against 1 for 160 in France.[6] The unique feature was that the Belgian parliament was composed of two directly elected chambers with equal authority over legislation. Chosen by the same electorate, the Senate was distinguished from the Chamber only in that a higher property qualification was set for eligibility. Furthermore, political participation was significantly more extensive at the municipal level, which was, as we shall see below, a very important political arena. Finally, the right to choose national and municipal representatives was accompanied by the right to organize and campaign on behalf of candidates.

The unusually high degree of freedom of association was itself derived from the application of the "exchange of freedoms" principle (which had made the revolutionary alliance possible) to the resolution of the potential conflict between church and state. Relations between them were settled by coupling "freedom of religion," dear to the liberals, with "freedom of education," cherished by the Catholics. Freedom of religion meant, from the Liberal point of view, that the Catholic church would not be granted a monopolistic position in Belgian society, and hence that legitimacy would rest, if not on a secular, at least on a pluralist spiritual foundation. From the Catholic point of view, it meant that the state would not supervise the church, as it had done under previously existing Concordat arrangements. In practice, the Catholics were willing to accept the primacy of civil marriage—a unique concession to the Liberals, which indicated to the world inside and outside Belgium the secular character of public authority—in exchange for public subsidies to maintain officers of all recognized religions and their houses of worship. Since the population was almost entirely Catholic, church authorities benefited immensely from the arrangement. But this was a price the Liberals were willing to pay in order to obtain what they considered a fundamental ideological victory, as well as to secure support of the local church hierarchy on behalf of the constitution in the face of thunderings from Rome against the "atheistic" Belgians.

Some time elapsed before the Holy See explicitly condemned the liberal political theory embodied in the Belgian constitution. But by

[6] Henry-T. Deschamps, *La Belgique devant la France de Juillet* (Paris, 1956), p. 375.

then the Belgian church was thriving on the arrangements, and the primate of Belgium counseled leaving well enough alone in this particular case. The results of the constitutional settlement remained so ambiguous that scholars still wondered in the middle of the twentieth century whether or not the Belgian constitution had separated church and state. It had not; but the formula was a unique solution to a major aspect of the crisis of legitimacy in the Catholic world.

PENETRATION

The pattern of settlement of issues related to legitimacy contributed to and was reinforced by the mode of settlement of several issues related to penetration. As indicated earlier, the other component in the compromise between Catholics and secularists was "freedom of education." Basically this meant that, in contrast to the situation that prevailed in the half-century preceding independence, the state would not monopolize the university (higher education, including the granting of degrees at the secondary level). That the Catholics interpreted it to mean that the state should stay out of secondary education altogether was a source of severe political conflict, as we shall see. Initially, however, the application of this principle was congruent with the basic formula underlying the constitutional settlement of spiritual issues. In the previous half-century, the state (Austria, then France, and then the Netherlands) had taken over the distinguished Catholic university in Louvain and created two additional institutions of higher education in Liège and Ghent. The Catholics now founded a new university in Mechlin. The Liberals quickly responded by creating the "Free University of Brussels," where "free" meant "freethinking," that is, founded on the principles of Freemasonry. A compromise was then worked out whereby Louvain was returned to the church, the Catholics abandoned Mechlin, and Belgium acquired a balanced system of two "neutral" state universities and two private universities, each oriented toward one of the spiritual camps. Although there were later skirmishes over authority to grant degrees, the formula stuck. Underlying it was the notion that Belgium consisted of a plurality of corporate groups, including the state and the church, with legitimate interests but with no claim to supremacy over the several spheres of Belgian society.

On the surface, since Belgium was a unitary state whose center operated on the basis of Napoleonic administrative law and practices, the pattern of spatial and functional penetration appears similar to the French one, which itself reflects a resolution of the crisis of penetration to the benefit of an indivisible center. Since such an outcome would be out of keeping with other components of the process that emerged from the resolution of the crises of political development in Belgium, we can hypothesize that significant differences in the Belgian situation should be found. Tentatively, two features, which warrant comparative examination, can be singled out. First, the Belgians institutionalized a distinct pattern of relations between the state and the municipalities. As in France, during the previous half-century Belgian territory had been divided into a large number of *communes* (municipalities), which constituted the lowest units in a hierarchical system of territorial government. There were local councils, but the executive was an administrator appointed by and accountable to central authority. In truly revolutionary manner, the provisional government of 1830 reversed this trend by instituting elected executives throughout the land. The king's desire to regain authority to appoint the mayor and his assistants was the source of increased tension between his government and parliament after independence. A compromise law, completed in 1836 after a total of 92 days of debate over a three-year period, was superseded by a law giving the monarch the authority he sought in 1842. This victory in turn reinforced the opposition and provoked a showdown that contributed to the emergence of party government a few years later.

Secondly, while the founders continued the Napoleonic institutional system, they seem to have completely rejected its spirit. First, they refused to create a French-type *conseil d'état*, leaving adjudication of conflicts between citizens and the state to be dealt with by ordinary courts, as in England or in the United States. Second, field administration was weaker than in France. Belgium was divided into nine provinces, corresponding to the division into departments during the period of French occupation; but the governors who headed them seem to have acted more as provincial ambassadors to the capital than as prefects. Third, at no time did the Belgians provide their state with mechanisms necessary for the recruitment and training of a stratum of *grands commis*. Not only was higher education not monopolized by the state, as we have already shown, but even the state universities developed somewhat autonomously of state needs. Finally, scattered evidence suggests that the bureaucracy underwent purges whenever there was a change of government, much as in the American spoils system, and that this was ultimately stabilized by allocating offices on a more or less proportional basis to the major political camps.

Diffidence toward the central executive extended to the organization of the Belgian army as well. While the monarch strove to monopolize manpower for the army, which he sought to transform into a reliable professional corps, the constitution makers advocated the maintenance of a civic guard during the Revolution, with elected officers from the middle class in Brussels and other cities. They argued that "since the public force of armies is an instrument in the hands of the central authorities, there must be a counterweight in favor of the country. It is therefore . . . indispensable to add an internal force which might, if necessary, become an army for the maintenance of our institutions as well as for the defense of the territory."[7] The guard, which also constituted an organization for the defense of class interests, remained an important component of the Belgian military establishment until after World War I. Parliament kept the army undermanned and regularly resisted the growth of defense appropriations. The belated (by Continental standards) institution of universal military service in 1909 was a victory for the central authorities; but it was also a victory for social progressives who sought a more equitable distribution of the burdens of military obligation among citizens of all classes.

The center that was in the process of being institutionalized was French. Although the founders included "freedom of linguistic usage" among the constitutional guarantees, they were firm assimilationists, committed to the view that a modern nation could be consolidated only if it had an unambiguously unilingual center. French was thus the sole official language of state administration, of secondary and higher education, and of the judiciary throughout the country. Constrained by the compromises discussed earlier, however, the Belgian rulers were unwilling or unable to reinforce central authority over elementary education and over municipal affairs, as required for the forceful implementation of an assimilationist ideology. Hence, although without legal standing, Dutch and Walloon were tolerated as the informal languages of local (municipal) services; Dutch was also the medium of instruction in the municipal primary schools instituted for the lower classes in the northern part of the country, whereas in the south, Walloon gave way to French. In any case, what mattered

[7] G. Verhaegen, "Les Institutions militaires belges," in J. Derhaveng, ed., *Histoire de la Belgique Contemporaine* (Brussels, 1930), II, 389.

was assimilation of the middle class. If Dutch-speaking Belgians were upwardly mobile, they were free to learn French; the state's obligation was to provide facilities for them to do so, particularly by fostering French-language public secondary schools in the relevant region. Others were condemned to live in what was becoming a cultural ghetto. There was little protest, except petitions from Flemish intellectuals active in philological and folklore societies for financial assistance or for the institution of literary prizes, which were granted by successive governments as a matter of course. There was no crisis.

Sequence

Although it did not resolve all issues pertaining to legitimacy and penetration, the Unionist compact, an early manifestation of the type of elite behavior believed to underlie "consociational democracy," formalized by the constitution and institutionalized through several key laws in the decade after independence, provided a framework that was valued by the participant elite, who were clustered into contending groups relatively free to maximize their ideological and material interests. They could strive for a portion of public benefits or for a sphere of institutional influence congruent with the political power they were able to muster. As this process became institutionalized, it confirmed that the Belgian state would not develop as a sovereign entity greater than the sum of its parts or as an autonomous actor above society and politics, but as the shared property of citizens organized into corporate groups. Identified as the government rather than as the regime, the state could be awarded to the winners of a regulated competition without too much danger to the other players or to the game itself. Issues that elsewhere still entailed either or choices were transformed in Belgium into more-or-less choices. Structured in this manner, political conflict tended to reinforce rather than to threaten the legitimacy of the regime.

During the first decade, the Catholics had the upper hand at the national level. The formal settlement of Belgium's international existence in 1839 freed the "Orangist" anticlericals of the past and enabled many of them to reenter the Belgian political arena by joining the Liberal camp. Although the change in the balance of partisan camps was not visible at the national level until the mid-1840s, recent research demonstrates persuasively that the sudden appearance of a liberal parliamentary wave was preceded by steady progress of well-structured coalitions of Orangist and Patriot anticlericals at the municipal level.[8] Growth of the liberal camp was stimulated also by more aggressive Roman pronouncements toward Freemasonry and liberalism more generally. In the 1840s, the monarch's victory on the issue of municipal executives, as well as adamant Catholic efforts to prevent the development of secular secondary education, provided the ideological flags around which electoral committees at the municipal level and public associations sponsored by Masonic lodges could rally under the leadership of partisan intellectuals at the Free University of Brussels to form a Liberal party.

The Unionists foundered on the secondary school issue in March 1846. Unable to find Union-minded Liberals willing to participate in a new cabinet, the king resorted to a government composed exclusively of Union-minded Catholics. Three months later, the Liberal associations, including some radical clubs, convened into a "congress" in Brussels. It was a shocking event. Writing to his son-in-law, Louis-Philippe viewed it as a "national convention constituted in a revolutionary manner," incompatible "with the existence of legal and constitutional government in the country."[9] Nevertheless, the Liberals were allowed to launch a political party which, on the basis of the above issues plus a commitment to the extension of suffrage to the next stratum of the middle class (expected to share the party's outlook), successfully contested the partial elections of April 1847 and appeared to have gained a majority in the Chamber. In June, after some hesitation and amidst rumors of his impending abdication, the king appointed a homogeneous Liberal government. The utopia of a republican monarchy seemed to have been achieved. European observers, especially the French, reported that Belgium had just achieved a successful revolution, a belief confirmed by the administrative purge immediately launched by the new government.

Whether or not it had a revolution in June 1847, Belgium was ruled by a reform-minded government when a revolution erupted in Paris eight months later. Within a week of the February events, the Belgian government proposed a law lowering property qualifications for the electorate to the constitutional minimum. This measure,

[8] See Els Witte, "Politieke Machtstrijd in en om de Voornaamste Belgische Steden, 1830-1848," Ph.D. dissertation, Rijksuniversiteit Gent, 1970. I am most grateful to Dr. Witte for allowing me to consult her dissertation.

[9] Quoted in Joseph Barthélémy, *L'Organisation du suffrage et l'experience belge* (Paris, 1912), p. 76.

unanimously approved in the Chamber within a week and passed by the Senate a week later, doubled the urban electorate and added one-third to the rural. Property qualifications were lowered even further for municipal elections—where no constitutional minimum was specified—and elected executives were restored. Belgium's middle-class civic guard, unlike its Parisian counterpart, cooperated with the government in repressing working-class agitators. The Liberals also purged the radicals from their midst.

Was the challenge to the Belgian regime less or was its staying power greater? Even if one takes into consideration differences between Paris and Brussels with respect to size and social structure, or other circumstantial factors, there can be no doubt that the significant differences between the two countries in the manner of settling similar crises of political development during the prior decades of the nineteenth century account for a large portion of the variance in outcomes. In any case, *not* having a revolution when the surrounding political world toppled was a salient historical event that strongly enhanced the legitimacy of the Belgian regime by demonstrating its effectiveness. What may have been due initially to a slight advantage greatly facilitated political development during the second half of the century.

The laws of 1848 had effects akin to those produced in Britain by the Reform Bill of 1832 and the subsequent reform of municipal government. The national electorate, which now included about five percent of the adult male population, doubled again without any change in the constitution over the next forty years; concurrently, about twice as many qualified to vote at the municipal level. More like England and less like France, Belgium experienced a relatively long period of parliamentary government with limited participation during which political organizations were able slowly to mobilize the electorate into stable partisan camps through a combination of ideological penetration and machine politics. The striking result is shown by the remarks of a papal Nuncio around 1880:

> Nothing is more interesting in Belgium than to witness municipal, and especially legislative elections. The two parties are better organized for battle than in any other European country. And this organization is the fruit of a long, patient, and tireless labor. Not only in all towns, but it can be said in all villages, there are permanent Liberal and Catholic committees which, throughout

the year, with daily care, prepare the ground for electors, protecting, if need be, their electoral rights, maintaining their loyalty to the cause, and seeking by all means to win partisans.[10]

Partisan mobilization of the electorate in turn provided the foundations for party government. Although the monarch retained personal influence, especially in the realms of defense and foreign affairs, executive authority was more and more clearly located in a cabinet accountable to the parliamentary majority. Liberals and Catholics alternated fairly regularly until 1884, when the Catholics began an uninterrupted thirty-year period of dominance. But while the Belgian pattern of government resembled the British, the issues with which government was concerned were those typical of a Continental Catholic society. The "spiritual conflict" did not abate; and it was only in May 1914 that the Belgian Parliament finally settled the educational issue of the 1830s: exchanging a commitment to subsidize Catholic education for a commitment to further develop the public secular sector, Parliament guaranteed to all families the effective right to educate their children in the spiritual camp of their choice. The underlying formula bore a striking resemblance to the one devised by the Unionists a century earlier.

CRISES OF MASS POLITICS: PARTICIPATION AND DISTRIBUTION

After 1848, lower-class demands for political citizenship remained on the agenda throughout Europe until universal suffrage was achieved. These demands were inseparable from demands for a greater share in economic benefits, for more secure and humane working conditions, and for the right to organize in order to obtain them. Since France extended political participation as early as 1848, and since class conflict was by no means less intense in Belgium, is it not surprising to find that in the twentieth century "the reconciliation of the Belgian working class to the political and social order . . . makes a vivid contrast with the experiences of France"?[11] A significant indicator is that, unlike German workers after World War I or French and Italian after World War II, the Belgian working class did not respond to the appeal of communism. Equally unexpected was the

[10] Quoted in Robert Demoulin, "Recherches de sociologie électorale en régime censitaire," *Revue Française de Science Politique*, 3 (1953), 701.

[11] Val R. Lorwin, "Working Class Politics and Economic Development in Western Europe," *American Historical Review*, 63 (1958), 348.

fact that the resolution of the crisis of participation in Belgium triggered off a major crisis of identity, which severely tested the stable process that resulted from the successful resolution of earlier crises of political development.

Demands for an extension of suffrage and for economic redistribution which arose as early as the 1840s provided incentives for the organization of a variety of working-class groups whose structure corresponded, generally speaking, to regional economic differentiation. Constrained everywhere by legislation against "combinations in restraint of trade"—that is, against collective bargaining—workers in Brussels and in Ghent tended to coalesce into mutual aid societies, craft associations, and producers' cooperatives, while the more class-conscious Walloon miners and metallurgists organized anarchist syndicates. A very extensive network of consumer cooperatives was developed, as well. The evolution of the Belgian working-class movement in the 1860s and 1870s seems to have been shaped by two institutional factors: first, the government's strategy of subcontracting the administration of social welfare to "responsible" associations reinforced mutualism; and second, opportunities to participate in municipal elections fostered the growth of socialist electoral associations founded on the network of available working-class organizations within each urban *commune*. Hence, the united Belgian Labor party, which was founded in Brussels in 1885, was a powerful amalgam of functionally differentiated structures encompassing numerous aspects of working-class life. Although the socialist leaders shared the anticlerical persuasion of the bourgeois Liberals, the Liberals' rigid class identification made impossible any cooperation other than limited tactical alliances against the Catholics.

In contrast with the Liberals, the Catholics, inspired by a corporatist ideology, successfully launched a network of associations designed to compete with the socialists for working-class support, as well as to mobilize the rural middle and lower classes. Furthermore, the Catholic camp now included a populist Flemish movement that had mobilized rural support in parts of northern Belgium. That movement emerged in the 1850s in response to disastrous economic deterioration, comparable to Ireland's. Flemish intellectuals shifted from a romantic concern with philology and folklore to demands for the material improvement of Flanders. By no means challenging the unilingual definition of the Belgian center, they urged that the four-and-one-half provinces located north of the linguistic frontier be recognized as a bilingual region where state and local services for the populace should be provided in the regional tongue. In the face of public indifference, they shifted in the 1870s from petitioning to local electoral action. Their contribution to Catholic victories in Antwerp and a few other key cities brought about a rapprochement between *Flamingants* and Catholics more generally. Although in the following decade the bilingual character of northern Belgium was acknowledged through a series of laws passed nearly unanimously, by then the more militant were demanding a redefinition of the center along the same lines. Adamant Liberal opposition further reinforced the Catholic-*Flamingant* alliance. The calculation that a further expansion of voting rights would totally transform the linguistic character of the Belgian electorate gave the Flemish movement a populist orientation. In the 1880s, therefore, it emerged as a Christian Democratic organization that coexisted in a state of tension with the established Catholic party.

Around 1890, when approximately 10 percent of the adult male population was qualified to vote in national elections and approximately 25 percent at the municipal level, the socialists triggered off a full-scale crisis of participation by organizing massive general strikes on behalf of universal adult male suffrage. The threat of civil disorder brought about a rapprochement between mainstream Catholics and liberals on older "spiritual" issues, but forced them to accept a compromise proposal sponsored by the Christian Democrats and the Progressives, a radical splinter within the Liberal camp, for constitutional revision. The reform of 1893 reflected Catholic and Liberal hypotheses concerning the political behavior of the Belgian population as well as Catholic parliamentary dominance. It entailed a tenfold increase of voters; but multiple voting (on the basis of tax, education, etc.) insured that 37 percent of the electorate had 58 percent of the votes. The Catholics insisted on mandatory voting in order to bring out the weight of putatively Catholic rural voters.

As anticipated, and in spite of a Christian-Democratic split, the system worked to the advantage of the Catholics, who won about two-thirds of the seats in 1894 with about half of the votes cast. In spite of the class bias inherent in multiple voting, the socialists obtained more seats than the liberals. Each party wished to further change the system to its advantage. The liberals, whose support was needed by the Catholics on class issues, successfully bargained for proportional representation in order to maximize the weight of anticlerical urban middle class voters; this subsequently somewhat weakened the Catholic party but strengthened the Christian Democrats. Unaffected, the Socialists continued to demonstrate their power in the streets. It was only in 1913, in exchange for a commitment to accept the rules of the parliamentary game, that their leaders obtained a commitment from the bourgeois parties to an open debate on the question of equal universal suffrage for males. Having entered the government of national union constituted at the outbreak of World War I, and having participated in the Belgian government-in-exile during the war, the socialist leaders finally secured equal universal suffrage and the right to bargain collectively as part of a new compact negotiated by the Belgian parties under the aegis of their monarch in November 1918.

These great victories, after two generations of intense struggle that consolidated working-class solidarity across spiritual and linguistic lines of cleavage, helped the established socialist leadership to maintain control over militants at a time when other parties in the Second International were torn apart under the challenge of the Russian Revolution. Paradoxically, the protracted struggle for participation in Belgium contributed to the integration of its working class into the established political game. So did World War I. Whereas French and German socialists were torn between patriotism and internationalism, Belgium was so clearly a victim of aggression that working-class leaders faced no dilemma. Furthermore, unlike France, where socialist participation in wartime governments left the leadership vulnerable to blame for sacrifices imposed on the workers, in Belgium guilt for ravages, privations, and repression could be placed squarely on enemy shoulders. But if the war contributed to the resolution of crises of participation and of distribution, it vastly exacerbated an incipient crisis of identity.

In the midst of the crises of mass politics, Belgium was in the process of acquiring a colony. Although the monarch's autonomous undertaking in Central Africa was the subject of protracted parliamentary debate, culminating in a division along partisan lines on a government proposal to transform the Independent Congo State into a Belgian colony (1908), colonial issues remained peripheral from the point of view of Belgian political development. At most, the Congo eased resolution of the crisis of distribution in the first half of the twentieth century because the Belgian economy as a whole benefited from the almost unrestrained predatory activities of its public and private entrepreneurs. Control of valuable mineral resources undoubtedly eased social strains after both world wars by facilitating

Belgian economic recovery. Conversely, loss of the Congo somewhat exacerbated the economic recession of the 1960s, which itself contributed to a revival of class tensions. Belgium's colonial experience is perhaps one of the very few cases—along with the Dutch experience in Indonesia—that confirm Lenin's propositions about the relationship of imperialism to the internal class struggle.

CRISES OF MASS POLITICS: IDENTITY

As anticipated, expansion of the electorate reinforced the power of the Flemish-minded. At the very end of the nineteenth century, nearly seventy years after the grant of "linguistic freedom," Dutch was recognized alongside French as an official national language. Although concomitant services were not provided until later, this indicated a formal commitment to the redefinition of the Belgian center as bilingual. But the resolution of an old issue of penetration did not solve what intellectuals now identified as a permanent threat to the survival of Flemish culture. They saw evidence that, even while *vervlaamsing* ("Flemishization") of public services and of education was becoming a reality, *verfransing* ("Frenchification") was occurring at a possibly higher rate through the interplay of upward mobility with assimilationist forces radiating from Brussels. So long as the Dutch-speaking region remained economically and socially backward in relation to the country as a whole, and so long as a choice between Dutch and French was available, within a couple of generations—often within a single lifetime—Dutch-speaking individuals, indistinguishable in other than linguistic respects from their compatriots, would continue to switch to French and stop being Flemings altogether. This might benefit them as individuals, but it would eventually mean the extinction of a culture, of a people.

In the process of groping for a more permanent foundation of identity, the *Flamingants* shifted from language to territory, from the rights of Dutch-speaking individuals to obtain services in their own language to the rights of a people, defined by its location on Flemish soil, to survive. The right to use Flemish became an obligation to do so. If many Flemings actually spoke French, this was an undesirable consequence of historical accident—as Geyl argued in the historiography he contributed to the movement around that time—and history should be reversed. The new battle cry was, *In Vlaanderen Vlaamsch.*

The Belgian state must recognize the exclusively unilingual character of the northern region. Since the threat evoked a more self-conscious commitment to preservation of the *status quo* among French-speaking Belgians than any previous demands for more equitable distribution of benefits, by reaction it enhanced their linguistic identity. On the eve of World War I, "Flemings" and "Walloons" were in the course of becoming antagonistic political communities. Some Flemish leaders collaborated with German authorities in realizing two important aspects of their program: transformation of the state university in Ghent into a Dutch-language institution, and transformation of linguistic regions into component units of a federal state. The growth of a Flemish protest movement among Dutch-speaking infantrymen serving under French-speaking officers at the front confirmed, in the eyes of the Walloons, that Flemings were not loyal Belgians. After the armistice, in spite of an interparty agreement to settle linguistic issues in the near future, there were further delays. Rallying around the issue of amnesty for their wartime leaders, the Flemings increasingly took to the streets.

It was only a decade later, under the constant pressure of street demonstations, that the Catholic and Socialist parties, which then represented about three-fourths of the electorate, accepted the principle of territoriality as the foundation for future legislation. In the 1930s, the principle *In Vlaanderen Vlaamsch* began to be implemented: the University of Ghent was transformed into a Flemish-language institution; Belgium was divided, for the purpose of general administration, education, and judicial organization, into two unilingual regions and a bilingual capital district, with a scattering of municipalities along the linguistic frontier whose status would be determined by decennial censuses; a knowledge of Dutch was required of all state officials, while hesitant steps were even taken to duplicate central administrative services into linguistically homogeneous sections; the reigning monarch regularly addressed Belgians in the country's two languages; and the political parties informally recognized the existence of linguistic-regional components in their midst. Linguistic affiliation was added to spiritual orientation and class interest as an element to be taken into consideration for the purpose of forming governmental coalitions.

Belgium thus acknowledged the existence of a Flemish people. But although the irritant that had provoked the crisis of identity was now removed, linguistic conflict rankled on, a source of intermittent crises down to the present. Had Belgium still not resolved its crisis of identity?

Tensions between the communities were exacerbated once again during World War II for some of the same reasons as during World War I. They grew even more intense afterwards, during the years of the "royal question" (1945-1950). Already in the late 1930s the recently crowned Leopold III antagonized the political class by pursuing an overly active role in foreign policy. Was he the prisoner of a leadership role unexpectedly developed by his father, the "soldier king" of World War I? In any case, Leopold's stubborn adherence to a policy of absolute neutrality after erstwhile neutralist politicians revised their stand provided the foundations for open conflict when Belgium was invaded. His willingness to sign an armistice considered premature by Churchill and the French, and his subsequent ambiguous wartime behavior under German occupation might have provoked a full-scale crisis of legitimacy had not the party leaders, fearing that such a crisis would play into the hands of the Communist party, kept the royal question within bounds by clearly separating the king as an individual from the monarchical role.

Although initially the royal question had little to do with language, mobilization occurred along existing lines of cleavage and contributed to their consolidation: a majority of Flemish Catholics sided with the king against a majority of Walloon and Brussels secularists. The linguistic settlement of the 1930s was itself questioned. It was only after the parties negotiated a pact shelving linguistic issues for a ten-year period that they were able to settle the royal question itself. It looked almost as if the leading players reasoned that too many lines of cleavage in play at the same time might overload the game: spiritual camps and classes, either of these with linguistic communities, but not all three. In 1950, the king was vindicated in a popular referendum, as the Catholics had hoped; but since regional breakdowns showed clearly that he was only king of the Flemings, and confronted by continued hostility of the united secular camps, he abdicated in favor of his son.

Having gained a temporary electoral advantage, which enabled them to rule alone for the first time since 1914, the Catholics reopened the spiritual issues settled by the educational legislation of 1913. The "school war" that raged for the next eight years was resolved by a return to the old formula and a pact among the parties to shelve spiritual issues for the next decade. Thus, in the late 1950s, the linguistic problem and class issues recaptured center stage.

By this time, changed economic and social circumstances affected the logic of political issues related to the linguistic communities. Between 1910 and 1961, the proportion of the total population living in what was now "Flemish territory" had grown from 47.2 to 51.3 percent. Located on the "European axis," with easy access to the sea and to the Rhine, Flanders was experiencing a genuine industrial boom as the result of Belgian and foreign investments. The status of Dutch as a language in relation to French benefited from the growing importance of English, to which it is closely related, as the international language of business, science, and international affairs, as well as from Belgium's participation in a multilingual European Economic Community that also contained ten million Dutch-speaking Netherlanders. No longer a numerical or status minority, Flemings had the upper hand in Belgium. The only threat came from Brussels. Having doubled in size during the previous half-century, the bilingual capital district contained sixteen percent of the total population of Belgium. It was a dynamic economic center that inexorably radiated French culture among its own population and, with perhaps the largest factor of daily commuters of any city in the world, into the Flemish territory that surrounded it almost entirely. It was now the Walloons who saw themselves as a deprived minority. The regional population shrank from thirty nine percent of the Belgian total in 1910 to thirty-three percent in 1961. Wallony resembled northern England, with which it had shared a history of precocious industrialization, in that its industrial plant was obsolete, its mines were depleted, and its location disadvantageous for new investments.

Altogether, these changes account for the transformation of the identity crisis into a new crisis involving distribution, participation, and penetration. The Flemings had no interest whatsoever in separatism. If things were allowed to take their course, the normal play of legislative reapportionment, based on a territorial headcount, would give Flemish constituencies a permanent majority in the Belgian parliament. The only threat would come from the use of linguistic headcount as the basis for legislation concerning public services, since that might lead to an expansion of the area defined as bilingual at the expense of Flemish territory. The most satisfactory solution, from this point of view, entailed a "freezing" of regional boundaries, coupled with genuine decentralization of cultural and economic policy-making to the regional level. The more regional autonomy, the more Flemings would retain their wealth and be free to operate in an international context in which Amsterdam, Cologne, or New York mattered more than Brussels. The Walloons, by contrast, feared being reduced to a shrinking political minority through reapportionment. With little bargaining power at the center, they would undergo more severe economic decline and become a "colony" in a country whose center was increasingly dominated by the Flemish. They might dream of reunion with France, but President De Gaulle seemed more aware of oppressed Frenchmen in the New World than on his own doorstep. Short of that, the Walloons also espoused a federal solution, but with economic and political guarantees for the smaller region. Finally, Brussels had a distinct interest of its own: it opposed the "freezing" of unilingual regional boundaries, since this would prevent the extension of bilingual arrangements into newly growing dormitory suburbs, and since regional autonomy would lessen its status and the economic benefits it derived from being the capital city of a unitary state.

But the Belgian political process does not involve the interplay of linguistic communities alone. Already in the 1930s, but increasingly in the 1960s, the political parties were torn between their immediate interests as national organizations involved in a game of coalition government (in which spiritual and class alignments were determinative), and the need to adjust to the interests of the linguistic communities with which their supporters also identified. Although they generally opposed any moves toward decentralization, since new arrangements were likely to lessen their control over the established political game, they must face loss of support to the benefit of political entrepreneurs who were free to emphasize regional interests to the exclusion of others. This dilemma affected each of the parties somewhat differently.[12] In 1961, for example, the Catholic party had 41.5 percent of the national vote; of this, it obtained 66.2 percent from Flanders, where it had an absolute majority. Since it was threatened in that region by the growth of militant Flemish movements that might undercut its national standing, the party tended to favor Flemish demands. But its leaders were constrained by Walloon Catholic fear of becoming a permanent minority in a socialist-dominant region. The

[12] The discussion is based on data presented by Val R. Lorwin, "Belgium: Religion, Class, Language in National Politics," in Robert A. Dahl, ed., *Political Oppositions in Western Democracies* (New Haven, 1966), pp. 412-15.

Socialist party had 36.7 percent of the national vote; of this, it obtained 44.1 percent from Flanders; but it was threatened in Wallony, where it was the leading party, by a communist revival and by the growth of a regional splinter group. The party's dilemma was even greater than that of the Catholics because decentralization would undermine the internal balance of ideological orientations which, so far, had enabled the leadership to maintain a middle-of-the-road policy. The Liberals were most militant in the defense of unitary Belgium and of the interests of the capital city.

By negotiating a series of linguistic laws that modified the arrangements of the 1930s in the direction of Flemish demands for a permanent freezing of regional boundaries, party leaders hoped in the early 1960s to postpone the day of reckoning. But after the elections of 1965 and 1968 revealed growing support for the new regional parties at the expense of the established players, especially among the young, the Catholics, soon followed by the Socialists and subsequently by the Liberals, transformed themselves into confederations of nearly autonomous regional parties. Seeking to preserve control of the Belgian political process in the face of new challenges, the parties reluctantly undertook the transformation of some of the political systems' traditional features. Between 1968 and 1974, Belgium moved toward the establishment of a pattern of institutional arrangements that has been dubbed "federalization without federalism." The country now contains officially recognized linguistic regions, cultural communities, and economic regions; voters cast ballots not only for one or the other of the regional components of the traditional political parties, but also for one or the other of the newer regional parties; and the process of governmental coalition making has become extremely complex. In the foreseeable future, linguistic and regional issues are unlikely to be settled, but neither are they likely to tear Belgium apart.[13]

Conclusion

Although this essay is mainly concerned with crises of political development in the past century and a half, some attention was devoted to an analysis of the political process that emerged in the Belgian region as the result of medieval and early modern transformations. A

[13] For a detailed account and interpretation of recent changes, see Aristide R. Zolberg, "Splitting the Difference: Federalization without Federalism in Belgium," in Milton J. Esman, ed., *Ethnic Conflict in the Western World* (Ithaca, 1977).

first sequence of crises of distribution, participation, and penetration undermined the foundations of feudal legitimacy and resulted in the institutionalization of conciliar government at the municipal and regional levels. This pattern of political life constituted a foundation that early distinguished the Netherlands region—along with England, Switzerland, as well as parts of France, Germany, and Italy—from the rest of the world.

As part of the Low Countries, Belgium experienced in the sixteenth century a first modern revolution and civil war that might have led, as it did in the United Provinces and a century later in England, to precocious parliamentary supremacy. Although the fortunes of war left Belgium instead among the countries subjected to an absolutist state-building strategy, the thrust of penetration was comparatively weak. Survival of important elements of the political process institutionalized earlier shaped the outcome of the second thrust of "modernization from above" in the form, successively, of enlightened despotism, of the revolutionary national state, and then of a restoration that constituted a mixture of the two. The kingdom of Belgium thus emerged as a strikingly liberal regime, as a "republican monarchy" in which parliamentary supremacy was rapidly institutionalized almost as if it were a natural outcome of Belgian history, repressed by centuries of foreign rule but always yearning to exist. This was, of course, a nationalist myth; but the myth contained enough historical truth to make it serviceable as a foundation of legitimacy and identity, as well as to justify the institutionalization of class as the sole criterion for political participation. Commercialization of land during the French Revolution had already resolved a major element of the crisis of distribution, so far as the participant class was concerned, while independence resolved another aspect. A bourgeois society *par excellence*, Catholic Belgium had the sort of rich associational life that Tocqueville and others ascribed to congregational Protestantism.

These internal features, as well as the international situation that eased the burdens of government and hence minimized the necessity of vigorous territorial and functional penetration, contributed to the settlement of the crisis of legitimacy in the first half of the nineteenth century, before Belgium experienced the full impact of the crises of popular participation and of distribution triggered off by industrialization and the establishment of universal suffrage next door in 1848. As in England and in the Netherlands, and in contrast with France, a consensus on regime among the ideological segments of the participant political class even while they engaged in political competition to maximize their interests enabled them to prevent the entrance of the lower strata into politics, while coopting the middle class into the system. The outcome of this "gradualist strategy" was the early institutionalization of party government. In this respect, Belgium turns out probably to be a unique Continental case, and undoubtedly a unique Catholic case, whose further analysis would contribute significantly to the revision of established propositions in political science and political sociology concerning the origins of political parties.

The early institutionalization of party government under conditions of limited political participation in turn facilitated the mobilization of the working class and of the peasantry into extensive associational networks *before* most of them obtained the right to vote. On the eve of World War I, political cleavages were stabilized along cross-cutting lines of class and spiritual orientations with an incipient linguistic dimension. A decade later, Belgium was in most respects a fully developed political community. The extension of political rights on an equal basis to the entire adult male population had been completed; the other half of the population was granted this right without difficulty a generation later. Although the right to collective bargaining did not bring about an immediate dramatic redistribution of material benefits, it did bring Belgium into the average category of liberal capitalist societies. There is no indication that its income inequalities were above the European average.

The first elections waged under equal universal male suffrage in 1919 established a modal pattern for the next twenty years. Nationally, the Catholics and the socialists each received a little over one-third of the total, while the remainder was split between the liberals and small regional groups. Although the Catholics had an absolute majority in the more rural Dutch-speaking provinces, mirrored by a slightly less pronounced socialist dominance in the more industrial Walloon region, with the liberals most powerful in the capital, all three parties had a genuinely national clientele. Under conditions of mandatory voting and with a well-mobilized population, electoral strategies dictated a concentration on each party's predictable clientele, rather than on "swing" voters. Procedures for voting by party lists insured that those who controlled party apparatuses could always get their man elected. Through a combination of these factors, party leaders emerged as the masters of Belgian politics.

This process was reinforced by the pattern of organization of the public services resulting from the earlier crisis of penetration. Although Belgium was formally a unitary state, responsibility for public services was shared between the central government and the municipalities; in addition, the allocation of public goods—especially social welfare—was increasingly subcontracted to a network of para-governmental organizations controlled by the political parties. The state bureaucracy was itself shared among the partisan camps on a more or less proportional basis. These features contributed to the organizational maintenance of the parties and their networks of ancillary associations, provided an incentive to the growth of membership, and insured that the partisan camps would retain a stake in the maintenance of the system as a whole.

Although the spirit of "compact" that presided over the founding survived, the development of stable partisan organizations led to its ever-greater formalization. For example, an agreement to settle the major issues that had arisen during World War I was negotiated by party leaders at a conference under the aegis of the king even before the government-in-exile returned to Belgium, much as if they were the executives of independent states engaged in diplomacy. "Treaties" of this sort were resorted to repeatedly after periods of crisis during the next half-century in order to provide the foundations for a period of normal coalition government. Although between the two world wars there were about thirty governmental "crises," there was never any serious doubt about the possibility of forming a new government.[14] Over half of the time, the government consisted of a relatively conservative Catholic-liberal coalition; for much of the remainder, Belgium was ruled by some form of "national union" made up of the more progressive elements of the two older parties and of the socialists. Pay-offs in this game did not involve control of government and of policy; rather, it involved the relative influence of party factions in a moving equilibrium of interests. In relation to policy, this meant that there was never a "combat" government, but rather an acceleration or a pause in the working out of specific issues.

The Belgian political process survived remarkably well the challenges stemming from the Russian Revolution and the rise of European fascism, probably less because there were significant differences in social structure between Belgium and other countries, where new mass movements of the left and of the right were more successful,

[14] Carl H. Höjer, *Le Régime parlementaire belge de 1918 à 1940* (Uppsala, 1946; reprinted Brussels, 1971), pp. 313-67.

than because, given the extensive prior mobilization of the relevant social strata into partisan networks (which was itself the outcome of the particular sequence of crises we have discussed) there was no substantial vacuum that these political entrepreneurs could fill in Belgium. Although distinct Flemish and Walloon protofascist movements inflicted some losses upon the established parties in 1936, the traditional organizations had remarkably recovered by the time the last prewar election was held in 1939. After World War II, further development of Catholic trade unionism, female suffrage, the elimination of regional-minded fascists, and the consequences of the royal question reinforced the Catholic electoral camp; labor unions became more important political actors, and the Communist party surged forward. But after some temporary disturbances, the traditional party system was reinstated in the late 1950s, with Catholic-socialist governmental coalitions as the new modal pattern. Within a few years, however, the stable Belgian political process was threatened by the inability of its institutional components to resolve the protracted conflict between linguistic communities.

We have attempted to demonstrate in the body of this essay that it would be misleading to regard manifestations of that conflict as evidence of a century-long crisis of identity. There was no significant crisis of identity in Belgium during the first half of the nineteenth century because the problem of nationality had been resolved for the participant political class in the course of gaining independence. Linguistic community consciousness, as manifested by the growth of a Flemish movement, initially concerned aspects of penetration and distribution rather than of identity. But the populist character of this movement contributed to the emergence of a crisis of participation, and the resolution of that crisis in turn precipitated a crisis of identity by revealing discrepancies between the numerical force of Dutch-speaking Belgians and their status in the national system. To the extent that the crisis involved an ideological transformation, which in turn fostered the redefinition of Belgium as a country containing two peoples, it was resolved in principle in the 1930s. The solution involved an application of the hitherto successful Belgian approach to political conflict: the transformation of an "either-or" problem into a "more-or-less" problem, which could then be resolved through reallocation of benefits on the basis of regular political competition.

Belgians have long known who they are: anti-clerical, French-speaking Brussels shopkeepers, many of Flemish ancestry, who regularly vote for the Liberals, or more recently for a local party which also defends their linguistic interests; militant Walloon workers, most of whom vote for the Socialist party, but some of whom vote for one of several Communist factions, or for a leftist Walloon regional party; comfortable, Catholic, Flemish farmers, most of whom continue to vote for democratic, Flemish-minded Catholic candidates; Flemish urban workers for whom being socialist is as much a way of life as being Catholic is for others, and so on. Perhaps in no other modern society are individuals so easily classifiable according to a few political, sociological, and cultural characteristics, and as aware of the identity these characteristics define. While responding with enthusiasm in the polling booth or occasionally in the streets to the slogans of leaders who reflect these divisions and help to maintain them, hardly any citizens have allegiances to a political unit other than Belgium. When they are engaged in conflict—which is about the only time the rest of the world becomes aware of their existence—Belgians rarely suffer loss of life or limb at the hands of their compatriots. Amidst permanent bickering, there is little room for hatred.

What, then, does the protracted linguistic conflict involve? In recent years, it has been mostly about participation in decision making concerning the cultural and economic life of the communities and the regions, and about distribution of resources to implement these decisions. The vigorous new regional parties are as concerned with spiritual and class-related issues as with the defense of culture. Hence it is doubtful whether Belgium remains in the throes of an unresolved crisis of identity. It is at the threshold of new crises of participation, distribution, and penetration, which it shares with most other industrial democracies, but which in Belgium are necessarily voiced in two languages.

The crises of political development provide a useful analytical framework for understanding the emergence of Belgium as a political community and for its subsequent transformation into a liberal industrial democracy of the "consociational" type with a specific political process. Throughout the essay, however, scattered references have been made as well as to the changing international context within which these transformations occurred.

The determinative importance of the international system during the preindependence period is obvious. In 1830, had the Dutch resisted effectively, or even had they decided to launch a serious offensive at any time during the next few years, or had the European powers not reluctantly thrown their weight on the side of the Belgian upstarts—England apparently in order to avoid the embarrassment of a Continental expedition during an electoral campaign—the Belgian regime might have been different; it might not even have survived at all.

Later, the country's guaranteed neutrality and international "low profile" facilitated the separation of domestic from foreign affairs, and hence eased the resolution of the crises of legitimacy, of penetration, and of participation in a manner conducive to an early transition to party government. Although the Belgian regime held fast in February 1848, it is unlikely that it would have survived for long under the impact of a successful French democratic republic. After 1851, Bonapartist designs on Belgium remained ambiguous and ambivalent. Having accidentally escaped being engulfed in the Franco-Prussian conflict a generation later, Belgium did not experience the exacerbation of class conflict that the war provoked within at least one of the belligerents. The "miracle" itself affirmed parliamentary resistance to increased defense appropriations and facilitated the further development of partisan political machines at the mass level. With the exception of contention between the monarch and the politicians over the acquisition of a colony and over universal military service, external affairs remained peripheral to Belgian politics until the eve of World War I. Surely, the contributions of nearly a century of peace to the resolution of the crises of development cannot be underestimated, any more than the subsequent contributions of two world wars and of consequent alterations of the international system to the outcome of Belgian crises in the twentieth century.

Generally speaking, during its formative period, as a small country located at the heart of the European balance-of-power system, Belgium was a political community whose fate was largely determined by decisions made elsewhere. Its regime was more permeable to the consequences of external factors than if Belgium had been a major actor, or than if it had been more isolated. On the other hand, in both the nineteenth and twentieth centuries Belgium was less likely than some of its larger Continental neighbors to experience the political costs of divisive foreign policy decisions and of the international obligations (including mobilization of human and physical resources) that such choices entailed. Although it is impossible to elaborate these considerations here, the Belgian case illustrates forcefully the necessity of overcoming what is by now an established theoretical convention in political science, the separate study of domestic and international politics.

Some Related Readings

Barthélémy, Joseph. *L'Organisation du suffrage et l'expérience belge.* Paris, 1912. A detailed monograph on electoral rules and procedures, elections and the origins of parties.

Chlepner, B.S. *Cent ans d'histoire sociale en Belgique.* Brussels, 1956. The standard work on the origins of labor organizations and on legislation relevant to the crisis of distribution.

Clough, Shephard B. *A History of the Flemish Movement in Belgium: A Study in Nationalism.* New York, 1930. Not as good as Elias, but more accessible as an introduction to the subject.

Demoulin, Robert. *La Révolution de 1830.* Brussels, 1950. A well-balanced, fairly modern reappraisal.

Deschamps, Henry-Thierry. *La Belgique devant la France de Juillet: L'opinion et l'attitude françaises de 1839 à 1848.* Paris, 1956. Very detailed analysis of French views as reported in the press and in diplomatic reports; although the author does not intend it, his monograph provides useful materials for a comparative analysis of the two regimes.

Elias, H. J. *Geschiedenis van de Vlaamse Gedachte, 1780-1914.* Antwerp, 1956. 4 volumes. A masterful account of the development of Flemish-minded movements and organizations with special attention to ideology, by an important leader tried for collaboration during World War II. An absolute must for the subject.

Gerard-Libois, Jules, and José Gotovitch. *L'an 40. La Belgique occupée.* Brussels, n.d. A key book for the understanding of the evolution of Belgian politics from 1936 on, including the events that gave rise to the post-World War II "royal question."

Geyl, Pieter A. *Debates with Historians.* New York, 1957. A full discussion of the Dutch-Belgian historiographic controversy on nationality.

———. *The Revolt of the Netherlands, 1555-1609.* New York, 1966. A segment of the author's major work, *Geschiedenis van de Nederlandsche Stam,* which states the "accidental" outcome thesis discussed in the essay; also excellent on the revolt itself.

Gilissen, John. *Le Régime représentatif avant 1790 en Belgique.* Brussels, 1952. A very useful, well-balanced overview of the origins and the development of constitutionalism.

———. *Le régime représentatif en Belgique depuis 1790*. Brussels, 1958. Equally useful for the recent period; good electoral tables.

Harsin, Paul. *Essai sur l'opinion publique en Belgique de 1815 à 1830*. Charleroi, n.d. Traces the development of the press during the period with special emphasis on the beginnings of "Union."

Höjer, Carl-Henrik. *Le régime parlementaire belge de 1918 à 1940*. Uppsala, 1946; reproduced in Brussels, 1969. A very interesting analysis of the Belgian political process and its components, including major issues.

Huyse, Lucien. *Passiviteit, Pacificatie en Verzuiling in de Belgische Politiek*. Antwerp, 1970. A unique attempt by a Belgian to analyze the rules of his country's political game within the framework of contemporary comparative politics.

Lebas, Colette. *L'union des Catholiques et des libéreaux de 1839 à 1847: Étude sur les pouvoirs exécutif et législatif*. Louvain, 1960. Detailed monograph on the end of Union and the emergence of partisan politics.

Lorwin, Val. R. "Belgium: Religion, Class and Language in National Politics," in Robert A. Dahl, ed., *Political Oppositions in Western Democracies*. New Haven, 1966, pp. 147-184, 409-416. Until the same author's forthcoming larger work is published, by far the best analytic and historical introduction to contemporary Belgian society and politics in any language.

Luykx, Theo. *Politieke Geschiedenis van Belgie van 1789 tot Heden*. Brussels and Amsterdam, 1964. A blow-by-blow descriptive political history with a focus on parliamentary life and succinct discussions of the legislative history of almost every issue as well as of elections. Thorough bibliography with useful appendices. There is no equivalent in French to this valuable handbook.

Meynaud, Jean *et al.*, *La décision politique en Belgique: Le pouvoir et les groupes*. Paris, 1965. Somewhat like Höjer, but for the period 1944-1964.

Palmer, Robert R. *The Age of Democratic Revolution: A Political History of Europe and America, 1760-1800*. Vol. I, *The Challenge*. Vol. II, *The Age of Struggle*. Princeton, 1959, 1964. Includes several chapters on Belgium based on the works of Suzanne Tassier and other Belgian historians, but casting Belgium in a revealing comparative context.

Pirenne, Henri. *Bibliographie de l'histoire de Belgique*. Gand, 1893. The preface is a major discussion of historiography.

———. *Histoire de Belgique*. Brussels, 1910-1926. 6 volumes. Remains the most stimulating general history, which views political development in relation to society and culture.

Res Publica, 10 (1968). *Numéro spécial*, "Les problèmes constitutionnels de la Belgique au XIXe siècle." Four articles on origins of the constitutions, church and state, political parties and social classes, the Flemish question.

Stengers, Jean. "Sentiment national, sentiment orangiste et sentiment français à l'aube de notre indépendance," in *Revue Belge de Philologie et d'Histoire*, 28 (1950), 994-1027 and XXIX 29 (1951), 66-90.

Van Houtte, J. A. *et al.*, *Algemene Geschiedenis der Nederlanden*. Utrecht, 1949-1958. 12 volumes. The modern collaborative history written by Belgian and Dutch scholars. Vols. X-XI, spanning the period 1840-1914, have very useful summary essays on political parties and movements by specialists on each subject.

Willemsen, A. W. *Het Vlaams-nationalisme: De geschiedenis van de jaren 1914-1940*. Utrecht, 1969, second edition. Picks up where Elias leaves off. A monograph of high quality.

Witte, Els. "Politieke Machtstrijd in en om de Voornaamste Belgische Steden 1830-1848." Doctoraats-verhandeling, Rijksuniverseteit Gent, 1970. 3 volumes. An original quantitative and analytic study of the origins of party organizations in the twenty largest Belgian towns.

Zolberg, Aristide R., "The Making of Flemings and Walloons: Belgium, 1830-1914," in *Journal of Interdisciplinary History*, 5 (1974), 179-235. A detailed examination, supported by quantitative evidence, of changing relationships cast within a developmental framework.

———. "Splitting the Difference: Federalization without Federalism in Belgium," in Milton J. Esman, ed., *Ethnic Conflict in the Western World* (Ithaca, 1977). Casts the constitutional revisions of the past decade in the context of changing social and political structures, with details on electoral and coalitional processes through 1975.

CHAPTER 4

Scandinavia: Denmark, Finland, Iceland, Norway, Sweden

FOLKE DOVRING

Scandinavia, or northern Europe, has been part of the world we call "modern" at least since it joined the medieval church. Through gradual adjustments, the area has been "modernized" as successfully as any. Gradual changes have continued over long periods, and there have been few overt crises. Historians and political scientists have traditionally focused their attention on dramatic episodes, of which there have been many in the history of all five countries. More recent interest in economic and social history, by contrast, emphasizes long-term processes. For the Scandinavian region, analysis of the "critical situations" offers more of interest when these situations are viewed as protracted problems (both analytical and perceived) rather than as turning points or as threats to the system. From a vast literature, some main points will be cited as reflecting a more or less general consensus of scholars, vague and implicit as that consensus often may be, without going into details of controversies still unresolved.

Scandinavia's "modernization" has been such a gradual process that no general "development syndrome" can be traced, nor any discernible "modernization threshold." Any meaningful treatment of most of these problems has to start in the middle ages, close to the beginning of recorded history in the area. But even medieval Scandinavia by no means fits any stereotype of "traditional" society as ridden with authoritative dependency relations. Some features that we think of as essential to a modern society were present, in crude and primitive beginnings, at a very early date. Some were introduced, reintroduced, or reinforced during the last two hundred years. The specific differences that do exist between the five countries, despite their intensive interaction in recent times, serve to underline the consequences of history, even on a generation that professes itself "historyless."

Scandinavia is more than a group of countries homogeneous enough

Crises of Political Development in Europe and the United States
0-691-07598-0/78/000139-23$01.15/1 (cloth)
0-691-02183-X/78/000139-23$01.15/1 (paperback)
For copying information, see copyright page

for comparative study. Several critical factors, especially those labeled identity and legitimacy, also apply to the entire area. The problems of Scandinavia as a whole are those most directly relevant to the problems of today's low-income countries. This aspect will be the focus of the conclusions to this paper.

Crises

IDENTITY

Within the Scandinavian-speaking populations, a national consciousness of sorts antedated national unity and national organization—a consciousness based on a common language. "Danish tongue" was once a collective name for all the Scandinavian dialects. This unity began to break up by increasing idiom cleavage at about the time when central political powers were established. The political entities created toward the end of the Viking age proved decisive for the language differences that were stabilized by national cultures. Icelandic, still close to the original common idiom, survived because of distance and isolation. Within the main body of Scandinavia, the cultural identities of Denmark and Sweden became coextensive with their political boundaries. Prior to the seventeenth century, border provinces, with intermediary dialects, sometimes vacillated in their loyalty. Economic interests could lead to "peasants' peace" across such borders, even as the kings kept on warring over issues of their own. The complex history of language in modern Norway further testifies to the importance of political unity for cultural identity.

Before literacy was made general through compulsory primary schools, national idioms were unified through the educational efforts of the church. Since the Reformation, the church in all the Scandinavian countries has been a national institution, subordinate to the Crown but in many ways the mentor of monarchs. Use of standardized vernaculars made the educational role of the church a strong nation-building element. This helped national identity in Denmark and Sweden, but led to critical situations in Finland and Norway.

In Norway, the Lutheran church failed to make the Danish language generally accepted. Neither did the church attempt to build a national language based on indigenous dialects. Following the rebirth of the Norwegian state in 1814, Norwegian nationalists began striving for a new national language based on old-fashioned dialects—those most remote from Danish and closest to Icelandic. The "speech strife" in Norway was a part of nineteenth-century romantic-nationalistic movements. It made the country bilingual in a puzzling way because "city Norwegian" and "country Norwegian" are neither sufficiently close for unity nor sufficiently dissimilar for true bilingualism. Repeated reforms of both, intended to bring them closer together, has increased the confusion as to what the national language is. Yet none of this has weakened the sense of nationality in modern Norway. The ability to endure the "speech strife" without lasting scars testifies to the strength of Norwegian identity—a feeling based on the striking geographic, historical, and cultural unity of the country.

In Finland, the educational approach of the church led to a critical situation for an entirely different reason. Swedish settlement never penetrated very far from the coastline. The bulk of the interior, along the numerous meandering lakes, was gradually and quietly settled by a peasant people speaking a Finno-Ugrian tongue—a conservative language with but moderate dialect cleavage. This quality of the Finnish language made it relatively easy for the Lutheran church to use it for Bible translation, hymnals, catechism, and sermons. The contrast with Russia is striking: no institution in the tsarist empire did anything similar to reach the non-Russian nationalities on their own ground. Thus it was because of the particular approach of the Lutheran church, to try and reach every soul individually, that Sweden became the foster parent of a new nation growing up on its eastern outskirts. Relations between the two language communities never took on the "colonial" aspect of eastern German settlement areas with Slavic populations. Civil equality was buttressed by the frequent army service of Finnish peasants, and the educated classes generally knew both languages.

When the Russian Empire, after centuries of devastating border warfare, used the turmoil of the Napoleonic era to take all of Finland away from Sweden, the conquest was, paradoxically, made easier because there had grown up within Finland enough of a separate identity to make separation from Sweden acceptable. In keeping with this, Finland obtained a special status within the Russian Empire, as a separate principality with the tsar as its monarch.

With peace on both boundaries through most of the nineteenth century, the Finnish nation was able to find enough identity and purpose to face the twentieth on its own. The country dealt with a two-sided conflict, identifying both with the East European heritage of language and peasant culture and with the Scandinavian heritage of individualism, personal freedom, and political constitutionality. All this made the elites of Finland—both the Swedish and the Finnish-speaking—search for identity so intensively that this identity now commands some grudging respect even from the leaders of the Soviet Union. In practical politics, the spiritual and political traditions inherited from Sweden have on the whole prevailed over nationalistic desires to emphasize distance.

With independence after World War I, Finnish chauvinism at times rose to considerable heights, among other things in the struggle over the language of instruction in the universities. As World War II renewed the threat from the Soviet Union, Finland found more domestic peace between the language groups.

The divisions of language groups came to the surface once more, however, in regard to the province of Åland, a complex archipelago in the Bothnian Gulf half-way between the Finnish and Swedish mainlands. Åland is purely Swedish in language, always has been, and belongs to Finland by historical accident only. After World War I, the people of Åland opted for Sweden, but the League of Nations gave it to Finland on the promise that its linguistic integrity would not be violated. When after World War II the people of Åland refused to accept Finnish refugees (from the eastern district ceded to the Soviet Union) as settlers in their province, the language conflict in Finland was revived to some extent.

PENETRATION

Organized civilian power was created and diffused early in most parts of Scandinavia, generally before documented history. Medieval society had a coherent system of law courts and rather comprehensive tax systems. The church, with its parish organization and its tithes, also contributed to strengthening society's secular powers. Main roads were built and maintained by a system of chores distributed among the local population.

Civilian infrastructure has been among the least crisis-laden long-term processes in Scandinavian development. The early appearance of "the king's men" in the middle ages stirred some negative reactions among local notables, and the further buildup of the civil service in the sixteenth century was also resented by the old nobility as a "secretaries' regime." Parallel with the civilian organization were the systems for raising manpower for the armed forces. At times this would shade over into the tax system, only to be followed by new techniques of conscription. In its various ways, the military organization strengthened civilian power because it increased the duties of common citizens. On the whole, there was little question that the affairs of the central authorities would be attended to, except where organized settlement had not yet penetrated.

Early medieval Scandinavia had vast wilderness areas. It is characteristic that land divided, water united. In early Scandinavia, people were drawn together by the numerous waterways. Inland wilderness was a hostile element, the home of outlaws and wolves. Penetration of southern and central Scandinavia was gradual and was largely accomplished before the end of the middle ages. Consolidation of inland settlement helped that of the separate national kingdoms.

Penetration of the high north is a more recent story, and one filled with more documented conflicts. Before organized Swedish settlement took hold along the shores of the Bothnian Gulf, free and lawless men had established exploitative trade relations with the pagan Laplanders of the vast northern inland. As Swedish farm colonization began to spread northward (fourteenth century), a political arrangement with the coastal traders was necessary lest these descend upon the settlers in bloody hostility. Not until two centuries later, with coastal settlement much better established, could royal power move to enforce the law upon the coastal traders and give some modicum of protection to the Laplanders.

The advances of the Crown were combined with those of the church. Ecclesiastical organization was spread thinly in the vast northlands, and its consolidation was promoted by political objectives of the Crown. Christianizing the Laplanders in the sixteenth and seventeenth centuries was prompted by the geopolitical purpose of staking clear claims to their territories, as well as to their loyalties. Then as now, nomadic Laplanders would roam across the lands between the Bothnian Gulf and the Arctic Sea. Newly consolidated royal power in both Denmark-Norway and Sweden-Finland, in the mid-sixteenth century and later, sought expansion in this remote wilderness, sometimes in competition also with Russian monarchs.

None of this turned Lapland into stable settled country. The Laplanders came to church at certain seasons only, between their extended hunting and fishing expeditions. Isolated mining ventures in the highlands had scant success until the vast iron ore deposits at Gällivare and Kiruna began to be worked in the nineteenth century. These mines have given rise to three middle-sized cities in the middle of nowhere—an impressive accomplishment if one compares, for instance, the mining areas in Canada's northern territories. Swedish and Finnish farm settlement was slow to expand in the northlands. Not until the pulp and timber industries began tapping the slow-growing virgin forests did northern Scandinavia become firmly penetrated by the economic and administrative systems of Finland, Norway, and Sweden. As farm settlement is now again receding, forest monoculture gives new emphasis to the problems of road maintenance and other overhead costs. Some of the northern railways never were self-supporting, and the "fleetways" for river transport of timber are becoming obsolete. Penetration of the northlands is, in fact, still dependent on geopolitical motives.

LEGITIMACY

Through most of the area's history, legitimacy in Scandinavia has had a twofold base—in secular arrangements and in the church. The monarchies of Denmark, Norway, and Sweden were organized at about the time when historical sources begin to provide the data for a somewhat coherent narrative for this part of the world. Details are often obscure and are best known for Norway, where the establishment of a central monarchy was followed by a sizable emigration to Iceland of those who refused to bow to the Norse king.

Settler life on Iceland was turbulent and in some ways resembled American frontier life in the nineteenth century. Eventually the settlers organized themselves as an aristocratic republic with a primitive parliament. This hints at what may have been the kind of polity in Scandinavia before the central kingdoms: a primitive "democracy" led by chieftains who were large owners of land and slaves, rather than princelings. Isolated glimpses in Swedish sources point in the same direction.

It is no mere coincidence that the creation of the territorial states came close in time to the introduction and victory of Christianity. The disappearance—on the surface, at least—of the pagan priesthood removed some of the functions of local notables, and the coming of the church supplied the territorial states with an additional source of support, more or less distinct from existing local powers. The transition is seen most distinctly on Iceland, where Christianity, after some individual proselytizing, was made the sole religion in the year 1000 through parliamentary decision—after a long and stormy debate, but still by constitutional deliberation rather than brute force. Elsewhere, conversion was not always peaceful. On the eastern outskirts of Finland, the fight was exacerbated by the clash with the eastern church, promoted by Russian monarchs.

We have few details on the transition from pagan local communities to Christian kingdom. The church for its part did much to destroy inscriptions and other artifacts bearing testimony to pagan culture. The identities of Denmark, Norway, and Sweden were in any event very real by the late middle ages. Despite episodes of fragmentation and dispersal of political authority (especially in the fourteenth century), royal power was sufficiently well established to serve as rallying points for renewed drives of consolidation.

The medieval kingdoms were constitutional, the powers of kings limited. Succession was by election rather than inheritance, even though most of the kings came from royal families. Dethronement was a constitutional option. Law antedated royal power in many areas, and there were limits as to how far these relatively weak kings could go in bending the will of local notables. These limitations on royal power were emphasized by the medieval church which, by its doctrine about *rex iustus* versus *rex iniquus*, tried to make itself the ultimate arbiter of legitimacy.

The early part of the sixteenth century saw a general strengthening of royal power. Both kingdoms became hereditary. Norway lost its constitutional identity and became a part of the Danish monarchy. These changes flowed from the general rise in princely power in Europe, which influenced political thought in Scandinavia as well. Important for Scandinavia was a concomitant decline of medieval powers with less distinct territorial identity: the Hanse cities and the Teutonic order.

The late medieval personal union between all three Scandinavian countries, though frequently broken, had served to protect them against encroaching German interests. Loose and rife with conflict, this union also delayed the coming of strong centralized power. This was especially striking in Sweden, where "the Union" cast doubt on the legitimacy of a separate king—several of the secessionist rulers merely called themselves "caretaker of the realm." Royal power could become strong in both kingdoms when they were definitely separate, and hence rivals for geopolitical dominance in the Baltic area.

The tradition that the law of the land stood above the king never died out. It could even be skilfully exploited to strengthen royal power, as it was by Gustav Vasa in Sweden (1523-1560). As a servant of the law, he argued, he was duty-bound to uphold it. Thus he must uphold all prerogatives of the Crown, including long-forgotten ones wherever they could be retrieved from oblivion. Among other things, this became a device for strengthening the tax system.

This tradition of primacy of law allowed civil freedom to survive in nearly unbroken practice. Even at the low point of peasant degradation in seventeenth-century Denmark, peasants—even bondsmen, on the islands—could still take their landlords to court and win.[1] The strengthening of royal power also meant strengthening the court system as a counterpoise to the license of landlords. As both kingdoms made the transition to absolute monarchies in the late seventeenth century, the kings remained guardians of the law and of the common man's rights.

In Sweden, the late medieval four-chamber Parliament continued to function even under the absolute monarchy, if for a time with only token powers. The time of this Parliament came again with the "Freedom Period" (1720-1772). Military defeat and losses of territory caused the downfall of absolutism in Sweden, but strengthened it in Denmark; there was less of an alternative. The eighteenth-century period of semimodern parliamentarianism in Sweden was turbulent and full of party strife, corruption, and cross-purpose dealings with foreign powers. The period began because a restive nobility had found the absolute king too concerned with the rights of peasants. The new system could function, after a fashion, as long as the nobility could keep the second and third estates (the clergy and the burgesses) aligned against the peasants, who were the fourth estate in Parliament. But when the three lower estates began joining hands in a struggle against privileges of the nobility, the first estate lost its interest in the rights of Parliament and supported a coup d'état that restored royal power from a rubber stamp (literally, "name block") to a position of leadership. The alliance of king and nobility did not last. Eventually, the monarch's conflict with the nobility led to a second coup, making the monarchy absolute again (1789). This led to the king's assassination (1792). Absolutism reached its peak under a reactionary camarilla that governed for the infant successor—an inept youth who was de-

[1] Hans H. Fussing, *Herremand og Faestebonde* (Copenhagen, 1942), see the summary, p. 456: Denmark was a society under the law.

throned after the loss of Finland. All of this led to the "revolution" of 1809, really a restoration that reinstituted and consolidated traditional institutions in a predominantly conservative spirit. The constitution of 1809 lasted, with amendments, until a few years ago. The intervening century and a half had few crises despite a great deal of change.

Both the shaky parliamentarianism of the Freedom Period and the doubtful legitimacy of revitalized royal power made Sweden more sensitive than Denmark to problems of legitimacy and social stability. Again, the position of the church is significant.

In both monarchies, Lutheranism was introduced in the early sixteenth century as a facet of the strengthening of monarchy. The advantages to the Crown were both political (bishops were no longer independent of the king) and financial (church property was added to the Crown domain). In return, the regular clergy gained complete monopoly of religious service. Gone were the unsettling forces of the late middle ages—the rabble-rousing friars and the disgruntled rural vicars whose opposition to the wealthy cathedral clergy had once prepared the ground for the Reformation itself. With doctrine properly cleansed of papal aberrations by Luther and the Book of Concord, religious truth was final, and there should be no need or room for variant interpretations. The strength of pure doctrine was such, so the tenet ran, that any properly instructed minister, not being a heretic, would serve equally well as the medium of the divine message. To enforce this salutary regimen, every subject (in both kingdoms) was duty bound, and required by law, regularly to attend the church of his parish and no other church. In the spirit of Luther's youth, each soul was invited to seek salvation on his own; but in the spirit of Luther's later years he was free to do so along the officially designated path only. With austere discipline, the ministers forced the common people to live under God's dictatorship—a paradox that would lend authority to an absolute king, or to a nearly absolutistic parliamentary oligarchy, whoever happened at the time to be the *Obrigkeit* instituted by divine grace. The claim to being sole custodian of the true religion gave the church a stake in legitimacy. The legitimacy of its own monopoly on faith and religious order became part of the legitimacy of the political order.

Lutheran discipline had its problems in the sixteenth century, especially in Sweden, where the matter was complicated by dynastic policy leading, for a time, to personal union with Catholic Poland. But in the seventeenth century, Lutheran discipline reigned unopposed among unending wars and bitter penury for the common people.

With this vested interest in the established order, the church was not very well equipped to change with the times. The coming of renewed dissent, with the Pietists and the Moravians, was met in paradoxically different fashion in Denmark and Sweden. Autocratic Denmark was stable enough to feel little threat from internal dissent; after some initial wavering, the new movements were quietly absorbed and became elements of the established order. But eighteenth-century Sweden, experimenting with political freedom (which might be risky enough), found freedom of faith and order too much to tolerate at the same time. The established church, feeling (rightly or wrongly) threatened in its privileged position at the center of the national establishment, rammed through the Conventicle Placard of 1726 to enforce its monopoly on organized spiritual guidance and discipline. Rejection drove a wing of the Pietists into even more radical dissent; but the lesson appeared hard to learn. Conflict with the Moravians, in the 1740s and after, might be doctrinally even less essential; but by insisting on the differences, the official church made its dire prophecies almost self-fulfilling: in the words of a church-inspired attorney-general, disunity of faith could have disastrous consequences for the whole state.[2] Placing so much faith in the purity of faith drove some radicalized dissenters into denouncing the official church as a "Babel."

A particularly acrimonious feud, and one highly symptomatic of the legitimacy problems involved, flared around the *Songs of Zion*, a hymnal used by the moderate Moravians in Sweden. The heat of the feud came from the mingling of theology and power politics. In their doctrine the Moravians were close enough to the official church so that they might have been quietly absorbed, as actually happened many years later. The power conflict had to do with church organization. In the 1740s, with party strife and constitutional problems among the ruling classes, the need to discipline the common people (most of whom were not represented in parliament) appeared all the more imperative. The sin of the Moravian preachers (some of them ministers of the official church) was to lure people away from their own parish churches, as if there could be more than one gospel. The

[2] Karin Dovring, *Striden Kring Sions Sånger och närstående sångsamlingar* (Lund, 1951), I, 52. Cf. *idem*, "Quantitative Semantics in 18th Century Sweden," *Public Opinion Quarterly*, 18:4 (Winter 1954-1955), 390.

acrimony was only exacerbated when it proved extremely difficult to identify any difference between the Moravian doctrine and the official one; the difference of spirit and resulting public behavior was obvious if elusive. Crude content analysis was used to detect differences of emphasis, and the dispute became a forerunner of modern quantitative semantics research in America. At the height of the debate, one minister of the official church saw fit to characterize a Moravian hymnal as "written by the Devil and printed in Hell"—and some of them were actually printed in Copenhagen, to avoid Swedish censorship.[3] "Truth squads" were sent into some churches to record any dissenting tenets used in the sermons, and rather subtle shades of meaning were denounced as a "contagion," the extermination of which was regarded as an important affair of state. Over such matters, honorable men had to recant or go into exile.

This struggle over ecclesiastical power was one of the first challenges to the legitimacy of the established church as a foundation of secular power in society. Its outcome was both a victory and a defeat for individual freedom. The dissenter movement of the eighteenth century began the attrition that was eventually to erode the strength of state religion. But in their own time the dissenters did not break that strength—the conflict rather served to demonstrate the church's essential function in the power structure of the day. As a residual, the now wilted state church leaves behind some basic attitudes of deference toward established authority in general. To this day many Swedish officials, such as university professors, school principals, and civil servants, tend to talk to the public as if *ex cathedra*. This feature is striking in the news announcers on the state-monopoly radio and television, who have inherited from the state church not only the role of bringing news of general interest to the community, but also some of the unction that carried over from announcing divine truth. The same attitude of inspired officialdom at times even affects spokesmen for the political party that was in power for several decades.

There is somewhat less of this in Denmark and Norway. The stability of an absolute monarchy left the church more peace to tolerate some dissent, to absorb it, and to be somewhat more responsive to the needs and sentiments of the population at large.

If Danish officialdom at times appears to have strong authority, too, this reflects the quiet manner in which the absolute monarchy was

[3] Karin Dovring, "Troubles with Mass Communication and Semantic Differentials in 1744 and Today," *American Behavioral Scientist*, 11:1 (January 1965), 11.

recast. Agrarian reform was initiated by the Crown, beginning in the 1780s. This start toward economic democracy was followed by political reforms originating from above; democracy came by royal decree. Having survived the storms of the Napoleonic era, the absolute monarchy eventually stepped down by itself. A temporary lapse into near dictatorship (under Prime Minister Estrup, 1875-1894) was merely a parenthesis in a continuum of constitutional development.

In Norway a brief legitimacy crisis arose in 1814. Denmark had ceded Norway to Sweden by one of the treaties concluding the Napoleonic era. Sweden claimed possession by right of conquest, but Norwegian public opinion did not see eye to eye with the "conquerors," who had not gained physical control of the country. A national convention proclaimed a new constitution establishing Norway as an independent monarchy. The crisis ended in compromise: the Norwegians accepted the king of Sweden as their monarch, and he accepted the Norwegian constitution. The union of the two kingdoms was thus relatively superficial, and this made possible its dissolution in 1905 without a revolution.

The Russian conquest of Finland in 1809 meant the birth of a new state but not a legitimacy crisis. Finland continued to live under its Swedish laws and constitutional arrangements. Even the four-chamber parliament continued to exist, at least on paper, right up to the Russian revolution. Technically, the change in 1809 was one of sovereign, as the tsar replaced the Swedish king. There was also a reconsolidation of the country: eastern regions that had been ceded to Russia in previous treaties were added to the new state. The downfall of the tsarist monarchy automatically meant independence for Finland, and Soviet attempts at conquest had to be construed as the spread of their revolution. The constitution of the Finnish republic, explicitly based on the "sovereignty of the people," and with democracy mentioned in the text itself, therefore meant no break in legitimacy.

PARTICIPATION

Before the coming of modern parliamentarianism, political participation was mainly limited to the propertied classes, usually a minority in the community. Early Scandinavian society was aristocratic and based on extensive use of slave labor. The vestiges of slavery faded out only in the fourteenth century. There were few political decisions to make, and participation in them was mainly at the local level. Outside village affairs, the most important function open to common laymen was to serve as members of the local courts of justice. This Scandinavian institution in some ways resembles the English jury system, but there are differences, as well. In the Danish monarchy, this function of the public died out gradually, to be revived in modern Denmark and Norway in the form of English-style jury systems. In Sweden and Finland the medieval system survived in unbroken practice, in which a group of community-elected laymen still forms a single judicial body with the judge.

Another community function was related to the election of a king. The election itself was by a small electoral group, but customarily the election was confirmed at local ceremonies in various localities. These were especially elaborate in Sweden; apparently the country had once been brought together from two main parts, the northerly of which had the prerogatives both of choosing the king and of dethroning him, while the southern regions had to pay homage at the new king's "all-realm progress." Descriptions of this function indicate a fairly wide community participation. In medieval Norway this ceremony was the only occasion on which peasant commoners are known to have participated in the political affairs of the entire kingdom. In Denmark participation was even more restricted; politics of the realm was mainly an affair of the leading noble families organized as "the council of the realm." This institution existed in Sweden too, but it did not become quite as prominent as in Denmark.

It is by no means clear when the custom grew up of gathering representatives of the public to "talks of the realm." In Sweden country-wide "Parliaments" including four estates (nobles, priests, burgesses, and peasants) began to be called together in the late middle ages, at least by the 1430s. This institution may have been solidified by the legitimacy problem of the period: Swedish "caretakers of the realm" needed a legal basis independent of the treaty-supported claim of the Danish monarch to be the head of the tri-state union. The use of voluntary peasant armies on the Swedish side of the "union wars" also tended to give the lower estates more influence.

Gustav Vasa (1523-1560), the Swedish king who made the breakup of the union final and then built a strong monarchy, also made good use of "the estates" as a source of legitimacy. In Denmark, there was no similar reason to seek the support of a broad constituency. In Norway, beginnings similar to those in Sweden atrophied for lack of political purpose, since the union with Denmark became permanent.

The central function of the Swedish four-chamber parliament remained the granting of extra taxes. In a country where freehold farmers were still a numerous class, their consent was of more than token significance. But even in its better days, the old Swedish parliament was far from being democratic in the modern sense. The first estate consisted of the heads of all noble families registered since 1626 in the "House of Chivalry," a rather stuffy institution that in the 1700s began to protect privilege by restricting new entrants—a sure way to the obsolescence that followed in the 1800s. The Estate of the Ministers included all bishops *ex officio*, plus representatives of the common clergy elected by their colleagues. The burgesses, property-owning merchants, and artisans established in recognized cities elected representatives to the third estate. The constituency of the fourth estate was limited to taxpaying farmers—freeholders and crown tenants—but excluded tenants of the nobility as well as the rural poor. Under the old four-chamber parliament, only a small percentage of the male population could vote for representatives; and the weight of the vote was different according to estate, wealth, and place of residence.

When the Swedish parliament was recast (1866) into a somewhat more modern two-chamber form, a condition the old parliament required before voting itself out of existence was that voting rights remained restricted. Thus constituencies were not really expanded. The newer parliaments in Norway (1814) and Denmark (1848) were also elected by limited suffrage. Finland's Swedish-style four-chamber parliament remained, essentially dormant, through the Russian period (1809-1917).

How the right to vote was gradually extended is a long story, the details of which can not be rendered here. Rising levels of income contributed something to extending the suffrage, and thus brought into the political game more of those who were committed to striking down the wealth and income barriers to the political franchise. There was at times considerable tension, but hardly any crises, over these matters. Norway, in the early nineteenth century mainly a society of peasants and fishermen with no indigenous nobility, led the way toward parliamentarianism and extended democracy in Scandinavia, with Denmark and Sweden somewhat more halting in their progress up to World War I. Breakthroughs toward general voting rights for men were made in Norway 1898-1901, in Sweden 1907-1909, and in Denmark 1915. Thus all three countries approached democratic suffrage before the upheavals of World War I had really been felt.

In the wake of the war there followed in rapid sequence supplementary reforms, among them the franchise for women. In Finland, a rash of democratization in 1905 (the Russian crisis) was abortive. Only after independence (1917) did Finland get one of the world's most explicitly democratic constitutions (1919).

DISTRIBUTION

If ever there was an egalitarian tribal society in Scandinavia, we lack any traces of it. The oldest clues that we have show Scandinavian society as highly structured and dominated by a wealthy upper class, owners of vast landholdings and numerous slaves. There were exceptions, mainly in areas settled late, but many of these eventually also came to have an aristocracy promoted by military organization and taxation. Only in the vast northlands was there poverty too stark to support any upper classes from farm rents or taxes. Except for the timber barons of the nineteenth century, northland communities remained remarkably free from class distinctions.

During the late middle ages there were some long-term trends to modify society's stratification by property and privilege. The distribution of property appears to have become gradually more unequal. The upper strata of landowners (the "big peasants" or chieftains of the earlier middle ages) continued to accumulate still more wealth. Eventually this landed artistocracy evolved into a formal nobility marked by some of the ceremonial trappings of European knighthood. Closing of ranks against new entrants came only centuries later. Some of the lesser families among the wealthy landowners of the earlier period declined into the ranks of toiling peasants—the penalty for not limiting the number of heirs to modest wealth.

These polarizing tendencies were in part offset by the rise of many serfs to become tenant farmers, eventually fusing with lesser landowners into a single peasant class. Rising taxes gradually became a burden comparable to that of farm rents paid by tenant farmers to landowners of the privileged classes (nobility and church). From this stage, class stratification evolved differently in Denmark and in the rest of Scandinavia.

In Denmark drawn-out wars of the late middle ages, and the consequent heavy burden of taxation, caused large numbers of peasants to seek the protection of local noblemen by giving up their freehold farms and receiving them back as copyhold—a procedure in some ways resembling the feudalization on the Continent centuries earlier. The bulk of all Danish peasants became tenants, those on the islands even subject to a mild form of bondage. From the fourteenth century until 1660, Denmark was in many ways a "noblemen's republic." In the dominant rural sector the distribution of wealth was as unequal as on the Continent; unequal, that is, between nobility and the peasants, but not among the peasants. This bimodal structure was broken up by the rural reforms begun in the 1780s, prompted by the Crown and by enlightened nobles who realized that increasing productivity required upgrading the downtrodden peasants.

In the other Scandinavian countries the peasantry never was as downgraded as in Denmark. Freehold peasants remained numerous. The ranks of freeholders were gradually increased by the settlement of forest areas, particularly in the northlands and the interior of Finland. Much of this expansion took place in areas where a landed gentry had never been seen, and in some cases never came. In Norway and Sweden, the physical frontier for settlement closed only about the middle of the nineteenth century, when emigration to America gained momentum and brought some relief from threatening rural congestion. In Finland the physical frontier remained open even longer.

The presence of settlement areas may have acted as a safety valve protecting tenant farmers from becoming bonded. In Sweden and Finland the approximate equality among the peasantry was strengthened in the fifteenth century by edicts prohibiting a taxpaying peasant from amassing more land than he needed for a "full-seated" farm.

The Reformation transferred most of the church's property to the Crown, thus increasing the resemblance between freehold peasants and Crown tenants. Reducing the clergy to a less privileged class than before removed one of the distribution problems of the late middle ages. Rising wealth of cathedrals and major monasteries, and the concomitant pauperization of country vicars had, as on the Continent and in England, spurred some "populist" discontent, which was part of the background to the Reformation.

In Norway the nobility had never been as important as in Denmark and Sweden. There was also, in the late middle ages, less of the kind of military situation that elsewhere served to justify the privilege of a landed gentry. Secularization of church property was followed by numerous sales of Crown lands to cultivating peasants. Many Norwegian noblemen moved to Denmark and eventually sold their tenant farms. Thus Norway became, from the seventeenth century, essentially a country of freehold peasants, in sharp contrast to Denmark. This difference followed in part from the economic weakness of Norway. The late medieval period was one of decline, possibly for climatic reasons (the "little Ice Age"). Among other things, this weakened the contact with Iceland (also on the decline) and with the Norse settlements on Greenland (which succumbed in the fifteenth century). Thus Norway emerged in the nineteenth century with a more democratic spirit than either Denmark or Sweden. Poverty had bred equality. Analogies may be found in the Balkans, especially Old Serbia.

The Swedish picture is more composite. In the best agricultural areas large parts of the peasantry were tenants, but in peripheral regions freeholds were predominant. Dominance of the aristocracy was furthered in the late sixteenth and early seventeenth centuries by the Crown's habit of donating the standing taxes from farms and entire districts to noblemen in exchange for their services in war or as pledges for loans. After the close of the Thirty Years' War, the question of the status of the peasantry reached crisis proportions. The Fourth Estate openly complained in parliament of the danger that they might become serfs. The Crown sided with the peasants to halt that tendency. The "Great Reduction," Sweden's only large-scale attempt at any kind of land reform, returned many farms from noble estates to the tax rolls. Events surrounding this great change led to the country's first period of absolute monarchy. It is sometimes theorized that the backward-looking economic philosophy inspiring the Crown to this reform may have contributed to the military defeats that a few decades later brought down the absolute monarchy. The free peasantry was saved, but the landed aristocracy was by no means eliminated. Today farms in Sweden still remain noticeably more unequal in size than in the other Scandinavian countries.

Finland, with its essentially Swedish institutions and social structure, democratized land holdings in two rounds of land reform in the early and mid-twentieth century—both inspired by the political crises of attaining independence after World War I and of nearly losing it in World War II.

Beneath and beside the landholding peasantry, there were other social classes. Rural paupers are mentioned in Icelandic sagas and in some early Swedish sources. Medieval laws prescribed support for the poor in various ways. Among the rich literary heritage from medieval Iceland is also an elaborate statute on care of the poor—not a very generous system (the realities of the time forbade that) but still an elaborate one. As a society of penury, the medieval polity in Scandinavia understood the basic truth that law and order would be in constant jeopardy, and justifiably so, if the propertyless were left without any help and forced to rob for self-preservation. A tradition of caring for the poor never quite died out. At times, harsh measures were taken to deal with the problem.

The standard device to support the poor and to control them at the same time was the "servants' code." Persons without property, tenure, or an established trade in one of the closed-shop craft guilds, were required to accept service to those wealthy enough to offer such employment. The hire contract was usually for a year. At the end of that term there was a free week—often a donnybrook of feasting and fighting—during which all could look for new jobs. Servants who had not at the end of the week landed a new position were legally obliged to accept the same terms from the same boss as the year before. Unemployment was thus absorbed at subsistence wages, accompanied by some features of a retainer system. In fully settled areas this system of control could function smoothly. In a sense, the economy of penury trapped the well-to-do as much as it trapped the poor.

The frontier areas to the north were somewhat more loosely organized amid bitter need and want. Where the worst that could happen would be to be childless on a wilderness homestead, peasant mores took a direction designed to maximize the birth rate. In some areas, parents would consent to a wedding only after the bride-to-be was safely pregnant. By being prolific, these people contributed more than their share to the rising urban proletariat—and to their mores.

There are no good statistics on income distribution until rather recently. Beyond any doubt, the early phases of industrialization led to a deepening of class contrast, even as the wealthier peasants rose to quite a decent level of living and often became employers of the rural poor. Attempts were made near the turn of the twentieth century to lessen rural poverty, and to halt the exodus of rural people to the cities and to America, by "internal colonization." Some of these attempts even tried to copy the American Homestead Act. In Denmark, later also in Finland, the internal colonization measures had some consequence—they were in fact partial land reforms. In Sweden the "homestead movement" turned into a mere palliative (creating poverty homes rather than farms) because there was no will to sacrifice the privilege of landed property. The class interest of the gentry here met that of the more prosperous peasants.

A real "crisis of poverty," similar to that in many low-income countries today, might have come in rural areas, if the impending congestion had not been relieved by the joint effect of industrialization and emigration—Norway and Sweden had, after Ireland, the highest rates of emigration in Europe. In its rural form, mass poverty remained essentially voiceless because the rural poor were too dispersed, and too closely tied to the gentry and the "big peasants," to form an organized social class.

It is not peculiar to Scandinavia that the poverty problem got its voice and the first attempts at its solution in and from the cities. Nor is it peculiar to Scandinavia that the urban industries, by increasing prosperity, were to supply the material means for ending mass poverty. Sparsely settled Scandinavia has, in fact, more of that phenomenon so often invoked and so seldom attained elsewhere—industrialization in rural areas.

Peculiar to Scandinavia, however, was the role of democratic socialism in redistributing income in a society essentially at peace. Especially in Sweden, where so much of the old aristocratic status system remained unreconstructed at the turn of the twentieth century, it is plausible to suggest that socialist agitation might well have led to a bloody revolution had not the socialist leaders been the level-headed pragmatists they were. Successful industrialization and the accelerated exodus from agriculture that eventually followed were the principal prerequisites for the mass affluence that is now commonplace in Scandinavia. But the orderly growth of the trade unions and of workers' influence through the Social Democratic parties were essential to the smooth transitions that have characterized Scandinavian society.

Economic growth under private capitalism has served these countries so well that even the socialists have long been hesitant about traditional demands for the "socialization of the means of production." What there is, since World War II, is "cold socialism": the state uses its multiple forms of leverage to enforce the common interest in the "macro" management of the economy, leaving the details of business management to private enterprise. With highly progressive income taxes, incomes have been redistributed more than wealth, and the traditional influence of established families is by no means eliminated. The coexistence of capitalist business with socialist labor and political organizations looks, as was said not long ago, like "an answer without a question." At the same time, it poses an unanswered question: who will lead the economy if the distribution of wealth is to be made much more equal?

Sequence

Political development in the Scandinavian countries has been largely parallel, as could be expected from the geographical closeness and the cultural similarities of the countries. Identity came early, except in Finland, where national consciousness largely evolved during the eighteenth and nineteenth centuries. Apart from provinces Sweden conquered from Denmark and Norway in the seventeenth century, the Scandinavian-speaking countries were rather clearly identifiable—to themselves and others—at the close of the middle ages. Penetration was accomplished somewhat later. With vast subarctic wilderness areas, penetration in Finland, Norway, and Sweden long remained incomplete and to some extent still is, as organized settlement recedes from areas becoming submarginal for agriculture.

Legitimacy crises typically occurred in what may be termed the semimodern period, from the early sixteenth to the early nineteenth centuries. Medieval society in Scandinavia would never for long have tolerated any power not grounded on its acceptance by essential elements of the community; nor has Scandinavian society done so in the modern period. The middle ages saw many minor crises over the legitimacy of this king or that caretaker of the realm, but never about the principle that kingship comes from community and is founded on native law. With the Reformation this tradition broke down, when new Continental concepts of political authority rushed into Scandinavia. The alliance of strong monarchy and state church in turn planted the seeds of a legitimacy crises over royal absolutism and the power of the "orthodox" church. For obvious reasons, Continental influence was strongest in Denmark, surrounded (as were the Continental powers) by strong contenders on all sides. Modern Denmark, reoriented toward free institutions, also drew more of its ideas from the liberal political philosophy of eighteenth and nineteenth-century Europe and less from native traditions handed down from the middle ages. Sweden, with its back toward the Arctic, was somewhat less pressed by the need for unity of action; thus some of the free institutions of the middle ages could more easily survive the pressures of absolutism and reemerge in modern time, with more continuity from times beyond memory.

Participation is, in fact, part of the same problem as legitimacy. To a limited extent, wide political participation followed from the medieval principles of community acceptance as the basis for authority. Yet participation long remained limited within the aristocratic social framework that the economy of penury appeared to render necessary —or so it appeared, at least, with some noteworthy exceptions. As a critical factor in Scandinavian development, participation on the whole comes distinctly after the legitimacy problems have been solved, but before much could be done about distribution. The early part of the Danish rural reforms is the main instance of a reverse sequence. It is characteristic that incipient rises in income would prompt extended suffrage before general affluence was sufficient to permit large-scale redistribution of incomes without political upheavals. The distribution problem, on the whole, had to await the prosperity of the modern period.

Conclusion

Scandinavia is a cluster of nations that might have become one country. Its political pluralism reflects several forces and sets of events. Nature made the region polycentric, with a potential for unity across water. Penetration across the inlands laid the foundation for separate political entities, with two decisive focal points: Copenhagen, the key to the Baltic Sea, and Stockholm, the key to medieval Europe's richest sources of iron and copper. Norway, less focused geographically, was unified by the ocean and by common overseas ventures, all of which was weakened by the economic decline from the fourteenth century (probably because of climatic change).

What nature both united and kept apart by the ambivalent medium of blue water might have become a single political entity had external pressures been strong enough. Located at the edge of the world, Scandinavia was subject to pressure mainly from the south and east, only incidentally from the west, and hardly at all from the north. The eastern pressure, of Russian states against Finland and the other eastern Baltic areas, was of vital importance to Sweden, but much less so to Denmark. The common interest that led to the formation of a tri-state union in the late fourteenth century was the pressure from the south: from German merchant cities and some German principalities. The faltering of the Hanse power at the time of the Reformation, and continued political fragmentation in northern Germany, removed or at least weakened this motive for the Scandinavian countries to remain in union. Had this pressure continued longer, the shaky union might have had time to jell into a single state, with its capital at Copenhagen.

The definitive breakup of the union in the 1520s made the two monarchies rivals for the *dominium maris Baltici*. The decline of Hanse power and the dissolution of Teutonic Order holdings on the eastern shores of the Baltic, and the continuing political fragmentation in northern Germany, gave scope for a struggle between Denmark and Sweden that rendered the contrast of nationalities deep and often bitterly resented. The cleavage turned out to be irremediable, for a very simple reason: with neither side strong enough to conquer the other in a single decisive operation, third parties would not stand by for a narrow victory. The point was made clearly in 1660, when Sweden might have won but for the intervention of the Dutch, who did not want the Baltic Sea dominated by a single strong power. The tables were turned a few decades later, when Denmark joined forces with Russia to help eliminate Sweden's hold on the eastern Baltic coast south of Finland. Scandinavian rivalry reduced both contenders to small-power proportions, stripped them of most of their non-Scandinavian possessions to the south and southeast, and facilitated the eventual emergence of Finland and Norway, and finally (during World War II) of Iceland as separate, sovereign states.

This kind of history leaves its marks on national images, and neighbors are easier to hate because they are easier to know. Long-standing hostility was fanned longer than necessary by the history textbooks. Chauvinistic historians continued to fight battles long lost, and thus artificially to maintain more animosity than would follow naturally from contrasts in accent, mores, and temperament.

The schoolbook vilifications were deliberately eradicated only as late as the 1930s. This may be surprising, for in the nineteenth century there was a good deal of romantic Scandinavianism in the universities, and among poets and their readers. "Student Scandinavianism" waxed strong and vocal during the years when Denmark's old unsettled affairs in the German border areas were called to account. Common Scandinavian sentiment ran high even in Norway, for a time mitigating the bitterness over the forced union with Sweden. But when Sweden-Norway did not intervene in Denmark's behalf and, in 1864, the uneven struggle for Slesvig was lost, this older Scandinavianism cooled, and its residual became commonplace and less articulate. Subsequently, Swedish royalty and high finance were drawn toward Wilhelmine Germany, while Denmark and Norway were more anglophile—a contrast that gave the chauvinistic textbooks a new lease on life.

It may be a paradox that Scandinavianism was reborn, with a different thrust, following the dissolution of the union between Norway and Sweden in 1905. Practical cooperation between three—later four—nations has since built more bridges than any military victories could have done, and created more integration than is sometimes found within vast territorial states. The backbone of this cooperation is in the gradual and purposeful homogenization of civil law in the four countries, systematically facilitating trade and free movement of people and goods. Without explicit federation, the Scandinavian countries are now enjoying many of the fruits of a federal state—especially the right for nationals of any one of the countries to seek employment in any of the others. People, goods, and ideas move freely across state boundaries, not without occasional irritation of narrow nationalism, but without major disturbance.

Together with this goes the positive benefit of some cultural diversity. Outsiders may overlook this, but differences in temperament and in art and literature among the peoples of the five countries are profound, yet not too large for mutual comprehension and appreciation. The position of the Scandinavian languages is characteristic: Danes, Norwegians, and Swedes are able, with some modest effort, fully to comprehend the languages of the other two countries; and it is accepted practice in conversation that each person speaks his own language, understanding the other without attempting to imitate it. Finns who know Swedish also participate in this multilingual conversation, and so do the many Icelanders who master one or another of the Scandinavian idioms other than their own. Academic and technical books often appear with some chapters in Danish, some in Norwegian, and some in Swedish, and newspapers are fully comprehensible across national boundaries. This unity in diversity lends a particular dimension of depth to Scandinavian life and culture.

This outcome of abortive empire building carries an important message to the world, especially to "nation building" countries that have not yet found their identity. In modern Scandinavia, no one deplores that the several countries did not become one. The unification of large national states has often meant the death of local languages, such as Provençal and Plattdeutsch, as well as degradation and atrophy of local culture; and it still threatens Catalan, Ukrainian, and many others. Is "national unity" worth such sacrifices? In the modern world no national state can become a world empire. We have to live with a polyglot international community; whatever its unity, it will have to be one in diversity. The Scandinavian lesson is this: the crises of identity and integration do not necessarily have to be "solved" in terms of a single legitimacy or at the price of oppression. There are worse things than political fragmentation, as witnessed by the many past tragedies when nation building turned into empire building. Scandinavia's freedom and unity in diversity blooms on the ruins of an empire that—fortunately—failed to materialize.

Some Related Readings

Anderson, S. V. *The Nordic Council: A Study of Scandinavian Regionalism* (Copenhagen, 1967).

Andersson, I. *A History of Sweden* (New York, 1968).

Arbman, H. *The Vikings* (London, 1961).

Castberg, F. *The Norwegian Way of Life* (London, 1954).

Christensen, Chr. A. R. *Norway: A Democratic Kingdom, 1905-1955* (Oslo, 1955).

Danstrup, J. *A History of Denmark* (Copenhagen, 1949).

Derry, T. K. *A Short History of Norway* (London, 1957).

Heldal, Halldor, ed. *Nordic Co-operation in the Social and Labour Field* (Oslo, 1965).

Johnson, S. ed. *Iceland's Thousand Years* (Winnipeg, 1946).

Jutikkala, E.K.I. *A History of Finland* (London, 1962).

Lauring, P. *A History of the Kingdom of Denmark* (Copenhagen, 1968).

Nordic Cooperation (Stockholm, 1956) Conference organized by the Nordic Council for International Organizations in Europe.

Roberts, M. *The Early Vasas: A History of Sweden, 1523-1611* (Cambridge, 1968).

Scandinavia Past and Present. 3 vols: I (From the Viking Age to Absolute Monarchy); II (Through Revolutions to Liberty); III (Five Modern Democracies) (Copenhagen, 1959).

Shirer, W. L. *The Challenge of Scandinavia: Norway, Sweden, Denmark and Finland in Our Time* (Boston and Toronto, 1955).

Sletten, V. *Five Northern Countries Pull Together* (Copenhagen, 1967).

Starcke, V. *Denmark in World History* (Philadelphia, 1962).

Wuorinen, J. H. *A History of Finland* (New York, 1965).

CHAPTER 5

The United States

J. ROGERS HOLLINGSWORTH

The most important fact to keep in mind when studying political change in America is that the United States is a product of a settler society. In many respects, its history resembles that of such other settler societies as New Zealand, Australia, South Africa, and Canada more than that of various European countries. Like the history of other settler societies, nineteenth-century American political history was very much concerned with developing a frontier, confronting a native population, lessening the ties with a colonial power, and transplanting social institutions from the "mother country."

In contrast to the Europeans, the Americans in their early history confronted no feudal society, no entrenched religious system, no rigid social structure. Where these circumstances occurred in Europe, centralization of political authority was necessary in order to break down traditional society and to develop a modern society. In America, however, a modern society could develop without a centralized political system. Indeed, it is the decentralized character of the American political system that has been its most distinctive and important feature.

To comprehend American political development, it is useful to note that American culture was a product of what Louis Hartz has called a "fragment society," that is it was only a fragment or a portion of English seventeenth-century society. And in America, it was this English fragment that developed into a whole society, and that gave rise to the dominant political culture, the political institutions, the language, the pattern of work and settlement, and many of the mental habits to which subsequent immigrants had to adjust.[1] As Samuel P. Huntington has suggested, American political culture and structure can only be understood in the light of traditions that had previously

Crises of Political Development in Europe and the United States
0-691-07598-0/78/000163-32$01.60/1 (cloth)
0-691-02183-X/78/000163-32$01.60/1 (paperback)
For copying information, see copyright page

[1] Louis Hartz, ed., *The Founding of New Societies* (New York, 1964), and "A Comparative Study of Fragment Cultures" in J. Rogers Hollingsworth, ed., *Nation and State Building in America: Comparative Historical Perspectives* (Boston, 1971), 10-26.

operated in Tudor England.[2] Analyses of the sequence of the five problem areas in American history must consider that they developed within a settler society dominated mostly by one settler group (the English), and in an environment in which no centralized power was necessary to dislodge the privileges of a feudal order.

Crises

PENETRATION

In Europe, there were many paths by which early state building occurred. And one can focus on the variations in European state-building activity to such an extent that he ends up with a configurative analysis of the penetration process. In an effort to be parsimonious, however, one might search for those few variables that most efficiently explain the variation in European national development. In this respect, there do appear to be three key variables that influenced the way in which early state penetration occurred in a number of European states. These were reflected in controversies involving: (1) the role of the church in each society; (2) the extent of landholding concentration and the subsequent relations between landowners on the one hand and, on the other, the bourgeoisie and the peasantry; and (3) the ethnic and/or linguistic conflicts that developed as various groups attempted to dominate the state-building process.[3]

In contrast with most European societies, perhaps the most distinguishing characteristic of American society was either the lack of conflict or the low intensity of conflict when cleavages did occur on these variables. Settled after the Reformation, American society never squarely faced the anticlerical crusades that several European societies encountered. In America, a country where it was possible to acquire vast landed estates, feudalism, for all practical purposes, never took root; and thus modernization in America did not require a conflict between a centralizing elite and feudal landowners—as was the case in several European societies. Even though American society became

[2] Samuel P. Huntington, "Political Modernization: America vs. Europe," *World Politics*, 18 (1966), 378-414.

[3] For a development of these ideas, see Stein Rokkan, "Dimensions of State Formation and Nation-Building: A Possible Paradigm for Research on Variations within Europe," in Charles Tilly, ed., *The Formation of National States in Western Europe* (Princeton, 1975), pp. 562-600; and *Citizens, Elections, Parties* (New York, 1970), pp. 72-144.

a mixture of ethnic groups, the Americans did not encounter the hostility of external powers attempting to incorporate their own nationals, a force that exacerbated the process of state building and the efforts to establish democratic government in several European states. Because there were no medieval estates, entrenched aristocracy, or powerful religious establishment in America, much less governmental penetration was needed in the process of American modernization than in most European societies.

When the new nation was established in 1789, there was a very weak bureaucracy. And because of the decentralized federal system, political parties were essentially locally oriented. Indeed, throughout the nineteenth century, most of the federal bureaucracy was dominated by a locally oriented party system, thus reducing the ability of the central government to penetrate the society. And it was the low level of governmental penetration into American society that encouraged the South to think that it could secede from the Union, a situation that led to the Civil War—the most serious crisis in American history. With the use of great force, involving the loss of over 600,000 lives, however, the central government enhanced its penetration into the South, thus preventing successful secession.

Once nationwide interest groups developed as part of the industrializing process, a vast governmental bureaucracy emerged, a bureaucracy that has become increasingly centralized and independent of the locally based party system. Even so, the governmental bureaucracy has penetrated much less into American society than have the bureaucracies of those European societies that have high levels of industrialization. Because of a tradition of weak and fragmented central government with low governmental penetration into the society, powerful interest groups have been able to penetrate the central bureaucracy and have become increasingly important in shaping public policy. It is the success with which interest groups have penetrated the federal government and the vast power that they exert in shaping public policy that led Andrew Hacker to remark that the "United States has as powerless a government as any developed nation in the modern world." Still, the penetration of the federal government into society has increased substantially during the twentieth century. This has occurred in response to the emergence of a national economy, and in response to the society's concern with the "cold war" in external affairs and with race relations and poverty in domestic politics.

IDENTITY

During the last two hundred years, the Americans have had a less developed sense of national identity than the British, the people of the Scandinavian countries, or those of other European states with populations that are relatively homogeneous ethnically. Throughout most of American history, there have been stronger ties to locality than to the national state, a condition resulting from the fact that the American political system is a federation of decentralized states. Because of the decentralized political system, various nationality groups have more easily identified with the political system and become integrated into it than would have been the case had a highly centralized system prevailed. In other words, the structure of government has facilitated the integration of various ethnic groups into American society, thus blunting the tendency of immigrants and their children to maintain a strong identity with foreign nation states. No doubt immigrants of many different nationalities could be assimilated into American society more easily than if it had been dominated by two, three, or four ethnic groups.

Because America has been a society with very fluid status lines and diverse ethnic groups, however, its citizens have had difficulty in developing a common sense of identity. Not knowing just what it means to be an American, Americans historically have been quick to engage in witch hunts designed to ferret out those who are not truly American. And the House of Representatives, along with numerous state legislatures, have had committees on un-American activities to help in discovering those who do not identify with accepted modes of conduct. Thus, the quest for an American identity has been exacerbated by the society's cultural and ethnic diversity.

Even so, certain events in American history have given meaning to a sense of American nationalism, facilitating the problem of developing a common identity from vast cultural diversity. Perhaps no set of events was more important in molding a sense of American nationalism than those surrounding the War for Independence. As a result of the war and the ideology embodied in the Declaration of Independence, a kind of utopian view of men's egalitarian relations helped Americans to understand who they were and what their role in the world should be. Because the American political system was created from the conditions surrounding the War for Independence, many of the nation's heroes, national holidays, and monuments have been derived from that period. That was an era in which elites espoused a rhetoric dedicated to the concepts of liberty and equality; and as subsequent generations have developed a sense of identity with the "Founding Fathers," the revolutionary rhetoric has remained alive. "Since all Americans are ideologically speaking, descendants of revolutionaries, Americans of the left and right remain utopian."[4]

Nevertheless, there have been identity crises in American history, the most serious one resulting in the American Civil War. As industrialization developed outside the South, the South's social processes diverged from the rest of the country. And as two different societies emerged, a distinctive regional identity developed in the South, thus leading to the first national identity crisis. With lines of cleavage sectionally based, secession was attempted and civil war erupted. Outside the South, the war stimulated a strong sense of identity with the national government. Men ceased to think of themselves primarily as New Yorkers or Ohioans, Easterners or Westerners, and increasingly viewed themselves as Americans, identifying with the nation as a whole.

In the South, however, the Civil War had the opposite effect, and it intensified a sense of regional identity. The violence of the war and the policies of Reconstruction, combined with the myths arising from both, encouraged white Southerners to see themselves as set apart from the rest of the country. Viewing themselves in a land of defeat, poverty, and pessimism, Southern whites found it very difficult to identify with the institutions centering in Washington that symbolized abundance, optimism, and progress. As C. Vann Woodward has observed, "the South had undergone an experience that it could share with no other part of America . . . the experience of military defeat, occupation, and reconstruction."[5] During the past twenty-five years, however, the South has become tightly integrated into the national economy; and as this has occurred, the South has lost its sense of having a separate identity and has increasingly shared a common identity with the rest of the nation.

Negroes, Indians, and Orientals have also encountered serious identity problems in the United States. While early American settlers

[4] Seymour Martin Lipset, *The First New Nation* (New York, 1963), p. 89.

[5] C. Vann Woodward, *The Burden of Southern History* (Baton Rouge, 1960), p. 170.

shared the enlightenment values that subsequently became the basis of the dominant value system for American society, white Americans did not apply this value system to nonwhites. Accordingly, a vertical type of stratification system existed in American society whereby nonwhites were rigidly ranked below white society. Because the nonwhites were considered to be outside the sphere in which enlightenment values applied, this system of stratification has historically been sustained by considerable force and brutality. Over time, it has resulted in a separate sense of identity among Oriental groups, Indians, and Negroes.

Historically, modern technology and high levels of economic development tend to promote education and new opportunities among subordinate groups, a kind of social change that usually brings the dominant and subordinate groups closer together and ultimately leads to the disintegration of rigid systems of stratification. High levels of technology generate and then diffuse universalistic, egalitarian, and achievement-oriented values among all groups in society. This in turn stimulates among subordinate groups a new leadership, usually from among the young who are skilled in manipulating the social system and who are dedicated to destroying the old stratification system. Because the old stratification system does not wither away quickly, however, strong emotions and loyalties are aroused among the subordinate group, leading to intense identity crises. And this is what occurred within the black and Indian communities of the United States during the 1960s. Black and Indian militants could identify neither with those within their community who had been forced to accept an inferior status in the society, nor with those who shared the dominant status positions in society. While an ethnic system based on rigid vertical lines may be reordered without a revolution, the disintegration of a rigid stratification system generates considerable societal tension, as the American case attests. That such a reordering of a stratification system has been taking place within American society without a widespread and violent revolutionary movement is due in large part to the enlightenment morality that demands that all citizens be treated equally before the law. In American history, that morality has slowly been extended to apply to all groups in society. Yet status distinctions based on language or religion generally disappear much more rapidly than those based on color—suggesting that the identity crisis involving minority groups will continue for some time.

PARTICIPATION

Problems posed by participation have been less critical for the American political system than for most European polities. In contrast to most European experience, high levels of participation occurred in America before industrialization was substantially underway. This meant that industrial workers never had to fight for the suffrage, and this does much to explain the conservative political culture in America and the low level of class consciousness among American workers compared to their counterparts in Europe.

Even in colonial America, when property holding was required for voting, very few white males were restrained from participating in the political process. With a fluid social structure and property widely distributed, conditions in America were unlike those in Europe. Even so, most voters in colonial America were willing to defer authority to social and economic elites. Despite the fact that few white males over twenty-one were denied the right to vote, an economic elite was able to assume political supremacy in colonial America, not because of a coercive authority system but because of the widespread acceptance of political norms, which held that those with the largest stake in society should be deferred to. However, the events leading to the War for Independence injected a new rhetoric as well as new practices into the political arena, with the result that democratic tendencies became more pronounced. And as organized political parties came into existence by the end of the eighteenth century, more and more voters were mobilized politically. As this occurred, the age of deferential politics declined and new patterns of political recruitment occurred, symbolized in the presidency of Andrew Jackson, who personified the values of a "mass public." While a participation crisis had not been necessary in order to promote widespread suffrage in America, high levels of political participation would subsequently increase the problems of maintaining political stability.

As Samuel P. Huntington has argued, political stability cannot be maintained if the expansion of political participation is not accompanied by the development of strong, complex, and autonomous political institutions (such as political parties).[6] Because increased levels of modernization (more urbanization, higher per capita income, higher rates of literacy) usually intensify and increase the levels of participa-

[6] Samuel P. Huntington, *Political Order in Changing Societies* (New Haven, 1968).

tion, one of the major problems in a modernizing society is to contain and organize mass participation in politics. In the United States, not only did political parties contain and organize mass participation throughout much of the nineteenth century, but increased industrialization also produced a pluralistic network of voluntary organizations and public bodies that assisted in mobilizing and channeling participation, aggregating interests, and serving as a link between social forces and the government. Despite the fact that electioneering has never seemed to cease in America—because of the necessity to fill local, county, state, and federal offices—a relatively high level of political participation was moderately well organized and contained throughout the nineteenth century, with the one exception that led to the Civil War.

In recent years, levels of participation have been quite high, but political and social institutions have not been very successful in organizing, channeling, and containing political participation. Group loyalties to communities, labor unions, churches, and other voluntary associations have become paper thin. Partly because nation-wide organizations have become so oligarchic in behavior, many of their members have lost all sense of meaningful identity with and participation in the society's institutions. This has led to a widespread sense of restlessness and alienation in American society, and has exacerbated the problem of identity. Widespread participation outside political parties and voluntary organizations easily leads to demonstrations and riots; and as this became an important characteristic of American politics during the 1960s, the United States was on the verge of a participation crisis. American history would suggest that a high level of institutionalization of complex organizations is necessary to promote political stability in the face of high participation. Recent American history suggests that when political and social institutions are better at holding the line than responding to political demands, despite widespread participation, instability may occur. During the 1960s, the United States may well have encountered an overinstitutionalization of complex organizations. Overinstitutionalization and the inadequate institutionalization of political participation are opposite sides of the same coin. In either case, political instability may occur.

DISTRIBUTION

High levels of urbanization, industrialization, literacy, and education generally extend political consciousness and broaden political participation. And this enhances the capacities for group organization, which in turn increases the intensity of demands on all levels of government for a greater redistribution of the society's resources.

The distributive role of the state has historically been much more restricted in the United States than in most European countries, however, despite the fact that political participation reached high levels earlier than in any other country. For example, in an effort to win the support of industrial workers, the German Reich was very generous in its welfare policies in the late nineteenth century. In the United States, however, the federal government provided very few welfare services prior to the "Great Depression." Aid to indigents was generally considered to be a local responsibility; and that aid, insofar as it was offered by local governments, was very meager. Contemporary America, in both the quality and quantity of its welfare programs, diverges from the practices of most countries in Western Europe. While one could demonstrate this in many distributive policy areas, the problem of old age pensions is quite illustrative: the United States appears to be the only highly industrial Western country in which, although a majority of the aged receive state pensions, a substantial minority do not.

During the past thirty years, however, there have emerged many new ideas and concepts about welfare, and as these views have been increasingly diffused on a world-wide scale, there has been an enormous expansion in distributive programs in the American political system. Historically, however, distributive programs have occurred in America more as a result of private than public activity, and even today are carried out more by voluntary than by state efforts, though the role of the state is increasing.

The American state has been less involved than other governments in distributive activities, for several reasons. First, the Americans have historically wanted the state to play a limited role in the society. And while historically there has been more state action than many of our history books would have us believe, especially in nineteenth-century developmental activity and in the field of education, Americans, compared with Europeans, have been inclined to use the state as "a sort of emergency apparatus, to be wheeled out only in the most extreme circumstances, and put back in its place, if at all possible, as soon as the emergency is over."[7]

Given the limited role that Americans have expected their govern-

[7] Anthony King, "Ideologies as Predictors of Public Policy Patterns: A Comparative Analysis" (paper presented at the American Political Science Association Annual Meeting, September 6-10, 1971, Chicago, Illinois), p. 30.

ment to play within the distributive area, discussions of distributive and redistributive activities have historically been very emotionally charged. Despite intermittent group demands for redistribution of societal resources, the structure and function of American governmental institutions have caused the level of redistributive activities in America to lag behind that in other countries. In other words, the American political system has certain institutional characteristics that maximize the opportunities for vetoing proposals for changes in governmental policies: the federal system, the separation of powers, the strong role of committees in Congress, and the Congressional seniority system. With so many different points of access to government, powerful interest groups have long had an opportunity for opposing and defeating redistributive measures.

LEGITIMACY

As the following section illustrates, the American government, like all new governments, faced the very serious problem of establishing legitimacy during its early years of existence. At the same time that they are weak in legitimacy, most new governments must establish new rules by which to govern, promote effective communication between political elites and the public, and establish new patterns of political participation and recruitment.

Unlike many new states of the nineteenth and twentieth centuries, the United States had the advantage of coterminous cultural, legal, and linguistic boundaries. Moreover, the timing of the establishment of the new national government did not undermine its legitimacy. With no highly industrial societies elsewhere to emulate, Americans did not place unreasonable demands on their government to establish a "modern society." As a result, the loads on the national government were relatively light, and because of the federal structure of government, many groups presented their political demands to their local and state governments. Partly for these reasons, the new government was able to survive challenges to its legitimacy during the first decades of its existence.

Throughout American history, problems of participation, penetration, identity, and distribution have raised questions about the legitimacy of the American political system. After 1815, however, the conditions leading to the American Civil War constituted the only serious legitimacy crisis in the history of the United States—that is, a challenge to the basic constitutional dimensions of the system and to the claims of leadership by those in authority.

Sequence

To comprehend the political development of the American political system, it is necessary to keep in mind that it evolved from thirteen separate systems and that it emerged from a colonial crisis of participation, penetration, and legitimacy. The key to understanding the colonial crisis is to be found in the type of imperial system that the British operated in America. Because the British during most of the colonial period were more interested in commercial growth than in imperial efficiency, they permitted the Americans to develop a high degree of self-government. Each colony had an impressive group of political leaders well trained in the art of leadership. In addition, the colonists developed extensive intercolonial trading, communications networks, an interlocking elite structure, and strong interurban ties. With a high level of political participation and a strong tradition of independence in the colonies, it was too late by the middle of the eighteenth century for the British to establish the type of penetration into colonial society that they were attempting. Each effort of the British to tighten control intensified the colonial tendency to realize that their society was different from English society, and reinforced a sense of colonial separation. And as Americans took on a new identity, a legitimacy crisis within the empire occurred, manifest in the Americans' increasing obsession with British corruption, their conspiratorial outlook toward British authority, and their millenial vision of a new society. By the 1770s, the colonists had reached a point of such common identity and passionate alienation from British authority that they were prepared to fight a war against the British and to establish new political institutions in order to gain their independence.

While the colonial experience had generated a desire for union, the colonists had nevertheless developed, as a result of their experience with the British, a strong distaste for centralized authority, and this, of course, was reflected in the new government that was established in 1789. Indeed, the new federal government reflected the American experience under the British Empire and during the government of the Confederation. The new government was to be strong enough to maintain peace against external and internal disturbances, and to tax and regulate interstate commerce, but otherwise most functions of government were to remain with the various states. During the early years of its history, however, the United States was confronted with several crises and with the need to solve simultaneously the crises of legitimacy and participation.

The most serious problem was that of establishing the legitimacy of the new government, a problem that reached crisis proportions during the Whiskey Rebellion of 1794, when the Alien and Sedition Acts were passed in 1798, and during the War of 1812, when much of New England threatened to secede from the Union. Even so, the political elites were able to cope with these problems, for they had certain advantages that some new states, especially those of the twentieth century, have lacked. First, the new government did not represent a major departure from tradition. There was no old order to overthrow. The new constitution represented a continuation of a constitutional tradition built on colonial experience. Moreover, there was a general consensus over the fundamentals of government: there should be representative government, elections at fixed intervals, separation of powers, checks and balances among various branches of government, and a written constitution. And unlike the newly emerging European states of the nineteenth century, there was no division over whether there should be a monarchy and hereditary privileges. In addition, most Americans were prepared to accept the idea of separation of church and state.

No doubt a general consensus over the ends of government resulted from the fluid social structure that minimized class conflict. In contrast to the more rigid class structure of Europe, American society offered the prospect of a politics of moderation and limited conflict. Unlike some new states where the political leaders have not been able to agree over the number of states in the federal structure, this problem was temporarily solved at the beginning of the American Republic, and was not a matter for serious dispute. Most of the boundaries of the American states had a certain legitimacy to them, and no leader seriously considered more or fewer than thirteen states.

One of the most important factors assisting the Americans in confronting their legitimacy crisis was their first president, George Washington. Without the intellectual genius of Hamilton and Jefferson, Washington appeared to be a very ordinary man. But most importantly, he was not a divisive leader. Skilled in the management of men, he was able to temper some of the clashes of philosophy and personality between Jefferson and Hamilton. Washington was a man of considerable prestige, devoted to promoting the new nation, and not possessed with the desire for personal power that moves many heads of new states. Indeed, he reluctantly served two terms as president, thus adding stability to the government, and then relinquished power, thereby establishing a precedent for the peaceful transfer from one administration to another.

Legitimacy was also enhanced by the fact that the nation's political elite were men who had worked closely together in the past in the War for Independence and the drafting of a constitution. Legitimacy could not have beeen established as readily had the Americans not been able to solve other problems that simultaneously emerged in the political system. As Sidney Verba has pointed out, the various problem areas are mutually reinforcing. What is done in one area affects performance in another. And in the early years of the Republic, one problem fed upon another. Eventually, a solution to one crisis helped to provide a solution for other problem areas.

Broadly speaking, participation was the other problem area in which the early Republic confronted a crisis. The authors of the Constitution believed that government should be structured so that no political unit would be powerful enough to shape public policy. To ensure against any group gaining sufficient power to control public policy, they devised a fragmented governmental structure that would permit various interests to be checked and balanced against each other. Governmental responsibility was to be divided between the central and state governments, and within the central government power was divided among the executive, the judiciary, and a two-house legislature. Not only did the architects of the Constitution believe in a government of sharply limited powers, but they also thought it was necessary to build into the system of government a set of checks and balances, automatic stabilizing devices that could counter interest group against interest group. And it would appear that the Founding Fathers did their work extremely well. It soon became apparent, however, that it was difficult to organize and to channel participation, and virtually impossible to develop coherent and unified policies in a governmental system that fostered and facilitated such fragmentation. Politics in such a poorly integrated system was a pluralistic, kaleidoscopic flux of personal cliques like those that came and went in New England, and half-invisible juntas, such as those in the capitals of southern states. In sum, there was a politics of constantly changing factional alliances; and, among factions, there was little continuity from election to election, with only a tenuous relationship between leaders in government and the electorate.[8]

Though suffrage was open to adult white males almost everywhere prior to 1789, the political role of the people was limited not only by property qualifications but also by the weight of habit and custom. Moreover, the linkages between political elites and the electorate were so poorly defined that the electorate did not believe that they could hold any group responsible for the direction of public policy. In response to the perils of fragmented government and a somewhat immobilized electorate, leaders such as Hamilton, Jefferson, and Madison worked to organize political parties in order to manage the machinery of government. Indeed, the new government survived largely because parties emerged to perform many of the essential functions of government: recruitment of political elites, mediation of disputes among competing groups, provision of vital connections among the various branches of government, linkage of political elites with the electorate, structuring the vote, and articulation and aggregation interests. In sum, political parties played an important role in solving a participation crisis in a political system that was basically fragmented. By organizing and channeling participation through mediating structures, parties reduced the amount of conflict that would otherwise have occurred.

Organized competition between parties stimulated the expansion of popular participation. In local politics, where parties were highly competitive and well organized, the electoral turnout increased significantly. Indeed, during the period 1804-1816, those voting in local politics varied from sixty-eight to ninety-eight percent of those eligible.[9] In some of the new nations of the twentieth century, such high levels of politicization have led to excessive demands on the political system and thus a certain instability. And while there were elements of instability in the early American republic, the institutionalization of complex and adaptable political parties tended to contain and discipline the electorate and to channel majority preferences through appropriate agencies of government. Thus parties contributed to con-

[8] William N. Chambers, *Political Parties in a New Nation: The American Experience, 1766-1799* (New York, 1963).

[9] See David H. Fischer, *The Revolution of American Conservatism: The Federalist Party in the Era of Jeffersonian Democracy* (New York, 1966).

tainment of the problems of legitimacy, participation, and integration.

While America may never have had a real revolution, the new government was born during an era colored by revolutionary rhetoric that espoused egalitarian principles. And because the War for Independence was successful, that rhetoric gained considerable legitimacy, which helps to explain why the political culture became participant-oriented. Not only did Americans believe that it was their right and duty to participate in government, but they very early believed that the government should be highly responsive to their demands. The persistence of this revolutionary rhetoric in the political culture of the United States helps to explain how certain of the problem areas have been handled. At the same time, it is from this "revolutionary" heritage that the basic paradox of American history emerges, for beneath the rhetoric of the Founding Fathers lies a counterrevolutionary tendency in American society. It is within the constant tension between the revolutionary rhetoric and the conservative political structure of the fragmented American political system that one must perceive much of American political history.

All new governments, in order to enhance their legitimacy, must be effective in dealing with the salient problems of the day. And partly because of the relatively high level of mass participation, there were significant challenges to the new government. For example, the problems of distribution teetered on the verge of crisis throughout the period from 1789 to 1840. At the national level, the following questions were hotly contested: should the national government assume the debts of the states, how should the federal debt be funded, how should revenue be raised, should there be a national bank? Eventually these questions were resolved, but the distribution problems were confronted more at the state level than at the national. Not only were the states older than the national government, but the people were more involved in and identified with their local and state governments. And for this reason, the public generally presented their demands to the state governments. Indeed, the state and local governments played a far more important role in the economic development of the United States than is generally assumed. State funds were extensively used to develop transportation, banking, and manufacturing. States awarded special franchises to private firms, making it possible for companies to operate with very little competition. The distinguished economic historian, G. S. Callender, estimated that during the first four decades of the new republic, the states increased a funded debt of more than $200 million.[10] Everywhere, local and state governments undertook the role of planner, promoter, investor, and regulator of the economy. In contrast to the new nation-states of the twentieth century, the demands that the central government develop the society economically were relatively light until well into the twentieth century.

The American nation also differed from more recent new nations in that it was born in a world of poor communications. Americans not only felt isolated but actually were separated from much of the world. Nor were they caught up in a syndrome of rising expectations and a belief that life was better elsewhere. To the contrary, most Americans believed that theirs was the world's best system of government; and when they wanted major societal changes, they were unaccustomed to looking to the political system for action. Expectations for private initiative and activity were high, while most Americans expected the role of government in society to be modest. Partly for these reasons, the American political system was not overloaded with demands that were impossible to fulfill.

By 1840, the legitimacy and participation crises facing the American political system appeared to have been solved. And the identity problems had simply not reached crisis proportions. True, there were numerous nationality groups in America in 1790, but the overwhelming majority of Americans had a British heritage. The people spoke a common language, and most Americans had a common religious and political tradition. In sum, it appeared to some observers that the United States had a relatively homogeneous population—despite the fact that scattered over the land there were many local ethnic conflicts.

Between 1840 and 1860, however, an identity crisis developed in America. Exacerbated by participation problems, it eventually became so serious that it led to a legitimacy crisis, so intense in nature that civil war resulted when the political elites were unable to cope with the crisis. From the beginning of the new government, men had identified more closely with their local and state governments than with the national government. As long as there were no serious internal value cleavages, identity problems were manageable. But in the half-century prior to 1860, two different nations, based on regional considerations,

[10] G. S. Callender, "The Early Transportation and Banking Enterprises of the States in Relation to the Growth of Corporations," *Quarterly Journal of Economics*, 17 (1902), 111-62.

slowly emerged in American society, with slavery at the root of the problem.

Slavery was not only an integral part of the Southern social and economic life, but it increasingly symbolized the diverging ways of life in the North and South. The South more and more was clinging to the past, while the North was struggling to enter the modern world. Each section became convinced that its society represented the direction toward which the "civilized world" would eventually move. Each was convinced that its was the virtuous life, the last best hope for mankind. In the past, men had been able to compromise over such concrete issues as tariffs, internal improvements, foreign policy, and so on. But during the 1850s, the realities of the world were distorted, replaced by abstractions. And once political elites permitted all issues to become symbols of good and evil, it was no longer possible for men to compromise their differences.

The problems of sectionalism were complicated by the high level of political participation that existed in America. Not only was turnout high in local elections, but by 1840, almost eighty percent of those eligible to vote in national elections did so.[11] With the federal system of government, campaigns at some level of government were constantly being held. Political agitation never ceased. There were more than thirty states, with as many different party systems. There was no central machinery capable of disciplining and controlling electoral activity, with the result that campaigning never ended. As Roy F. Nichols has written, politicians "egged one another on to make more and more exaggerated statements to a people pervasively romantic and protestant, isolated and confused. . . . The emotional complex which was created by the variety of these attitudes, and the tension which their antagonism bred, added confusion to that already provided by the chaotic electoral customs and poorly organized parties.[12] Political participation had simply exceeded the level of institutionalization of political parties. And this situation, combined with the emergence of two separate nations, was beyond the capability of political elites to manage. As people identified with their region more than with the nation as a whole, the identity crisis led to a legitimacy crisis.

The resulting civil war did more than any other single event to

[11] Richard P. McCormick, "New Perspectives on Jacksonian Politics," *American Historical Review*, 65 (1960), 288-301.

[12] Roy F. Nichols, *The Disruption of American Democracy* (New York, 1948), pp. 503-504.

solve the identity crisis, however. The war effort and Lincoln's assassination stimulated people outside the South to identify with the national government, though in the South people still tended to identify more with their local governments than with the one in Washington—a trend which was to continue well into the twentieth century. Because the power of the South was broken, however, the failure of its citizens to identify with the national government posed no serious problems to the national government following the Civil War and during the period of Reconstruction.

Following the Civil War–Reconstruction era, there were no governmental crises until well into the twentieth century, though incremental changes in the institutionalization of politics constantly took place. Once again, political parties played the most important role in carrying out the functions of government. And the intricate relationships among parties, governmental bureaucracy, and interest groups do much to explain why a period of stability followed the Civil War–Reconstruction era.

Undoubtedly, parties would not have been so important in coping with the five problem areas in nineteenth-century America had the governmental bureaucracy not been so weak when the new government was established in 1789. When the new government began, there was no national bureaucracy—no army, no navy, or postal service, treasury department, central bank, and so on. Because there was no entrenched and independent bureaucracy, political parties were from the beginning much stronger vis-à-vis the governmental bureaucracy than has been the case with most new nations of the nineteenth and twentieth centuries. Indeed, the bureaucracy in national, state, and local politics was virtually dominated by political parties. This of course helps to explain why, historically, Americans have been participant-oriented toward their political system and somewhat suspicious and resentful of government officials.

With a political system oriented more toward license and freedom than toward order, parties tended to use the various governmental bureaucracies as opportunities for patronage and graft, without which it is difficult to imagine that American political parties would have been sufficiently galvanized to integrate the complicated machinery of government. True, a bureaucracy so dependent on political parties was generally inefficient and uneconomical. But such a system of government was responsive to public demands, perhaps more so than a government with an entrenched bureaucracy guided by formal and highly rationalized rules for dealing with public policy.

A bureaucracy dominated by partisan considerations did much to enhance the legitimacy of the political system. This point is demonstrated by the relationship that existed between political parties and bureaucracies during most of the nineteenth century. Had millions of immigrants arrived in America and found it necessary to deal with strange and alien but highly efficient bureaucrats, no doubt it would have been much more difficult for the newcomers to identify with their new government. As it was, the decentralized nature of the American federal system permitted local party officials to appoint the governmental bureaucrats from among the local population. Partisan identification and party loyalty as well as ethnic affiliation were usually the decisive factors determining who received an appointment to public office. Thus, the loyal Democrat who happened to be Irish was likely to receive a public office in an area dominated by Irish, whereas a German, Czech, or Italian would be unrewarded. Most immigants tended to locate not only where others of the same ethnic identity resided, but also where governmental operations were manned by people of their own nationality. As a result, most immigrants quickly viewed the government as their own. In sum, the decentralized nature of the American political system facilitated the newcomer's becoming participant-oriented toward governmental affairs.

Immigrants were thus socialized and recruited into the process of government much earlier than a highly efficient and rule-oriented political system would have permitted. Moreover, the party system within the context of American federalism meant that one party, when it won an election, did not leave the minority party powerless. One party could capture the Congress and/or the presidency, and another could win control of state, county, or local governments.

Parties not only helped immigrants to resolve identity problems but continued throughout the nineteenth century to play an important role in problems of legitimacy and distribution. The integration of minority groups into the political system enhanced its legitimacy, and the political machine was especially important in this respect. The immigrants, who were the bulk of the urban machine's clientele, came largely from the European peasantry. As peasants, they required extensive acculturation simply to come to terms with an urban-industrial environment. In return for their votes, the immigrants received recognition for their personal problems and wants. As federal, state, and local governments provided few public welfare agencies, the political machines filled the void by making available to their followers a host of vital services. Charges of municipal corruption and graft were winked at, even applauded by the machine clientele, who viewed the social banditry of the machines as something like the work of an urban Robin Hood.[13] Indeed, machine inducements were especially appreciated by those newly arrived and disoriented, who received the quick helping hand of the political party. In their heyday, the power of machines reached prodigious levels. For example, the Martin machine in Philadelphia during the late nineteenth century provided 15,000 people with public jobs, and "each of these 15,000 persons was selected for office because he could deliver votes, either by organizations, by parties, or by families."[14]

As it was necessary for the machine to offer numerous social services to its followers, money was of course indispensable. And the most lucrative source of money was graft, usually in the form of "kickbacks" in contracts for public construction. Moreover, numerous business enterprises considered it good practice to make periodic contributions to the machine. While those who cooperated with the machines received rewards, those who crossed its path could expect punishment. The most common penalties included loss of jobs, police harassment, rigorous enforcement of construction codes, high tax assessments, and revocation of business licenses. Relying on ascriptive and particularistic criteria for making decisions, whether at the city, state, or county level, the machine was a most inefficient—though effective—means of confronting the political system's distribution problems.

The late nineteenth century was a period of widespread economic dislocation, serious economic depressions, and mass unemployment. Without the emergence of the political machine to promote the integration of the previously fragmented local and state political systems, it is indeed difficult to imagine how the centrifugal and complex forces of social change could have been contained. Machines reached their highest levels of development where ties to the community were weak and the potential for violence was considerable—in other words, in areas where the political system was poorly integrated. Machine bosses were in essence brokers for com-

[13] James C. Scott, "Corruption, Machine Politics, and Political Change," *American Political Science Review*, 63 (1969), 1142-58.

[14] Lincoln Steffens, *The Shame of the Cities* (New York, 1957), p. 146.

peting values, and served to protect ideological and ethnic pluralism within the confines of a single governmental system. Moreover, machines were able to narrow the cleavages in the society by fostering interclass collaboration. Though the machines frequently "milked" the the treasuries of local governments, they nevertheless lent a high degree of order and stability to public affairs.

By the end of the nineteenth century, political parties had transformed the operation of the American government in ways never contemplated by the authors of the Constitution. In many respects, parties had greatly simplified one of the world's most complex systems of government. Parties had done much to integrate a government that was extremely fragmented, had helped to institutionalize mass participation, had assumed major responsibility for assisting immigrants and other highly mobile people to identify with the political system, and had established links between elites and masses that permitted the central government to penetrate the society with enough effectiveness to govern. In sum, parties had assumed the major responsibility for keeping the various problem areas at a low level of salience.

But in the latter nineteenth and early twentieth centuries, basic changes were taking place in American society, changes that eventually altered the nature of the political system. These were: 1) the emergence of nationwide and powerful interest groups as a result of increasing industrialization; 2) a nationwide reaction against political machines, which resulted in the weakening of party organization; and 3) an expansion of the political bureaucracy, which became increasingly independent of political parties but intricately tied to powerful interest groups. These changes were to have a significant effect on the nature of political participation, the integration of the political system, the penetration of the political system by pressure groups—and, ultimately, its legitimacy.

In most economically underdeveloped countries, there are not numerous organized interest groups capable of influencing legislation. And people outside them usually attempt to influence government at the enforcement stage, where officials have considerable discretionary power. So it was in the United States where political machines existed. Groups were usually too weak to shape the writing of legislation, but they could influence its implementation. In many respects, the machine was similar to a business. At the enforcement stage, particularistic rewards were purchased in exchange for monetary or electoral support.

As late as 1870, most industrial firms in America serviced an agrarian economy. These firms tended to be small, and they bought their raw materials and sold their finished goods locally. When they manufactured for a market more than a few miles away from the factory, they bought and sold through commissioned agents who handled the business of several firms. By the beginning of the twentieth century, however, major industries were dominated by a few firms, as the day of powerfully organized, nationwide interest groups arrived.

Influence exerted in an effort to shape legislation has historically been referred to as pressure group politics and in the American context has been viewed as quite legitimate. Influence exerted at the enforcement state has historically been viewed as corruption. In America both processes have clearly been at work. When groups have been powerful, they have resorted to pressure-group tactics; and when they have been weak, they have attempted to influence legislation at the enforcement stage.[15]

As economic and industrial development proceeded in America, new types of loyalties and perspectives emerged. Powerful groups shaping the new industrial order often became much more concerned with making policy and exercising influence at the legislative stage than with influencing the implementation of policy. They were anxious to use government to plan and regulate certain types of economic activity. Their demands were serious and reflected tensions in distribution and penetration, which led to new forms of institutionalization, although crisis proportions were not reached. For these groups, occupational and professional affiliations became more important than ethnic considerations. If new forms for institutionalizing participation and penetration had not come about, certainly in these areas the scale of activities involving organized pressure groups had increased.

Most middle-class Americans saw nothing disturbing in the rise of these new aggregations of private power, but by the early years of the twentieth century they became convinced that the organized power wielded by political machines was evil. As long as America was relatively underdeveloped economically, most Americans were willing to tolerate a political system that rewarded parochial loyalties, encouraged short-run material inducements in order to gain public support, and made little effort to recruit the most qualified men to public office.

[15] For a very useful development of this point, see Scott, "Corruption," pp. 1142-58.

Caught up in the new industrial order, middle-class Americans mounted a confused and somewhat disorganized campaign against corruption during the first two decades of the century. Among the objects of attack were political parties. Those who mounted the attack on political parties had two major goals, somewhat inconsistent with one another. One was to make the political system more democratic, "to return government to the people," to break up large concentrations of political power. Somewhat antidemocratic, the other goal was to promote centralization in government in order to achieve more efficient and economical government.

To democratize government, the reformers introduced the direct primary, the initiative and referendum, a commission form of city government, and even nonpartisan elections. The direct primary would assist in upsetting the system by which a handful of party leaders could choose the candidates for important offices. The initiative and referendum would check the corruption of the state legislatures. And the commission plan of city government would smash the city machines. Believing that parties led to bosses, waste, and corruption, many reformers were convinced that more competent men would seek public office if they were not subjected to the practices of party politics. As a result, several hundred cities quickly adopted a nonpartisan type of city government. The net effect of all these changes was to weaken party organization.

On the other hand, some reformers attacked parties, and in particular, political machines, not because of faith in democracy and in the political wisdom of the electorate but because they believed that only the man of trained intelligence, the expert, could bring the necessary knowledge to bear on society's problems. As a result, numerous governmental agencies were established to regulate aspects of the enlarging industrial society, especially those in which the problems were highly technical and complicated. At first, the regulatory agencies were established in local and state politics, but eventually in national politics as well.

In the early days of the Republic, the country had needed a government that would integrate its diverse groups into a single nation state. Parties and administration had been intricately tied to one another in a fashion that had not stressed governmental efficiency and rationality, but placed a premium on representing ethnic groups, different classes, and competing regions, thereby winning public trust that strengthened the government's legitimacy, as a centralized bureaucracy probably could not. But now that large-scale corporate enterprises had emerged in the private sector of the society, there were strong demands that parties and administration not be so intricately involved with one another. The bureaucratized sector of the American economy now demanded a governmental administration that emphasized expertise, rationality, and professionalization. As party organization was weakened, bureaucracies and governmental employees became increasingly independent of political parties. Though partisan considerations were still of some importance in staffing governmental bureaucracies, universalistic and achievement criteria now became much more important.

However, many of the reforms did not have the consequences intended, and some resulted in the very opposite. For example, the weakening of the party organization did not bring about the immediate democratization that some reformers desired. With the breakup of state party organizations, powerful special interests became more influential within the political process than when they had to make demands upon well-organized political parties. Indeed, in the twentieth century it has become possible for powerful interest groups to shape much of public policy. This process was accelerated during the 1940s when, as a result of the most serious economic depression in American history, the political system was confronted with a distribution crisis of considerable magnitude. In response to the crisis, the government passed legislation that benefitted the most powerfully organized groups in American society. And in this fashion, the New Deal legislation successfully confronted the crisis situation.

But the success with which powerful interest groups have been able to shape public policy has, in turn, contributed to bringing the American political system to the verge of other crises. In almost every regulatory agency, the experts, the people with sufficient technical knowledge to operate the agencies, have generally been recruited from the interest group that is to be regulated. As a result, the regulatory commissions have usually ended up representing the interests of the group to be policed. The significance of this for the political process has been profound. First, the interests being regulated have had a governmental agency to articulate and aggregate their demands. Second, it has no longer been necessary for certain powerful interests to approach fragmented political parties for support. With regulatory commissions intricately tied to their clientele, elements of bureaucracy have been rendered all the more independent of political parties—a major departure from American political development of the nineteenth century.[16]

The way in which policy making has been turned over to private groups is visible in other sectors of the political system as well. For example, the power of the individual legislator has increased as party organization has weakened—especially if the legislator has seniority and is chairman of a legislative committee. True, legislators have held committee chairmanships by virtue of their party identification. But in the twentieth century, the importance of party discipline in shaping activity in legislative committees has diminished. With party discipline declining, legislators have carved out fiefdoms that they have tended as best they can. In response, powerful pressure groups have built up close working relationships with key legislators, who in many instances have, like numerous governmental bureaucrats, become the spokesmen for powerful interest groups.

In an effort to democratize the political process, twentieth-century reformers have arranged for state governments to have numerous elected offices. Those commonly elected have been directors of education, agriculture, labor, insurance, mines, land, public utilities, taxation, highways, public welfare, and health. While the voters have usually believed that they are participating more widely in the political process, the net effect of such a multiplicity of elected administrative officials has been to defeat public control. In the absence of strong parties, the elected officers were often members of different parties; and when they were not, the parties have been too weak to shape policy. As a result, administrators have increasingly become accountable primarily to a narrow constituency consisting of the group or groups most directly and intimately affected by the agency's activities.

The weakness of parties has been clearly paralleled by the weakness of state governors. Where parties have been weak and numerous, administrators have been elected by the public. Through the fragmentation of administration into autonomous agencies, the governor has been reduced to impotence in the government he ostensibly heads.

While the fragmentation of authority has made it increasingly difficult at the state and national level to govern in the interest of the entire society, the problems at the local level have come to be among the most serious ones facing the American political system. One could

[16] For more lengthy discussions of this subject, see Grant McConnell, *Private Power and American Democracy* (New York, 1966); Theodore J. Lowi, *The End of Liberalism* (New York, 1969); and David B. Truman, *The Governmental Process* (New York, 1956).

argue that in metropolitan areas there are many publics but no polity. Some years ago, Robert Wood counted 1,400 governments in the metropolitan area of New York City. For the smaller area around Chicago, in 1960 there were 1,060 governments, 995 of which had legal power to raise taxes. With so much fragmentation of authority, it has become increasingly difficult to govern.[17]

Functions involving transportation, health, water and air pollution, and land-use patterns have been shared by many agencies in each of these and other cities—making a coherent policy a virtual impossibility. And in many cities, powerful vested interests have been intricately tied to the public agencies. For example, the federal government has attempted to deal with housing problems through programs such as public housing, urban renewal, and FHA-VA mortgages, which powerful interest groups have both consciously and unconsciously controlled in such a way as to remove Blacks and other lower-class groups from desirable locations and to shift them into ghettos. The framers of these programs certainly did not intend them to be used in this manner, and Washington is far removed from an *apartheid* policy, but one commentator has observed that "the social state of American cities could be only a little worse if all the Federal agencies had been staffed all these years with white secret agents from South Africa."[18]

The sheer multiplicity of organized groups in private life, many with influence sometimes amounting to control of public agencies, and many with power through ties to particular legislative committees, meant that by the middle of the twentieth century it had become increasingly difficult in the United States for elected officials to implement policies that would benefit in any significant fashion the entire society. Indeed, decisions that had beneficial consequences for the entire society usually turned out upon close examination to have been largely the unanticipated consequences of previous and lesser decisions made in response to the pressures of some powerful interest group.

As these changes have taken place, organized interest groups and bureaucracies have become more important in the total political process as the role of legislatures has declined. As industrialization has made America an increasingly complex society, the problems facing legislators have required technical and expert knowledge in more and more fields of knowledge. Elected assemblies have increasingly deferred to

[17] Robert Wood, *1400 Governments* (Cambridge, 1961) and Lowi, *The End of Liberalism*, pp. 197-98.

[18] Lowi, *The End of Liberalism*, 251.

the knowledge of the expert whose information was believed to be indispensable for the maintenance and promotion of order and welfare. As administrators have gained their independence from political parties, bureaucratic officials have treated official business as confidential, thus increasing the difficulties of having their work inspected and controlled by political leaders. The Departments of State and Defense are only two areas in which this tendency has been especially pronounced.

By 1970, not only was the American political system poorly integrated, but it had encountered troubles in performance areas as well. Indeed, the political system was on the verge of a participation and legitimacy crisis. And the exclusion of groups from certain benefits of public policy raised serious distribution problems—especially within the black community. Parceling out policy making decisions to the most powerful in American society had meant that in many areas the rest of the public felt excluded. In programs in which administrative agencies had dealt primarily with powerful interest groups, the administrators became accountable to powerful pressure groups first and only secondarily to a president, a governor, the Congress, or a state legislature. Partly as a result of this process of dividing up the society's resources, there had slowly been developing a crisis in public authority in the United States. There had been building up for some time serious doubt about the efficacy and justice in the processes of policy making, leadership selection, and implementation of decisions. Sit-ins, demonstrations, and riots occurred as efforts of unorganized groups to participate in shaping the outcome of the political process.

But there were other reasons why America in the late 1960s was on the verge of a participation and legitimacy crisis. High levels of urbanization, industrialization, literacy, education, combined with an extensive mass media network had caused levels of political participation to rise. In most societies, there is political instability when there are high levels of participation and the organization of political parties is weak. And this set of circumstances had come into play in America, as a highly politicized society with a low level of party organization led to pockets of anomic politics.

Modernization has brought about two countertendencies in American society. On the one hand, it has led to government by the trained specialist, and a decline in the power of elected assemblies and political parties. America has become a society of giant organizations in labor, industry, government, and education, and in each sector the individual citizen has yielded to the power of the organization. In the process he has felt increasingly helpless. On the other hand, modernization has provided social conditions that increased the politicization of the masses. As voters have been uprooted by urbanization and industrialization, freed of a stable class structure and increasingly deprived of meaningful primary-group associations, the mass base of American politics has become somewhat volatile. Survey research indicates that partisan identification in America has been highly stable over time, but the political behavior of voters in recent years has oscillated from party to party.[19] And the number of voters unattached to any party has been rapidly increasing, especially among younger people.

Modernization not only has broadened participation and extended political consciousness in America, but it has given rise to enhanced expectations and demands for equality. For example, the countercurrents brought about by modernization have been clearly visible among welfare recipients. Confronted by a highly differentiated bureaucratic system, groups on welfare have demanded greater participation in managing welfare programs. The bureaucratic apparatus emphasizing achievement and professional values has usually resisted these demands. But denial of the welfare recipient's right to participate in decisions involving his life led to confrontations between clients and the professional administrators. And this tension between bureaucrats and frustrated clients has involved not only the poor but many groups that feel they have no control over "establishment" officials who "manage" society.

In response to social and economic modernization, the American political system has become highly differentiated. But the political system, instead of being well integrated, is becoming more fragmented. As Samuel P. Huntington has pointed out, the United States is the most modern society on earth, but has never developed a modern political system.[20] Ironically, the decentralized and fragmented character of the American political system facilitated legitimacy and stability in its early history. But these same characteristics make it difficult to cope with some of the society's most pressing urban problems

[19] Angus Campbell, Philip E. Converse, Warren E. Miller, and Donald E. Stokes, *The American Voter* (New York, 1960); V. O. Key, *The Responsible Electorate* (Cambridge, 1966); Walter Dean Burnham, *Critical Elections and the Mainsprings of American Politics* (New York, 1970).

[20] Samuel P. Huntington, "Political Development and Political Decay," *World Politics*, 17 (1965), 386-480, and "Political Modernization: America vs Europe," *World Politics*, 18 (1966), 378-414.

in the middle of the twentieth century. Indeed, the high level of demands for social, economic, and political equality have created a serious distribution problem.

Not only structurally, but psychically, American society has become fragmented. Indeed, as the level of modernization has increased, the problem of maintaining a society with commonly shared values has become one of the most critical challenges facing the American political system. A high level of modernization has meant that for many Americans traditional values of status, prestige, and morality have been eroded. As a result, American political elites have increasingly found it difficult to engage in symbolic activity that maintains a national consensus on major issues.

Not only have science and technology—the forces of modernization—progressed further in America than elsewhere, but in contrast with Europe, America has fewer traditional institutions, thus making it possible for the effects of modernization to be more volatile. Obviously, the effects of modernization have manifested themselves in many different ways, but it is the frequent resort to violence that has frightened the society and has threatened to increase the intensity of crisis. Indeed, one recent study of comparative violence concludes that "in numbers of political assassinations, riots, politically relevant armed group attacks and demonstrations, the United States has, since 1948, been among the half dozen most tumultuous nations in the world."[21]

Conclusion

Table 5.1 demonstrates the sequence with which crises have occurred in American history. By definition, a crisis requires the institutionalization of a new level of governmental output if there is not to be an overthrow of the elite structure of the society or a changing of the society's boundaries. There have been problem areas that were highly salient to elites and electorate, but were not so serious as to threaten the political system with a breakdown. The salient problems as well as crises are demonstrated on the table.

Because the United States was a settler society, most of the issues giving rise to crises have been different from those in European history. Because Americans did not have an encrusted traditional society, it was not necessary to develop a centralized state in order to promote

[21] Hugh Davis Graham and Ted Robert Gurr, *The History of Violence in America* (New York, 1969), p. 798.

TABLE 5.1: THE SEQUENCE AND SALIENCE OF POLITICAL PROBLEMS IN UNITED STATES HISTORY

Type of Problem	*1775-1789*	*1789-1815*	*1815-1840*	*1840-1865*	*1865-1928*	*1928-1940*	*1940-1970*
Legitimacy	x			x			(x)
Identity				x			(x)
Penetration	x		x	x			
Participation	x	x		x			(x)
Distribution		(x)	(x)			x	(x)

x Salient at crisis level.
(x) Salient enough to be serious problem.

a modern society. For this reason, Americans, prior to the twentieth century, did not develop a tradition of turning to government for solving the society's problems, as these were expected to be handled by private initiative and voluntary organizations. As a result, relatively few demands were placed on the government, and historically few problems have become salient enough to erupt as full-blown crises.

After the constitution was ratified, the first crisis—that of generating support for the new government—was a difficult one; and for several decades it was touch-and-go as to whether the experiment in new government would succeed. Like most new nations, the American government encountered several crises simultaneously. However, all problem areas did not become crises at one time, as has often been the case with new nations in the twentieth century. For example, the new government faced crises of participation and legitimacy during the years 1789-1815. After confronting these crises successfully, it then faced a crisis of penetration, 1815-1840. Serious problems of distribution, which did not reach crisis proportions, also occurred during the 1789-1840 period.

There was no model of development that the Americans were attempting to duplicate. Nor was the government faced with a revolution of rapidly rising expectations based on the belief that life was better elsewhere. As a result, political parties were able to cope with the various problem areas. But had all the problem areas become crises simultaneously, the political system would have been overwhelmed with political demands, and political parties undoubtedly would have been unable to cope with the situation.

The identity problem remained unsolved, however—that is, most Americans continued to identify with their region or with state governments to a greater extent than with their national government. As two distinct nations emerged during the 1840s and 1850s, the identity crisis became serious. And because weak performance in one problem area affects performances in other areas, the identity crisis promoted crises of participation, penetration, and legitimacy. When the elites were unable to cope with the crises, the result was the breakdown of the American party system—the one institution that had been able to cope with the various problem areas since the 1790s. The consequence was the American Civil War.

As a result of the war, people outside the South developed a strong identity with the national government, the political system's effectiveness of penetration increased, and parties were once again able to contain the high levels of political participation in American society. These effects were to promote relatively high levels of legitimacy and stability in the American political system until the 1920s. Of course there were factors other than political that were responsible for stability in American society. For example, as a high level of economic development began to take place, there was a tendency for people to have overlapping and multiple memberships in complex organizations, a factor that tended to reduce the ethnic, religious, and sectional cleavages in the society.

But in the twentieth century, modernization, having reached a relatively high level, has been responsible for introducing serious tensions into the American political system. A highly urban and industrial society required a governmental bureaucracy manned by experts, and the power of parties and the legislatures declined. Meantime, the forces of modernization had politicized the population, bringing the country to the verge of a participation crisis by the 1960s. Modernization also was responsible for the weakening of such primary institutions as the family and the church which, like political parties, had been a force for political stability.

Because the society became highly politicized, the demands for equality reached new heights—bringing the political system to the verge of a distribution crisis. No doubt, it could have responded with greater capability to the demands for equality made by the end of the 1960s were it not so fragmented. Specifically, the highly differentiated system could not cope adequately with the demands stemming from the metropolitan areas. The perceived failures of the distribution mechanisms, combined with the changing values of many Americans, brought many groups to the verge of a serious identity crisis. Blacks, the young, and the poor were only a few of the groups that felt a lack of common identity with the political system. As a result of their challenges, political elites found it increasingly difficult to engage in effective symbolic activity, and the binding together of culturally and socially discrete groups into a peaceful whole had become a Herculean task.

From the vantage point of the early 1970s, the American political system had come almost full circle. The consequences of modernization had brought it squarely to the edge of multiple crises—a situation that previously had existed only during the early days of the new nation and on the eve of the Civil War.

Some Related Readings

Several studies that attempt to explain why American social and political development have differed from those in European states are Louis Hartz, ed., *The Founding of New Societies* (New York, 1964); Samuel P. Huntington, "Political Modernization: America vs. Europe," *World Politics*, 18 (April 1966), 378-414; and Seymour M. Lipset, *The First New Nation: The United States in Historical and Comparative Perspective* (New York, 1963).

The best studies dealing with the participation and legitimacy crises of the early Republic are William N. Chambers, *Political Parties in a New Nation: The American Experience, 1776-1809* (New York, 1963); Lee Benson, *The Concept of Jacksonian Democracy* (Princeton, 1961); William N. Chambers and Walter Dean Burnham, eds., *The American Party Systems: Stages of Political Development* (New York, 1967); Richard P. McCormick, *The Second American Party System* (Chapel Hill, 1966); and David H. Fischer, *The Revolution of American Conservatism* (New York, 1965).

While the literature of the American Civil War is voluminous, two very useful studies are Roy Nichols, *The Disruption of American Democracy* (New York, 1948) and Avery O. Craven, *The Coming of the Civil War* (New York, 1942). For a statement covering the shortcomings of the literature on the civil war, see Lee Benson, *Toward the Scientific Study of History* (Philadelphia, 1972).

Perhaps the most useful book on American political culture is Alexis de Tocqueville's classic *Democracy in America.* Other valuable studies of political culture are Louis Hartz, *The Liberal Tradition in America* (New York, 1955) and Daniel J. Boorstin, *The Genius of American Politics* (Chicago, 1953).

For the relationships among political parties, bureaucracies, interest groups, and public policy during the late nineteenth century, see James C. Scott, "Corruption, Machine Politics, and Political Change," *American Political Science Review*, 63 (1969), 1142-58; Seymour J. Mandelbaum, *Boss Tweed's New York* (New York, 1965), and Moisei Ostrogorski's two-volume work, *Democracy and the Organization of Political Parties*, first published in 1902 but recently edited by Seymour Martin Lipset (New York, 1964).

For the twentieth century, the following are the most important: Theodore Lowi, *The End of Liberalism: Ideology, Policy, and the Crisis of Public Authority* (New York, 1969); Grant McConnell, *Private Power and American Democracy* (New York, 1966); David B. Truman, *The Governmental Process* (New York, 1951).

For excellent studies of the distribution problem in the twentieth century, see H. L. Wilensky and C. N. Lebeaux, *Industrial Society and Social Welfare* (New York, 1965); G. V. Rimlinger, "Welfare Policy and Economic Development: A Comparative Historical Perspective," *Journal of Economic History*, 26 (1966), 556-71; Solomon Fabricant, *The Trend of Government Activity in the United States since 1900* (New York, 1952); and Margaret Gordon, *The Economics of Welfare Policies* (New York, 1963).

The participation problem in twentieth-century America is very well discussed in Walter Dean Burnham, *Critical Elections and the Mainsprings of American Politics* (New York, 1970), and Richard Dawson and James A. Robinson, "Inter-Party Competition, Economic Variables, and Welfare Policies in the American States," *Journal of Politics*, 25 (1963), 265-89. For a more general treatment of electoral behavior in American history, see Joel Silbey *et al.*, *The History of American Electoral Behavior* (Princeton, 1978).

CHAPTER 6

Spain and Portugal

STANLEY G. PAYNE

The instability of modern Spanish government and its failure to develop a viable representative polity on the British or Scandinavian models have usually been attributed to certain inherent deficiencies of Spanish society. These include the supposed lack of a middle class, the assumed strength of the church, the entrenched power of a vaguely defined "oligarchy" of land and wealth, the backwardness of Spanish culture in terms of literacy and technological training, and the slow growth of the economic system. The conventional view of non-Spanish scholars tends to assume that the left has by and large played a progressive and constructive role, and that conservative or rightist groups are the main villains of modern Spanish history. The most serious and scholarly statements of this conventional attitude are by Gerald Brenan and Gabriel Jackson,[1] and center on problems of participation and distribution.

The major one-volume treatment of modern Spanish history, Raymond Carr's *Spain 1808-1939* (Oxford, 1966), is conceived in different terms. It centers on the failure of Spanish liberalism to achieve a viable constitutional system in the nineteenth and early twentieth centuries, but its approach is broader and more empirical. Carr does not employ the terminology of the present analysis, for he never mentions the concept of penetration, uses the word identity very rarely and then in a limited sense, and employs the term legitimacy only with reference to competing dynastic claims. Nonetheless, by means of his particularistic, no-nonsense historian's approach he deals with the same kinds of problems posed by the identification and analysis of crises in our current study; for he stresses disagreements over the definition and the goals of the Spanish state and of a changing society (the problem of identity), protracted conflict over the acceptability (or

Crises of Political Development in Europe and the United States
0-691-07598-0/78/000197-22$01.10/1 (cloth)
0-691-02183-X/78/000197-22$01.10/1 (paperback)

[1] Gerald Brenan, *The Spanish Labyrinth* (London, 1944); Gabriel Jackson, *The Spanish Republic and Civil War 1931-1939* (Princeton, 1965).

legitimacy) of constitutional monarchy and its successors, and also the persistent problems of government services, taxes, finance, and economic policy (the problems of penetration and distribution). Analysis of such issues receives much more attention than do descriptions of Spanish backwardness, while moral denunciations in his work are rare. He does not attempt to establish any simply defined interpretation of the causes of political conflict and frustration, but suggests that the failure was above all "political"—that is, a failure of political culture, structures, and dominant personalities—rather than the consequence of specific social groups or the inevitable result of a slow rate of economic development.

In general, modern Spanish historiography is much less developed than that of the other large European countries (save Poland). Major monographic gaps inhibit the formulation of soundly based interpretations and also render consensus among general commentators difficult. Though the formal political history of modern Spain has been written to some degree, we still know comparatively little about the social and economic bases underlying surface phenomena. The only mass movement of nineteenth-century Spain, Carlism, has never been systematically studied; and the most crucial single topic of all—religion and the church—has been almost ignored by serious research. There is still too much generalization about Spain as a whole, though in fact the country is more severely divided by manifold regional differences than any other in Western Europe. The whole issue of regional differences and differential rates of regional development has been very little studied, despite its crucial role in the problems of modern Spain.

Crises

IDENTITY

Common Hispanic "identity" dates from Visigothic times and persisted through the middle ages, based on geography, common religion, certain common cultural forms, and also a common mission, the affirmation of Hispano-Christian identity and values against the Muslim presence in the peninsula. These factors served to some extent to transcend the medieval division of Christian Hispania among five separate kingdoms.[2] Union of all the Hispanic kingdoms save

[2] On this problem see José Antonio Maravall, *El concepto de España en la Edad Media* (Madrid, 1954).

Portugal under a common Habsburg state in the sixteenth century created a partially coordinated governing system, but nothing approaching an integrated nation.

The creation of a unified, largely centralized Spanish state, together with the basis for a common civic identity, was the work of the eighteenth-century Spanish Bourbon monarchy. This new regime abolished the regional parliaments and separate courts of the Aragonese principalities, and developed an increasingly efficient centralized administration and coordinated economic policy, largely on the French model. It was only after the initial establishment of this integrated Spanish polity at the close of the War of Succession in 1713 that the Portuguese ceased to participate in the broader Hispanic geographico-cultural identity and finally gave up the use of the generic term "Spanish." For the remainder of the century there was remarkably little discord in Spanish society over either political or economic matters. To speak of the growth of a common civil identity *per se* would probably be an exaggeration, since the civic role in Spanish society was largely passive and unmobilized. There was, however, unqualified acceptance of Bourbon monarchism, of Catholicism, and of traditional Spanish (not merely Castilian) legal usages and culture, combined with an enlightened new development policy that complemented the interests of most, though perhaps not all, of the diverse regions of Spain. Loyalty to the crown and to the church were the simplest and most obvious manifestations of this identity, but a more conscious sense of common purpose and interrelationship in terms of a single state structure and integrated policy was also beginning to take root. The simpler, relatively undifferentiated ties to crown and church were, however, the bonds of common identity most clearly displayed during the harsh trials of the wars with revolutionary and Napoleonic France. In the War of Independence, 1808-1813, the Spanish generated the first modern guerrilla war of popular resistance and set the example of a kind of popular prenationalism that helped to inspire the German resistance against Napoleon.

The subsequent political history of Spain, following the introduction of the liberal parliamentary system, was the most turbulent of any country in nineteenth-century Europe. The manifold crises, pronunciamientos, breakdowns, and overthrows of cabinets and of entire regimes did not, however, necessarily reawaken the intrinsic question of a common identity, which remained largely undisputed until the last years of the century. Even the emergence of the notorious "two

Spains" after 1820—one Catholic and traditionalist, the other secular and modernist—created a profound conflict within the broader Spanish identity, and led several times to civil war, yet neither side ever proposed any form of partition (either of institutions or the state) or the rejection of a mutual civic identity.

This issue only began to reemerge at the very close of the century, after the disaster of the Spanish-American War of 1898 and the loss of the remainder of the overseas empire (save in northwest Africa) reawakened the whole question of the nature and identity of the Spanish polity and its viability. Spain seemed to be the least successful country in western Europe; and in its most active, most rapidly modernizing region—Catalonia—there emerged a regional nationalist movement that rejected Spanish identity altogether. The flexibility and cooptive capacity of the system was nonetheless revealed during the generation that followed, for the constitutional monarchy managed to retain the cooperation of the moderate Catalanists and even offered to establish a reasonable statute of regional autonomy in 1919, though this enterprise was rejected by Catalan maximalism.

Collapse of the restored parliamentary monarchist regime in 1923 through military pronunciamiento resulted not so directly from internal stresses as from the neocolonial problem in Morocco. The cancer of protracted colonial war in the Moroccan Protectorate had, among other things, raised the issue of Spain's mission and identity in the modern world, and it is almost axiomatic that countries with latent internal identity problems are less able to face foreign crises. The seven-year dictatorship of Primo de Rivera (1923-1930) that followed undid much of the work of the preceding half-century, which had partially stilled the identity problem by accommodating large sectors through participation, access, and compromises in penetration. The dictatorship followed a diametrically opposite course.

Collapse of the monarchy and introduction of the second Republic in 1931 at first seemed unrelated to issues of identity, for what was initially at stake was simply the legitimacy of the monarchist regime and the breakdown of participation due to the dictatorship. However, in the ensuing political vacuum, power at first fell into the hands of a radical middle-class "Republican left" that challenged the entire fabric of liberal compromise, Catholicism, and individualism on which the preceding regime had been based. Together with their socialist allies, they posed the issue of a new Spain: anticlerical, socially radical, and semicollectivist, as opposed to a Spain still Catholic and middle class-individualist. The cleavage was profound and reached critical dimensions touching all the major categories of modern political conflict. The identity of Spain was at stake in the realms of ideology and values, structure of regime, and even continued national existence. Catalonia was given regional autonomy in 1932, and a major Basque nationalist movement developed. By 1936 the Spanish Communist party, then the maximal agent of national disintegration, proposed as feasible that Catalonia, the Basque country, and Galicia establish themselves as sovereign states. Nearly every region of Spain began to draw up its own demands for autonomy. In the civil war that followed (1936-1939), Spanish nationalists came to label their struggle a "crusade" to "save Spain" in the most elementary sense of that verb.

Full national identity on the French or English model has never developed in Spain. It should be noted that Spain is very nearly the only country in modern Europe never to have registered a strong nationalist or proimperialist movement. The main reasons for this are internal conflict coupled with extremely low mobilization, low rates of economic development and, equally important, an almost absolute lack of involvement in the international power conflicts of modern Europe (due in large measure to Spain's marginal geographic position). This last factor is in marked contrast to Spain's perpetual and ultimately fatal involvement in literally every single one of the major international power conflicts of sixteenth and seventeenth-century Europe, and underscores the extent to which the interminable involvements of the earlier period were the artificial consequences of Habsburg dynasticism, little related to the vital interests of Spain itself.

Similarly, despite the enduring reputation of so-called "Spanish fascism," Spain was the country in continental Europe which—after Scandinavia—registered the least support for political fascism prior to the outbreak of the civil war in 1936. In the elections of February of that year the Falange gained only one percent of the vote. Its electorate and total membership were proportionately much smaller than those of the fascist parties in France and Belgium. Falangism gained support only as a defensive reaction against the revolutionary left in 1936-1939, and then completely failed to win decisive power within the Franco regime.

After 1939 the Franco regime imposed its own definition of national identity on Spain, emphasizing traditional religion and culture under pluralistic authoritarianism. The result has been at least as innovative as it has been reactionary, for the regime's welfare and developmental policies have made possible greater integration as well as a more extensive differentiation of national society. The Franco regime has not "solved" the identity problem, for regional feeling remains strong in Catalonia and the Basque country, while mounting secularization alters the basis of Catholic identity. Fundamental issues of participation and distribution await solution in the future, while past experience indicates that major conflicts over such problems, if carried far enough, can reawaken the question of national identity.

National identity was established earlier in Portugal than in Spain. Portuguese historians have argued that during the twelfth and thirteenth centuries theirs became the first nation state in Europe. Such terminology is exaggerated, but a common and fairly well integrated Portuguese identity did take shape during the middle ages. It was based on political unity under a strong and rather efficient monarchy, on relative geographic unity under the shelter of the northeastern mountains that cut Portugal off from the main part of Castile-Leon, on a common language that was early employed in the vernacular for state and legal business and was never severely divided by dialect differences, and finally on a sense of social and institutional difference from the dominant power in the peninsula—Castile—whose control was feared and resented.

LEGITIMACY

Legitimacy conflict first appeared in modern Spain in the form of dynastic quarrels and rivalries; but, after the inception of the first liberal polity in 1810, involved broader questions of identity, privilege, participation, and centralist penetration and distribution. Legitimacy conflict has been more endemic to Spanish politics throughout the modern period than in the history of any other Western European state. In the most general sense, this has been due to protracted cleavage within and between the national elites over fundamental norms and goals. More concretely, four factors can be pointed out: a) the intensity of religious identity and its social and political power in Spain, reenforcing the legitimacy conflict between liberals and Catholic traditionalists to a greater degree than almost anywhere else in nineteenth-century Europe; b) the persistence of regional identities, loyalties, and even of socio-economic structures, building a deeply rooted resistance, especially in the Basque country, to the legitimacy of the centralist liberal regime; c) the extraordinary political duplicity and ineptitude—there are no better terms for it—of Fernando VII

(1808-1833) and Isabel II (1833-1868), which greatly hindered the establishment of legitimacy; and d) the nature of Spanish social styles and values. Status has long been of overweening importance in Spain, and is associated with deeply personalist attitudes[3] that hinder compromise and acceptance of the legitimacy of attitudes or legal structures with which one disagrees in whole or in part. Much of Spanish political conflict has been over epiphenomenal issues of personal status rivalry rather than objective problems.

The original legitimacy crises between liberalism and traditionalism were protracted, if intermittent, and took the form of three separate struggles during the periods 1807-1814, 1820-1823 and 1833-1840. After 1840 the liberal principles of constitutional monarchy and parliamentary representation achieved a fairly general consensus thanks to victory in the civil war, permeation of liberal ideas among nearly all the elite, and new social and economic changes oriented toward entrepreneurial market economics. What remained, however, was severe cleavage over participation and access within that system.

The second period of sharp legitimacy conflict occurred at the end of Spain's first regular constitutional monarchy, the Isabeline regime of 1833-1868. The legitimacy crisis of 1866-1868 was due almost exclusively to the fact that, despite the earlier general acceptance of the regime, it had completely failed to resolve the issues of participation and access. This reawakened the fundamental question of the legality of such a narrow, exclusivist system, which was finally overthrown by a fairly broad liberal-democratic coalition. The latter inaugurated a new constitutionally democratic monarchy under a Savoyan prince, Amadeo (1870-1873).

The main defect of the democratic monarchy was that it was too democratic in a country riven by elite dissidence and without a developed structure of interest representation. Lacking a real *poder*

[3] The common notion that the Spanish are highly "individualistic" is, on the other hand, quite misleading and is due to defective terminology and superficial analysis. Spain's leading historical anthropologist, Julio Caro Baroja, has put the matter well: "The Spanish are not individualists, but personalists, which is quite different. The individualist in effect believes that society is constituted by individuals who have or ought to have more or less the same rights and duties. He asks that his be respected and agrees to respect those of others. The personalist sees each person as isolated (beginning with himself) with a series of distinct characteristics and has no scruples about abusing some and favoring others, since he sees them all as inherently different, some of them sympathetic and attractive to him and others not. The personalist starts from a boundless, instinctive and capricious ego to judge his neighbor and determine what he does or does not deserve." *Los judios en la España moderna y contemporánea* (Madrid, 1961), III, 258-59.

moderador (moderating power), the liberal factions fought each other tooth and nail over issues of access, status, and patronage. In addition, the new Radical party raised questions of penetration and distribution, and after two years the conflict was so deep that the very legitimacy of the regime was once more in question. Abdication of the king and establishment of a federal republic resulted in eighteen months of virtual chaos that was only ended after restoration of the regular Bourbon dynasty in 1875. One lesson from this experience was that legitimacy could be neither achieved nor maintained without a constitutionally powerful moderating force able to uphold legality and regulate access.

Despite a potentially severe legitimacy problem at the beginning, leaders of the restored constitutional monarchy of 1875-1923/31 managed to avert a new legitimacy crisis for more than half a century. The legitimacy of the preceding regimes had broken down under severe pressures of access, participation, and to some extent penetration. The restored monarchy proved much more skillful—at least for two generations—in handling these problems. It was only after the total exclusion of participation and excesses of penetration by the Primo de Rivera dictatorship that a genuine legitimacy crisis appeared in 1931.

This was the fourth in modern Spanish history, and quickly led to the inauguration of the second Republic, but not to any enduring resolution of the legitimacy issue. This was somewhat paradoxical in that initially the legitimacy of the Republic was scarcely contested at all, even by most conservatives. Here again it was conflict over the entire range of problems, from participation to distribution, that soon became so severe as to open the question of legitimacy itself.

Portugal has experienced two distinct modern legitimacy crises that roughly but not exactly parallel the first two in Spain. The initial legitimacy crisis of Portuguese liberalism, which, as has been suggested above, involved a sort of crisis of identity as well, was resolved between 1820 and 1834. That this conflict emerged a decade later than in Spain was due to the slower development of the Portuguese political intelligentsia and the lack of alternative foci of political activity in a country largely dominated by two cities, Lisbon and Porto. The Portuguese conflict was also less protracted due to the small scale of the country and the exiguous size of the Portuguese elite, more easily coopted into the new regime. These same factors—the relative lack of differentiation of interests and the compactness of the political intelligentsia and agrarian bourgeoisie—helped to avert any real problem about legitimacy until a complex series of pressures converged to undermine the regime in 1908-1910.

The First Republic from 1910 to 1926 experienced a constant succession of government crises, but it is doubtful that any of them should be labeled as a legitimacy crisis *per se*. Even when the parliamentary system was finally overthrown, the new military government insisted that it was only correcting basic republican institutions. This vague but general acceptance of republican legitimacy was due in large part to lack of alternatives. The monarchy was thoroughly discredited because of its failure to raise Portugal's international status, carry through economic modernization, or maintain political stability. In a still undifferentiated peasant and middle-class society—without a powerful upper class, a strong political right, or working class movements—there seemed no other option but some form of middle-class republicanism. The subsequent emergence of Salazar's "Estado Novo" in 1933 was not the result of a critical break or confrontation but an undramatic transformation worked out over a decade.

PARTICIPATION

The growth of political participation in modern Spain has been paradoxical. The early establishment of a common state and relative administrative uniformity created enough sense—perhaps illusory—of civil integration to encourage the new liberal elite to introduce what was in 1812 the broadest system of electoral participation in the world. Though indirect, suffrage was to be exercised by all heads of households. Meanwhile, a very broad process of nonelectoral participation in a kind of civic referendum was carried on by means of the guerrilla struggle against Napoleon. Yet Spain had one of the lowest literacy rates in Western and Central Europe, and its population was not well prepared to engage in direct political activity. Forces of conservatism and/or reaction were quite strong in a landlord-and-peasant society. Armed strength was used to choke off the liberal participatory system in 1814 and 1823, and a major effort was made once more after 1833. It should be recognized, however, that what most opponents contested was probably not so much the concept of participation—though that was also resisted—as the domination of a new elite who would manipulate that system.

The Isabeline regime began in 1833-1834 with an extremely restricted suffrage, but this, together with the pressures of the First Carlist War, quickly led to a participation crisis that broke out in the riots and revolts of 1836. Though the latter produced a broadening of the suffrage under terms of the new constitution of 1837, the basic principle of direct, censitary suffrage limited to the elite—whether somewhat broader or somewhat narrower—was accepted by the bulk of political opinion for the remainder of the Isabeline period.

The elements who participated, in fact or in theory, were the middle and upper classes. It is a commonplace that the instability of politics in the Hispanic world is due to the "lack" of a middle class, but in essence this frequently heard assertion is nearly a contradiction in terms, since modern politics in Spain—and in much of Spanish America—is the product of the middle classes. Part of the problem is that the customary definition of "middle-class" is based on the Anglo-Dutch model of the entrepreneurial bourgeoisie. Such a bourgeoisie was almost completely absent in nineteenth-century Spain. What did exist was the peculiar Spanish middle-class structure of bureaucrats, professional men, merchants and shopkeepers, provincial landowners, unemployed intellectuals, and, last but not least, army officers. The traditional aristocracy had lost privilege and power, and was merging with the new upper middle class, from whom a new "bourgeois nobility" was being created. The base of Spanish political participation were these heterogeneous middle classes, for whom the exact terms of suffrage varied considerably (see Table 6.1), pressure for universal male suffrage only beginning to build during the final crisis of 1866-1868.

TABLE 6.1: VARIATIONS IN SUFFRAGE IN SPAIN, 1836-1867

Date	*Eligible voters*	*Percentage of total population*
1836	65,067	.52
1837	257,984	2.09
1839	342,559	2.78
1840	423,787	3.44
1846	97,100	.79
1850	121,770	1.11
1851	122,700	1.11
1857	157,725	1.01
1858	157,931	1.02
1863	179,413	1.14
1864	166,291	1.06
1865	418,271	2.67
1867	396,863	2.38

Source: Diego Sevilla Andrés, *Historia política de España (1800-1867)* (Madrid, 1968), p. 234.

Instead of major electoral participation conflicts, the Isabeline regime suffered perpetual conflict over access among the elite, due to the narrowly restrictive politics of the Crown and the governing cliques. A special role was played by the politically active minorities within the army officer corps, for in a country lacking strong, expanding middle classes based on new wealth, sectors of the army played the role of a sort of modernizing elite. Beginning as early as 1817, the army was persistently called upon by civilian liberals to sustain initiatives of which the latter were incapable. Thus, politicized officers were of crucial importance both in trying to establish the new legitimacy and in regulating access, though they ultimately failed in both endeavors.

Another major problem of access and integration had to do with the role and influence of the church. The advent of ideological and institutional liberalism coincided with—and partially provoked—a genuine religious crisis, involving a drastic shrinkage of the clergy and decline in vocations. Along with the downgrading of the church's legal and political power came the expropriation of nearly all church lands in the 1830s and 1840s. In that sense the Carlist War also coincided with a sort of distribution crisis. For a full generation the most important nongovernment institution in Spain was completely alienated from the liberal regime. A tentative rapproachement only began with the negotiation of a new concordat in 1851.

Conflicts of access reached major proportions in 1840-1843 and 1854. In 1840 the Progressives overthrew the Moderates and established a temporary military-led regency over the issue of extending local self-government to the provinces, though this was more a crisis of penetration than of participation *per se*. Exclusion from access brought another successful revolt in 1854 and a two-year Progressivist government.

After the democratic interlude of 1868-1874, the restored constitutional monarchy of 1875 once more restricted the suffrage, though not so narrowly as the Isabeline regime, limiting it to between five and seven percent of the population. Universal male suffrage, in effect from 1869 to 1874, was again restored in 1890. At that time, the bulk of the adult population was still illiterate, and nominal democracy resulted in a new kind of access problem—a problem of "common" rather than "elite" access through distortion of the basic electoral process. The name commonly given this is *caciquismo*, a vague term covering a half-dozen different kinds of local political forms: domination by notables, total apathy, clientage, rigged elections, buying of votes, and so on. *Caciquismo* was largely a reflection of civic immaturity, and declined more and more as a problem in most parts of Spain during the early twentieth century.

"Elite" or "governmental" access was handled with relative skill for the first four decades of the restored monarchy. Access demands became unresolved on a major scale only under the pressures of the First World War. In 1917 elements that were being denied governmental and legislative (not electoral) access tried to set up a counter-parliament in Barcelona and attempted to pressure for basic constitutional changes, indirectly encouraging a protorevolutionary wave among the expanding worker movements.

The revolutionary insurrection of 1934 that nearly wrecked the Second Republic two years before the Civil War was in a sense the result of a participation crisis in which the left was trying to deny governmental and legislative access to the right. Yet it was also much more than that, constituting one of the best examples of a concurrent multicategory crisis in modern Spanish history. At the same time, a sort of penetration crisis existed in two different dimensions, the regionalist-centralist and church-state education issues. Drastic changes in wages and benefits during the preceding three years, together with a new effort made by the right to roll them back, amounted to a distribution crisis. When cleavage became total, the left temporarily rejected the legitimacy of the constitutional Republic (which they had borne primary responsibility for building) because democratic participation helped to legitimize the activities of the right and give the latter governmental access. The interaction of all these conflicts led to a crisis in the very concept of civic identity as originally accepted by most of the population only three years earlier.

Participation crises in modern Portugal have been rarer than in Spain, in large measure because of the small size of the Portuguese elite, which could be more fully accommodated within a restrictive system. The only electoral participation crises *per se* broke out in the two major revolts in the early history of Portuguese liberalism, the Septembrist rebellion of 1836 and the "Patuléia" of 1846. Both were also crises of penetration and, to some extent, of distribution. By the mid-nineteenth century, a system of limited suffrage had been established that satisfied most of the elite and was somewhat broadened during the remainder of the century. Access problems were less severe than in Spain because of more enlightened royal arbitration, less fragmentation among the elite, and the sketching out after 1852 of what later became a "rotativist" system between the two major parties. (By contrast, the Spanish *turno* was not established until the 1880s.) The overthrow of the monarchy was to some extent the result of participation conflict, since the suffrage had been notably reduced in recent years (see Table 6.2). At first, however, the subsequent Republican

TABLE 6.2: VARIATIONS IN PORTUGUESE SUFFRAGE, 1864-1918

Year	*Requirements for voting*	*Total number of eligible voters*	*Percentage of total population*
1864	Males over 25 with 100 *reis* annual income	344,173	11.1
1878	Literate males and male heads of families	580,214	13.9
1890	Literate males over 21	874,528	18.7
1910	or with 500 *reis* income	650,341	11.6
1911	Literate males over 21 or heads of families	782,292	13.9
1913	Literate males over 21	379,714	6.7
1915		450,322	8.0
1918	Universal male suffrage		

Source: Adapted from Souza Junior, *Censo eleitoral da metropole*, in Bento Carqueja, *O Povo portuguez* (Porto, 1916).

system broadened the franchise very little, apparently to minimize the influence of "ignorant," "clerical" voters. The First Republic never experienced a genuine participation crisis in popular terms, though its entire history might be written in the framework of protracted conflicts between status rivals and factions.

PENETRATION

The achievement of greater and more efficient penetration was a major goal of the modern liberal polity in Spain. At issue were the usual objectives of administrative reform and regularization, legal coordination and equality and, in the Spanish case, the opening of institutional and communal land to the private market. During the first full decade of liberalism, this led to a penetration crisis that hinged on two issues: seizure of church lands, and central administration of provincial and regional affairs. The former aspect exacerbated the identity and legitimacy conflicts facing the new polity, while the latter aspect divided the liberal forces after their victory over the Carlists. The penetration crisis, which began in 1836, was resolved after 1843 with a complete victory for orthodox elitist liberalism on both issues. Several reasons may be adduced to explain this triumph: concerning the first issue, clerical traditionalists were a minority even in Spain as a result of the cultural and socio-economic changes of the two preceding generations. Moreover, the two major constitutional monarchies of Europe, Britain and France, lent strong support to the liberal cause. Second, with regard to the conflict between elitist centralism and Progressivist provincialism, the elitist centralists represented the dominant agrarian interests of Spain and had better leadership and coordination. They stood for politico-administrative rationalization and modernization as they understood it, and, in part because of the excesses and incompetence of their foes, gained the support of the dominant faction in the army. Progressivist decentralizers tended to fall between two stools: they were not democrats and could not develop sustained mobilization, yet their intermittent willingness to call out the mob and encourage provincialist radicalism elicited forces that they could not control or coordinate.

After 1843 the Spanish polity did not face a full-scale penetration crisis until the first liberal cycle ended in the chaos of the Federal Republic. What it did register, however, was a failure of efficient penetration in most of the main areas. During the mid-nineteenth century, underpenetration was not yet a problem in itself, for the society had not yet generated major demands that could only be met by more effective penetration. The only penetration problems were those denounced as excessive penetration in certain areas, such as excises and the military draft—two of the most common complaints on the popular level—and the question of local self-government. Major problems of underpenetration—such as deficiencies in public services and the paucity of state measures to stimulate economic government—were emphasized by comparatively few spokesmen. Underpenetration in itself became critical only in 1873, when it reached the extremes of provincial anarchy under federalism, destroying the entire structure of civic integration and reawakening the issue of legitimacy itself.

The last six years of parliamentary government under the restored parliamentary monarchy (1917-1923) were a time of protracted crisis in problems of penetration. This was a result of changing patterns of social and economic structure that required new services, stimuli, and regulation. Though the mechanisms of state penetration were steadily improving, the rate was still too slow. The system had resolved its problems of legitimacy and participation (though not all issues of access) but failed to meet the new challenges demanded of state penetration in the twentieth century. The resultant conflict, when it reached critical dimensions, was a major factor, as in 1873, in reawakening the basic problems of participation and legitimacy.

The failure of penetration was most apparent in two areas: social and economic affairs, and regional and provincial administration. Lack of governmental resources and of determination seriously hampered development of effective means of regulation and arbitration that were being demanded with greater and greater urgency. With respect to the regionalist issue, the weakness of penetration was partially responsible for growing demands for regional autonomy, mobilized with great vehemence by Catalanists who insisted that the state relinquish nearly all administrative control of their region. On the one hand, centralization precluded local administration and self-government. On the other hand, it failed to provide in the Spanish case the kind of leadership and services that might have made it palatable to the more advanced and demanding regions. Centralism worked in France because it stood not merely for politico-administrative control but as a vehicle for creative penetration and development. In Spain the latter aspect was poorly developed.

The Second Republic lived amid a perpetual penetration crisis that contributed in large measure to its breakdown. This had three facets: the determination of middle-class radicals to subjugate the church, even within its own sphere of education; the aim of the socialists to employ major state intervention to achieve economic redistribution; and the goal of the Catalan and Basque regionalists to achieve autonomy. Even after an autonomous system was created for Catalonia, it proved very difficult to balance the latter's demands with the remaining minimal requirements of central penetration.

The modern Portuguese polity also encountered a penetration crisis of sorts immediately upon its establishment. The terms of this almost exactly paralleled those of the penetration crisis occurring at the same time in Spain, save that once more the Portuguese crisis was somewhat more readily resolved. During the remaining history of the Portuguese parliamentary monarchy, penetration was even more ineffective in its productive aspects than in the case of Spain, but also led to less conflict. The resultant Portuguese fiscal problem was, however, even more severe than that of Spain. Initially, the most serious penetration problem of the First Republic stemmed from its determination to subjugate the church. This was not achieved, but it never led to a thorough crisis in itself, and after 1918 an autonomous *modus vivendi* with the church began to be worked out.

DISTRIBUTION

The nineteenth-century Spanish polity did not experience a full-scale distribution crisis. The major economic redistribution of that period was the sale of church and common lands to private owners. This provoked serious peasant discontent in some areas, but its effects were diffuse, and peasant society in most parts of Spain remained completely unmobilized. During the remainder of the century, there was much intermittent conflict over issues of distribution; but none reached critical dimensions. The nineteenth-century middle-class parties did not present major challenges to the distribution pattern (the partial exception might be the Federal Republicans), and working-class movements remained weak in Spain until the time of the First World War. The absence of a distribution crisis until that time may be explained in part by the lack of new wealth to redistribute, and also by the relative stability and partial self-sufficiency of the smallholders of northern and central Spain. The most miserable members of Spanish society—the landless peasants of the south and south-center—were largely illiterate and lacking in the means for mobilization. Their plight, however, had actually grown worse by the early twentieth century, due to rapid population increase unrelieved by the sizable emigration that worked as a sort of safety valve in the north. Even so, the growth of labor organization only developed effectively among the anarcho-syndicalist CNT in the industrial northeast (especially in Catalonia), and only after special opportunities and pressures created by wartime industrial expansion. Emergence of the CNT as a mass movement in 1917-1918 precipitated the first major strike wave in Spanish history, provoking a genuine distribution crisis. The last two years of the second Republic were also a time of latent or actual distribution crisis. At issue was a fundamental redistribution of wage incomes and farmland, some aspects of which were revolutionary in scope.

In Portugal, by contrast, it is not clear that there has ever been a genuine distribution crisis. During the nineteenth century much of the Portuguese population was composed of a virtually self-sufficient peasantry. They complained about penetration in the form of central administration and excises, contributing to the penetration crisis of the early liberal period; but aside from the sale of church lands, there were no major new redistribution demands from any sector. An urban working-class movement, centered on the two main cities, developed slowly after the turn of the century. Labor disturbances contributed marginally to the crisis that overthrew the monarchy, then intensified greatly under the First Republic. Even so, there was never a full-scale systematic crisis over the distribution issue.

Sequence

The study of crisis sequences is simplest and most effective when dealing with a single political system or cycle, and ideally with a country that has had one major or even continuous political regime. Though most European countries do not meet this desideratum, the case of Spain is particularly difficult, since its modern political structure has gone through three distinct cycles: a) the first liberal polity, which required three different tries to get started, then ranged through three distinct regimes only to end in total bankruptcy with a federal Republic—the years 1808, 1820, 1833-1874; b) the restored constitutional monarchy of 1875-1923/1931; and c) the shortlived but politically frenetic second Republic of 1931-1936.

Converting the identification and dating of crises suggested in the preceding sections into a chronological chart (see Table 6.3) does not

TABLE 6.3: CHRONOLOGY OF SPANISH POLITICAL CRISES, 1807-1936

Identity	1700-30								1934-36
Legitimacy		1807-40[a]			1866-68	1873-75		1931	1934-36
Participation[b]			1836-37	1854	1866-68		1917		1934-36
Penetration			1836-43			1873-75	1917-23		1934-36
Distribution							1917-23		1934-36

[a] The years of overt crisis were 1807-1810, 1812-1814, 1820-1823 and 1833-1839.

[b] The establishment of a coordinated, centralized state system in the early eighteenth century obviously involved crises of participation and penetration for the Aragonese principalities, but these were part of the resolution of political problems in the traditional constitutional systems of the peninsula (which may be termed either medieval or early modern, depending on definition) and refer to a different period and level of political development that we are not concerned with here.

establish any neat patterns, but it does illustrate an approximate sequence. The first point, that the establishment of a national identity is necessary for further civic development, is tautological. In the Spanish case, however, the creation of a limited civic identity under the monarchy made possible the precocious introduction of a liberal system at a time when neither national culture not social and economic interests was prepared to sustain it.

The first legitimacy crisis was precipitated more by foreign invasion than by domestic political pressures. After this provided opportunity to prepare a revolutionary liberal system (1810-1812), there soon developed a full-scale domestic crisis of legitimacy. Each successive effort to reestablish liberal constitutional monarchy (1820-1823, 1833-1840) involved a crisis of legitimacy. The first genuine participation crisis occurred a distinct third in terms of chronological inception (1836). The first penetration crisis (as distinct from a legitimacy crisis *per se*) occurred at the same time as the first participation crisis, but took six years longer tentatively to resolve. In terms of duration if not of date of initiation, it came fourth. Moreover, a new participation crisis developed in 1854, though legitimacy and identity were not at issue.

Failure to resolve new problems of participation and penetration at length reawakened a legitimacy crisis in 1866-1868. The legitimacy of the new democratic monarchy of 1868 quickly received wide acceptance, but the failure to resolve problems of access and penetration soon led to a renewed legitimacy crisis by 1873.

After 1874 the restored constitutional monarchy was able to establish a tenuous legitimacy, and for long to avoid a serious crisis of participation or penetration. A participation crisis finally occurred in 1917, accompanied by crises of penetration and, for the first time, of distribution. Though the participation crisis was seemingly resolved, it proved more difficult to resolve those of penetration and distribution. This failure was a major factor in the process that led to reopening the issue of legitimacy in 1923.

The legitimacy crisis of 1931 was an outgrowth of that of 1923, which had not been resolved by the intervening Primo de Rivera dictatorship. Yet the new Republican regime soon led to new crises of participation, penetration, and distribution. By 1934 this resulted in a new crisis of legitimacy so profound as to reawaken a basic crisis of identity. That in turn led to the distintegration of the polity within two more years.

This analysis serves to reconfirm the common observation that political systems cannot be overloaded with multiple crises and still function. In the Spanish experience, no polity could handle major crises in more than two—or at most three—categories at a time. Sequence does seem to have been important, for if problems of participation and access had not already been resolved, penetration and/or distribution became much harder, indeed almost impossible, to solve. Once the overload stage was reached, the earlier problems of legitimacy and eventually even identity once more reappeared. Resolution of participation was vital for dealing with penetration problems under the first liberal cycle, but failure to resolve penetration was even more fatal for the handling of distribution problems in a second liberal system.

A brief look at the suggested chronology of Portuguese crisis sequence reveals something of the same pattern, save that the mobilization of the Portuguese polity was so limited that the pattern there seems of less significance. Inception of the modern Portuguese political system in 1820 involved crises of both identity and legitimacy. These were solved by 1834; only after that did crises of participation and penetration emerge. Since the first two problems were in no way at issue, resolution of the two succeeding crises was somewhat easier. In Spain, by comparison, participation became a major problem before legitimacy was resolved, and penetration problems began to pile up as well. This made the first tentative resolution of participation more difficult, whereas the Portuguese polity was able to avoid multiproblem convergence to the same extent, and retained relative stability through the second half of the century. The crisis attending the eventual overthrow of the monarchy involved all four problem areas, though here again the fourth—penetration—while not exactly coming last, was the most protracted.

However, one major kind of crisis, sometimes the most telling of all, that cannot be provided for in a self-contained crisis sequence theory built strictly in terms of a domestic model is the effect of international pressures of war, competition, and colonial involvement. This has perhaps been more influential in modern European polities as a whole than any single common domestic factor, and must always be kept in mind. In Spain it was, in the immediate sense, responsible for both the beginning and the end of the century of constitutional monarchy, the country's classic modern political system.

Conclusion

This analysis suggests that the five-crisis sequence theory tends to a considerable extent to be corroborated by the experience of the modern representative polity in Spain. Though this conclusion might earlier have been surprising to some, it seems in no way extraordinary when one considers that the nominal political structures and goals of modern Spanish affairs have followed a very standard pattern in terms of the civic modernization theories of classic western liberalism. That modern Spanish politics have long been considered unintelligible and "labyrinthine" is because until recently they have not been seriously studied. It is generally assumed outside Spain that the liberal political system there was either a complete failure or a mere caricature. In fact, Spain has lived under liberal parliamentary government longer than any other large European country save Britain and France. The personalist attitudes of Spanish society and culture undoubtedly hindered political functioning, but in view of the overall levels of cultural and economic development, the liberal polity in modern Spain has in proportionate terms functioned about as well and as "naturally" as in other countries.

Modern European nation states—excluding the multinational empires of eastern and central Europe—have tended to function in one of three basic political patterns: a) the traditionalist-evolutionary constitutional monarchies of Britain, Holland, Belgium, and the Scandinavian countries; b) the centralist, post-Napoleonic, semirevolutionary pattern of the constitutional monarchies, and later republics of France, Spain, Italy, and Portugal; and c) the nationalist polities of Central and Eastern Europe, whose development was uniquely conditioned (or more precisely, warped) by extreme pressures of international rivalries and threats. In the case of the latter, the sequence of problems was gravely affected by foreign pressures, so that Prussia/Germany, for example, had to face and resolve penetration before other kinds of crises emerged. The traditionalist-evolutionary polities might evince a pattern that more nearly corresponds to the five-sequence theory, but in their case the time spans and intervals were much greater and have less applicability. The new centralized regimes of southwestern Europe in the nineteenth century form a more useful and appropriate basis for generalizing about the political problems of new states of the mid-twentieth century, few or none of whom have evolutionary structures, and most of whom are less directly beset by nationalist rivalries and pressures than those of Eastern Europe. The southwestern European countries, in short, present the nearest thing to a "classic" model of "normal" political development of modern new representative polities.

Some Related Readings

Most of the work done in modern Spanish history is essentially narrative. There has been comparatively little effort at serious conceptualization and comparative analysis, and the field has been largely ignored by political scientists. Study must begin with general accounts, among which the classic is Raymond Carr's *Spain 1808-1939* (Oxford, 1966). It deals with both political and socio-economic history, and is remarkable for the insight with which available materials are used. A balanced, if very limited and general, treatment will be found in Salvador de Madariaga's *Spain: A Modern History* (New York, 1957). Diego Sevilla Andres' *Historia política de España (1800-1967)* (Madrid, 1968) is uneven but contains much detail and considerable quantitative data.

The best general study of the period in which the modern Spanish polity began is Miguel Artola, *La época de Fernando VII* (Madrid, 1968). J. T. Villarroya, *El sistema político del Estatuto Real* (Madrid, 1968), offers an exhaustive investigation of the initial phase of the Isabeline regime. Its counterpart, Carlism, has never received objective or professional historiographic attention, but see Román Oyarzun, *Historia del carlismo* (Madrid, 1940). The best exposition of the problem of dynastic legitimacy is Jesús Pabón, *La otra legitimidad* (Madrid, 1967). Jose Luis Comellas, currently the most active historian of nineteenth century Spanish politics, has among other works written a study of the central phase of the Isabeline regime, *Los Moderados en el poder (1844-1854)*, (Madrid, 1970). V. G. Kiernan, *The Revolution of 1854 in Spanish History* (Oxford, 1968), is the chief account of that crisis, presented in a narrative context. The best treatment of the last phase of the first liberal cycle is C.A.M. Hennessy's *The Federal Republic in Spain* (Oxford, 1962). The role of the military has been studied in Eric Christiansen, *The Origins of Military Power in Spain, 1800-1854* (Oxford, 1967), and S. G. Payne, *Politics and the Military in Modern Spain* (Stanford, 1967).

The only electoral and party-system study for a major period of modern Spanish politics is Miguel M. Cuadrado's excellent *Elecciones y partidos políticos de España (1868-1931)* (Madrid, 1969), 2 volumes, but see also Juan J. Linz, "The Party System of Spain: Past and Future," in S. M. Lipset and S. Rokkan, eds., *Party Systems and Voter Alignments* (New York, 1967). Detailed narrative accounts of the political history of the restored constitutional monarchy will be found in two major political chronicles by Melchor Fernandez Almagro, *Historia política de la España contemporánea 1868-1902* (Madrid, 1968), 2 volumes, and *Historia del reinado de D. Alfonso XIII* (Barcelona, 1934). Carlos Seco Serrano, *Alfonso XIII y la crisis de la Restauración* (Barcelona, 1969), is especially useful on the problem of access during that period. See also Maximiano Garcia Venero's *Santiago Alba* (Madrid, 1963). The best treatments of the problem of participation and penetration with regard to regionalism will be found in Garcia Venero's *Historia del nacionalismo catalán* (Madrid, 1967), 2 volumes, his *Historia del nacionalismo vasco* (Madrid, 1968), and Jesús Pabón's superb biography of *Cambó* (Barcelona, 1952-1968), 3 volumes.

The best overall history of the second Republic is Ricardo de la Cierva's *Historia de la Guerra civil española*, I, "Antecedentes: Monarquía y República, 1898-1936" (Madrid, 1969). See also Gabriel Jackson, *The Spanish Republic and Civil War 1931-1939* (Princeton, 1965). Special treatment of the political problems of left and right will be found in S. G. Payne, *The Spanish Revolution* (New York, 1970), and R.A.H. Robinson, *The Origins of Franco's Spain* (London, 1970). Edward E. Malefakis, *Agrarian Reform and Peasant Revolution in Spain* (New Haven, 1970), explains one of the major dilemmas of penetration and redistribution under the Second Republic. Javier Tusell *et al. Las elecciones del Frente Popular en España* (Madrid, 1973), 2 volumes, provides the best analysis of the climax of electoral conflict in Spain.

CHAPTER 7

France

DAVID D. BIEN AND RAYMOND GREW

THE QUESTIONS raised by the search for crises of development are in many respects closer to those that preoccupied historians of France in earlier generations than to the ones that evoke the greatest excitement today. Michelet, looking for the roots of French character, or Carlton J. H. Hayes, writing about how the French schooled a nation of patriots, might have readier answers to questions about identity than contemporary historians fascinated by local customs or family structure. Studies of royal officials and the spread of the king's justice have given way, as favorite dissertation topics, to criminality, mendicancy, migrations; penetration is likely to be called social control. Crises of distribution attract more interest in terms of markets, social structure, and climate than government policy; for historians (perhaps especially historians of France) appear to have become less respectful of the autonomy of politics. Often more attention is paid to the social origins of officials than to what they did. The emphasis on local history, on dissidence, on the anonymous people who sustain a culture not taught in schoolrooms, on social structure, on the long-term drifts of demography and economic cycles tends to make politics peripheral. It does not deny the importance of government, but the focus is different. Ministers, parties, cabals, and political debates are less studied today in part because they have been well investigated in the past (and no nation's history has been more richly interpreted than France's) but also because the critical connections that form society are now sought lower on the social scale.

In these terms, the age-old question of the relation between state and society remains, like the standard question (a tradition on examinations) that asks about change and continuity between the *ancien régime* and modern France, well worth asking. Both questions are central to any discussion of the crises of political development in French history. If most recent work has not dealt with them directly,

Crises of Political Development in Europe and the United States
0-691-07598-0/78/000219-51$02.55/1 (cloth)
0-691-02183-X/78/000219-51$02.55/1 (paperback)
For copying information, see copyright page

it has established that the answers will now be more complex and diffuse.

Crises

IDENTITY

Precise measures for detecting a sense of identity in early periods do not exist. Behavior as the test is ambiguous. What, for example, does rebellion signify: resistance to the wider identity (whether by medieval Burgundians or today's French in Montreal), or so strong a national identity that a group's visible representatives are required to embrace it? The behavior itself will never tell us. And especially when we move back to the day when most rebels could not write, how can one tell about motives and ideals? Indirect evidence and some sympathetic supposing may help.

Everywhere in Europe in the middle ages the two most evident realities to men were at first what was very local and knowable, within a day's walk, and what was universal. Marc Bloch once noted that strangers who appeared in the local community were likely to be wanderers, persons on pilgrimmages, or traveling emissaries of the universal church. Between them and the familiar faces of neighbors at the local market, however, agents or travelers from units later thought to be basic—from the province or nation state—were seldom seen. Until the later twelfth century the popular tales (for example, the Charlemagne legend from the *Song of Roland*) glorified warriors who represented the tribe or the universal religious culture rather than what was specifically or exclusively French.

From the late twelfth century to the end of the middle ages, the broad sense of a French identity surely grew, but the landmarks are few. Perhaps Joan of Arc evoked and crystalized a developing popular awareness of French identity against the English. A common language no doubt facilitates the absorption and cultural assimilation of the peripheral areas and provinces that had their own traditions and dialects. By contrast to England, this absorption was slow. In France provincial loyalties and institutions had time to harden into local habit before the provinces were taken over by the crown whose power grew slowly out of the Paris region. In England an imported and therefore more uniform feudalism that had kept the king visible at the center, favored the earlier growth of centralized state power and had the effect of uniting Englishmen from various regions or making them aware of one another through their common fear of rough intrusion on fief and property. But in France, where counts of Toulouse, for example, did not see a French king for a period of 150 years, local institutions and attitudes grew naturally into diverse cultures. The growth of national culture, slower and later in France than in England, seems nonetheless steady and impressive by contrast to other regions of Europe.

For the literate the sense of a unifying and cosmopolitan culture grew more rapidly in the sixteenth and seventeenth centuries, when secondary schools (*collèges*) proliferated. The new education did not at first stress a specifically French formation or teach about the French past, but the literary formalism and related skills in expression that it fostered made possible the growth of a whole historical literature. The rising frequency of complaints that students learned more about ancient Rome than they did about their own more immediate past reflected a broad awareness of the importance of national community for the elite. Increasingly the rapidly growing body of venal office owners and holders, usually trained in law, lined their bookshelves with works on French history. Law codifications, even when they spoke of Roman law and admired its method and unity, stressed the substance of general French practice and experience. At the popular level the evidence from pedlars' literature is that already by the seventeenth century the historical tales and myths that circulated rested heavily on the anachronistic view that Charlemagne was a Frenchman.

What seems clear, then, is that the growth of French national consciousness was steady and unmarked by the kind of crises of doubt and assertion that Germany, for example, experienced later. If there was a crisis of national identity with lasting significance in France, it would no doubt be located in the sixteenth century. For it was then that localism and feudal magnates, in league with religious universalism, whether Catholic or Calvinist, looked outside France for military aid and for spiritual community and brotherhood. In many regions a majority of the nobles and others wondered whether they in fact shared more with the Spanish, Italians, Dutch, Swiss, or English than they did with other Frenchmen who would obey a "heretic" king. The consequences—civil war over religion—tore France apart for decades late in the century, and the issues that would lead some to call for foreign intervention, mainly Spanish, persisted through nearly half the seventeenth century. The perceived effect of civil war was heightened in the minds of Frenchmen who would impute to religious division and supra-French definitions of community the troubles that in fact came also at the time from a severe Malthusian crisis. Against this background the romantic and heroic figure of a Henri IV, surrounded and encouraged by a brain-trust of *politiques*, seemed to have saved France. In so doing they convinced subsequent generations that only a secular and independent national state was safe. Social and political peace seemed to require that one be French above all, French before being Catholic or Protestant. The memories persisted. Favoring an independent Gallican church and revoking the Edict of Nantes that had given Calvinists toleration made perfectly good sense to even quite secularist administrators who increasingly distrusted religious enthusiasm and sects at the end of the seventeenth century. If the awareness of being French was not new in the sixteenth century, it received then a powerful reinforcement through specific events, and was raised to the level of conscious and continuing concern.

With the seventeenth century the culture of *collèges* and salons expressed itself in an outpouring of literature that generated in France a persisting national pride. National identity and pride, however, if important for practical reasons, were mixed with universalist assumptions. The dominating cultural notions were Cartesian, and in all areas of thought men borrowed from science and mathematics the idea that diversity and appearance are deceiving and that a basic quantitative uniformity always underlies seeming difference. The large elite educated in *collèges* absorbed a religious and classical culture in which the best the ancient world had to offer mingled easily with the highly creative works of French literature. The new Académie Française attempted to establish rules and to codify a language that seemed appropriate for expressing the universal truths of human psychology and behavior. French cultural supremacy came from the superior expression of truths that were everywhere and always the same. Racine, Molière, La Fontaine, and the rest wrote for all time. Later Voltaire would express a general pride among Frenchmen who believed that the association of growing political and military strength with high intellectual achievement properly made Louis XIV's France the school for humanity.

The eighteenth-century French Enlightenment was more humble in its assumptions. Chastened by what seemed the disasters of the wars at mid-century, and inclined to seek moral explanations for the failures, the French turned to a close and obsessive examination of foreign models. Sometimes the examination reflected xenophobic tendencies:

these fed the hostility to Jesuits, seen as nonnational and part of a threatening international conspiracy emanating from Rome. The Jesuits were expelled in the 1760s by magistrates who felt themselves heirs to the national traditions of a Gallican church that was specifically French in customs and values. England, Prussia, Poland, and America were especially interesting to Frenchmen, the more so within the current of new ideas that stressed the environmental formation of man. Human nature was now thought less rigid, fixed, corpuscular, universal; it was malleable. Men and their *moeurs* would vary according to time and place. The character and habits of Frenchmen might be changed if institutions were made over, or perhaps the distinctive local habits shaped over centuries of history would be persisting and unyielding. Montesquieu held for history and the environmental formation of a special national character—it took him no more than a page in the *Esprit des lois* to dispose of the state of nature and the innate qualities imputed by Hobbes to man in general. Others felt less secure with history, but still expressed outrage in the 1770s when the minister of war, Saint-Germain, introduced for soldiers the "Prussian" discipline of beating with the flat of the sword. It was argued that such punishment suited only foreign despotisms and did not fit, could even destroy, the French national character. But whatever the way of arguing the point, in the eighteenth century a distinctive national identity became an object for explicit analysis and comparison within the broader spectrum of varying national types.

With the growing sense of a unique national identity, even the nation's boundaries came to be seen as "natural" by the nineteenth century. The conquests lost with Napoleon's defeat, even the second reduction in French territory after Waterloo, produced little anguish among Frenchmen. The new departments spread across Europe had not been really French; they had been annexed to France but not, after all, identified with *la patrie*. Neither the possibility of annexing Belgium in 1830 nor the nationalistic visions of extending France's frontier to the Rhine that tempted Napoleon III ever won extensive support. Nor for that matter was there much irredentist fervor in the annexation of Nice and Savoy. Alsace and Lorraine, on the other hand, were considered an intrinsic part of France; and their loss in 1870 remained an unquenchably bitter theme of French politics until they were regained in 1918. Modern Frenchmen have enjoyed a comparable confidence about their culture. Intellectuals might argue about how that culture compared to others or about the perdurable qualities of French character; but unlike the nationalists of most countries, they never had to meet charges that their culture was either an ancient memory or a recent invention without autonomous vitality. Furthermore, the boundaries of the French state, of French culture, and of French speech (at least among the educated) have been so nearly coterminous as to create little of the conflict over identity that plagued the national movements of Eastern Europe. Territorial and cultural identity has not been effectively challenged either by regional divisions, however important, or local dialects, however current.

Long associated with the state, French national identity was a source of strength in the *ancien régime*; but with the French Revolution the reciprocal claims of identity became the basis of the most effective political and social mobilization European government had yet achieved. Ceremonies and symbols of song and flag and costume sought to invoke in each Frenchman a sense of obligation and personal pride. The needs of the nation justified sacrifice and discipline, tested civic virtue, defined one's enemies. The nation itself was thus the nexus of all social obligations, the source of that equality that conceived of each individual as citizen. The nation's integrity required the elimination of institutions and orders intervening between citizen and state, just as it implied obeissance to the voice of the people.

In this way the sense of national identity became the core of a political ideology that, at the height of revolutionary fervor, excluded aristocrats, nonjuring priests, and "reactionaries"; such opponents were considered as foreign as opposing armies. Indeed one became French through conviction as much as by birth; Thomas Paine and Jeremy Bentham were *citoyens*. The confluence of national and ideological identity, unique to France and the United States in the early nineteenth century, remained to a large degree even after revolutionary ardor cooled and after the compromises of Directory and Empire. Thus political identity in France since the Revolution needs to be discussed on two levels, one traditional and implicit (reflecting a sense of shared destiny, of common language, culture, and national interest) and one more demanding, ideological, and explicit.

This older national identity never lost its political vitality. It was part of the strength of Napoleonic *gloire* (with which both Louis Philippe and Louis Napoleon later sought to associate themselves), underlay the universal commitment to paying off the indemnities of defeat and to removing foreign troops from French soil in 1815-1818 and 1870-1873. Reinvoked in the "*union sacrée*" of World War

I, it has proved its durability in modern Gaullism. With the common belief that France has some peculiar historical mission to fulfill (clearly reflected of course in the justifications of imperialism), this traditional identity easily shades into the ideological one that since the Revolution has generally been associated with the democratic left: the victories of revolutionary armies and the nearly total mobilization sought under the Reign of Terror, the return to the tricolor and the national guard in 1830, the fiery patriotism of Gambetta and the Paris Commune arising out of the siege of Paris, the initial appeal of General Boulanger, and the frequent calls to rally to the Third Republic from the 1880s to the Popular Front of 1939—an association revitalized in the resistance movements of World War II and reflected in the postwar need to establish that the Vichy regime was not truly French.

Conservatives found the need for an explicit political ideology in itself less congenial. The Bourbon restoration tried to associate Catholicism and aristocracy with the monarchy, but the White Terror was hardly a broadly popular movement. The church slowly learned to maintain some distance from political lost causes. While reinstating themselves as central to many established institutions and in local society, members of the aristocracy found it difficult to transmute influence into political power. Count Gobineau's historical justification of the aristocracy in his *Essai sur l'inégalité des races humaines* was more widely read and admired in Prussian barracks than in France. On the one hand, traditional identity was clear and strong enough not to require misty racial definitions which, on the other, were inadequate to sustain a political ideology. When the Count of Chambord insisted on returning to the white flag of the Bourbons, that symbol of an alternative ideological identity proved fatal to a monarchical restoration in the 1870s. Still, the effort to evolve a conservative ideology of identity to compete with that inherited from the Revolution continued. Seen in this light, the Dreyfus Affair was the major effort of the century to mobilize the French in the name of an ideological identity that defined the Revolution itself as fundamentally alien—like Jews or petty-bourgeois, professional (and corrupt) politicians. The claim that France's true identity was rural, racial, aristocratic, and Catholic was defeated—but barely. Conservatives and aristocrats lost out in France (as in Italy) in their effort to capture power through modern mass politics at about the same time that they reasserted their dominance in Great Britain and Germany. The alternative ideological identity they offered was never without supporters, however; and it was strengthened by the excesses and the weaknesses of the Republic and then by fears of socialism and communism. Promulgated from many a pulpit, by the *Action Française*, and by the right-wing leagues of the 1930s, it became official in the France of Vichy.

A strong traditional identity has, usually, helped pull the French together—one reason that the moderate regimes of the July Monarchy, the Second Empire, the Third and Fifth Republics have so frequently sought to invoke it. De Gaulle's Fifth Republic, like the Third, proved to be the regime that divided Frenchmen least. External danger can also call into play this traditional identity. The effect is different, however, when issues of foreign policy resonate strongly with the conflicting ideological identities,[1] for then they may weaken the regime itself as happened with the Italian policy of Napoleon III, the Spanish Civil War and the relations with the Soviet Union in the 1930s, the Cold War, and policy in Indochina and Algeria after World War II.[2] Traditional identity has similarly shown its strength in French schooling. *Instituteurs* and priests in the nineteenth century, even while locked in combat, promulgated an almost identical curriculum connecting French and classical culture and jointly condemning regional dialects as the mispronunciation of the ignorant. As an instrument of ideological identity, however, education became a socially divisive issue.

Since ideas tend to be universal as places are not, ideological identities underscore the element of universality in French patriotism and encourage a tendency to accept as essentially French anyone who speaks the language properly and holds the right values. Such attitudes have helped France absorb more immigrants than any other European nation, have favored doctrines of imperialism that were assimilationist, and helped sustain relations with former colonial peoples after their independence. On the other hand, ideological conflicts, when associated with something so fundamental as identity, tend to intolerance. Opponents are almost by definition potential traitors. Nor

[1] Despite the insistence by many that Algeria was an integral part of France, the crisis over Algeria raised few problems for the mainland French about the definition of who was French, while dividing them deeply over what it should mean to be French.

[2] Note Jean-Baptiste Duroselle's concept of "introversive goals" in Stanley Hoffman *et al.*, *In Search of France* (New York, 1965), p. 306. Richard F. Hamilton, *Affluence and the French Worker in the Fourth Republic* (Princeton, 1967), pp. 53-67, finds that French workers in the 1960s differed from other groups in attitudes toward politics and government more than in attitudes toward foreign policy or domestic welfare.

does there seem to be any escape from such divisiveness. Identity remains the most fundamental and durable base for mobilizing mass political support and extracting resources for governmental use. Historically, France was a pioneer in the discovery that this was so, in large part because her own national identity was so little disputed. The revolution that sought to expand patriotism so as to transform an entire nation into a community of shared belief thus introduced a second stage in the political use of identity. Ideological identity in turn opened a conflict never wholly resolved.

LEGITIMACY

Every society surely believes that some authority is legitimate, but that authority need not have been the central state, which is what concerns us here.

In the middle ages two sometimes inconsistent sets of ideas—the feudal and the Christian—combined to build and to strengthen the institution of kingship around which the state developed. At first glance this is surprising: feudalism would seem to have worked against assigning legitimacy to a unified state, and only local and visible authority could be effective. In France, where feudal decentralization of authority in the ninth and tenth centuries was more complete than elsewhere, the idea of kingship for a time persisted only through hearsay and romantic legend, in the popular stories that circulated about Roland and Charlemagne, and (in the south) also in the law that was Roman. The feudal experience in the regions that became France built attitudes that, without entirely denying him his place, would slow and limit the king in his later attempts at consolidation. To succeed at all, the king had to seem just, a defender of law, a protector. If he did not, he ran into a resistance that based itself on custom, contract, and a new view of the vassal's fief that contemporaries mistakenly thought was very old. In the ninth and tenth centuries the fief had been transformed: once the property of the feudal lord who might give it or take it back as he wished, it fell to the patrimony of the vassal and became hereditary. Giving the fief to the vassal's son, at first only a convenience, quickly became custom and thus law in a nonliterate society where law was no more than what men saw and could remember having been done. By the eleventh century, the practice repeated several times, the vassal began to think he owned the fief his ancestors had merely held as a temporary grant. Although vassals clearly owed some services and money to their lords, they had generally been specifying and cutting down the once unlimited obligations whose original justification was lost. As the higher, conferring authority lost full control of the fief, however, there was a grave problem for the state—the fief was much more than land; it was also local control and legal jurisdiction over men, a part of what the Romans and we would define as public authority. Now, if the fief belonged to the vassal, a king who wished to consolidate and extend authority was quickly in trouble. Any attempt to unite legal jurisdiction and powers in his own hands seemed an attack on the fief, and thus on the property of vassals everywhere. Only a very slow change in habits, and not impulsive action that would stir general resistance, could strengthen kings.

But if feudalism limited kings, it also made them legitimate and secure when they did not violate the ideal too conspicuously. However different may have been the reality, the feudal lord was legitimate and entitled to his place and his vassals' support when he respected their expanded rights, property, and jurisdiction. The ideal feudal leader was a hero—generous, but brave, strong, tough; above all he defended the law, but a law that guaranteed his own rights (including the feudal payments owing to him), no less than those of his vassals. These qualities of the good feudal leader were of course easily transferrable to the king.

In this view, then, an authority, even a central authority, was legitimate and necessary, for when working well and correctly it acted to preserve law and the rights of all. The vision of the king as supreme feudal overlord was the logical extension to a broader territorial scale of feudalism itself. But since the rights of vassals, great and small, filled most of the area we call public, a basis for continuing conflict was assured from the time when the idea and machinery of kingship began to expand. Kings, like lords everywhere, should live mainly on their own. Their place, their moral and legal authority, were assured and proper, but steady growth in their power was not proper. Their frequent demand for feudal dues, or for irregular payments that made often enough might become taxation, seemed an unwarranted attack on the legal principle of property and local or personal ownership of public functions. It is perhaps no accident that during the twelfth century the view of kings that feudal lords enjoyed hearing about in the literature shifted. When at the end of the century Philip Augustus became the first king to show serious centralizing intent over a wide area, the lay elite began to take comfort or find amusement in the romantic tales that portrayed the king as cuckold; they lost interest in the earlier heroic vision of the warrior-leader that infused the *Song of Roland*. For all that, a feudal king, if prudent and unaggressive, was fully legitimate.

The second line of legitimacy derived from Christianity. Our attention to the struggle between the ecclesiastical and the secular powers in the middle ages sometimes misleads us. The term secular must not be used anachronistically. If the medieval state operated in the world, it did so as one of the competing jurisdictions within the broad and overarching framework of Christian society. Opposed sometimes to the church, the state was nonetheless itself fully Christian. In France, although kings never claimed the power to distribute grace by administering the sacraments, they did take on a supernatural air as legends grew about the miraculously curative power of the king's touch. The church's officials had rare skills—they could read and write—and the secular royal state relied heavily on them for advice and administration. When later, at the end of the thirteenth century and subsequently, French kings came into conflict with the church, sometimes at home but more frequently at Rome, independence for the secular authority did not mean secularism in the sense in which we have understood that term since the eighteenth century; it had to mean instead an increasing reliance on the argument and theory of divine right. With independence from the church, the king's personal and direct link to God was seen as closer. Christian purpose and rhetoric were essential to the legitimacy of king and state.

The Christian component of legitimacy grew steadily in the middle ages. Early feudal society believed in law, an unchanging and rigid law of custom, but in that society conflict was endemic and brutal. As we saw, law existed only in the minds and memories of the illiterate elite, and memory is of course flexible, deceiving, sometimes self-serving. The impossibility of verifying by written evidence what was the law gave rise to ambiguities and uncertainties over who had what rights and obligations, and then to habits in which the frequent exercise of violence seemed normal. By the twelfth and thirteenth centuries, however, standards for behavior were changing, and churchmen advanced ideas of Christian peace and God's higher law. This law, broader and more universal, was more easily embodied in a king than in a local authority. The figure of Louis IX—St. Louis—was central to the process by which Christian prestige and the expectations of the faithful came to be centered on the king. If, like others, he used the feudal contract and royal claims to be theoretical feudal overlord of all, he did so to enforce broader, suprafeudal ideas of Christian peace. A saint on the throne was difficult to resist, and his memory, together with that of Henri IV, was the one that came to mind most readily to Frenchmen when they counted their favorite kings, at least until late nineteenth-century positivist secularism dulled the image.

In the sixteenth century the civil wars of religion tested and strained both feudalism and Christianity as sources of legitimacy. Internationalist Protestants and Catholics, reviving feudal forces based in the provinces, burned and tore the country.

In the seventeenth century, the grounds for legitimacy began to shift. If the trappings of the "Most Christian Monarch" and feudal formalism remained, the argument from utility became more important. Louis XIV expelled Huguenots and crushed deviant Catholic tendencies, but when he did so, contemporaries began to think that these actions had less to do with religious truth and the salvation of Christians than the felt need to protect society from political and social subversion. In their view, only potential rebels would make a fuss over small points of theology—any peaceful person could be an orthodox Catholic without difficulty. Insistence on sectarian differences must have reflected other than religious concerns. And just as God was receding from the new mechanical universe, the king also became distant, closed up in Versailles at the same moment when his agents were becoming more numerous, active, and powerful. Authority through persuasion and friendship and popularity, the style of Henri IV who had been the colleague and companion of nobles, survived only in the nostalgia felt by men who in fact were looking for something else. The popularity of Thomas Hobbes' writings among literate Frenchmen reflected a wider sense that concentration of power was needed. Civil wars, frequent popular rebellions, the Fronde, and new ideas about nature worked together to make order an overriding concern. Even the heirs to the feudal classes turned to new principles of unnegotiated obedience and did not seem to worry when the central state expanded its military force tenfold. As subject replaced vassal in the political understanding, the test for legitimate authority shifted to effectiveness in the use of power to quiet and control unruly and dangerous human nature.

In the Enlightenment the secularism that appeared in seventeenth-century thinking remained, but there were some important changes. The police function of the warfare state was still there, even expanded, and contemporaries did not find it odd when regiments of the army put down grain riots or when the rural mounted police gathered in and jailed vagabonds. But the exclusively gloomy picture of man in the seventeenth century began to fade when rebellion and civil war were no longer current events. Seen most clearly in the writings left by theorists, the new views were expressed also in routine statement and action by many others who were administrators, judges, lawyers, army officers, even churchmen. Bad men, men raised the wrong way, might need to be controlled, but another generation might be conditioned into sociability, virtue and happiness. The state would have to play a growing role in society, and it would be held responsible for forming men and for their condition. Plans and proposals proliferated; some thought, for example, that the state might take over "useless" Benedictine monasteries to make of them schools where peasants, under the right conditions of temperature and humidity, would learn to work harder, to be more productive, and to be trained into happiness through limiting their desires and learning hatred for cities and luxury. Sparta more than Athens was the model. But however one argued, whatever the program, the debate about men and society that was opened took place in terms that supposed a central and formative role for a state that should fix the environment. On all sides, by the eighteenth century the state itself seemed more than legitimate; its absence was almost unthinkable.

The state, then became steadily more essential, its legitimacy as a force unquestioned. But with the change in its role, the state's particular form turned into a matter for active, even passionate, concern. Some kinds of state, it was thought, were more useful and therefore more legitimate than others. The choice of regime was critical, for that was what would determine how society was shaped. After 1789, the state lived on; its monarchical form seemed illegitimate and had to go. If no one before the Revolution had actually planned to replace the monarchy, Montesquieu's and Rousseau's writings were only part of a long discussion over the relation between a government's forms and the specific and varying moral values and habits to which it was thought to give rise. Under the broad cover of the French Enlightenment's assumptions, many programs and views of society could be and were derived. Some presumed only a small change of initiating ideas within existing forms, and others were more radical. But for all, the very shape of society and morality seemed to depend on the nature of the government and regime. Perhaps the Enlightenment did not *cause* the Revolution, but it provided the broad ideas within which changes from absolute monarchy to constitutional monarchy, then republic, and finally empire could take place, matter, and become tied to more bitter struggles. The eighteenth and nineteenth centuries look much alike in their common tendency to link the varying shape of values and habits to the specific regime, to the particular objects for emulation it dignified. The Enlightenment's approach affected even those who were later called Romantics, Liberals, Conservatives, and so on. The ideas and conflicts of the eighteenth century lived on, then, into the nineteenth and twentieth, turning practical questions of political organization into broader issues of morality and the good society. From 1789 no single regime would or could seem legitimate to all Frenchmen.

In this sense, then, the Revolution crystallized not a single ideology, but an approach, from the Enlightenment. Shifting forms of government and regimes were linked in men's minds to their likely success in maintaining not only order, but liberty and virtue. The fall of the monarchy, and even more the public execution of Louis XVI, of course shocked the king's subjects, but they made very clear that the range of alternatives in government was dramatically broadened. Inheritance and custom as the basis for legitimacy gave way to measures and tests that were immediate and visible in the behavior of men. And every order, to be legitimate, had now to acknowledge the demands for participation in government and its decisions by some or many citizens. The welfare of citizens—moral and intellectual no less than physical—was too important to be left to priests alone and provided an additional test of a government's legitimacy. In these terms uncertainty over what welfare and morality meant would henceforth be a source of instability for governments, if not the state.

Legitimacy was a preoccupation of Napoleonic rule, and the emperor characteristically sought to make use of every prop to legitimacy then available. Without abandoning his claim to be the heir of the revolution, he used an imperial title, family marriages with established royalty, and peace with the church to add those more traditional supports of legitimacy, as well. Utility, now measured in the more demanding terms of "revolutionary" or "modern" efficiency, was his strongest claim, however, and that was undermined by the military defeats of 1814-1815 and the victors' preference for monarchy. Although the legitimacy of Valois and Bourbon kings had survived wars lost, that of the Bonaparte "usurper" did not. The basis of legitimacy itself had shifted, and military defeat, taken as the clearest measure, of some larger moral and practical failure, would prove fatal to other regimes in 1870, 1940, 1945, and 1958.

Restorations, almost by definition, base their legitimacy more on claims to historic continuity than on abstract values; and the Bourbon restoration of 1815 sought to renew the magic of royalty and to tie throne to altar, efforts neatly symbolized in the elaborate coronation of Charles X in 1824. Not unlike Napoleon, however, the Bourbons recognized other tests of legitimacy. Although they did what they could to restore the aristocracy as a prop to monarchy, even the most reactionary could hardly imagine a restoration of feudal reciprocity. Instead, they accepted the revolutionary substitute of a constitutional contract to guarantee against the abuse of power and admitted the principle of participation, however limited. From the Bourbons to this day every French government has based its legitimacy on a series of explicit claims not always easily reconciled: continuity and formal legality, a constitution duly adopted, the participation of citizens, and general efficacy, taken to include both general competence in managing a highly centralized state and an ability to meet the major challenges facing it. From the Bourbons to this day every French government has seen its legitimacy challenged on one or more of these grounds. Legitimacy, however, like virtue, is increasingly subject to debate and denial, the more explicitly it is defined.

Two characteristics of modern French politics follow. First, a significant segment of French public life has actively denied the legitimacy of each regime. So commonplace did such rejection become that it ceased in itself to be revolutionary. Thus familiarity has had an effect like tolerance, often allowing even fundamental opponents to maintain some peripheral contact with the political system. At the same time, issues of conflict that might be resolved or subject to compromise within the system are likely instead to be raised as a challenge to the regime itself. Second, each new regime, aware of its shaky legitimacy, stresses as much as it can its continuity with its predecessors in law, institutions, and even personnel. This has had a paradoxical effect. It has reinforced the remarkable continuity across eight regimes in 160 years. The Bourbons kept much of the Napoleonic system of government; Louis Philippe was declared king of the French by a rump of the parliament elected under Charles X; the Second Republic was ratified in a parliament elected under Louis Philippe; Louis Napoleon was elected under the constitution of the Second Republic; the

Third Republic was quietly born out of the acephalous monarchy established in 1871; Marshal Pétain was elected by deputies of the Third Republic (which the Free French also claimed to represent), much as Charles De Gaulle was chosen by those of the Fourth. Ironically, this concern for legality reinforces the durable prestige and legitimacy of the state, while exposing the fragile legitimacy of the regime. Identity and legitimacy, which thoroughly overlapped in the old regime, have been more separate since the Revolution, with traditional identity also strengthening the state's legitimacy rather than the regime's. This separation has allowed aristocrats, Bonapartists, republicans, army officers, even bishops and socialists to serve the legitimate state while intransigently and publicly opposing the regime. It has relieved such fundamental opponents of the need to be very specific about their own positive programs and has allowed regimes in France to fall almost as quietly as cabinets that lost an election.

Formal legality and institutional continuity have thus not proved sufficient supports of legitimacy in times of crisis. Neither have constitutions, although every regime since 1792 has seen the need to have one (and the Fourth Republic was seriously weakened from its start by the narrow vote in favor of its revised constitution). Especially at their beginning, many regimes have in fact violated their fundamental laws (as did Louis Napoleon, republicans battling Boulanger, or Charles De Gaulle),[3] but it is important to the history of French liberty that most regimes have not dared such presumption for long but come—like the liberal empire, the defenders of the republic during the Dreyfus affair, and De Gaulle's successors—to treat their constitutions seriously. The charge that participation was unjustly restricted proved fatal to legitimacy in 1830 and 1848, and was then used by Louis Napoleon in burying the Second Republic. Since adoption of universal male suffrage in 1848 and the acceptance of its will in 1875-1876, that much formal democracy has remained essential to legitimacy. There is also the test of efficacy. The very legitimacy of the state provided a basis for denying the legitimacy of any regime believed to serve it badly. Political corruption (the Wilson scandal of 1887, the Panama scandal of 1892, or the Stavisky scandal of 1934), treachery or injustice as in the Dreyfus case, the economic and foreign policies of the Popular Front, the colonial disasters and instability of the Fourth Republic quickly became questions of regime. Finally, cen-

[3] Roy C. Macridis and Bernard E. Brown, *Supplement to the De Gaulle Republic* (Homewood, 1963), pp. 44-45.

tralization, which reflects the strong legitimacy of the state, has been balanced by tacit limitations on what the state can do.[4] Republican attacks on the army or the church, threats by the Popular Front to the interests of business and the banks, even affronts to wine growers or Bretons, can immediately raise threats to legitimacy—what Crozier has called the practice of a kind of blackmail.[5]

The government's legitimacy can be attacked from so many directions because, since the Revolution, it has been conceived in so many ways. For all his cynicism, Talleyrand recognized the irreversible change that had occurred as he argued at the Congress of Vienna for a narrowed interpretation that made legitimacy rest primarily on historical continuity and popular acceptance. The *doctrinaires* followed a similar line of reasoning, extending it to require representative government; but if a government's legitimacy rests on its electorate, democrats argued, an electorate of all the people would provide the fullest legitimacy. From these views of legitimacy come France's early adoption of universal suffrage and emphasis upon legal form. A second approach emphasizes traditional authority and social custom. Like good men of the Enlightenment, de Maistre and de Bonald assessed a government according to the moral coherence and stable order of the society it governed. Too rigid to win broad support, their ideas were echoed in visions of a Christian commonwealth that many French Catholics refused to abandon even after Leo XIII (with a pragmatism like Talleyrand's) recognized the legitimacy of the Third Republic. This emphasis is related, however, to the acceptance of a hierarchy and authority within the French state no longer found in French society. Finally, radicals, too, have judged politics in moral terms, insisting that political legitimacy requires social justice. If no French regime has quite accepted that test (the constitutions of the Fourth and Fifth Republics make notable bows in that direction), the principle has justified resistance to bourgeois government while pushing it to accept ever broader social responsibilities.

Each of these concerns—continuity and popular acceptance, authority, and social justice—leads to statements of principle that political reality can hardly match. Each can justify the rejection of any regime's legitimacy; yet something of each is necessary to sustain legitimacy at all. The importance of ideology in French politics has thus not been a mere peculiarity of Gallic rationalism but a very practical matter. So

[4] Hoffmann, *In Search of France*, p. 12 and *passim*.
[5] Michel Crozier, *The Bureaucratic Phenomenon* (Chicago, 1964), pp. 258-59.

have the myths and symbols in which each regime wraps itself, even though they evoke the ideological identities that divide Frenchmen. The "revolutionary tradition" that has bemused so many English commentators on French instability is thus an effort to establish the legitimacy that can sustain stability.[6] Republicans marching to the Hotel de Ville, Bonapartists hailing plebiscites, monarchists and Catholics building Sacré Coeur, and socialists mourning the Commune were all staking their claims to legitimacy.[7] Nor is this mere wishful thinking on their part. If modern France has experienced a remarkable number of crises of legitimacy, it has turned back many more. When such challenges are effectively met, succeeding governments—whether led by Waldeck-Rousseau, Clemenceau, Blum, or Gaullists after De Gaulle—often enjoy brief periods of unusual strength.

On the whole, the persistent problem of legitimacy that underlies much of the divisiveness and instability of politics in modern France has also contributed to the striking continuity noted with pleasure, despair, or a slight sneer by astute observers, from de Tocqueville and Michelet to contemporaries: "Behind a constantly changing facade of feudalism, absolutism, constitutional monarchy, empires, and a whole series of republics, the great institutions and corporations of this state—and the state itself—have remained essentially the same."[8]

PENETRATION

Given the historical literature, this problem needs recasting. If older ideas about man in a state of nature—either aggressive or virtuously cooperative, Hobbesian, or Rousseauistic—seem today naive, they nonetheless have conditioned a good deal of the writing. This is especially true of the Hobbesian view. The assumption that self-interested man is naturally in conflict with his fellows, disorderly, and "anarchic," has always fitted neatly with the view that the expansion of the central state saved him from destructive feudalism and localism. The march of history has been from disorder toward acceptance of authority, toward "pacification" of unruly and uncontrolled men who, left alone, would and did tear one another apart. The growth of the state is matched only by the rise of the ubiquitous bourgeoisie as the

[6] G. Lowes Dickinson, *Revolution and Reaction in Modern France* (London, 1892); Lord Elton, *The Revolutionary Idea in France, 1789-1871* (London, 1923); John Plamenatz, *The Revolutionary Movement in France, 1815-71* (London, 1952); E. L. Woodward, *French Revolutions* (Oxford, 1934).

[7] See J. Lucas-Dubreton, *Le culte de Napoléon, 1815-1848* (Paris, 1960).

[8] Herbert Leuthy, *France against Herself* (New York, 1957), p. 15.

thematic staple for textbooks covering any century from the tenth to the twentieth. For us, however, the Hobbesian assumption can only be misleading. What we call penetration is in fact less the imposition of new authority over unruly man than the shift to the central state of functions of governance previously exercised elsewhere. Some of the forms of social control once located in family, tribe, church, seigneury, feudal relationships, or local and provincial states gradually and increasingly became the responsibility of the centralized national state. Thus, it is not authority and the breaking to civilized habits of innately aggressive man, but the simple location of authority that is here at issue. Widely diffused changes in habit and receptivity made penetration possible, but those had to do with where men would look for social norms and from where they would expect actual power to emanate.

For France, as for other medieval societies, the process began in a concentration of legal jurisdiction, followed only later by the building of an enforcing power. The first monopoly that the king and the state sought was in justice. To attain it the king encouraged appeals from feudal, seigneurial, and church courts to royal ones. The practice grew rapidly in the thirteenth century and continued thereafter. Basing itself on something like the general welfare clause in the American constitution, royal authority steadily expanded the number and kind of cases that it would define as public and secular and, thus, within its jurisdiction. By the eighteenth century the royal secular courts were routinely intervening in matters concerning the administration of sacraments and the teaching of theology on the grounds that they involved the property and status of individuals or the public security. To enforce the decisions of magistrates and to keep the peace, a central machinery of bureaucratic and police control did grow, more rapidly in France than in England, but very slowly. As late as the eighteenth century even substantial cities were likely to have only a handful of ill-equipped and ill-trained part-time policemen, and at the Revolution the whole vast countryside in France was patrolled by no more than two to three thousand members of the *maréchaussée*, or rural mounted police.

Significant changes in the degree of penetration by the central state did come in the seventeenth century, however—changes so considerable that we can speak of a crisis of penetration at that time. Its measures lie principally in the areas of military organization and taxation. The army expanded ten times over during the century, and its character changed. It became not only large but permanent, requiring barracks scattered in provincial cities and fortifications in frontier provinces. Aimed outward, it brought many years of almost continuous war; but aimed inward, the new, more professional army, better disciplined and more isolated from the civilian population, could be used to play the role of riot police to control collective, if not individual, violence.

The army was expensive, and to support it dramatic changes in taxation occurred simultaneously. Regular taxation developed only very slowly during the fourteenth and fifteenth centuries, and the yield from the land tax (*taille*) seems even to have diminished in real terms in the first half of the sixteenth century. Badly collected by the king during the civil wars, especially in regions that went over to Calvinism,[9] its weight grew heavier everywhere only in the seventeenth century. Across the ministry of Richelieu, whose mercantilist ideas also required for their implementation an expensive navy, the land tax leaped from a little more than 15 million livres under Henri IV to 55 million in Mazarin's day. This growing burden rested on a peasant population suffering the effects of population growth, the attendant rapid inflation of the bread price, and a sharp decline in real wages. For the lower orders, famine was frequent, debilitating disease endemic. Under Richelieu the frequency of local rebellions rose, and in them peasants and artisans joined local notables, often nobles, concerned to defend local rights and their own jurisdictions. Whatever differences of status and interest divided the participants, they agreed in upholding violently a partial truth: the growing burden of the state, and the tax collector as its agent and symbol, was the source of all their ills. "Vive le roi sans gabelle," was nearly everywhere the saying. The crisis of penetration was reflected in local violence and the Fronde until after the middle of the century.

Out of the crisis came several responses. The army continued to grow in size exponentially, and it developed large supporting civilian services. Local charges to pay for maintaining barracks and fortresses in the outlying, frontier regions had the effect now of equalizing somewhat the heavy financial burden by extending it to peripheral provinces where awareness of the central state rose. The bureaucracy expanded in numbers and, far more important, its attitudes, habits, and capacity

[9] Those regions, it is true, had then to pay substantial sums to Calvinist magnates, and popular habits of paying almost certainly did not diminish. See Martin Wolfe, *The Fiscal System of Renaissance France* (New Haven, 1972).

for work changed dramatically. Recruited from the Royal Council were intendants, once only roving investigators on commission, now placed permanently in the provinces where they in turn recruited their own agents (subdelegates) into a growing administrative network. One could measure quantitatively the change from about the 1670s on, by noting the roughly tenfold rise over the next century in the number of cartons per decade that the departmental archives house in the series for administrative correspondence on almost any subject. There was a veritable bureaucratic "takeoff." Municipal finance, affairs of Protestants, assessment of the *taille*, rural or urban unrest, the grain supply, militia, forage for the army's horses—in these and dozens of other areas the intendants and subdelegates began to exercise routine supervision and control. The habit of referring local matters to the central administration for decision, by both parties to local quarrels, grew rapidly. At the very local level, in parishes, peasant inhabitants were aware that it was no longer the wealthy local notables who owned offices of *trésorier de France* in the *bureaux des finances* who would decide how much tax each parish should pay, or who would supervise their forced work on the roads. They could hardly fail to know that the intendant, or his agent, was the one responsible and that appeals should go to him. Real power directed from a distant center was felt throughout society in the late seventeenth century.

Change in degree of penetration, then, was vast in the seventeenth century, and continuous thereafter. By 1700 rebellion was no longer a political act to end in negotiation, but a criminal act whose perpetrator would be hanged, or, if noble, beheaded. Why did the change occur so rapidly? It is puzzling to know why the feudality yielded as it did, now acquiescing in, if not applauding, the expansion of the royal state. Simple power does not explain it, for the machinery for real police control did not exist. The military revolution and increased costs, of course, had to be paid for. Cartesian ideas, quantitative and admiring of uniformity, distrusting variety perhaps dignified the bureaucrats' view of the world, and played a role. Social fear may have contributed: the trends of the price revolution and the demographic explosion that was its motor had fragmented the peasantry into wealthy kulaks who sold grain in the market and the land-poor masses; when those trends were reversed in the seventeenth century, all suffered. To the rural noble elite, later in the century, the peasantry no doubt came to seem at once more unified and solid, and more threatening. Maritime and commercial expansion provided groups of newly wealthy men who, in exchange for privilege, would place their credit at the state's service. Whatever the reasons, the administration, and receptivity to it throughout society, grew rapidly in the seventeenth century. If attitudes in 1600 seemed medieval, those in 1700 seem already quite modern.[10]

During the eighteenth century the expectation that the state would act more frequently and in wider areas clearly rose. But equally clearly there were some limits to penetration. Mainly these limits involved control of the bureaucracy. When in the 1760s and 1770s the government resolved to free the grain trade, local police officials, who believed in a policy of regulation when the supply was short and conscious neglect when it was not, simply did not carry out what the ministers wanted. Sometimes they did not get their orders; sometimes the orders were garbled or could be interpreted as being ambiguous. In any case, the radically liberalizing economic effort over nearly two decades, one that did not fit the tastes and habits of officials or the expectations of the populace, was regularly impeded and sabotaged by local officers who could not be watched from the center. A second limit was the spread of privileged corps and their membership of venal officeholders. These provided unlimited pretexts for questioning orders, for verification that orders squared with other jurisdictions whose privileges had been bought and paid for, for negotiation, for endless delay. Chancelleries, *parlements*, provincial estates, a bewildering variety of tax courts whose areas of competence overlapped, municipalities, guilds, syndicates of tax farmers—all these bodies had designated revenues and rights, would be needed for financial purposes again, and could not be bypassed easily for simple administrative convenience. The existence of a myriad of corps established by the state itself no doubt made many people at all levels of the social hierarchy, even in regions distant from Versailles, aware of the central state. The involvement of tens of thousands of persons in corps whose functions were often redundant aided penetration as a matter of habit and as a psychological fact. But it did not help in controlling a bureaucracy and in having implemented efficiently or rapidly those policies that were decided at the center.

In what sense was the Revolution of 1789 a crisis of penetration?[11]

[10] J. Russell Major, *Representative Institutions in Renaissance France, 1421-1559* (Madison, 1960).

[11] Franklin L. Ford gives such a question a very positive answer in "The Revolutionary-Napoleonic Era: How Much of a Watershed?" *American Historical Review*, 49 (October 1963), 22-23.

Bureaucratically its effects were large, and failure to transform the administrative structures would no doubt have produced paralysis sooner or later. Before 1789, financial and other corps abounded. Composed usually of wealthy persons who held ennobling offices and in effect lent their money to the state, then collected independently the state's revenues, these bodies insisted on their rights collectively and if they worked at all, worked badly. In the Revolution these gave way to a modern bureaucracy organized hierarchically, subordinates taking orders from superiors all up and down the line. The independence of church and clergy, who were so important for royal administration, disappeared with the sale of church lands. A more responsive and efficient bureaucracy grew, one that would carry out new laws that denied privilege and variety, and stressed equality and uniformity. Could the *ancien régime*'s government have carried through the law establishing uniform weights and measures? Probably not. Following on the abolition of noble status, privilege, and regional legal differences, came war in defense of the new democratic order in 1792. Even heavier demands on the people through taxes and conscription were imposed on a new scale, and led sometimes to resistance and internal counterrevolution. But what surprises is how well the French accepted their unprecedented burdens. The remarkable *cahiers des doleances* with their lists of grievances and aspirations, both very specific and idealistically general, reflect a well-established tradition of looking to the state to guarantee the bases of legal equality. In that sense they were a demand for greater penetration, and the crisis of penetration during the Revolution was met effectively, with the aid of a modernized form and ideology of participation—democracy.

In the past two centuries France has shared in all the social changes that have swept Europe and has seen her governments fall with a frequency unmatched in any other major nation; yet the state's essential monopolies of force and law have been little challenged in principle and only peripherally in practice. From Joseph Fouché, who supervised domestic order for both Bonaparte and Bourbon, through the police established under Guizot and the various republican *gardes*, these civil forces have, like the army itself, maintained institutional integrity and, except for brief moments, remained generally effective. Similarly, the judicial and legal system has for one hundred and seventy years maintained a quite Anglo-Saxon continuity of personnel and practices, subject to piecemeal reform but amazingly little direct attack (or attention from social historians). Penetration, then, has been the category in which the French system has been strongest, after identity; and just as the opponents of any regime have tended to challenge its legitimacy, so governments have almost instinctively relied on the traditional strength of penetration.

Political penetration through stable, respected, and hierarchical institutions reaching well into departments and communes has, however, included rather consistent limits rooted in these institutions themselves, in their relationship to the larger society, and in the policies they have been allowed to pursue. Prefects, inspectors of finance, foreign service officers, and army officers have evolved their own traditions and corporate loyalties that strengthen continuity and sustain some significant autonomy. Dominated from 1815 to 1830 by the aristocracy, the upper administration subsequently renewed an older tradition of state service in which officials' careers depended less on local social roots than on their record of efficiency and loyalty (evidenced by political caution). This process of professionalization accelerated in the Third Republic, with greater emphasis upon formal training and competitive examinations as the means of access to the *grands corps*; and in the last century there appears to have been somewhat less movement in France than in most countries from bureaucratic offices to parliamentary politics and back again, or from a career in one corps to a position in another, although this matter deserves more analysis than it has yet received. Bureaucrats, attached to their procedures and favoring promotion from within, have tended to resist sudden new directions imposed from outside, have used their expertise more to dominate less durable politicians than to alter society, and have been more impressive in their routine than in their capacity to effect change.[12] Such influence can have unanticipated results, favoring some policies over others or even, as in the evolution of the Conseil d'État, leading to strong protections for individual or traditional rights against the state.

The price of autonomy, however, can be isolation. In France a strong administration of great ability, rectitude, and skill has generally been but weakly connected at either end to society at large. At the top it has not necessarily been tied to parliamentary leaders or the broader political and intellectual community by those interconnections of social class and life style that have created in Great Britain political, business, and intellectual elites that speak the same language and meet at the same dinner parties. At the bottom, too, officials of the French state

[12] Crozier, *Bureaucratic Phenomenon*, pp. 251-57.

have remained somewhat alien from local society, more inclined to negotiate than to mingle with local notables. This may be one of the reasons that great cleavages over ideology or policy (such as those of the Dreyfus case or the 1930s or the Fourth Republic) have, when echoed within administrative structures, seemed to threaten the very regime. Without the overlapping of social connection and political function found in English (or Prussian) officialdom, modern French administrative institutions were limited in their capacity to influence those outside their realm. When administrators bend to pressure groups, politicians, or local influences, that therefore seems more an explicit concession than a "natural" compromise and is likely to be construed as weakness or even corruption. Yet such "outside" influences have necessarily remained strong in a pluralistic society with a stable social structure. Because the administrative system has in many respects been stronger and more stable than the political system, penetration more sure than participation, a great many of the compromises of French public life occur through the supple administration of laws less flexibly intended. Isolated, the administrative apparatus is sullied by its responsiveness to social reality and suspect for its internal rigidity; to cabinet ministers and parliamentarians it stands as a barrier as well as an instrument.

In a society in which the state is apparently so strong, this has often seemed surprising and sometimes unacceptable. By their reluctance to purge their politically suspect members, the great corps have—in the Third Republic, under Vichy, and since protected important values as well as their corporate integrity just as, by insisting on uniform practice and centralization, they have limited the influence of the special interests with which they deal. But the vision of an efficient state obedient to the commands of the people's representatives has made bureaucratic conservatism (the administrative elite reflects the values of the upper-middle class of which it is an important part) shocking to many, and cries of outrage have rung out in every generation at the discovery that the trusts, the banks, the Catholic hierarchy, or innumerable special interests remain largely unfettered by a supposedly powerful state.

More limited in practice than its revolutionary origins suggest, the modern French state has proved adequate to most of the tasks assigned it, able to mobilize the resources of society to meet new challenges. If the growth of the state has been a universal phenomenon in modern history, that growth in France has been more gradual and less disruptive than in most societies. French governments spent an impressive eight or nine percent of GNP from 1815 to 1870, expanding to eleven or twelve percent during the fifty years from 1870 to the 1920s (except for a sharp rise during World War I). The social programs of the depression and the Popular Front and the onset of World War II brought another sharp rise to the present level of some twenty percent or more. This means that those notable increases in penetration accompanying the educational and economic policies of the Second Empire; the expanded educational programs, professionalized bureaucracy, and public works achieved at the turn of the century; and the social programs and economic planning of the last thirty years were paid for largely by increased prosperity.[13] The demands of technology and commerce for better communication were met more slowly by France than by many of her neighbors; yet her railway network was essentially completed by the turn of the century. France lagged even more notably in social programs, from policy as much as any lack of means, but there too expansion has been steady, placing minimal strains on administration or society. No nation during World War I excelled France's social and economic mobilization. Made possible by the patriotism of wartime, it was also a triumph of penetration, a measure of the high level of ability and of the efficient structures that marked French administration. As France moved into the realm of more formal economic planning (the first Four Year Plan was launched in 1946), she did so with an impressive wealth of talent and expertise employing, with characteristic continuity, many of the programs and personnel developed within the *grands corps* during the Vichy period. Thus crises of penetration caused either by challenges unmet or by sudden disruptive increases in governmental demands have been uncommon in the history of modern France.

One of the most severe penetration crises, perhaps, was that centering around the conflict between church and state from the 1880s to about 1906. That conflict had, of course, an ancient history; and the carefully contrived arrangements of the Napoleonic Concordat, successful as they proved to be, provided grounds for endless contention over the appointment of bishops, the authorization of religious orders,

[13] They were also paid for largely through indirect taxes; since 1870 direct taxes have been the largest single source of revenue only during the interwar period. All these figures, extremely approximate, are from calculations based on the data in B. R. Mitchell, *European Historical Statistics* (New York, 1974), including the estimates by Markovitch reprinted there, p. 797.

and the proper political, social, and educational role of the church. Three distinct trends came together in the clash at the end of the nineteenth century. One was the steady process of secularization whereby the state had absorbed more and more social functions once performed by the church, from keeping registers of births and deaths to running prisons and hospitals, and providing public education. A second was the state's insistence on social penetration as it demanded that national institutions be purveyors of uniform, national, and republican values. The third, and most dramatic, was the immediate political clash of Catholics and anticlerical republicans. Characteristically, the conflict subsided with the separation of church and state, a compromise disguised as total victory for the republican state and administered with notable moderation. There were also secondary crises in particular institutions, especially the army after the Dreyfus affair and during the conflict over Algeria. Again and again, however, contending groups came to accept the claims of an efficient and ostensibly neutral state as less dangerous than their opponents.

In general, opposition to governmental policies has been expressed through politics and not through direct crises of penetration. If the Algerian crisis that brought De Gaulle to power and produced a kind of mutiny in the army is an exception, it took very weak governments and highly organized oppositions to produce it. The relatively rapid restitution of government reliably administered may be equally instructive. Political penetration in France continues to benefit from the dominance of Parisian ideas and institutions creating a culture more sensitive to the center and more homogenous even in its divisions than that of most European nations. Traditions of uniform national policy and administration remain so generally accepted that De Gaulle's gestures toward regionalism were suspect on both left and right. Since the 1960s, however, attitudes toward the state so exalted by the Fifth Republic may have begun to change. Attacks on the arbitrariness of state authorities, on the governmental monopoly of radio and television, on its handling of education and of urban and regional development have all brought issues of penetration more to the fore than at any time in fifty years. Although 1968 may not have opened the new era students envisioned, it did see a briefly effective challenge to penetration. Nevertheless, the historical record is one of somewhat isolate administrative structures that have greatly strengthened governments otherwise weak, even while protecting special interests. A bureaucracy designed to impose change proved a major element of continuity.

PARTICIPATION

No one doubts that it was the issue of participation that produced France's greatest crisis. Well into the twentieth century, the great French Revolution of 1789 served as the model for revolution, cheering the left and frightening the right. At the heart of the principles and practices of 1789 lay not only equality before the law—an idea that could find legal expression even in authoritarian regimes—but participation. What was startling in 1789 was that equality implied an active citizenship or democracy, an order under which all citizens shared not only equal rights as individuals *against* the exercise of power but equal rights *in* formation of the policy that power should apply. Popular sovereignty meant no less than that. Neither booted aristocrat nor shoemaker should be excluded from the right of active citizenship on the basis of what he did or who he was. The land too large for direct democracy, the French elected representatives as their temporary agents and through them citizens voiced their opinions and concerns. Of course not everyone cared; and in practice wealth, and the education that wealth could buy, counted for much. But the principle and practice of participatory democracy were established in 1789 and astonished Europe.

The history of participation is of course long and not uniquely French. In the middle ages, specialists remind us, the need at all levels by authorities, local ones no less than kings, to consult other notables when making decisions was essential to the implementation of those decisions. The strongest authority was the one that through some combination of moral attraction and fear could force others to participate in councils or assemblies, there collectively to pass on information, give advice, and try in a nonliterate society to remember what was the law. Feudal assemblies existed not to resist authority, but to strengthen it; they gave publicity to decisions, and by involving themselves in the decision, they made it seem right and legal for the authority to enforce the decision on others. Visible acquiescence in decisions by strong men made it more difficult for smaller ones to avoid their obligations.

Participation through representatives in national assemblies developed in France, as elsewhere, from the fourteenth through the mid-seventeenth centuries. The Estates General were called at first only to prepare public opinion for the real negotiations that the king's agents would conduct for him at the local level. These negotiations fixed the size of expected feudal aids or other assistance that important individuals or, increasingly, corporate groups would pay. The Estates General met in 1614 and Assemblies of Notables several times thereafter. Regional representative bodies were active in many provinces. This was the moment when one imagines that the aristocracy, strengthened by rising incomes that came from the higher rents a growing population produced, might have been absorbed constitutionally into the government. Elite participation and constitutionalism based on representative institutions seem then to have been a possibility. But if provincial representative bodies continued to meet in Bretagne, Bourgogne, and Languedoc until the Revolution, the great age of national representation and participation evidently ended with the rise of the absolute state in the seventeenth century.

How then do we explain the extraordinary happenings of 1789 and after, the Revolution that, no one doubts, was an unexpectedly renewed crisis of participation? England and the French past provided models for participation by elites in the political process of making decisions, but no one was prepared for democracy. A constitutional revolution to make the king obey a law prescribed by the aristocracy or by propertied men was, if not exactly foreseen, nonetheless within the range of what contemporaries could understand. And the possibility of popular rioting and violence was always real and on the minds of administrators and better-off people. But shoemakers voting? To explain this scale of participation, so different from the efforts at institutionalizing essentially aristocratic representation in the late middle ages and Renaissance, we will need to look for a moment at France's particular form of political modernization and its consequences.

The French state from the seventeenth century was absolute, but like all states, it needed money to finance the new military machine that seventeenth-century warfare demanded. In France, as elsewhere, taxes, if much heavier in the seventeenth century, were still insufficient to pay the new state's costs. Wherever urban and mercantile interests and resources existed, the solution was for states to borrow what they needed, thereby establishing what by the eighteenth century in England, for example, was already called a national debt. But providing suitable guarantees to investors that their money was safe required in England that men who understood and ordinarily possessed substantial property be in a position to check and to verify what the money was used for and, more important, to control the taxation that gave the assurance that one's capital and interest would be paid. Parliament and political participation by the landed elite played that guaranteeing role in England, and thus the state there had the confidence of investors and could borrow easily from its subjects at a low rate of interest. In France, however, political participation by the noble elite seemed dangerous, retrograde, a principle linked to the religious fanaticism and feudal localism that had once torn France apart. But the history of absolute kings was one of regular repudiations of debt. How then could the new state raise the money it needed? How could it borrow if it had no Parliament whose propertied, substantial members had both the inclination and power to protect investors.

The solution in France was one that enormously reinforced and extended the regime of privilege and corps that characterized French society under the *ancien régime.* Provincial estates, privileged municipalities, sovereign courts whose offices conferred nobility and tax exemptions on their holders, guilds of small producers and tradesmen who had monopoly rights for local sales, non-functional tax courts, chancelleries whose members frequently had never seen the city where their offices were established—all this and more, the whole apparatus of venality, privilege, and corps—if not wholly new in the seventeenth century, was then vastly extended. All up and down the social scale privileged communities and bodies proliferated, buying their privileges again and again as the king and his ministers alternately assigned and revoked them, providing forced loans for the crown. The sums advanced by the corps grew larger until we can, by the eighteenth century, discern a system of privileged corps that borrowed money locally on their own credit and in turn loaned to the king at low rates of interest. The corps' credit, stronger than the king's own, rested on the local visibility and connections of their members and on the security provided by the price of offices, a price inflated and sustained by the privileges they carried. In France privileged corps played the same role for the state's borrowing as did Parliament and the Bank of England across the channel.

But in France the consequences of the state's massive borrowing through the corps would be profoundly different, and in the end extremely important for extending ideas and habits of participation to groups all up and down the social scale. Take the local guilds, for example. Their survival was assured by the debts they had accumulated in the king's behalf. They had bought and retired the extra masterships, inspectorships, even the offices Louis XIV created to oversee debts they acquired to buy the other offices. Within the guild all masters were in principle equal, both economically and as voting members of the organization that managed their collective affairs. Ordinary people, the "little" people who were the heart of revolutionary democracy either participated in, or saw at work nearby, organizations within which all individuals voted and were equal. The regime of corps that the needy absolute state fostered preserved ideas, built habits, and provided an education for broader democracy, an education unknown elsewhere, even in England. In tax courts, oligarchic municipalities, *parlements* filled mainly by nobles, all bodies filled by persons sharing with other members identical privileges, the same principles operated and the same lessons were taught. Even learned societies and academies in Paris and the provinces mirrored the corporate institutions and worked the same way—there nobles and commoners, socially differentiated by the laws of precedence in the larger society, gave their opinions equally and in simple order of seniority. Institutions proliferated within which Frenchmen, many of very modest means, were equal to one another and participated in making decisions. The shells of corporate institutions once dissolved in 1789, the habits of the corps were easily transferable to the broader political society and susceptible to expression on the national scale. It was surely no accident that the first, still awesome, crisis of participatory democracy came in France, growing there in rich ground prepared unwittingly by the absolute state.

The crisis of 1789 was of course prepared also in the better-known ways. *Parlements* insisted on verifying royal edicts to see that those edicts conformed to the kingdom's putative "fundamental laws." First on religious questions involving Jansenists and Gallicans early in the century, then increasingly in financial matters, the court in Paris and the older provincial *parlements* issued remonstrances that questioned the crown's policies and even intent. As aristocratic corps, intermediate between king and people, the sovereign courts thought they provided a kind of protection and representation for the people, one not very different from the "virtual representation" that was the best most Englishmen could, in fact, hope for. Historians have often noted the importance of the *parlements'* printed remonstrances in diffusing the message that the king should be under law, that unchecked authority is dangerous, and that some body to represent the people was needed. In part to bypass the dangerous *parlements*, the king's ministers experimented with other forms of representation in the last years of the *ancien régime*. A hand-picked Assembly of Notables—princes, some generals, bishops, mayors, *parlementaires*—proved less pliable at Versailles than Calonne had hoped; there they showed little interest in his plan to establish in the provinces assemblies of landowners whose main function was only to distribute taxes locally. Ideas for new forms of participation were in the air, however, as 1789 approached.

Calling the Estates General immediately raised the issue as to who or what should be represented, and how. The three estates—the clergy, nobility, and third, that is, everyone else (in fact, mainly bourgeois notables)—were never really workable as the framework for representation. Now, as the Revolution began, it was quickly clear that newly politicized lawyers, nonnoble officeholders, noncommissioned officers in the army, some merchants, and many others would not accept the traditional organization. Representatives of the less than two percent of the privileged population in the first two estates would not be permitted jointly to block what those of the other ninety-eight percent wanted done. Doubling the number of deputies for the Third Estate raised broader democratic hopes; and with the help of crowds milling in the Versailles streets in June, the new democratic order was born when Louis XVI yielded the main point—the orders were to meet together in a new assembly, a national one, and members now voted equally and together regardless of their personal status. Soon the deputies represented only citizens, not orders or corps.

At the heart of the Revolution was the message that all men were equal, and all should therefore participate equally as citizens in political life. Monks and bachelors were thought bad—egoistic, selfish, sunk in luxury, antisocial, lacking in virtue because locked into their private worlds. Virtue should be public. But there agreement stopped. The internal tensions of the Revolution were closely tied to the working out of what democratic participation meant. Do-it-yourself, grassroots democrats in the popular societies, the Jacobin clubs, and entrenched in the Paris sections did not always trust the men at the top, in the National or Legislative Assemblies, even in the Convention. Federalists in distant cities did not always receive quickly or accept the message from Paris—their concern for local interests and views sometimes looked counterrevolutionary from the capital, but at home it could look democratic. In the National Assemblies it became obvious after 1792 that the increased penetration (taxes, conscription) brought by the ideologically inspired wars with the aristocratic powers required that better-informed representatives take actions that might not carry in a referendum. Louis XVI would surely not have been executed had the question been submitted to decision by all the people. Differences in views on the proper degree of participation and form of representation grew sharp, and led to conflict that was social no less than political.

Since that time, however, no government of France has disavowed the need for some regularly elected assembly, although its role has varied from absolute supremacy in the First and Second Republics to a shadowy and insignificant existence under Napoleon and Marshal Pétain, with parliamentary influence on the executive considerably restricted during much of the nineteenth century under the constitutional monarchies of Bourbons and Louis Philippe and the empire of Napoleon III. Despite such variety, every regime save Vichy has honored the principle of representation; and the direction of change from Charles X to Louis Philippe or from the early Second Empire to the liberal empire and then the Third Republic suggests that the pressures to do so were great. The revolution of 1830 can fairly be taken as a crisis of participation; so to a large extent were the crises of 1848 and 1875-1876. Participation at the national level had been essential to the legitimacy of government in France for nearly two hundred years; and since 1848 universal male suffrage, a very radical step at the time, has been its *sine qua non*.

In France, therefore, the continuing and important disputes about participation have centered on the complicated questions of how it should be institutionalized. The claims of the aristocracy to represent the nation were rejected at the beginning of the Revolution; for many, however, representation itself would never be wholly satisfactory; the great days of the Revolution, after all, were made by people acting directly. The representative assemblies and limited suffrage of the constitutional monarchies never lost the appearance of a somewhat artificial, Anglophile compromise between royal authority and democracy. Men like Thiers and Guizot took parliament very seriously; but the regime of *notables* proved to have shallow roots, and those who demanded (and won) increased suffrage intended it to increase the prestige and power of parliament. Since 1870, the deputies sitting in the Palais Bourbon have represented their nation as accurately and with as high a standard of probity and intelligence as any representative body in the world. Yet they have remained suspect, and even more so have been all those devices—political parties, electoral distortion, coalitions of special interests, and parliamentary compromise—by which coherent majorities are produced. It is as if the voice of the people is best expressed when all the deputies speak at once. While many have worried, in and out of France, that no nation can afford to represent its divisions so fully,[14] no criticism has more threatened the legitimacy of the Republic—from Boulanger to the students of 1968—than that it was not representative enough.

Such paradoxes are sustained by parliament's separation from the nation at large. Out of its own sense of importance (and a certain institutional defensiveness) it evolved traditions as compelling as those of the House of Commons, but less ritually explicit and less public. Bertrand de Jouvenel's famous remark that two deputies of opposite beliefs have more in common than either has with his partisans outside the Chamber reflects both an institutional strength and a source of weakness. In France, the important compromises that make legislation possible have tended to take place in committees and corridors rather than in the public eye, and even the most statesmanlike parliamentary accord can seem corrupt to voters attracted by more intransigent stands on the hustings. The lack of autonomy in local government means in addition that parties are likely to be perceived less as institutions tying local politics to national issues than as intervening ones independently distorting the popular will. Early in the history of the Third Republic voting by party list was favored by those, like Gambetta and Boulanger, who wanted to mobilize the *nouvelles couches* and were distrustful of the monarchist sympathies of local notables. But *scrutin de liste* was quickly abandoned and multiple candidacies outlawed when Boulanger showed their political potential. Despite occasional returns to elections by party list (in the hope of increasing governmental stability), the single-member constituency remained the form favored by deputies determined to be free of "external" restraints.[15] National parties continued to grow in importance with improved communication, but their weak discipline and multiplicity reduced their impact on parliamentary politics. Impermanent coalitions—cartels, blocs, national unions, popular fronts—were a preferred device preserving more of the autonomy of individual deputies, while capturing some of the benefits of stability and visibility associated with strong parties. Significantly, these coalitions were resorted to increasingly in the interwar years. In contrast, the Fourth Republic was from

[14] See Alfred Grosser, "France: Nothing but Opposition," in Robert A. Dahl, ed., *Political Oppositions in Western Democracies* (New Haven, 1966); and Mark Kesselman, "Overinstitutionalization and Political Constraint: The Case of France," *Comparative Politics*, 3 (October 1970), 21-44.

[15] *Scrutin de liste* was used in 1871-1875, 1885, 1889, 1919.

the beginning a regime of parties (although only the Communists among the three dominant parties maintained much coherence of policy or tactics), and so to assure representativeness it added proportional representation to the fragmenting devices of French elections.[16] On the whole, the development of stronger parties—like the growth of lobbying as organized interests speaking for imperialists, bankers, businessmen, and farmers became increasingly adept at influencing legislation from the 1890s on—tended to increase the feeling of parliamentary isolation.

For those not deputies, a sense of political participation was in many respects strongest at the local level. Here, too, however, its effects were awkwardly indirect. The authority of communal and departmental councils (and of mayors who, in all but the largest cities, were directly elected from 1884 on) was severely restricted, although one of the prefect's major responsibilities was to assess and accommodate to local sentiment. Political vitality extended deep into the French countryside, but the connection between local politics and actual policy, local or national, remained (like the parliamentary process itself) indirect and quasi covert. The deputy who voted on national questions in Paris had often been elected on the basis of local issues, and he carefully nurtured local ties politically more important than party. The Radical party, with its reliance on local notables and weak party discipline, was in this sense as well as others superbly adapted to the Third and Fourth Republics.[17]

The proper connection between parliament and an executive has been still more disputed. In the Revolution, radicals sought to make the church and army more reliable by resting their hierarchies on election, a faith faintly echoed a century later when church properties were placed in the hands of elected committees, and republicans sought to reform the army. The Third and Fourth Republics were content to keep the political executive weak. If governments depended for their strength on an efficient centralized administration bequeathed by Na-

[16] Hoffmann, *In Search of France*, p. 49, sees the effect of this combined with the dominance of parliament increasing a fatal *immobilisme*. One is reminded of the tendency within French big business to favor measures that will sustain its smaller and inefficient competitors. The addition of *apparentement* to favor more centrist coalitions and *panachage* to allow voters to express their preference for individual candidates had little effect but to express a reluctance to achieve stable majorities by reducing the voter's freedom of choice.

[17] Francis de Tarr, *The French Radical Party from Herriot to Mendes France* (London, 1961), p. 241. Hoffmann, *In Search of France*, pp. 96-99, sees the drying up of these networks as fatal to the Fourth Republic and related to the failure of recent regimes to foster participation.

poleon, parliament in normal times sought to control the civil service, granting extraordinary but temporary powers to strong leaders (such as Clemenceau, Poincaré, Doumergue, Pétain, and De Gaulle) in times of crisis. Such expedients, which break the participatory tie, could not be allowed for long, however; even plebiscites and referenda skillfully used by Napoleon III and De Gaulle as substitutes for representation, soon lost authority as effective expressions of the popular will.[18] One obvious alternative, an executive directly elected, proved unforgettably fatal to the Second Republic, and runs directly counter to much in the ethos of participation that developed in France since 1870.[19] The fact, unparalleled in French history, that since 1965 three presidents have been elected by popular vote may therefore represent so major a shift in the meaning of participation as to suggest that the Fifth Republic was above all an effort to resolve one special type of long-term crisis of participation.

Parliamentary approval of particular ministries has rarely lasted long. The governments of the Third Republic on the average endured some eight months, those of the July Monarchy slightly less, and those of the Fourth Republic barely five.[20] If the French political system compensated for this instability by allowing considerable continuity of politicians and policies between governments, it also tended to accept rapid turnover (which often increased dangerously when the issues in dispute became more divisive) as an assurance that participation was real and the executive under parliamentary check. Yet, perhaps because participation was associated with volatility, its very devotees have been willing to exclude significant sectors of opinion. Ex-communards and anarcho-syndicalists suffered direct repression in the early decades of the Third Republic; Communists were allowed no place among governing coalitions during most of the Fourth Republic. A great deal of the anticlericalism of the Third Republic was

[18] De Gaulle's boast in his speech of April 6, 1962 (cited in Macridis and Brown, *Supplement to the De Gaulle Republic*, p. 37) that "we have accomplished by referendum three major changes, which it had been impossible to bring about until then in spite of countless trials and endless debates" somewhat defensively points to the indecisiveness of parliament but without attacking its legitimacy.

[19] Particularly after the collapse of General Boulanger, whose political fortune first rose on the cry for constitutional revision to strengthen the executive.

[20] The figure for the July monarchy excludes the shortest (the "three day ministry" of 1834) and the longest governments (the several years of Marshal Soult and Guizot). Robert O. Paxton, *Vichy France: Old Guard and New Order* (New York, 1972), pp. 199-200, points out that under Vichy ministries turned over more rapidly yet.

rooted in the fear that the Catholic masses could be mobilized by conservatives. And the belief that women would be likely to follow their priests at the polls delayed women's suffrage.[21] By a similar process, leaders who strayed too far from the political center or simply antagonized too many of their colleagues have suddenly found themselves ostracized. Few polities could afford so heavy a toll of famous names: those who made the mistake of once thinking Algeria French, of opposing De Gaulle on other grounds, of being too attached to the Fourth Republic, too close to Vichy, or too often losers in the conflicts of the Third Republic.[22] Among other things, all these excluded groups and leaders were often charged with unrepublican inflexibility and indifference to the popular will, a claim that at least faintly echoes revolutionary cries for direct democracy. At the heart of the French political system there lies a residual distrust of all institutions, interest groups, or parties that threaten to come between citizen and state. Even in the Third Republic most republicans blushed for the influence of Freemasons, and conservatives apologized for political activity by army or church.

The mystique of participation, which can support presidential democracy or parliamentary supremacy while excluding from the political game those said to endanger it, can also justify extraparliamentary participation through demonstration. Indeed, the very suspicion that parties and parliament are isolated and moved by their own interests has given a surprising legitimacy in French political life to those who march in the street. That, too, is participation. The very proper banqueteers of 1847, Déroulède and his several *ligues*, Dreyfusards and anti-Dreyfusards, syndicalists and sometimes the CGT, the *Cagoulards* and *Croix de Feu* and *Action Française* in the 1930s, and more recently communists, Gaullists, and students have shared in common the cry that theirs was the true voice of the people, that parliament was a self-serving fraud.[23] Extraparliamentary "participation" has thus seemed an effective means not so much of influencing parliament as of challenging its legitimacy while daring the government to violate its own liberal norms. As if drawn by a magnet, the most rad-

[21] It was easier in the French system to make occasional concessions of legal rights to bank accounts and property than to extend the vote to women.

[22] Rudolf Binion, *Defeated Leaders: The Political Fate of Caillaux, Jouvenal, and Tardieu* (New York, 1960).

[23] F. F. Ridley, *Revolutionary Syndicalism in France* (Cambridge, 1970) argues that antiparliamentarism was central to that movement.

ical of such groups have since 1792 marched toward the Chamber of Deputies, making the test of their cause mass as against institutionalized participation.

When applied to France, the concept of crises of participation thus becomes complicated and rather special. Such crises, in their simplest and presumably classical form—when the survival of a government was threatened by demands for increased participation (usually enlarged suffrage) that it was reluctant to meet—have been of little importance except for the sixty years from 1789 to 1848. In large part this is because the society as a whole has placed so high a value on participation that governments had to adapt to or find ways of manipulating the forms of participation.

In whatever form accepted by the state, participation has seemed simultaneously threatened and inadequate—threatened because important groups denied its validity (and thus had to be excluded from full participation), inadequate not only because it was limited but because it failed to have the full integrative effect expected of it. The ties between local and national politics, between interest groups and policy, between parties and government have been more personal than institutional, and therefore appeared more private than public. The resultant system, unclear in principle and uncertain in practice, has never won from Frenchmen or foreigners, political scientists or public, the sort of praise variously accorded that of Great Britain, the United States, imperial Germany or fascist Italy. It has been a system in all the modern republics liable to overloading as major cleavages cut across the weaker ties that allowed the system to operate. Yet, on the whole, it has worked remarkably well, sustaining a lively and highly intelligent political life, providing remarkable continuity, reasonable effectiveness and adaptability to new needs, while maintaining the major democratic liberties. Participation, never high enough to make the regime legitimate in everyone's eyes, has nevertheless generally been sufficient to let government rest on an equilibrium more social than political, achieved through alternation more than accord.

DISTRIBUTION

For individuals and families real crises of grain shortages and hunger, sometimes on a national scale and frequently on the regional one, were regular occurrences in traditional France. These crises were ordinarily short-run, seasonal, tied to a bad harvest; they sometimes produced violence, rioting, seizure of grain convoys; and they led to regular demands for provisioning and regulation of the grain price by the king, the father of his people, whose expected role was to restrain the merchants and potential monopolists who had a stake in rigging shortages and keeping the people hungry. For all that, no single distribution crisis threatened the regime or political order itself until nearly the end of the eighteenth century.

The long-run movement that conditioned distribution in France, as elsewhere, was demographic. The population that may have reached 17 million toward 1300, having fallen below 10 million in the mid-fifteenth century, began to rise sharply before 1500, and more than doubled during the next century. A peak of 20 to 22 million in about 1625 represented a ceiling below which population then oscillated until nearly the middle of the eighteenth century. After about 1740, a decline of some 15 percent in infant mortality renewed growth and carried the population to a total of 26 or 27 million by 1789.

In the eighteenth century one of every six Europeans was French, and the country was, after the Netherlands, the most densely populated in Europe. Productivity of the land rose almost not at all between the middle ages and roughly 1830—the agricultural revolution once assumed to have taken place in the eighteenth century has been shown to be a myth.[24] Further growth in numbers and greater prosperity for the at least two-thirds of Frenchmen involved in agriculture were limited by a kind of Malthusianism that was conditioned by cultural and institutional factors. Jacques Dupâquier has argued that France could have fed 30 to 40 millions in the eighteenth century but for the limits tied to the system of ownership and exploitation of the land: large exploitations and tenures (owned by nobles, the church, some bourgeois) producing grain were mixed with small, family-size holdings farmed more intensively. The amount of land allocated to family-size holdings in effect fixed the population ceiling. A peasant family could supplement its income to some extent, through the wages paid them for part-time work by larger cultivators, payments for artisanship, or sometimes a supplement for wet-nursing babies from the city. But the time came, as population expanded and the share of land available for family tenures was fixed, when no further subdivision of small holdings was possible. Thus, no further population growth.

In periods when the number of persons was rising—in the sixteenth

[24] Michel Morineau, *Les faux semblants d'un démarrage économique, Agriculture et démographie en France au XVIIIe siècle* (Paris, 1971).

century or after 1740—the distribution of wealth would shift. Pressure of people on land, given the inelasticity of supply and demand, forced up the price of food, especially the cheaper grains; competition for land by a larger population similarly forced up the price of rents. What went down, at least in purchasing power, was the price of a day's labor. Thus, two groups were favored: those, mainly but not exclusively nobles, who lived from rents or produced enough food to sell a surplus in the market; those merchant-entrepreneurs who could take advantage of the cheaper labor in the countryside to produce more cheaply and sell more widely. The conflict and partial merger of the two rising groups, one old and one new, in such a situation ordinarily generated social tensions, reflected toward 1600 in the rise of duelling and the appearance of sumptuary legislation, and in 1781 by the Ségur *règlement* that excluded from officerships in the reforming army those persons who could not present pedigrees detailing four generations of paternal noblesse. Middling peasants blessed by having either more land or small families got along. Those who were hurt were, of course, most of the population—wage earners and small producers in town and countryside. The growth in the number of vagrants and "floating population," the uprooted from the countryside—numbering about one million by 1789—is a sign of what was happening, as was the shift in the wanderers' characteristics, mainly older women and children seeking charity in the city early in the century, mainly grown men later.

In the long interval between periods of population growth and inflation, roughly the century between 1640 and 1740, there were of course hard times. Higher taxes, disease, almost continuous warfare until 1713, especially cold weather during the 1690s, the difficulties of organizing trade and production without sufficient specie and in the absence of paper money that inspired confidence, generally falling prices punctuated by killing famines in 1693-1694 and 1709-1710—all seemed to conspire to bring distress to many groups. Perhaps social fear rose when the peasantry looked more uniformly miserable. Earlier and later, in times of growing population and a rising grain price, one could be cheered by the sight of better-off peasants, the *laboureurs* or kulaks, selling their grain in a good market; these were the visible peasants, and one could almost forget the others, who were not seen until they took to the roads to become a police problem. But in Louis XIV's day the peasantry must have seemed more homogeneous and threatening, and if so, that fact helps to explain the acquiescence of the previously turbulent and touchy rural elite in the rapid expansion of the centralizing state's administrative, police, and military apparatus.

Misery, however, is not automatically a crisis, and there is little sign that sheer misery of people posed a threat to the regime or constituted a crisis, in the sense in which we are using the term, until quite late in the eighteenth century. Even then the issue is not clear cut. There were some new features in the situation from the 1760s. The size of the population was larger than before and raised problems on a larger scale. No less important, new ideas and policies of reforming ministers (most conspicuously Turgot, but several others as well) favored freeing the grain trade. This was to turn bread, the basis of life itself, into a simple object for domestic and international commerce, to give merchants and producers freedom to buy and sell as they wished, even in secret. The king and the state would play no role, just let market forces operate, in principle benevolently. The new policy and intent was shocking to many: it shook confidence in the paternal and moral character of political authority. Heartless economists working from theories and an indifferent king would now let greedy hoarders and monopolists get rich by starving and poisoning the decent little people. Wild stories about the "famine pact" circulated widely, and the political authorities, if rational and clear in their economic ideas, had done much to erode the confidence of millions who were raised in the traditions of Saint Louis and Henri IV ("A Chicken in Every Pot").

In 1789, and in the years immediately preceding, there were severe economic troubles, although in specific political terms the crisis of distribution can be seen as having come only during the Revolution. Historians still dispute the extent and meaning of the seigneurial dues peasants refused to pay in 1789, and that the nobles renounced on the celebrated Night of August 4. Regional variety was large, and what were substantial payments to one's lord in one place were insignificant, only symbolic payments elsewhere. In either case, the peasants' attack on seigneurial dues was thorough and violent in 1789. Chateaux were burned. For the moment the wealthier peasants and the more numerous poorer ones were linked by their common hostility to nobles (or sometimes landed bourgeois who were also fief holders). The actual condition of that majority of peasants who did not produce enough to feed themselves was worsening through the interplay of impersonal demographic and market forces—the higher rents had nothing to do with seigneurialism or "feudalism." But the bad will of the local seigneur, often absentee, was convenient as explanation for the discomfort felt by persons suffering also from the bad harvests and unemployment that struck in the late 1780s. At all levels in the peasantry the hope and ambition was of course for unfettered land, but also for land itself. Peasants looked covetously at the church lands, used as security for the new currency and tied also to the liquidation of royal debts.

In cities the economic difficulties of 1788-1789, and of the 1790s—unemployment, episodically high bread prices—raised as always questions of provisioning, regulating prices, seeing that grain was sent to the city markets, especially Parisian, and thereby angered the peasants whose grain stocks were seized or who had themselves to buy bread in the nearby village. On all sides, now in the 1790s more than ever, it was the state whose role in the economy would be seen as critical—the noble villains in whom one could once take comfort as explanation either had disappeared, or their "feudal" powers had. Older routine regulations of the grain supply and occasional price fixing in the Revolution became the issue of the Maximum over which contemporaries (and historians since) disputed the nature of the regime and government. The whole range of views, from liberal and laissez faire to the protosocialist views of the Hébertistes, found expression through these specific issues. Were objective conditions worse than they had been under the *ancien régime*, or was it rather the mentalities that were more heated, the categories of political discourse and dispute transformed and expanded? Take your pick, but probably the latter.

The recollection of peasants marching up the hill to burn seigneurial records, and of the demands of the Conspiracy of Equals have fed the hopes of the French left and the fears of French conservatives ever since the Revolution. The Second Republic was sapped by the violence of the June Days, at least in its noisiest aspects a distribution crisis, as was the Commune from whose ashes the Third Republic rose. Evidence as well as ideology has made it tempting to write the history of modern French politics in terms of classes clashing over whose interests the state should foster. Yet distributive issues have not often provided the clear central axis on which modern France's frequent political crises have turned. The Second Republic's new taxes antagonized the peasants, while its abandonment of the National Workshops alienated workers; but questions of participation had been the crucial ones in the initial success of the Revolution of 1848. The

Commune arose only in the very special circumstances following the seige of Paris; and its radical programs and brutal suppression were, like the June Days, primarily a Parisian affair. It is not hard to show that the Third Republic, which gained in acceptability from its conservative origins, generally favored the prosperous over the poor; yet its governments, rocked by so much else, were not shaken by issues primarily distributive until after World War I. Even then, defense of the *franc* brought conservatives to power and appeared to strengthen the regime. Demographic stability and slow industrialization in a nation of small factories, small towns, and fertile agriculture had eased the tasks of government despite the vigorous denunciations (from left and right) of liberal capitalism. Only in the 1930s did distributive issues reach the crisis stage of requiring a sudden shift in policy. That was begun with impressive adaptability, then eroded amidst social tension and distrust that contributed to France's defeat in 1940, even though international pressures had helped to hide its seriousness. On the whole, however, it is the absence of political crises of distribution that needs to be explained.

Three general factors stand out. The Revolution, by the elimination of legal privilege and the encouragement of peasant ownership of the land, left the countryside less liable to violent, political mobilization. Second, by the standards of the time, France has been a very prosperous country with little unemployment and relatively high wages, whose slow demographic growth in the nineteenth century (itself in part a measure of the widespread acceptance of bourgeois attitudes) and relatively slow pace of industrialization had similar effects on political life in the towns. Few of them were new factory towns, fewer still had to cope with great hordes of new arrivals seeking work. Urban politics, through most of the century, thus tended to rest on artisans and small shopkeepers who respected private property and trusted local notables. Third, until the end of the century, few even of the most disadvantaged expected governments to resolve inequities or alter the laws of economics, so that steady (and well-publicized) attention to public works, national support for roads and schools, taxes that did not rise too rapidly and tariffs that did not drop too quickly were in general enough to keep other sorts of issues at the forefront of politics. (The most likely basis for mobilizing village and rural opposition to the government was in fact religious.)

Since 1870, the political system itself has worked to keep distributive issues from threatening the regime; groups insistent on radical changes

—communards, syndicalists, socialists until 1936, and communists since—have been kept outside the quotidian political calculus. Highly politicized (because their survival demands it), they in effect often transmute immediate conflicts into matters of party or ideology.[25] Very real anger about the distribution of economic and social benefits in French society is thus twice deflected: from questions about distribution to challenges of the government's legitimacy (much as the Communists have done since their exclusion from the governing coalition in 1946), and from specific issues of employment, wages, and legislation to political strikes, demonstrations, and support for parties of the left. Political alienation, even if rooted in differences of social class, is (like misery) not sufficient for a crisis of distribution. Syndicalists did not seek solutions in parliament. Manufacturers, bankers, farmers, and wine distributors, of course, expected their interests to be protected, but that could usually be accomplished through lobbying rather than more risky public remonstrances. French governments are normally responsive to such groups, providing the hidden subsidies of high tariffs (few regimes dared the resentment produced by the Second Empire's adoption of the Cobden-Chevalier treaty in 1860), farm supports (democratic France, like the United States, was among the last of the industrial states to adopt comprehensive programs of social welfare, but among the first to adopt support for farmers), and vigorous "national" stands within the European Common Market. The brief flurry of the movement led by Poujade in the 1950s reflected the outrage of small businessmen and producers threatened by new standards of efficiency upon discovering that the government no longer could or would protect them from the threat of change.

Until World War I, governments had, from conviction as well as weakness, accepted a very limited role in the distribution of wealth. Budgets were balanced on the basis of limited social programs and unintrusive indirect taxation. Slowly the old balance changed, and the role of government increased from free schooling and public health to the sudden acceptance of a partially directed economy in wartime. The stalwart efforts after the war to return to a more modest role, probably doomed by economic and social change in any case, were undermined by the Great Depression. That crisis, which ended the

[25] This is not limited to the left. The *école unique*, which could easily be seen as a vital matter of social equality and mobility, has been discussed instead in terms of religion, culture, and social ideology. See John E. Talbott, *The Politics of Educational Reform in France, 1918-40*. (Princeton, 1969).

illusion of France's economic autonomy and brought the socialists into governing circles, was more clearly a crisis of distribution than any since the Great Revolution. The Popular Front effected a fundamental change, not only with social programs (social security had first been established in 1928) and the recognition of collective bargaining, but with the direct intervention of the state, symbolized by Blum's negotiation of the Matignon accords. Yet even socialists accepted much of pre-Keynesian orthodoxy, and their own high hopes had begun to fade even before the bitter resentment of their opponents brought the government down. The distribution crisis of the 1930s was less resolved than submerged in the still more threatening international danger facing a divided republic. Affection for the old interests and the government's "neutrality" in economic matters had little place among the parties that emerged from the resistance, and they were free to build on the *dirigiste* structures developed under a Vichy regime hardly inhibited by liberalism. The Fourth Republic, so much like the Third in its political outline, was fundamentally different in the economic and social role it assumed. Although traditional interests eventually learned again to make their views politically effective, prosperity made them less resistant to change. The great distribution crisis of modern France was in a sense resolved for it, rather than by the political system; and the outburst of 1968, unable to win as much support for its attacks on "consumerism" as for its denunciation of an arbitrary government, suggested in its failure much the same thing as the electoral successes of the Gaullists: the new patterns of distribution had won an acceptance comparable to that which sustained the old one under the Third Republic.

Sequence

Despite the belief of many historians that the lasting changes brought by the French Revolution have been exaggerated, 1789-1815 remains the great divide of French political history. It is tempting therefore to look for two cycles of crises, one before and one the result of the Revolution.

Medieval kingship rested on legitimacy, and was hard to distinguish from it. Based in feudal rights and obligations and ideas of a Christian commonwealth, legitimacy was strengthened by the sacral character of the crown, by a slowly evolved but increasingly explicit and complex system of law and of legal jurisdictions, and even by claims rooted in memories of Roman order. It was reinforced by a hierarchical social structure that granted specific privileges to particular social groups, regions, towns, and corporations. The legitimacy of the state thus expanded and became more explicit in its rights and demands with the expansion and consolidation of the king's realm. Severely tested in the wars of religion, its most identifiable crisis of the *ancien régime*, legitimacy became a formal attribute of the state as well as the monarchy, requiring more in the way of loyalty, internal order (and taxes) from all the king's subjects. This allowed a certain shift in emphasis with the Enlightenment, as the state's efficiency and its subjects' well-being were added to the measures of its legitimacy. By the 1790s defenders of the Crown's legitimacy could make the awesome claim of a millennium of continuity.

French national identity developed in a similar evolution, but its firm beginnings may have been somewhat later (if events and institutions are the measure, rather than the misty claims about Caesar, Franks, and Gauls, and the eldest daughter of the church favored by nineteenth-century writers). Some signs of national identity certainly can be seen in the Hundred Years War, but the clear watershed came with the Wars of Religion (and the standoff against Charles V) in the sixteenth century. By the seventeenth century the integration of language, religion, culture, institutions, and territory—and of all these with the state, all of them "French"—seemed so solid and "natural" as to become the model of the nation throughout the continent.

A crisis of penetration followed shortly after the consolidation of the state's legitimacy and of French political identity. With the acquiescence of the aristocracy, the state, in order to meet growing military demands and the need for increased revenue, reached deep into French society with a loyal and efficient administration and myriads of regulations. Europe's greatest absolute state was established.

This occurred without demarked crises of participation or distribution. Not that participation did not exist or was not important or that the economic problems and tensions of society and state were not pressing, but in neither was a new national, political pattern established or required. A kind of "failed crisis" of participation in the sixteenth and early seventeenth centuries left French elites without the nationally institutionalized forms of participation that might have been established. A more modest military policy following the wars of Louis XIV allowed the state to weather the incipient crisis of distribution of the early eighteenth century. In both categories, however, pressures for change continued to build until the Revolution.

The crisis of 1789 opened as a crisis of participation, one whose (brief) resolution in democratic assembly led to a crisis of legitimacy that culminated in the beheading of the king, and that opened a crisis of distribution marked first by the abolition of the remaining formal feudal ties and by an (often violent) redistribution of land. Faced with the threat of foreign invasion, the new regime extended its radical changes in distribution with the confiscation of church lands and inventive fiscal measures. By the time of the Terror it sought a significantly different standard of penetration (initiated early in the Revolution with the establishment of departments and uniform weights and measures), and had come to associate revolutionary belief and ideological loyalty with national identity.

If the Revolution was a crisis in all five categories, the Directory and Napoleonic regime attempted some compromise in each. A heightened but predictable and stable level of penetration was sustained by a professional, hierarchical administration (organized on a clear military model) operating from uniform legal codes. The major distributive changes of the Revolution were kept, but with a stable currency, frank acceptance of profit making, and enormous armies supported as much as possible from foreign conquest. Although propaganda and symbols were used to evoke an ever strident sense of identity, ideological intolerance was softened, as in the acceptance of noble titles and the compromise with the church. The variety of solutions to problems of legitimacy and participation that were tried from 1795 to 1815 bespeaks the failure to find comparably stable compromises in these matters.

Since 1815, two monarchies, three republics, an empire, and the mixed nonconstitution of Marshal Pétain have fallen to revolution, military defeat, or sheer incompetence. Eight regimes in one hundred sixty years is, at the very least, an almost perpetual crisis of legitimacy. Crises of participation underlay this instability in 1830, 1848, 1850-1851, the 1860s, 1871-1876; but the adoption of universal male suffrage in 1848 and the acceptance of republican government resting on an elected assembly in 1876 proved essentially irreversible. By that date a century-long crisis of participation can be said (with some qualification) to have been resolved. The qualification has to do with the difficulty in establishing an effective, stable executive without denying participation, the problem that brought the fall of the Fourth Republic and one that raises issues of both legitimacy and participation. Despite a long record since 1815 of strikes, demonstrations, and collective violence, despite the martyrs of the June Days and the Commune, France had no political crisis of distribution requiring a major change in governmental policy for over a century. The crisis of distribution marked in 1936 by the programs of the Popular Front lasted for more than a decade, resolved in part by the strange hiatus of war and occupation, and then the adoption of systematic state economic planning and higher levels of public welfare. When distributive demands erupted in violence, it is the state that triumphed, and then later proffered ameliorative measures under Napoleon III and the Third, Fourth, and Fifth Republics. French identity, transformed least by the Revolution, has never been fundamentally challenged since; but its capacity for political mobilization has invited the political use of more demanding ideological identities, which have proved divisive and have helped sustain denials of any particular regime's legitimacy.

The sequence of crises, then, would be one of early resolutions of legitimacy and identity (by the fifteenth and sixteenth centuries), followed by a crisis of penetration (early in the seventeenth). A crisis of participation at the end of the eighteenth then opened crises in four categories (with something of a crisis of identity, but at a different, ideological, level). Of these, the crises of penetration and distribution were relatively quickly resolved, that of participation was resolved after a century, and legitimacy was unresolved in any enduring sense, but remained more or less salient from the Revolution to the present.

Despite short lives, most modern French governments have ruled reasonably effectively while unevenly adapting to changing needs and demands. Even sudden death has not kept them from bequeathing durable institutions and legislation to their successors. Perhaps such continuity can be interpreted as related to strong identity and penetration, supported by the acknowledgment of demands for participation. Perhaps this can serve as the beginning of a description, though clearly not an explanation, of a tradition of limited but efficient, isolated but able government in a divided society. The pattern of crises may even suggest why most French governments could not survive simultaneous challenge in several categories, but the analysis of political processes must, to go much further, give more attention to the society that produced them.

Some Related Readings

GENERAL

Bowditch, John, and Raymond Grew, eds. *A Selected Bibliography on Modern French History 1600 to the Present.* Ann Arbor, 1974.

FRANCE

Bloch, Marc. *French Rural History; An Essay in Its Basic Characteristics.* Berkeley, 1966.
Curtius, Ernst Robert. *The Civilization of France.* New York, 1932.

ANCIEN RÉGIME

Bloch, Marc. *Feudal Society.* Translated by L. A. Manyon, Chicago, 1961.
———. *The Royal Touch: Sacred Monarchy and Scrofula in England and France.* London, 1973.
Bosher, J. F. *French Finances, 1770-95.* New York, 1970.
Church, William F. *Richelieu and the Reason of State.* Princeton, 1972.
Cole, Charles W. *French Mercantilism.* New York, 1943.
Dent, Julian. *Crisis in Finance: Crown and Society in Seventeenth-Century France.* Newton Abbot, 1973.
Ford, Franklin L. *Robe and Sword.* Cambridge, 1953.
Fox-Genovese, Elizabeth. *The Origins of Physiocracy: Economic Revolution and Social Order in Eighteenth-Century France.* Ithaca, 1976.
Gay, Peter. *Voltaire's Politics: The Poet as Realist.* Princeton, 1959.
Goubert, Pierre. *Louis XIV and Twenty Million Frenchmen.* New York, 1970.
Gruder, Vivian R. *The Royal Provincial Intendants.* Ithaca, 1968.
Henneman, John B. *Royal Taxation in Fourteenth-Century France: The Development of War Bureaucracy, 1322-1356.* Princeton, 1971.
Kaplan, Steven L. *Bread, Politics, and Political Economy in the Reign of Louis XV.* 2 volumes. The Hague, 1976.
King, James E. *Science and Rationalism in the Government of Louis XIV.* Baltimore, 1949.
Le Roy Ladurie, Emmanuel. *The Peasants of Languedoc.* Translated by John Day. Urbana, 1974.
Price, Jacob M. *France and the Chesapeake, a History of the French Tobacco Monopoly, 1674-1791, and Its Relationship to the British and American Tobacco Trades.* 2 volumes. Ann Arbor, 1973.
Rothkrug, Lionel. *Opposition to Louis XIV.* Princeton, 1965.
Rule, John C., ed. *Louis XIV and the Craft of Kingship.* Columbus, 1969.
Salmon, J.H.M. *Society in Crisis: France in the Sixteenth Century.* New York, 1975.
Shennan, J. H. *The Parlement of Paris.* London, 1968.

Strayer, Joseph R. *On the Medieval Origins of the Modern State.* Princeton, 1970.

———, and Charles H. Taylor, *Studies in Early French Taxation.* Cambridge, Mass., 1939.

Tilly, Louise A. "The Food Riot as a Form of Political Conflict in France," *Journal of Interdisciplinary History*, 2 (1971), 23-57.

Van Kley, Dale. *The Jansenists and the Expulsion of the Jesuits from France, 1757-1765.* New Haven, 1975.

THE REVOLUTION

Brinton, Crane. *The Jacobins.* New York, 1961.

Furet, François, and Denis Richet. *The French Revolution*, Translated by Stephan Hardman. London, 1970.

LeFebvre, Georges. *The French Revolution.* 2 volumes. New York, 1962-1964.

———. *Napoleon.* 2 volumes. New York, 1960.

Palmer, Robert R. *The Age of the Democratic Revolution.* 2 volumes. Princeton, 1959 and 1964.

———. *Twelve Who Ruled.* Princeton, 1959.

Soboul, Albert. *The Parisian Sans-culottes and the French Revolution.* Oxford, 1964.

Tocqueville, Alexis C. H. de, *The Old Regime and the French Revolution.* New York, 1955.

1815-1939

Bertier de Sauvigny, Guillaume de. *The Bourbon Restoration.* Philadelphia, 1966.

Cameron, Rondo. *France and the Economic Development of Europe.* Chicago, 1966.

Chapman, Brian. *Prefects and Provincial France.* London, 1955.

Chapman, Guy. *The Third Republic of France.* New York, 1962.

Clough, Shepard B. *France: A History of National Economics, 1789-1939.* New York, 1964.

Dansette, Adrian. *Religious History of Modern France.* New York, 1961.

Duveau, Georges. *1848: The Making of a Revolution.* New York, 1967.

Edwards, Stewart. *The Paris Commune of 1871.* Chicago, 1971.

Greene, Nathanael. *Crisis and Decline: The French Socialist Party in the Popular Front Era*. Ithaca, 1969.

Guerard, Albert L. *Napoleon III*. Cambridge, 1943.

Johnson, Douglas. *France and the Dreyfus Affair*. New York, 1966.

———. *Guizot: Aspects of French History, 1787-1874*. London, 1963.

Larmour, Peter J. *The French Radical Party in the 1930's*. Stanford, 1964.

Lorwin, Val R. *The French Labor Movement*. Cambridge, 1954.

McManners, John. *Church and State in France, 1870-1914*. London, 1972.

Pinkney, David H. *The French Revolution of 1830*. Princeton, 1972.

Rémond, René. *The Right Wing in France from 1815 to De Gaulle*. Philadelphia, 1969.

Rothney, John. *Bonapartism after Sedan*. Ithaca, 1969.

Seager, Frederic H. *The Boulanger Affair*. Ithaca, 1969.

Weber, Eugen. *Action Française*. Stanford, 1962.

———. *The Nationalist Revival in France 1905-14*. Berkeley and Los Angeles, 1959.

———. *Peasants into Frenchmen*. Stanford, 1976.

Wohl, Robert. *French Communism in the Making, 1914-24*. Stanford, 1966.

Wright, Gordon. *France in Modern Times, 1760 to the Present*. Chicago, 1960.

Zeldin, Theodore. *France, 1845-1945*. 2 volumes. Oxford, 1973 and 1977.

———. *The Political System of Napoleon III*. London, 1958.

SINCE 1939

Ambler, John S. *The French Army in Politics, 1945-62*. Columbus, 1966.

Earle, Edward Mead, ed. *Modern France*. New York, 1964.

Ehrmann, Henry S. *Politics in France*. New York, 1976.

Hoffman, Stanley, *et al. In Search of France*. New York, 1965.

Hughes, H. Stuart. *The Obstructed Path: French Social Thought, 1930-1960*. New York, 1968.

Leuthy, Herbert. *France against Herself*. New York, 1957.

Paxton, Robert O. *Vichy France: Old Guard and New Order, 1940-44*. New York, 1972.

Pickles, Dorothy. *The Fifth French Republic*. New York, 1963.
Pierce, Roy. *Contemporary French Political Thought*. New York, 1966.
Soucy, Robert. *Fascism in France*. Berkeley, 1972.
Williams, Philip M., and Martin Harrison. *Politics and Society in De Gaulle's Republic*. London, 1971.

CHAPTER 8

ITALY

RAYMOND GREW

THE ISSUES of modern Italian history are largely ones of modernization, and the most significant controversies among historians of Italy have often been about the nature (and incompleteness) of that process. In the nineteenth century Italian nationalism presented itself as the natural awakening of a people long suppressed by foreigners, ignorance, and poverty. General progress, then, accounted for development; and historians sought to determine when changes in Italy were essentially autonomous or the result of foreign influence. Liberal historiography, dominant from unification through the 1950s, measured development more concretely in terms of constitutional guarantees, administrative efficiency, individual liberties, representative government, and economic growth. Nearly all agreed that these goals required the overthrow of the old regimes, and only a minority criticized as excessive the degree of political centralization that replaced them. The controversy between federalists and unitarians, however, has echoed through the historical literature, and the conflict between Cavourians and Mazzinians—between the liberal right and the liberal left—has been kept alive in historical assessments of the political means the Cavourians used, the role of popular forces in the Risorgimento, and the extent to which unification meant the disguised expansion of Piedmont. Such issues have stimulated some of the most important historical research.

Scholarly controversies surrounding Italian economic development grew out of the increasing recognition of the special problems of the south, where Piedmontese dominance was slow to undermine preindustrial structures, allowing the area to fall further behind the more advanced north. Such criticisms, including the powerful jeremiads of Gaetano Salvemini, led to a revisionist history of the Risorgimento as a *revolution manquée*, in which social and political changes stopped short of the fundamental transformation required to create a truly mod-

Crises of Political Development in Europe and the United States
0-691-07598-0/78/000271-40$02.00/1 (cloth)
0-691-02183-X/78/000271-40$02.00/1 (paperback)
For copying information, see copyright page

ern state. Developed after World War I, most influentially perhaps by Piero Gobetti, this reappraisal was, like much Italian historical writing, also a part of current controversy in a nation for which assessment of the past has remained a vital part of politics.[1] A related view emerged in the writings of Antonio Gramsci, whose subtle and sophisticated Marxism has replaced the liberal (and optimistic) idealism of Benedetto Croce as the most pervasive influence in Italian historical writing. In the twentieth century both liberal and Marxist historians have tended to measure Italy's past against ideal standards that justify indignation while explaining failure.

Analysis of the era of the liberal state, from 1860 to 1922, has varied according to whether one interpreted the period as the continuation of the Risorgimento (leading to a gradual increase in political participation and economic growth) or as a progressive breakdown of the compromises of a limited liberalism (leading to fascism). The Fascist experience has been seen as the continuance of nineteenth-century nationalism with new forms (a view the Fascists themselves often encouraged); as the determination of powerful interests, especially of the industrial, landholding, and lower middle classes to protect themselves against the radical threat of a rising proletariat (a Marxist position); as the effect of a momentary crisis resulting from the war, the entry into parliament of two new mass parties, and the corrupt incompetence of a tired elite (a liberal interpretation); and as the rejection of the liberal state by those who had been affronted since 1860—Catholics, aristocrats, peasants—led by modernizers who promised the benefits of economic growth without the threat of revolutionary change (a view congenial to developmental theories that make of fascism a transitional phase of modernization). The latter two schools of thought also stress the importance of antiliberal ideas and attitudes by no means unique to Italy. Although these interpretations are not necessarily exclusive, each makes somewhat different assumptions about natural patterns of development and about the condition of Italy after the first world war.

Italian political development since the second world war has been sufficiently uneven to offer additional evidence for each of these views: Italy's relative stability and her economic miracle are as undeniable as her deep ideological and social divisions, or the persistence of such

[1] Piero Gobetti, *Risogimento senza eroi* (Turin, 1926); *La rivoluzione liberale* (Turin, 1950).

familiar problems as southern backwardness and administrative inefficiency. The persistence of old problems in the midst of clear achievements has helped, however, to open the way for historical analysis somewhat further removed from political controversy, while the influence of the social sciences and of Marxism have combined to spur more intensive study of social structure. The effort to establish some pattern in the crises of Italian development can, therefore, be more informed now than it would have been in the past; but a historiography as varied and ideologically engaged as the history it encompasses also labels in advance any such undertaking as a highly personal matter.[2]

Italy is, of course, a very special case of modernization. Her institutions and culture have always been part of the Western European mainstream. However backward her governments, much of Italy was after 1815 politically and culturally more like France than was most of the Austrian Empire or Spain. Italy's conscious and rapid political modernization began (in contrast to most other nations') when Western liberalism was still in vogue, and sought to make Italy more like Britain and France (rather than to escape their dominance). On the other hand, modernization in Italy produced particular strains. National unification required a conscious turning away from a past in which the proudest achievements were associated either with city states or a universal church. Whatever its accomplishments, Italian society was constantly measured against the "more advanced" examples across the Alps—and found wanting. Worse, even as Italians achieved a centralized state, liberal institutions, and modern industry, those accomplishments were being newly challenged in the nations that had experienced them first.

By any general standard Italian modernization has enjoyed significant "successes," yet from unification to the present a high proportion of the population has indicated its radical rejection of Italy's political system. Local violence, voting patterns, the disaffection of intellectuals, the instability of single ministries, and the simple refusal to cooperate have constantly reminded Italian governments of the opposition they faced, an opposition only rarely submerged in outbursts of patriotism. A developmental pattern so classic, and yet

[2] The best introductions to this literature in English are Charles F. Delzell, ed., *The Unification of Italy, 1859-1861* (New York, 1965); and A. William Salomone, ed., *Italy from Risorgimento to Fascism* (New York, 1970).

with results so mixed, should be a useful test of any theory of modernization, particularly one centering on crises, for Italians tend to consider crises endemic to their political life.

Crises

IDENTITY

Although Italy is a relatively young European nation, Italian identity is conceived in millennial terms, for the culture has maintained a sense of continuity from ancient Rome to the present. Many Renaissance leaders called themselves Italian, though the degree of modern nationalism in that term can be disputed. By the nineteenth century few denied the existence of an Italian culture, and patriots who denounced the dominance of French letters or found the Etruscans at the origin of Western civilization were arguing that Italian culture was independent and creative. For Italians, increased national consciousness did not require unearthing forgotten literature or learning to write some unprinted tongue. It was, in fact, dangerously easy to forget that Italian was the formal language of an elite, and that Italy's overwhelming majority of illiterates spoke only their native dialect.

This sense of a common and admirable Italian culture was reinforced by religion. However international Catholicism was, the papacy remained an Italian institution; and when Mazzini spoke of the "Third Rome" he was both dreaming of a new Italian state and boasting of the "Italian" influence of the Catholic church and the Roman Empire. Religious conflicts took place not between religions but among nominal Catholics (if Jansenism was an issue, Protestantism really was not), and tended, like anticlericalism, to extend across the peninsula rather than to divide regions. Even the multiple political divisions of Italy helped to establish cultural identity as independent of politics, for nearly every educated Italian had traveled in some state not his own yet indisputedly Italian. The administrative and legal practices of the various Italian states were not only similar, but the policies of one were copied in others; monarchs and aristocracies frequently intermarried, and the several courts regularly borrowed each other's statesmen. Eighteenth-century reformers and reform programs were remarkably similar in Lombardy, Tuscany, Parma, or Naples.

When Metternich offered his famous quip that Italy was a geographical expression, he infuriated Italian nationalists; but he also conceded something Czechs or Poles might have envied. The geographical boundaries of Italy were "natural" ones, less subject to major controversy than those of most European states. Regional differences, in dialect and custom, were great, though probably no more so than those between Wales and Yorkshire, Brittany and Provence, or Catalonia and Andalusia. The unity Italy lacked seemed more tangibly and simply political. Tuscany, relatively prosperous and progressive, was closely tied to Austria, as were the Duchies of Parma and Modena. The Papal States, poorly governed but centrally located, were supported by traditional ties to France and Austria and by the loyalty of Catholics everywhere. The declining but proud Venetian republic lost its independence in 1799, first to Napoleon and then to Austria; Lombardy, too, became a part of the Austrian Empire. Political fragmentation could, in short, be attributed to international politics, for only the kingdoms of the Two Sicilies (Naples) and of Sardinia (Piedmont) played in European diplomacy the independent role of sovereign states.

The first Italian experience of political unity in modern times, or at least of something approaching it, came with Napoleon. Even he never permitted all Italy a single, unified state; but he introduced uniform institutions and practices, put Italians into a single army, and gave them a common coinage as well as high taxes. However self-serving these policies, they left behind more common institutions, better roads, numerous academies, a standard of administrative efficiency, and even some experience of representative bodies—a kind of first installment on the gains to be expected from revolutionary and enlightened principles. By 1815 literate Italians believed as deeply as Europeans anywhere that effective government was the key to social well being. The period of the Risorgimento, from the eighteenth century to 1870, was therefore one of politicization; and the movement for national unification created a classic crisis of identity. The Risorgimento benefitted from the economic development of Lombardy, Piedmont, and Tuscany, and the resultant pressures for common tariffs, better transport, scientific farming, industrialization, and improved education; but it made the benefits from all such changes seem dependent upon political unification. Eventually, the achievement of unity appeared more important than the means by which it was achieved or the policies that the new state might pursue.

Many aspects of the Risorgimento follow from this emphasis upon politics. First, for all the fervent rhetoric the movement evoked, it was so essentially political as to seem prosaic. *Italianità* did not really have to be defined (and Italians heard relatively little of racial doctrines); but the emphasis upon politics, and realistic politics at that, dimmed the sense of ethical and cultural mission so vibrant in Mazzini. After unification, the government's ability to mobilize support even among the middle classes was reduced by the impression that the state itself was the product of tawdry political deals.

Second, the emphasis upon politics allowed the Cavourian coalition of liberal aristocrats and middle-class lawyers to make use of revolutionaries and radical reformers without permitting them a real share of power. Radical goals were not formally rejected, but their consideration was carefully postponed until a unified state—a state acceptable to the other European powers and to the most cautious Italian nationalists—could be created. The social changes that followed unification were thus the byproduct of moderate liberalism and slow economic modernization more than political initiative.

Third, the skill that marshaled the diffuse forces of nationalism prepared the way for serious disillusionment. There was a tendency to expect too much of politics, to promise prosperity, justice, and a cultural flowering from the achievement of a national political system.[3] For a society in which a competent bureaucracy and political stability were not yet achieved, such expectations could be explosive.

Still, unification proved a far more effective response to the crisis of identity than any of the alternatives. After 1815, Austrian policy sought to deny that nationalist feelings were important, but neither repression nor the substitution of other benefits (a relatively efficient bureaucracy, efforts to stimulate economic growth, or attempts to placate the intelligentsia) proved sufficient to the challenge. The politicization of Italian identity threatened any foreign presence; and after 1848, Austria recognized more clearly than ever that her position rested upon military force (and therefore on the acquiescence of the other European powers). Projects for an Italian federation in the 1840s offered a way out for the "native" states, but required a liberalizing gamble few were willing or able to take. The papacy went far in 1846-1848 to assuage patriotic sentiment, but the church's universal responsibilities and determination to maintain her own conservative rule in central Italy made sufficient accommodation im-

[3] Raymond Grew, *A Sterner Plan for Italian Unity* (Princeton, 1963), pp. 141-66, 476-79.

possible. Although the political and military weaknesses of federalism were dramatized in 1848-1849, the Neapolitan and Tuscan governments still had a chance to establish their place in an Italian union during the fifties. Both failed to do so, the first unwilling to adopt the necessary domestic reforms, the second unable to assert the required independence in foreign policy. Cavourian policy and the mistakes of the other states left Piedmont the only established regime that could survive the creation of an Italian state. That solution was in many respects a compromise; it emphasized national identity at the expense of a democratic revolution, and it accepted a disappointingly piecemeal creation of an Italian polity, including only the north (without Venice) in 1859, extending to the south (without Rome) in 1860, adding Venice in 1866 and Rome in 1870. Garibaldi's efforts to capture Rome without waiting for French approval created serious crises in 1862 and 1867; yet the government survived by rejecting Garibaldi in favor of diplomacy. A failure to take part in the Austro-Prussian war in 1866 or to take advantage of the Franco-Prussian war in 1870 would, on the other hand, undoubtedly have precipitated still greater crises.

With the taking of Rome, Italy's gravest identity crises were over. Irredentism was, to be sure, often strident, especially after the 1880s; memories of Nice and Savoy, insistent demands for extensive territorial gains from World War I, the Fiume crisis of the twenties, and the issue of Trieste in the 1950s, all evoked problems of identity. Each of these issues in some ways weakened the government of the time; yet even the noisiest propaganda rarely succeeded in making these questions the central ones of Italian life. The Italian state, which has not had to deal with issues as divisive as those that have rent Ireland or Belgium, represents the durable solution of an identity crisis—a solution that survived international Catholic opposition, military disaster in Ethiopia in 1896 and the strikes and repression of the following years, the strain of World War I, the rise and fall of fascism, and the creation of a republic.

Two amendments must be quickly added. First, Italian identity has remained limited, so much so that Italy's statesmen for a century after 1860 frequently behaved as if the state itself might come apart as quickly as it had been put together. Although Catholicism, regional loyalties, and a tradition of distrusting all governments have not often directly challenged Italian identity, they have—more than in most parliamentary regimes—restricted the claims that could be made on the citizen in the name of the nation. Catholics early learned to separate their patriotic feelings from cooperation with the secular government, and in that they have been followed by socialists and communists.

Italy's famed regionalism (and especially the *campanilismo* so despised by progressives) has often seemed to threaten the national polity. Yet that regionalism, partly perhaps because formal policy usually ignored its existence, is also easily exaggerated. In 1870 fewer than 1 percent of Italians had a mother tongue other than some form of Italian, and even with the territories annexed after World War I that percentage had barely doubled. Language does not measure identity, but by analogy at least it does speak to the problem: no other *national* identity challenged *italianità*. Serious separatist movements have been limited to the periphery—the Alto Adige, the Val d'Aosta, Sardinia, and Sicily—and even then have been sporadic and more recently reduced by international agreements, grants of autonomy, and linguistic concessions. But language also suggests the limits of identity. Outside Rome and Tuscany the Italian common tongue was used primarily in written and formal discourse; perhaps only 2.5 percent of the population employed it easily and habitually in 1861, some 40 percent by 1900.[4] Regional loyalties, like dialects, have eroded slowly and offered, even as they did, cultural support for resisting an intrusive state. Identity, like language, is a social phenomenon related in large part to literacy, communication, and social class. Italian politics, like the Italian language, have for much of Italy's brief history been the tool of a narrow elite.

The gravest of Italy's regional divisions, that between north and south, has scarcely denied Italian identity, despite the anguished discoveries in succeeding generations of two races, two nations, contrasting social systems, or a dual economy. Such sharp differences have, however, both encouraged centralization and limited its effectiveness, weakened the state and dominated its politics.[5] If many southerners quickly learned to view the state as a Piedmontese employment agency, Italians in all parts of the peninsula were inclined to distinguish between the government and national identity. Not surprisingly, efforts to evoke national feeling in behalf of the government—whether

[4] Tullio De Mauro, *Storia linguistica dell'Italia unita* (Bari, 1970), pp. 1-10, 28-37, 135.

[5] Regionalism and centralization are discussed by Denis Mack Smith in Edward R. Tannenbaum and Emiliana P. Noether, eds., *Modern Italy* (New York, 1974), pp. 125-46).

Crispi's anticlericalism and imperialism, Giolitti's Libyan campaign, or his opponents' interventionism in World War I—were only partly successful. Even fascism could not consistently overcome such limitations, despite its strident efforts to make identity more intense by redefining it, by extending it to all forms of public activity through official ideology and new institutions, and by demanding that everyone serve the national good as defined by the government.

Nevertheless—and this is the second amendment to any statement about a durable Italian sense of national identity—that identity has often appeared inadequate because governments have so often invoked it to strengthen themselves, especially in their resistance to demands for social change. Thus problems better understood in other terms have been treated as questions of identity. The "brigands" whose guerrilla warfare in the south bloodied the postunification years (and cost the Italian army more men than all the wars of unification) were, to be sure, supported by Carlists and to some extent by the papacy. But their strength was social, the angry alienation of peasants suspicious of any imposed order. They were met, however, more like a foreign army than a socialist protest. Similarly, Crispi saw in the peasant riots of the Sicilian fasci a few decades later a threat to the existence of the state rather than a complaint about its policies, and cold war leaders viewed the Communist party as more a foreign menace than a domestic opposition. For a century, belief that Italy's political identity was in danger encouraged reliance on police measures and further compromises with local elites. Such policies were costly, for they weakened the government's legitimacy, lessened effective participation, and led the state to accept very restricted penetration into society. The modernizing social changes the government meant to favor were slowed, while distrust of the state increased.

LEGITIMACY

The wide-scale acceptance of a governmental system as natural or good can evolve in many ways, but it is clearly strengthened by historical continuity associated with military or cultural glory (an element in the stability of all Europe's great monarchies), by intense and coherent ideologies (as in Calvin's Geneva or many revolutionary regimes), or by a consistent record of providing effectively for the general welfare and security (Switzerland and Canada may be examples of this). With the invasion of armies from revolutionary France, the weakness of Italy's governments in all these categories was clear, despite the special aura of Rome, the republican traditions of Venice, the military exploits of Piedmont, or the many ties between Italy's rulers and the crowns of Europe.

The problem of legitimacy had concerned Machiavelli, and Italian regimes from his day to the Risorgimento tried all the devices from religious sanction to military power to strengthen their claims to legitimacy. Often they relied upon the prestige and military strength of Spain, Austria, or France, or upon regal institutions of the approved European type and a place in international relations strengthened by family connection. Such efforts aided the process whereby the various city-states had gradually succumbed to larger units, usually with the aid of foreign arms; yet in the eighteenth century Italian properties could still be exchanged among Europe's royal families. The political stability achieved was largely imposed. In fact, the separate Italian states could endure only so long as internal opposition was diffuse, the pressures of economic change were slight, ideological assaults were rare, and external arrangements saved them from any serious test of their military power.

When restored by the allies in 1815, the legitimacy of regimes that had toppled before the French was still more vulnerable, visibly weakened by discontinuity and dependence on Austria. Talleyrand was so aware of this, particularly with reference to Italy, that he attempted at the Congress of Vienna to win the powers to a broad, new definition of legitimacy combining duration of rule and domestic acceptability, but even that seemed dangerous in the eyes of Metternich and Tsar Alexander.[6] After 1815, the governments of Italy rested primarily upon the influence of the aristocracy and the military power of other governments, especially Austria. Every revolution in France would threaten their position. Piedmont was strengthened not only by the regime's historic continuity and traditional autonomy, but by the loyalty of an aristocracy with a proud tradition of service. The papal government and the Bourbon regime in Naples attached the legitimacy of their rule to the church as well as to their aristocracies, but without claims to administrative efficiency. In Tuscany the aristocracy had greater prestige and perhaps greater legitimacy than the state, and in Lombardy the aristocracy was effectively deprived of political independence by the strength of the Austrian Empire. Else-

[6] It may be significant that Talleyrand's search for an ideology of restoration has tended to be taken most seriously by Italians; see Guglielmo Ferrero, *Ricostruzione: Talleyrand a Vienna* (Milan, 1948).

where, the "Court party" was often only a faction of the aristocracy, and the state depended more upon indifference than active support. Generally, there were hardly other groups capable of testing or challenging the government. Only Rome had a bureaucracy not dominated by the aristocracy, and priests were hardly the ones to reject papal discipline. On the other hand, the very special claims to legitimacy of a state ruled by the Vicar of Christ, although not enough to preserve the Papal States, echoed long after Italian unification.

In 1821, young officers and Bonapartists were able briefly to challenge the state in Piedmont, Naples, and Modena, but revolution was most threatening where governments resisted reform, lost the support of the liberal aristocracy, and could appeal neither to national nor regional identity: Sicily ruled from Naples, the Romagna ruled from Rome, and somewhat later in Lombardy-Venetia ruled from Vienna. New, imported standards of legitimacy had showed their dangerous power in 1799, and thereafter visions of economic progress and ideas of nationalism gave new weapons to those who wished to deny the legitimacy of the established regimes. In 1848 they fell, even in Rome, with remarkable ease. Restored once more, all except Piedmont's henceforth rejected any claim that legitimacy was related to the popular will—a stand so fatal that in 1859-1860 these governments were hardly capable of self-defense. They collapsed as old leaders withdrew, even before local revolution could take shape or foreign armies could arrive. The dukes who, like Charles X and Louis-Philippe in France, climbed into their carriages and headed for the frontier, epitomized a crisis of legitimacy long brewing.

The new Italian monarchy based its legitimacy upon three awkwardly combined claims: the historic legitimacy of the royal House of Savoy, Italy's right to be a nation, and the popular will expressed in the plebiscites by which each area of Italy voted to join the new state. These diverse claims to legitimacy, each of which could be disputed, were brought together in legal codes, constitutional procedures, and representative government, enabling the liberal regime for sixty years to sustain its legitimacy against challenges so frequent as to make the achievement notable. Garibaldians and Mazzinians denied the legitimacy of a government that sought only piecemeal unification and that rejected democracy. Catholics declared the despoilers of the church illegitimate rulers and boycotted elections to make their point. By the turn of the century, anarchists and socialists had joined the assault. Military humiliation from Austria in 1866 and in Ethiopia twenty years later, scandals and charges of corruption such as the *Banco di Roma* affair of 1893, the strikes and riots of 1898 all fostered renewed attacks on the regime's legitimacy. Yet it survived, the opposition slowly reduced by diplomatic gains, parliamentary investigations, or the extension of civil liberties, suffrage, and welfare.

The Italian state has defended its legitimacy primarily by emphasizing formal legality and by asserting its vague but ultimate dependence on the popular will. The new nation gave great weight to continuity. Victor Emmanuel II of Piedmont kept that title as king of Italy, and the legal codes of Piedmont continued in the new nation, much as laws of the fascist monarchy remain on the books of the contemporary Republic. For a century most of Italy's leaders (and a majority of her elite generally) have been trained in a highly formalistic jurisprudence that informs Italy's general culture as well as her bureaucratic and political procedures. Even after years of violence and the ugly charade of the March on Rome, Mussolini was careful to become prime minister and to acquire his extraordinary powers in formally correct ways. Similarly, care was taken to make his deposition and replacement by Marshal Badoglio meticulously legal.[7] Palely reflected in the numerous and elaborate official ceremonies of the Republic (borrowed from an era of regal authority), this sense of the state's legal roots remains closely intertwined with Italy's political identity as well as its cumbersome bureaucracy.

The state's claim to rest on the popular will, expressed in the plebiscites of the Risorgimento, depended only partially on a parliament elected by limited suffrage, and has remained something vague, beyond mere representation. Yet it was critical in forcing an end to the political repression of 1896-1900 in order to avoid a crippling crisis of legitimacy; and it was central to the bafflement of antifascists faced with a regime that acquired power legally and boasted of its own extraparliamentary ways of embodying the popular will. Significantly, the Matteotti crisis was the gravest challenge to its legitimacy that Fascism faced until the Allied invasion twenty years later. Mussolini's dramatic capture by the Germans and the brief life of his Salò venture attached Fascism more firmly than ever to the Nazi occupation, and the resistance of the partisans did more than the king to make it clear that legitimacy lay elsewhere. The difficult crisis raised by opposition

[7] Carlo Ghisalberti, *Storia constituzionale d'Italia, 1849/1958* (Bari, 1974), p. 382; the book as a whole is an excellent discussion of Italy's legal and constitutional tradition.

to the monarchy was then rather smoothly settled by referendum. Italy's present republic, like the monarchy it replaced, rests upon a formal vote conducted but once; and though the procedures used in the nineteenth-century plebiscites could be questioned and the returns of the twentieth-century one were hardly one-sided (54 percent of those who went to the polls, 51 percent of those eligible voted for the change), the results of those votes have been accepted as the voice of the people.

Since 1870, however, the legitimacy of Italian governments has been denied by significant and vocal groups—on general ideological and moral grounds, as not in fact reflecting the popular will, and for failing to fulfill its functions. The challenge from principle has generally been weathered—at the high price of a divided political culture and widespread distrust of politics.[8] Although Mazzinians, Catholics, and Marxists have not brought the government down, their rejection of its legitimacy has made compromise more difficult, leaders more cautious, and turmoil more common. Italian governments have learned not to add to their enemies by threatening the established interests of local notables, capitalists, the church, or the bureaucracy. If legitimacy has rested on the sense of identity and tradition, the forms of legality, and some allusion at least to the popular will, it may in practice have required the state's rather limited penetration into society.

That the liberal state did not reflect the true desires of its people was asserted by Catholics and, in more limited terms, by Mazzinians from its beginning. But the passing of the old Cavourian right with its air of personal rectitude exposed the politics of *transformismo* to a less ideological but more widespread attack: that in Italy the political process was inherently corrupting, the echo of private interests rather than the expression of public needs.[9] Such charges, all too often well founded, were more than a spur to reform; for they tended to pull moderate conservatives, moderate Catholics, and moderate socialists toward opposition to the regime itself, thus narrowing further the basis of its legitimacy.

[8] Joseph LaPalombara, *Interest Groups in Italian Politics* (Princeton, 1964), pp. 53-62.

[9] Salvemini's philippics are the most famous and most insightful: Gaetano Salvemini, *Il Ministro della mala vita e altri scritti sull'Italia giolittiana*, edited by Elio Apito (Milan, 1962); but Sidney Sonnino, *Scritti e discorsi extraparlamentari 1870-1902*, I, edited by Benjamin F. Brown (Bari, 1972) shows the political disaffection of a moderate conservative from 1872 on. See also Gabriele de Rosa, *Vescovi, popolo, e magia nel Sud* (Naples, 1971), pp. 215, 243-45. Giovanni Spadolini, *I Radicali nel'Ottocento* (Florence, 1963), pp. 152-59, notes the vilification of Depretis.

The ultimate test of any government's legitimacy is its capacity to perform essential functions. That the Italian government failed to meet this test was asserted from the 1880s on by some who cited the unsolved social problems of the poor and of the south, and by others who cited nationalist goals unmet and internal order not maintained. But the dismal record of World War I, the disappointing peace, and the domestic disorder thereafter made this a more central issue, which fascists exacerbated and then capitalized upon. The legitimacy of the Republic has also been challenged on these grounds in the 1950s and the 1970s. Each time new standards of political capacity have been imported—with the Enlightenment, the French Revolution, nineteenth-century liberalism, democracy and socialism, and the European Common Market—Italian governments have faced some crises of legitimacy. There have been few moments in modern Italian history when a crisis of legitimacy was not a real possibility. Such frequent threats on so many fronts should not, however, obscure the equally striking fact that some consensus as to its legitimacy has reinforced a legalistic tradition, preserved for the state some aura of awe, and remained an important source of strength for Italian national governments.

PARTICIPATION

Italy's long urban tradition made both voting and political demonstrations a common experience there earlier than in most of Europe, and since 1848 participation in plebiscites and elections has been a major source of legitimacy. Thus when Catholics withheld their participation in the first generation of unification, all sides recognized the seriousness of that challenge; and the Aventine secession, when opposition parties withdrew from the Fascist chamber, may have been weakly symbolic, but the focus on participation was characteristic.

The extension of the franchise in national elections marked a gradual progression to democracy of the sort textbooks usually associate with England. After the plebiscites of 1859-1860, conducted by universal suffrage, the Piedmontese electoral law was calmly extended to united Italy in a remarkable act of conservatism, giving the vote to approximately two percent of the population: all literate men over twenty-five who paid high, direct taxes—a measure of the narrow elite upon whom national unity seemed to depend. In 1881 the electorate was more than trebled (from roughly 600,000 to 2,000,000, or seven percent of the population) by lowering the voting age to twenty-one, by reducing the taxes required for eligibility to just over one-third the former figure, and by permitting all who had university degrees or held certain major offices to vote in any case, a characteristic definition of the political elite. That extension of the suffrage was a major promise of the old left that supplanted the Cavourians in 1876. Figures of lesser influence and independent social status, they compensated by building a broader political base. Following the repression of 1894-1900,[10] Giolitti's liberal governments sought to appeal to Catholics and all but the extreme left. In 1912, Italy adopted what was essentially universal male suffrage (all men over thirty could vote; those between twenty-one and thirty had to meet the old requirements); by the election of 1919 all men over twenty-one could vote, and proportional representation was added. With the dominance of a Catholic party that did not share traditional fears of clerical influence, adult women were given the vote in 1948. Thus every generation witnessed a significant increase in eligible voters. The conservative caution with which this occurred may even have contributed to stability and (much as in Belgium) allowed representative forms to take root. Certainly the disenfranchisement of peasants reduced attention to regional questions and allowed an impoverished government to avoid facing the difficulties of the southern question. The exclusion of workers similarly postponed some of the political complications of industrialization, and the abstention of Catholics made public education and *de facto* arrangements with the Vatican easier to establish.

Until 1876 Cavourian liberals were free to insist that good government meant balanced budgets and civil liberties. Then until World War I, Italian politics were characterized by *trasformismo*, a system of shifting parliamentary majorities (not unlike that in England under Walpole or France under Guizot) in which a certain amount of electoral corruption, innumerable personal political deals, and skillful shifts in political programs prevented the formation of an effective opposition.[11] That system also excluded most Italians from any direct part in national politics, while increasing the distrust of politicians and alienation from politics so often noted as a characteristic of Italian

[10] It is significant that Crispi, di Rudinì, and Pelloux did not dare a direct reduction in the suffrage, although they were certainly tempted. The return to single-member constituencies and concommitantly stricter residency requirements in 1894 did, however, reduce the number of eligible voters by almost 29 percent (from 9.4 percent to 6.7 percent of the population, a disenfranchisement of more than 800,000 men).

[11] Raymond Grew, "Il trasformismo: ultimo stadio del Risorgimento," in Vittorio Frosini, ed., *Il Risorgimento e l'Europa* (Catania, 1969), pp. 151-63.

society.[12] Of the important cleavages in Italian society, only the regional ones were effectively represented in parliamentary life; and the relatively homogeneous political elite encouraged distrust of organized national parties. They achieved a central institutional role relatively late in Italian political history. The new parties and alignments that developed with universal suffrage did not have time to produce an effective alternative system before the disruption of world war and the rise of fascism. Since 1948, Italian politics has been dominated by highly organized mass parties, especially the Christian Democrats and Communists. To many a voter, however, party bosses seem no more responsive than local notables.

From 1871 to 1922, the Italian political system managed its transition to broader participation relatively smoothly; and it has shown remarkable centripetal attraction, gradually winning Catholics, then socialists, and now possibly Communists to cooperation and compromise within the system. In part this has resulted from the greater accessibility of local politics. In the nineteenth century, suffrage was more generous in local elections (which Catholics did not boycott and in which some socialists won local positions long before the party was nationally prominent), and currently the case for Communist responsibility and moderation is based in great part on the party's effective leadership in cities such as Bologna and the regional governments of central Italy. This gradual expansion of suffrage from local to national levels, and there by stages, has also, however, come at high cost. Illiteracy, poor communication, and an underdeveloped economy, which were used to justify gradualness, also made it possible; and the groups excluded from formal political life included a high proportion of those inclined to think in national terms and to be sensitive to social issues. Before each extension of the suffrage save the last, excluded groups had already proclaimed their alienation. Working-class parties, militant Catholics, regional and rural groups arrived on the national political scene experienced in combat and with little loyalty to the established system.

[12] Gabriel A. Almond and Sidney Verba, *The Civic Culture* (Princeton, 1963); Alberto Spreafico and Joseph LaPalombara, eds., *Elezioni e comportamento politico in Italia* (Milan, 1963); Joseph LaPalombara, "Italy: Fragmentation, Isolation, Alienation," in Lucien W. Pye and Sidney Verba, eds., *Political Culture and Political Development* (Princeton, 1969), pp. 282-329. Samuel H. Barnes, "Italy: Oppositions, Left, Right, and Center," in Robert A. Dahl, ed., *Political Oppositions in Western Democracies* (New Haven, 1966), pp. 303-31; Giovanni Sartori, "European Political Parties: the Case of Polarised Pluralism," in Joseph LaPalombara and Myron Weiner, eds., *Political Development* (Princeton, 1966), pp. 140-53.

Voting in Italy has perhaps been more important as a symbolic act than as an expression of choice. Nearly 80 percent of the adult males of Italy voted in the plebiscites of the Risorgimento, almost unanimously for unification. In national elections from 1861 to 1924, approximately 58 percent of those eligible, on the average, troubled to vote. The Fascists made much of the act of voting (and the legal penalties they established for not participating have, significantly, been kept in the Republic); since 1929 every national election has brought 89 percent or more of the eligible voters to the polls. Furthermore, these impressive turnouts have occurred across the nation.[13] Yet the parliaments thus elected have remained distant; governmental pressures clearly affected the results, especially in the south, and the prime minister has been more a parliamentary arbiter contriving his majority than a national leader.[14] Parliament in turn has often been bypassed at the most critical times. The decisions to extend Piedmont's administrative codes to the entire nation were taken in 1859 under the wartime powers parliament had bequeathed to the nation; Crispi ruled for a tumultuous year with parliament prorogued, and the decision to enter World War I was put only indirectly to a parliament that then had little to do with its conduct. The examples can be multiplied, and Mussolini's demands for extraordinary powers and rigged majorities were thus in themselves less shocking than they might have been.[15]

Voting was not, of course, the only or necessarily the most important form of political participation in Italy. The Risorgimento itself was a triumph of demonstrations: of tricolor bunting dropped from opera balconies, taxes withheld, patriotic funds solicited, and piazzas filled with cheering throngs. These organized public expressions could be as important politically as any election. Political life, in short, was always bursting the narrow bounds of formal procedures, and the demonstration was often a political act, even a political achievement, in its own right. Similarly, strikes in the decades before World War I and since were protests as often political as economic.

[13] Based on statistics in the Appendix of Ghisalberti, *Storia costituzionale*, and in *Statistiche del Mezzogiorno d'Italia, 1861-1953*, published by SVIMEZ, Associazione per lo Sviluppo dell'industria nel Mezzogiorno (Rome, 1961), pp. 944-60.

[14] On the role of prefects in the elections, see Robert C. Fried, *The Italian Prefects: A Study in Administrative Politics* (New Haven, 1963), pp. 247-49, 255-59; on the nature of participation in the contemporary south, see Sidney G. Tarrow, *Peasant Communism in Southern Italy* (New Haven, 1967), especially pp. 74-81.

[15] The importance of the decision on intervention as background to the rise of fascism is noted in Carlo Morandi, *I partiti politici nella storia d'Italia* (Florence, 1946), p. 76; and Roberto Vivarelli, *Il dopoguerra in Italia e l'avvento del fascismo, 1918-1922*, I (Naples, 1967), pp. 40-42, 552.

Such demonstrations implied, of course, that the legal political system was unresponsive, and the conviction that it was spurred the development of alternative forms of participation. The Catholic Action movement that developed in the 1880s and has continued in various forms to the present is one example. Groups of laymen formed cooperatives, mutual aid funds, lending libraries, societies for defense of the faith, and charitable organizations—but always they saw themselves as a militant interest group, striving to influence (or defend itself against) the state. The workers' organizations known as *Camere di lavoro*, similarly diffuse in membership and aims, sponsored cooperatives and unions, recreation centers, and edifying lectures on everything from history to hygiene. In the 1890s they taught a whole generation to see itself as a class excluded, and like Catholic Action, they were extrapolitical organizations seeking ends in large part political. The Fascist regime institutionalized extrapolitical participation into a mode of government, and the Communist party and the church now sponsor a wide array of cultural, economic, and recreational organizations as a means of mobilizing political strength outside politics. Such alternative participation, while putting useful pressure on politicians, tends also to withdraw important political forces from the arena of political negotiation and thus to lessen the flexibility of the political process itself.

In addition to this alternative participation, there has also been in Italy a kind of apolitical participation based on informal relations through which political purposes can be achieved with minimal direct or public connection to established politics. The now much-studied networks of patron-client relationships are prime examples, but other interest groups have operated similarly. People in such networks participate in social and political life, while recognizing little connection between local or personal goals and national political issues, and while playing by rules quite different from those of the formal political system. Such apolitical participation requires political sophistication and is more than merely backward, or "traditional" rejection of change; yet it similarly resists the penetration of rational policy or central organization.

These various modes of participation have reached more deeply into Italian society than the national political system. From 1871 to the present, Italy's political leaders have, like the upper bureaucracy, usually been members of a rather isolated professional class, trained in a rigid legal tradition. While awkward at appealing to a broad public, they were comfortable in dealing with local elites; and thus the Italian political system has almost uniquely combined an isolated elite with mass mobilization in which voting is seen as a very limited form of participation, a momentary and often angry declaration more than the selection of a representative to the legislature. With the introduction of universal suffrage, those hardened in the politics of alternative participation continued to undermine the old system until fascism obliterated it. Since World War II the traditions that emphasize voting, that preserve the distance between citizens and rulers, and that seek alternative forms of participation have found expression in sprawling, bureaucratized parties.[16]

PENETRATION

Since unification, problems of penetration have proved the most intractable of all those faced by the Italian state. All societies offer some resistance to governmental intrusions, but that resistance has been particularly broadly based and skillful in Italy, where the linkages between state and society have been weak and the Italian bureaucracy has rarely been an effective instrument of change. From its beginnings, the Italian state faced many groups determined to oppose or subvert its policies. The aristocracies of the several smaller states had, after all, long resisted the pretensions of their own rulers and of foreign governments, and the Catholic hierarchy excelled in the tactics of opposition. Local notables, while sometimes willing to side with the state against the first two orders, first made sure that national government would not undermine their own often shaky positions. In addition, artisans and workers had good reason to welcome the leadership of radicals who made their careers opposing established hierarchies; and communities only tenuously connected to the outside world could offer the most formidable barrier of all through patron-client networks that absorbed the agents of central government, of commerce, or of national parties into the complex web of local interests.

The Risorgimento itself brought a crisis of penetration with the extension of uniform laws and bureaucracy to the entire peninsula. Even then, patriotic enthusiasm and a successful army only effected political change at the top; the social pyramid, if somewhat truncated, re-

[16] On the role of parties, see Giovanni Sartori, *Il Parlamento* (Naples, 1963); and Stefano Passigli, "Italy" in R. Rose and A. J. Heidenheimer, eds., "Comparative Political Finance," special issue of *Journal of Politics*, 25 (August 1963), 718-36.

mained essentially unchanged. Holding the nation together continued to be the central concern of Italy's moderate leaders, and their own insecurity was reflected in the adoption of a highly centralized administration on the French model, but at the same time one in which the prefect did not enjoy all the powers of his French counterpart (for example, the regional agents of each ministry reported directly to ministerial superiors in Rome rather than through the prefect).[17] The sporadic and bloody challenge of southern brigands was only slowly overcome by military means and the use of ancient patron-client networks. From necessity as well as conviction, the state generally chartered a course of accommodation with the church, whose territory it had absorbed and monastic lands it sold, despite sporadic thrusts at anticlericalism. With the outburst of the Sicilian fasci in 1894, Crispi again attempted a military solution of armed repression and a state of seige, but the crisis thus begun became a crisis of legitimacy that eventually led to a reaffirmation of liberal politics. Thus an attempt at increased penetration without modernization or increased participation had threatened legitimacy; stability was better assured by the old compromised system, whose policies reached the citizen muffled by the voice of a local patron.

Even the bureaucracy, at first dominated by the Piedmontese, had taken on a less alien tone as it absorbed officials from the regimes overthrown. Within a generation most prefects were natives of the regions they administered;[18] and a growing proportion of officials came from the south, where backwardness and respect for rank made a government career especially attractive. The inefficiency and lethargy of Italian bureaucracy, which lacked traditions of Napoleonic expertise or Prussian service, became the target of every reformer. In an economy plagued by underemployment and a society keenly sensitive to social status, its very cumbersomeness rested on the social structure it could not command.

The unheroic achievements of this approach were nevertheless real. Until World War I, the proportion of public expenditures devoted to administration increased but slightly;[19] yet a national administration

[17] Fried, *Italian Prefects*, pp. 120-46; Isabella Ianni Rosiello, *Unificazione politica e amministrazione nelle "Provincie dell'Emilia" (1859-60)* (Milan, 1965), pp. 199, 265.

[18] Ernesto Ragionieri, *Politica e amministrazione nella storia d'Italia unita* (Bari, 1967), pp. 127-29.

[19] Istituto Centrale di Statistica, *Sommario di statistiche storiche dell'Italia, 1861-1965* (Rome, 1968), pp. 139, 142.

was created and preserved, a national army effectively recruited, indirect taxes at least regularly collected, roads and railroads built and maintained, a national system of education slowly extended and improved, the basic services provided with standards of domestic order and justice probably at about the level enjoyed by most Europeans. From the Risorgimento on, however, politically conscious Italians had expected much more; and they tended to blame the state for the absence of forced modernization, efficiency, and public integrity. By such standards, Italian government was weak and immobile; even the establishment of a modern, national banking system required a generation of discussion, a number of bank failures leading to the crisis of the nineties, and extraparliamentary arrangements with German capital.[20] Dissatisfaction had reached dangerous proportions even before the outbreak of world war, a challenge that staggered every state in Europe, and for which Italy did just mobilize sufficient resources to survive.

The strikes and agitation of the postwar period, which seemed to threaten revolution, also measured the government's incompetence. While fascism played effectively on such fears, a confused and weak government faced the need for decisive action unsure of how its own officials or the army, the king, the church, and most political leaders would respond to any clear command. Afraid to act with speed, it gave way to the Fascists without a real test of strength. If the Fascist "revolution" succeeded during a crisis of penetration, fascism's promise to resolve that chronic crisis was an important part of its appeal. It attempted to accomplish this through a single, authoritarian party (and discovered that in Italy a single party could so quickly fall prey to careerists that membership had to be restricted), through a near monopoly of cultural and recreational activities (and soon had to make an exception for the organizations of Catholic Action), and through a corporative system intended to extend the government's will into all the economic structures of society (a system that was for the most part captured instead by the large industrial interests). Still, Fascism was a truly radical attempt to increase penetration through tyranny; and the regime that even battled the mafia undoubtedly managed to touch the lives of more Italians than its predecessors; but unity and efficiency proved easier to achieve as an illusion of propaganda than as a social reality. If world war is the test of those qualities

[20] See Giordano dell'Amore, "Il processo di costituzione della banca centrale in Italia," in *L'Economia italiana dal 1861 al 1961* (Milan, 1961), pp. 360-77.

that Fascism declared it to be, Italy slipped farther behind her neighbors in the second than the first. In the bitter days of his Salò Republic, as Mussolini flailed against the monarchy, church, business, and bureaucracy that had once supported him, he described a failure of penetration.

The monarchy and army, whose sympathetic inaction had helped him to power, were still free to dump the Duce in 1943. Constitutionally, those institutions had always escaped clear subordination to parliament; and Sidney Sonnino's famous call in 1897 for a return to the *Statuto* (as understood in 1848) evoked the sense that only through such autonomy could the state exercise effective authority. With a more modern vision, Fascism made its most lasting contribution in the creation of other autonomous organizations of state, like the industrial holding company, the *Istituto per la Riscostruzione Industriale*. Since 1945 the example has been vastly extended; IRI, the enterprising energy corporation ENI (*Ente Nazionale Idrocarburi*), the *Cassa per il Mezzogiorno*, and scores of other subsidiary and parallel organizations have played a central role in Italy's remarkable postwar economic growth. These autonomous state organizations, like the great political parties, both inhibit governmental penetration and in some sense compensate for its weakness, reaching into society while prodding and resisting parliament and bureaucracy to assure policies in their own interest.[21] Even as Italy has experienced breathtaking economic and social modernization, her government has never been far from the crisis of penetration its numerous outraged critics loudly predict. Corruption, though real, has been exaggerated; inefficiency, though grave, has been increased; indecisiveness and instability, though serious, have been accentuated by opponents of left and right, who have learned over the past one hundred years to test the state's weakness while denouncing it.

DISTRIBUTION

There were throughout the nineteenth century strong economic arguments for unification; but these were primarily that a national market and free environment would unleash those natural forces certain to produce prosperity. After unification, the demands of national defense, limited penetration, and general poverty kept the government

[21] Joseph LaPalombara, *Italy: the Politics of Planning* (Syracuse, 1966) discusses the "parentela" by which these agencies influence government, the resistance to penetration, and the continuing need for buraucratic reform.

pressed for money. Until the 1880s, three-fifths of the government's expenditures were devoted to the military and the national debt; amounts allocated to public works and education could not meet the nation's needs.[22] Although dedicated to economic growth and industrialization, Italy's cautious liberal leaders had no consistent vision of the government's role in promoting these ends.

It was expected, of course, that the national government would be less wasteful than those it replaced, by eliminating both duplication and the aristocratic taste for extravagance. In practice, however, liberal parsimony produced no enormous savings. The confiscation of church lands stands, therefore, as the most notable distributive policy of the new Italian state, and it was considered a single, surgical measure for putting important resources into "productive" hands and for weakening a dangerous enemy. The government did not feel responsible, however, for determining who should acquire the new land or how it was used. In fact, the concentration of land holding decreased only slightly, and the sale of church lands was more notable for stimulating an emphasis on quick profit (through deforestation, for example) than on long-term improvement. The distinct land-holding systems of the Po Valley, the center, and the south remained much as before. Similarly, a national market brought an automatic extension of Piedmont's low tariffs, and most southerners (followed since by many historians) have seen this as an economic disaster for the south, spiking any chance for that region's early industrialization. If Italy's policies favored the northern middle classes, they merely followed the economic dogmas of the day. Despite some subsidies to railroads, shipbuilding, ports, and heavy industry, the government was more inclined to divest itself of such economic responsibilities in the interest of a balanced budget.[23]

It was, in fact, uncertain as to which distributive issues were legitimate subjects of national politics. Peasant hunger for land was part of the revolutions that helped create the nation and of the brigandage that quickly challenged it, but the issue was allowed little direct voice within the moderate regime. The relations of peasant and landlord continued to be fixed by the sanctity of property and local custom. Labor agitation from the 1860s through the 1880s over such issues as a ten-hour day, wages, and union recognition was officially viewed more as a local challenge to order than a national concern. On the

[22] Rosario Romeo, *Risorgimento e capitalismo* (Bari, 1959), p. 141; *Statistiche storiche*, p. 139.

[23] These policies are discussed in Romeo, *Risorgimento e capitalismo* and in *L'Economia italiana*.

other hand, nationalist denunciations of the old regimes had made much of retarded economics and inadequate public services, and a variety of old hopes haunted the new regime; but some distributive issues could be ignored and most postponed so long as suffrage was limited.

Even tax policy was considered more as a matter of desperate necessity than as part of any larger economic vision. Reluctantly, Italy's leaders declared government bonds unconvertible and resorted to the hated grist tax, even though they recognized it to be regressive and unjust, promising merely that it would be temporary. A policy that so evoked the old regime and that made the poor pay to balance the budget gave the opposition a clear issue and contributed to the fall of the Cavourian Right; by 1880 the measure was repealed. Increasingly in the eighties southern politicians demanded protection for agricultural goods if they were to accept tariffs against cotton textiles, iron, and steel. Tariffs thus became, like the political assignment of bridges, railroads, and new schools, part of the complex trading on which parliamentary majorities were built. The agony of emigration rather than any government policy was the most imporant response to southern poverty. When the social effects of the policies effected proved too painful, as in Crispi's tariff war with France, they had to be altered. But on the whole, distributive policies were not often explicitly at issue or central to political conflict before rapid industrialization and the growth of trade union movements and workers' parties at the end of the century. Strikes, for example, were increasingly an angry demand for different patterns of distribution, and they threatened very serious political crises. The government's initial response, the suppression under Crispi, Pelloux, and di Rudinì, was abandoned by the turn of the century in favor of Giolitti's effective return to a liberal solution: the government would proclaim neutrality in battles between management and labor. In imitation of its northern neighbors, the government also undertook limited programs of accident and old-age insurance and improved public services, but the most effective response remained the removal of distributive issues from politics. That would become more difficult as prosperity brought more wealth to distribute (the cost of industrialization was until 1900 paid for by low *per capita* consumption)[24] and suffrage broadened.

The socialist vision of what the state should do, the needs of the first world war, and the example of the Soviet revolution all signaled

[24] Roberto Tremelloni, "Gli ultimi cent'anni dell'industria italiana," *L'Economia italiana*, p. 225.

the change. Strikes in the twenties appeared more threatening to society precisely because they were part of a rising demand for broad social, economic, and political changes. A crisis of distribution in an economy suffering the dislocations of war and rapid industrialization, and in a political system still adjusting to universal suffrage, contributed to the breakdown of the Italian political system in the postwar period. The Fascists, like the socialists, insisted upon the state's central role in all issues of distribution; and they encouraged the view that social and economic injustices had political solutions. At the same time, they stressed the spiritual merit of sacrifice in behalf of the national interest. In practice this meant a number of things. Autarchy was favored, whatever its economic effects, as in the Battle of Wheat. Elaborate public works and an expanding military were paid for primarily by the poor, while the government cooperated with the largest industrialists (whether they favored efficiency or not) in discouraging "wasteful" competition and in keeping wages down. Wage cuts, both direct and indirect, were measures no representative government would have dared, and family allowances and well-publicized special projects had by 1939 but barely compensated the workers for their earlier losses. Under Fascism the redistribution of resources that accompanied the growth of the twenties almost wholly favored capital.[25] The urgent demands of war as well as internal dissension and the lack of any clear program prevented much fuller development of a fascist economic policy.

After the second world war, there could be no question of the government's critical involvement in issues of distribution. The old barriers to government involvement were gone, and the revival of a war-torn economy (including the disposition of foreign aid) required drastic and planned government intervention. Social justice, like employment, was a promise of the Italian constitution. Socialists and Communists, with nearly half the popular vote, put strong pressure upon Christian Democratic governments, which already accepted in principle the government's general responsibility for economic and social conditions. Furthermore, many of the structures developed in the Fascist era remained to be used for different purposes, and new ones like the *Cassa per il Mezzogiorno* were quickly added. A high proportion of Italy's principle industrial firms are now controlled by the state, although they do not often behave very differently from their private competitors, and the government is committed to elaborate pro-

[25] Edward R. Tannenbaum, *The Fascist Experience* (New York, 1972), pp. 101-12.

grams of social reform, ranging from the redistribution of land to education and welfare.

Neither Italy's industrial "take off" at the turn of the century nor the economic growth and modernization of the last decades can, however, be confidently credited to state action.[26] The chasm between north and south, inadequate housing, rural poverty, urban neglect, inefficiency, and peculation instead offer daily justification for the widespread discontent that is partly reflected in the continued strength of the militant left. But those elected for their distributive policies have been largely excluded from the chance to carry them out. If much has been done, performance continues to lag behind promises and the example of most other Common Market countries. Despite some outstanding economic experts and some remarkable entrepreneurs who have earned a major role for the public sector in the Italian boom, Italy does not have a cadre of planners and technical experts comparable to those of France, nor do they exercise so free a hand or direct an impact on society.

Since the Risorgimento, issues of distribution have helped to sustain an atmosphere of impending crisis; and they were important in the rise of the old left in 1876, the crisis of the 1890s and the rise of Giolitti, the postwar crisis and the rise of Fascism, the strength of the left since World War II, the "opening to the left" in 1962, when the Socialists were given a voice in government, and the pressure for an historic compromise with the Communists. Yet Italy's governments since the Risorgimento have generally resisted demands for radical redistribution, preferring to narrow the field of politics to exclude the most difficult distributive isssues from immediate policy, and relying on the support of established interests and piecemeal compromise to preserve stability. Timid programs not always competently pursued by governments weak in penetration and short of funds might nevertheless be viewed as evidence of the flexible and sometimes skillful adaptation possible within the political system. In Italy they are more often cited to prove the need for fundamental change.

Sequence

These five categories of political functions, taken as crises in a particular sequence, suggest a periodization—1860-1896, 1900-1921,

[26] Alexander Gerschenkron, *Continuity in History and Other Essays* (Cambridge, 1968), pp. 118-19, and his *Economic Backwardness in Historical Perspective* (Cambridge, 1966), pp. 79-86; George H. Hildebrand, *Growth and Structure in the Economy of Italy* (Cambridge, 1965), pp. 388-404.

1922-1943, 1946 to the present—conventional and obvious enough, except perhaps for the emphasis upon the turn-of-the-century crisis. The first period follows from the Risorgimento, in which there were crises to some extent in all five categories. The leading one, of course, was identity, a crisis that had grown steadily from the late eighteenth century, reaching its peak in the period 1846-1860 but continuing to 1870. It was accompanied by a major crisis of legitimacy (especially 1796-1815 and 1848-1870), and a somewhat lesser one of participation (particularly notable in 1848-1849 and 1859-1860). Not only was the identity crisis lastingly resolved with the creation of an Italian state, but that resolution was closely tied to a liberal, constitutional view of legitimacy that included at least some expression of the popular will through plebiscites and regular consultation of a narrow electorate. If monarchy and limited suffrage were political compromises, they gained acceptability as the price for creating a national state amidst many conflicting pressures (even radicals feared the clerical influence that broad suffrage might bring). There was a crisis of penetration in the 1860s, dramatized by the war against brigands and efforts to extend a national administration across the peninsula, but the new state could respond with energetic if unimaginative measures strengthened by patriotic commitment and the belief that Italian identity itself was under attack.

Subsequent issues of participation, distribution, and penetration were handled within the parliamentary framework, although Cavour's successors found parliament difficult to work with and lacked Cavour's ability to reach the wider public. In the last government of the old right, the finance minister, Quintino Sella, pushed through a program as technically consistent as it was politically dangerous. Following liberal canons, he reduced the bureaucracy, raised taxes, and spurred the construction of railroads and the building of a merchant marine. But even narrow suffrage could not maintain a majority to support such Spartan policies in behalf of capitalist development. So concerted an effort to extract the costs of modernization from society at large was attempted only once again, under Mussolini.

When the old left came to power in 1876, however, it faced the same problems with less confidence and few new ideas. The change was rather one of tone, which brought the first broadening of the electorate and the development of new techniques for maintaining a parliamentary majority, the *trasformismo* practiced by Depretis (for all but two years of the period 1876-1887), by Crispi (1887-1891 and

1893-1896), and by Giolitti (primarily in the period 1903-1909, 1911-1914). Governments used electoral pressure, patronage, and deals with individual deputies to win and maintain a core of followers, but the system took its name from its tendency to construct shifting majorities for different issues and to prevent thereby the formation of formal political parties or a coherent opposition. Such politics required rare skills as well as the evasion of the most divisive issues. In practice, it led to stable government and flexible administration tainted with favoritism and the sense that deputies represented interests more than opinions or policies. The political system was not so unresponsive as its opponents charged, but in twenty years the old left had accomplished little to justify earlier hope that reforms would make Italy richer, the state stronger, and politics more democratic.

Italy's disastrous defeat in Ethiopia (the most dramatic such European defeat in that era of imperialism) brought Crispi's fall in 1896, but his position had already been growing steadily weaker. While doing much to frighten Catholics and conservatives, he had responded to rising peasant and labor unrest with military force. The conservative governments that followed him took a similar course, believing that the state's very legitimacy was threatened. Emphasizing national strength and order, a revived right called for the strong measures promised by the governments of di Rudinì and General Pelloux in the period 1896 to 1900. Amid strikes and riots, the crisis of distribution brought repression that sparked a crisis of legitimacy, and underscored the weak penetration of a regime poorly informed and ill-equipped to handle such crises or to ease the resentment of citizens excluded from effective participation in politics. Violence in Sicily and workers' risings in Milan in 1898 were met by troops, mass arrests, and the closing of "subversive" newspapers and organizations, socialist and Catholic. The government thereby created a more dangerous legitimacy crisis as it broke its own rules to infringe civil liberties; then a kind of electoral and parliamentary revolt drove the right from power. Unlike the anti-Dreyfusards in France or the propagandizing imperialist, peasant, or naval leagues in Germany, Italian conservatives failed to win a mass following. In 1900 the Italian political system, still isolated from the masses, righted itself with a reaffirmation of liberal constitutionalism.

The new period, which carried Italy through World War I, was in many respects analogous to that of 1876-1896. Governments showed themselves more sensitive to social issues and democratic sentiment.

The extension of the suffrage in 1911 represented, like that of 1880, a crisis of participation well manipulated, and Giolitti succeeded in drawing Catholics into political life (benefitting from their fear of a socialist left much as earlier governments had benefitted from the left's fear of a clerical right). The urgency of distributive issues was reduced by piecemeal but significant welfare measures; the state's capacity for penetration was increased by measures making administration more efficient, accompanied by a more purposeful and systematic use of local corruption. Indeed, all the indicators agree that from late in the nineteenth century to the 1920s Italy was undergoing impressive modernization. Yet for that very reason distributive issues continued to press, and sometimes to threaten, the government itself; demands upon the state increased, and organized vociferous oppositions questioned the state's legitimacy anew. Nationalists denounced its dull weakness, reformers decried corruption and inefficiency, and the left campaigned against its conservatism and the social system it supported. The evolution toward democracy which may have prevented far graver crises took place in a crisis atmosphere.

More than any nation, Italy faced World War I free to chose neutrality or intervention on either side. Such freedom of choice, however, was a further political strain. In their Libyan venture, the Giolittians had experimented with the healing qualities of a nationalist and imperialist war (a not uncommon effort to shift conflict over distribution and participation toward agreement on political identity). Now they were joined by much of the old political elite in favoring neutrality (very few candidly favored joining the Central powers), but democratic reformers hoped that alliance with Britain and France would weld the nation into a unified democracy of the Western type. This division was further complicated by noisy nationalists, soon joined by Mussolini, who welcomed the cleansing experience of bloodshed, while the growing mass movements of the left, the Catholic Popular party and the socialists, opposed intervention. Territorial gains offered by the Allies tipped the scale; but Italy, a divided society in painful transition, was ill prepared for total war. If survival through three years of fighting was in its way an achievement, it proved an inglorious one. Nor did the Allied cause support within Italy that apparent resurgence of the democratic left associated with the rise to power of Lloyd George, Clemenceau, and Wilson.

The most nearly defeated of the victors, Italy was as disillusioned with the peace settlement as with the war. Yet in the elections of 1921 a country still in social shock gave a clear majority to liberals and democrats, while making the Socialists and the Catholic *Popolari* the two largest parties. Universal suffrage seemed to have pointed Italy once more on the path of liberal government and stepped-up political and social reform. Instead, the majority was divided on most important issues, including the disappointing rewards of the peace conference; *Popolari* and Socialists refused to work together, and the Socialists, whose chronic divisions were increased by the experience of war and the Soviet revolution, could agree only in opposition. In an atmosphere of political confusion, social instability—including demobilization, unemployment, peasant occupation of farmland, bitter sitdown strikes—and nationalist agitation, the political system collapsed through inaction.

This can be explained in part by noting that it simply faced too many crises at once. The loudest, a crisis of identity, was perhaps the least fundamental. But politicians of the center and right had for a generation sought to evoke nationalist feeling, and the war had reestablished patriotism among the highest of political virtues. Thus the irredentist campaigns and D'Annunzio's antics in Fiume had a broad and disruptive echo throughout the nation, a demonstration of vigor and nationalism that denounced liberalism for leaving an ethical vacuum and justified the resentments of unemployed veterans. Most important, however, was the long-term crisis of distribution. Italy's governments in the previous twenty years had done far more than their predecessors in social matters, but extremes of modern industrial wealth, urban unemployment, dislocated populations, and rural poverty were greater than ever. Again and again, single issues of distribution, land reform, taxes, or education, had nearly crippled the political process until some compromise finally reduced the pressure and shifted attention to another issue; but after the war all facets of distribution bred critical problems.

There was also a kind of delayed crisis of participation, for universal suffrage produced new, mass parties that campaigned in unprecedented ways and maintained a discipline destructive of old techniques of *trasformismo*. Giolitti's instinct, predictably, was to absorb these new groups too; but he had begun too late to win the socialists, who could not afford his taint, and he encouraged instead an effort to domesticate the fascists. A party of direct action and political maneuver, Fascism achieved by the very contradictions of its doctrine a tactical flexibility no other group could match. Given the chance, it devoured its hosts.

All three new mass political movements had in a sense been hardened in the traditions of alternative opposition, and the old system had little time and probably not the capacity to make use of the forces they represented. Fascists and communists, of course, did their best to inflate the crisis; and the Fascists who employed violence denounced a state that could not prevent it. Fear—the fear of businessmen before strikes, of an isolated elite, and of the respectable generally—did the rest.

But in the most immediate sense, the triumph of Fascism followed a crisis of penetration. A government that had so long postponed so much, that everyone believed to be feeble, whose capacity to penetrate society was notoriously weak, whose bureaucracy and responsibilities had expanded during the war without increased efficiency, could not win the confidence either of the masses or of the leaders themselves. The pervasive social-political crisis was enough to incapacitate political response. Political leaders, even as they came to feel that representative government was in danger and to suspect they wanted to save it, could not be sure their commands would be carried out. In the months of uncertainty many in high places, like hundreds of officials below them, began to tolerate and even connive with the Fascists. Mussolini's arrival in power was formally legal, but the March on Rome was staged precisely so that all would recognize that the old state had fallen, its legitimacy effectively challenged.

The events of 1921-1922 thus cut across all five categories of analysis, an indication perhaps of the seriousness of the larger crisis. But the point is too easy and may exaggerate the inevitability of political collapse. Most of the specific political problems the nation faced were not new and have not since been wholly resolved, but in other contexts they have not been fatal to constitutional government. Some conservative businessmen then and many Marxists since have insisted that fascism was necessary to save private property; the claim is doubtful, but it makes the point that Italy's crisis was social and psychological as well as political.

What fascism provided was not the structural changes that follow revolution but apparent decisiveness, and it came to power ambiguously claiming the glory of revolt and the security of legal succession. Fascists tried to correct the inadequacies of penetration that had limited and weakened the Italian state since its founding, and to resolve the issues of distribution that had plagued Italian politics since the crisis of 1898. They substituted for parliamentarism an organized militance modeled on the prewar alternative participation of Catholics and socialists, based on a party, to be sure, but one tied through its military hierarchy to the state. They created corporate institutions to handle problems of distribution outside electoral politics, and sought in ideological identity the basis of totalitarian unity. Despite police and propaganda, however, there were signs of rising crises in these areas even before World War II. The legitimacy of Fascism, strengthened by the elections of 1924 and threatened during the Matteotti affair, was increasingly accepted with the passage of time and the regime's successes in church-state relations and in foreign policy. Yet legitimacy remained a sore point, too often sustained by naked power and the strident insistence of those who protest too much. Indeed, the cautious handling of church, business, and monarchy revealed fears later justified by the ease with which the regime fell in defeat. Great gains in penetration in the late twenties and again in the thirties nevertheless stopped short before traditional obstacles, and a bureaucracy supposedly freer of social restraint frequently risked breaking down into separate fiefdoms. Its own ambitions led the Fascist state to a perpetual crisis of penetration. Propaganda and power were used to prevent public conflict over distributive issues, but economic development, social rigidity, and Fascist boasts about welfare policies promised to make such problems irrepressible.

For Italy, the second world war was a disaster that exposed the hollowness of Fascist boasts. The state, dedicated to militarism and political control, did less well in meeting the growing demands of total war in the 1940s than its predecessors, suffering a rising crisis of penetration. The Allied invasion in 1943 spelled the fall of Mussolini and a new crisis of legitimacy. He was forced out of office in secret by the leading figures of the regime—much as the old regimes in 1859 lost the support of the liberal aristocracy. And like the dukes of Modena, Parma, and Tuscany eighty years before, Mussolini fled before an invasion of Western power, putting his hope in the military strength of his German-speaking ideological kin. The parallels between the two crises of legitimacy underscore the extent to which Mussolini's initial fall was first an event within the upper echelons of government, and the extent to which new leaders therefore faced the immediate need to establish their own legitimacy on a new basis, as had the liberals of the Risorgimento.

In fact, Mussolini's successors, though obviously dependent on the Allies, moved rapidly to do so. Whereas the Garibaldians had been quickly dropped after unification, the antifascist Resistance was recognized as a source of legitimacy and a central element of postwar politics. Despite British resistance, the referendum of 1946 was held and the monarchy made to pay for a generation of cooperation with Fascism. Two points are worth stressing: despite the gravity of the 1943-1946 crisis, which included many of the aspects of a civil war, the sources of legitimacy were recognized to be the traditional, constitutional, liberal ones rooted in the Risorgimento. And no real national crisis of identity emerged despite questions about Italy's frontiers in the Tyrol and the Dalmatian coast (which waxed hot at war's end, again a decade later, and are not yet entirely resolved) or demands for autonomy so strong that some Sicilians could talk of making Sicily the forty-ninth American state.

The postwar period brought great emphasis on participation, supported by the mobilizing efforts of highly organized, modern political parties. Even some degree of decentralization as a means of strengthening participation was accepted in principal in the forties and cautiously put into practice in 1972. Yet the sense of separation between the governing classes and the rest of the nation remains strong in Italy, and the institutionalization of increased participation has shifted the locus of coalition building from parliament to party offices. Postwar governments have faced the overwhelming problems of economic recovery, the needs of a rapidly changing and prospering society, and the insistent demand for major political and social reform enshrined in the constitution itself. Even with the help of the Allied presence, remaining fascist structures that reached more deeply into society than those of earlier liberal regimes, and the major parties' ostensible commitment to reform, Italy's governments have continued to be plagued by problems of penetration. Demands on government run constantly ahead even of improved performance. This is made more apparent to all by the continuing crises of distribution around which the parties of the left have consistently captured between forty and fifty percent of the vote.

In the 1960s and 1970s, then, the pattern of Italian politics has been much like that of 1898-1912. Communists have replaced Catholics as the great minority excluded from government but, like the Catholics of that period, are being drawn closer to the official political process. Rapid economic growth in both periods has accelerated demands on government but also perhaps done more than governmental policy to keep the crises of distribution below the level of explosion. Efforts at increased penetration alternate between structural reforms and the use of police power, with extremes in either direction prevented by the political system itself and the organized voices of protest.

Italian and foreign commentators have made much of the weaknesses of the Italian political system, but the concept of a *sequence of crises* may also help to explain its notable elements of continuity and stability. The Risorgimento had established political identity as fundamental, and a dramatic crisis of identity was lastingly solved with the formation of the Italian state. Political legitimacy, though more weakly established, was attached to this identity, so that usually they proved mutually reinforcing. Furthermore, serious crises of distribution occurred later in the sequence after patterns of compromise had been established. Thus the first generation after unification was relatively free of crises threatening the entire system, despite the serious problems faced by the new nation. In the period 1860-1896, a kind of political equilibrium was achieved with identity not at issue, legitimacy well established but not strong enough to provide much help in meeting other crises, participation slightly increased through broader suffrage, but thwarted by *trasformismo* and almost overshadowed by alternative extraparliamentary forms of participation, and distributive demands not great. Thus a crisis of penetration could be dealt with alone, and became less threatening as minimal penetration was assured by military force, and as the government learned not to demand more effective authority. Often, new challenges could be contained by adjustments that included specific measures of limited penetration, enlarged participation, and the reaffirmation of constitutional legitimacy. When, however, toward the end of the nineteenth century and again after World War I, distributive demands were added to issues of penetration and participation, customary responses proved inadequate.

From 1900 to 1921 identity remained strong, and governments sought increasingly to tap this strength by mobilizing the nation through patriotism. Legitimacy was much strengthened, thus making possible significant concessions to democratic participation and to distributive demands, but World War I strained this balance, creating demands for penetration and distribution Italian governments could not meet and opening crises in all five categories at once.

The fascist years, 1922-1943, brought an effort to resolve the crises of penetration and distribution by new forms of participation and new efforts to mobilize the nation (identity), but threatened crises of legitimacy led once more to compromises that brought some relaxation of efforts to increase penetration and conservative policies of distribution.

After 1943, Italian political identity having shown its continuity and strength, dramatic issues of legitimacy were rather quickly resolved and participation was given structure through strengthened parties. Penetration, while greatly increasing, tends to lag behind the demands put upon it in another period of rapid change; and when distributive issues are not reduced by growing prosperity, the entire political system is threatened.

The periods of gravest political crisis (1896-1900, 1918-1922, 1943-1946) have been marked by some divisive identity problems that weakened political responsiveness (and those seeking to overthrow an Italian regime have always sought to create an identity crisis); but in all three periods legitimacy became the critical issue. In terms of sequences then one can say that Italian crises of identity were resolved first, that legitimacy and participation crises—less firmly resolved—have been sufficiently reduced to produce stability except when reinvoked by crises of penetration and distribution, and that issues of distribution—usually avoided within the system—have often had to be raised from outside it, while weaknesses of penetration have remained one of its leading characteristics.

Conclusion

Beyond this, however, it is hard to go; for any list of the order in which single crises in Italy emerged and were settled would be open to overwhelming objections. This may reflect something important about Italian politics, in which crises are reduced but not resolved, their persistence in itself a part of the political culture. But the difficulty seems also to indicate some limits beyond which the idea of crises and sequences should not be pushed. The measures of a crisis remain vague and rather subjective, leaving scholars as much room for varied interpretations as they enjoyed before. The concept of crisis may be too limited to describe all the political process, too ambiguous to permit precise dating, and too broad to allow one often to declare any crisis "resolved." Nevertheless, the application of the idea of the five crises to the Italian case is suggestive, inviting revised emphases and comparative analysis. Treated as five sorts of political problems, these categories seem even more useful; but there are some factors, both external and internal, that this approach is likely to slight.

The timing of phylloxera blights, agricultural depressions, or monetary crises have been critical to Italian politics, but outside its control. The standard of military power necessary for survival is set by other nations, but their influence can also delimit internal policy, as in Italy the French did during the Risorgimento, the Germans in the years of the Axis, or the Americans after World War II. Italy's geographical position, her special problems as the least of the great European powers, her sensitivity to European opinion, were reflected in the concern for foreign policy so often dominant in the thinking of Cavour, Crispi, and Mussolini. Domestic sacrifices were often justified in terms of international requirements, while defeats, loss of face, or mere disappointment at Lissa in 1866, Adowa in 1896, or Paris in 1919 had profound effects on domestic politics. Even in normal times, the available choice of international ties affects domestic alignments, and Italians divided bitterly in their responses to Napoleon III and Bismarck, or the conflicts of the Cold War. For a nation struggling against colonial domination, such problems become crises of identity; but for a sovereign European nation, especially one of less than first rank, they may have comparable importance without raising issues explicitly encompassed by the five crises.

Similarly, the implicit emphasis upon decision making and crisis management in the idea of crises of development can invite an underemphasis on certain elements of the domestic political environment, including the relations and organization of social classes, enduring cleavages in the social structure, and the role of competing ideologies. The sharp distinction between the culture of the elite and of the masses has persisted from the era of aristocratic dominance through the Risorgimento, despite public education, economic growth, and mass communication. Regional loyalty and the social contrasts between north and south have remained strong. Italy's early urbanization or a century's tradition of migration and immigration are important subjects still too little studied, about which the broader concept of crises of development says little. Liberal goals and promises won in Italy a very wide, if contested, acceptance; and the rejection of those values by mass movements constitutes a kind of crisis (throughout the West) worthy of independent attention.

Because the institutions and ideas of modernization are not seen as wholly alien within any European nation, responses do not come in neat terms of acceptance or rejection. This means that those whom the state attempts to manage in the name of modernization can resist in the same terms and with great flexibility. In Italy monarchy, the church and business, like interest groups of the urban north or agrarian south, have known how to combat, resist, and infiltrate the government. Concentration on the response of the political elite to the crises of development must not obscure the sophistication of other groups. With reason, observers of Italy generally suspect that the Catholic church and the local elites have long been practiced in political skills that would challenge any government. Centuries-old traditions of avoiding the state or using it for individual ends have been preserved at many levels of society, even by those who advocate change.

Like all late-developing nations, Italy has faced the challenge of imported standards as to what governments should do, how society should be organized, and the way the economy should grow. These views have been quickly codified in ideologies simultaneously borrowed and indigenous (and Gramsci's genius in relating Marxist theory to Italian reality has been central to the strength of communism). This adaptation of general European currents complicates the political process: all sides can argue in the name of progress; quite specific and even local issues are rasied in the context of rigid ideologies. Domestic problems have been complicated by experience elsewhere; labor unrest, for example, was confused with the Paris Commune or the Russian Revolution, liberal government with the social insensitivity of French or English liberals a generation or two earlier. Thus political conflict tends to be expressed in ideological clashes that not only hide the real responsiveness within the system but create a tension as wearing as the rigidity they encourage. Some of the attractiveness of the politics of *trasformismo* or of Fascism was its avoidance of such public conflict. It is not surprising, then, that Italian politics is marked by continuing attitudes that extend beyond her crises: the insecurity of her leaders, the tendency to be fascinated with politics and to politicize almost every issue, a public cynicism about the political process, and a dissatisfaction with the nation and its government that seeks bold policies but makes them difficult to effect.

In sum, close concentration on the five categories of crisis could inadvertently direct attention away from some elements critical to Italian politics—external factors first of all, economic ones of trade, investment, and finance, and ones of international pressure, diplomatic and military. Domestically, too, the concept of crises does not in itself invite analysis of the independent effects of social structure, of the special characteristics of the internal opposition that has challenged the Italian state, of the particular circumstances faced by a "late developer," or of the peculiar attitudes and composition of Italy's political class. Yet the inclusion of such matters is essential to any explanation of the outstanding features of Italian political history. Three examples will make the point. Italy has an extraordinary pattern of short-lived governments but dominant individual leaders. In the 120 years since Cavour became Piedmontese prime minister in 1852, he has had thirty-nine successors; but just six (Cavour, Depretis, Crispi, Giolitti, Mussolini, and De Gasperi) held office for half of that time. Only nine others were prime minister for a total of more than two years, and only four of them served such a period uninterruptedly. Analysis in terms of these five categories offers little explanation for such extremes of instability and durable leadership. If it casts some light on the rise of fascism, it can say little about why Italy was the birthplace of that important phenomenon. Nor can it add much to our understanding of the contribution politics made to the Italian economic miracle of the 1960s or of why such rapid change has not had more dramatic effect on the political system.

The five crises of development appear more effective for a description of the Italian political system than for an explanation of its peculiarities. Political identity proved a fundamental, if limited, source of governmental strength; and that made it tempting to use war or the threat of war to draw upon that support. Legitimacy, more often called into question, has usually been sustained by identity, legalism, the forms of participation and tradition. A kind of legitimacy as alternative participation has even been granted to Catholic, communist, rural, and regional opposition to the government. Participation within this system has been important but circumscribed. A narrow suffrage depriving the left of an effective voice, the exclusion and withdrawal of Catholics, the totalitarian measures of Fascism, and the subsequent exclusion of the communists from power has been a heavy price to pay for making politics more comfortable. Such practices have weakened legitimacy and inhibited penetration. The bureaucracy, like its leaders, has in practice negotiated more than given orders. The tradition of working with particular interests has kept Italian government flexible, as well as liable to corruption; able to endure ideological cleavages and extreme social diversity, as well as insecure in a nation hard to mobilize and a society highly resistant to directed change. Distributive issues have been dealt with timidly when faced at all, more threatening to the system as a whole than attended to within it, where compromises, more private than public, tend to strengthen elements opposed to fundamental change. Yet this Italian pattern allows other forces to move society in directions politics apparently cannot. If in Italy the call to revolution makes sense, its failure to arrive is also understandable.

Italian history is rich in crises not even recognized until very late (such as the growing differences between north and south), as well as crises feared—regional separatism and proletarian revolt—that may not have been serious threats at all. Yet Italy's history is a useful reminder that crises do not always have to be recognized or resolved once seen, and that it is easy to exaggerate what politics can or should accomplish. The freedom of politicians is limited, and they frequently act to narrow their own independence. For all the turmoil, defeats, misadventures, and dissatisfactions of Italian political history, a tradition has evolved that usually preserves a certain stability while producing conciliatory measures that preserve the state, if they do not strengthen it.

In Italy political failures and weakness have even helped to preserve a society in which culture is conceived to be independent of the state, in which power is limited even before it is exercised, and in which social and ideological diversity is a way of life. The tension between a traditional heritage and modern practice can, after all, be fruitful, a stimulus to crafts as well as industry, to futurism and *verismo* both, to social criticism and humane administration—provided, of course, that a whole society can accept frequent frustration and constant confusion.

Some Related Readings

The historical literature on Italy available in English remains surprisingly uneven, reflecting older interests in Italian unification or more recent concern with fascism, but offering much less on politics in other periods and reflecting little (except in some remarkable anthropological studies) of the most recent and best work on economic and social or local history.

A. William Salomone, ed., *Italy from Risorgimento to Fascism* (New York, 1970) and Charles F. Delzell, ed., *The Unification of Italy, 1859-1861* (New York, 1965) provides good introductions to interpretations of Italian unification, with excellent bibliographies. Among the older English-language classics on the Risorgimento still well worth reading: G. M. Trevelyan, *Garibaldi and the Thousand*

(London, 1910) and *Garibaldi and the Making of Italy* (London, 1911); William Roscoe Thayer, *The Life and Times of Cavour*, 2 volumes (Boston, 1911); Gaetano Salvemini, *Mazzini* (Stanford, 1957); Kent Roberts Greenfield, *Economics and Liberalism in Risorgimento* (Baltimore, 1965). Newer works include: Luigi Salvatorelli, *The Risorgimento: Thought and Action* (New York, 1970); Derek Beales, *The Risorgimento and the Unification of Italy* (London, 1971); Denis Mack Smith, *Cavour and Garibaldi 1860* (Cambridge, 1954) and *Victor Emmanuel, Cavour, and the Risorgimento* (New York, 1972); Raymond Grew, *A Sterner Plan for Italian Unity* (Princeton, 1963).

For the liberal monarchy the best general works in English are: Denis Mack Smith, *Italy* (Ann Arbor, 1969), which covers the period from unification to the present; Christopher Seton-Watson, *Italy from Liberalism to Fascism, 1870-1925* (London, 1967); Benedetto Croce, *A History of Italy from 1871 to 1915* (Oxford, 1929); Shepard B. Clough, *The Economic History of Modern Italy* (New York, 1964); and Edward R. Tannenbaum and Emiliana P. Noether, eds., *Modern Italy: A Topical History of Italy since 1861* (New York, 1974). Good analyses of Italian political life in practice and of the issues in conflict can be found in: A. William Salomone, *Italy in the Giolittian Era* (Philadelphia, 1960); John A. Thayer, *Italy and the Great War* (Madison, 1964); Richard Hostetter, *The Italian Socialist Movement*, I, *Origins, 1860-88* (Princeton, 1958); Daniel L. Horowitz, *The Italian Labor Movement* (Cambridge, Mass., 1963).

Representative of some of the recent work on fascism are: Renzo De Felice, *Interpretations of Fascism* (Cambridge, Mass., 1977); Federico Chabod, *A History of Italian Fascism* (London, 1963); Adrian Lyttleton, *The Seizure of Power: Fascism in Italy, 1919-29* (London, 1973); Edward R. Tannenbaum, *The Fascist Experience* (New York, 1972); Roland Sarti, *The Axe Within* (New York, 1973); Sir Ivone Kirkpatrick, *Mussolini: Study of a Demagogue* (London, 1964); Richard A. Webster, *The Cross and the Fasces* (Stanford, 1960); Alan Cassels, *Fascist Italy* (New York, 1968). There is also a quite extensive literature on special topics, especially foreign policy, but perhaps more fruitful for the general reader are some of the interpretative studies of fascism as a phenomenon, although Italy is only one of the cases considered in the first issue of *Journal of Contemporary History* (1966) and in the works written or edited by Nathaniel Green, Ernst Nolte, Eugen Weber, John Weiss, and Stuart J. Woolf.

The most stimulating introduction to contemporary Italy remains H. Stuart Hughes, *The United States and Italy* (Cambridge, Mass., 1965). Giuseppe Mammarella, *Italy after Fascism* (Montreal, 1964), and Norman Kogan, *A Political History of Postwar Italy* (New York, 1966) are more attentive to politics. Among the more specialized studies, Joseph LaPalombara, *Interest Groups in Italian Politics* (Princeton, 1964); Sidney G. Tarrow, *Peasant Communism in Southern Italy* (New Haven, 1967); Donald C. M. Blackmer, *Unity in Diversity: Italian Communism and the Communist World* (Cambridge, Mass., 1968); Donald C. M. Blackmer and Sidney Tarrow, *Communism in France and Italy* (Princeton, 1975); Robert C. Fried, *The Italian Prefects* (New Haven, 1963); Giorgio Galli and Alfonso Prandi, *Patterns of Political Participation in Italy* (New Haven, 1970); and F. Roy Willis, *Italy Chooses Europe* (Oxford, 1971) are particularly relevant to this essay.

CHAPTER 9

GERMANY

JOHN R. GILLIS

THE "GERMAN QUESTION," interpreted either as a problem of international relations or as a purely internal affair, has traditionally been approached in a comparative manner, the frame of reference being the development of the Western European nation states. During the eighteenth century and for a good part of the nineteenth, France and England set the standards by which Germans judged their own political institutions. Later, as a more nationalistic mood replaced the earlier cosmopolitanism, Western models were increasingly rejected as unsuited to Germany's particular geopolitical requirements. But, even at their most xenophobic, German academic and political leaders continued to employ a perspective that was implicitly comparative, using the development of other Western nation states to isolate the supposedly uniquely Germanic elements that they wished to amplify. These same preoccupations are still reflected in such terms as "belated nation" or "faulted nation," a language loaded with normative connotations, which continues to dominate contemporary discussion of German political history.

The terms of comparison available today are no longer purely Western in origin. So much of the recent scholarship in the field of political development has been based on the experience of non-Western countries that the perspective is practically reversed, the European nation state no longer representing the norm but rather the exception. In the light of this new approach, the German case no longer seems so exceptional. As a country that felt itself to be "backward" in the European context of the eighteenth and nineteenth centuries, Germany experienced many of the problems characteristic of developing polities today. Like those former colonial states that upon independence inherit relatively well-developed central institutions, including an efficient bureaucracy and powerful military, but little in the way of national unity or stable sense of legitimacy, Germany was, as Alexis de Tocque-

Crises of Political Development in Europe and the United States
0-691-07598-0/78/000313-32$01.60/1 (cloth)
0-691-02183-X/78/000313-32$01.60/1 (paperback)
For copying information, see copyright page

ville described her, a modern state superimposed on a "thoroughly gothic" society.

England entered the modern period with the problems of identity and legitimacy already settled. France's great upheaval of 1789 left unresolved important questions about participation and legitimacy, but at least created the boundaries of a national consciousness within which these issues could be fought out. Germany, on the other hand, began the nineteenth century with none of these crucial nation-forming experiences behind her. During the course of the next one hundred fifty years all the problems involved in aspiring to the condition of the modern nation state emerged one by one, yet none was resolved in any final sense. Indeed, it would seem that the intervening series of political regimes only served to exacerbate Germany's societal disunity, leaving it in 1945 no closer to the achievement of national consensus than at the beginning of the modern period.

Crises

In Germany's case, the sequence in which the problems of penetration, participation, legitimacy, distribution, and identity became salient —that is, became areas of urgent political debate and conflict—and the sequence in which they became actual crises were two different things. Borrowing Sidney Verba's definition, I mean by crisis an event involving major institutional change designed to meet or resolve some pressing problem. When one compares the sequencing of problem recognition with crisis innovation as such, one is struck by the disparity in the timing and sequencing. If we start with the recognition of problems, it is clear that penetration, participation, and identity were already salient early in the nineteenth century, coincidental with the advent of liberal nationalist movements in the various German states. Liberalism raised questions about participation; nationalism represented a fundamental rethinking of the boundaries of the political unit. Because both liberalism and nationalism developed outside and in opposition to the governing elites of the existing German states, they tended also to raise the issue of legitimacy. Nevertheless, in the early nineteenth century the primary threat to the German states was the expansion of France, not the small, weak revolutionary movements within Germany itself. Thus, it was not until much later that fundamental questions of legitimacy and distribution were raised. Even in 1848 the direct challenge to the legitimacy of the existing states was insubstantial. A more direct challenge awaited the rise of the socialist movement later in the century, an event that opened new areas of conflict. By 1918, all five of the major problem areas were subjects of public recognition and agitation, a condition that persisted throughout the brief history of the Weimar Republic and into the era of the Third Reich.

If we turn to the sequencing of crises, however, a somewhat different order appears. We find that as far as actual institutional innovation was concerned, penetration comes first in time and importance in almost every instance, absorbing or containing changes in institutions affecting participation, national identity, the distribution of material welfare, and even legitimacy. As we shall see, the Reform Era (1806-1819) was primarily a penetration crisis. Problems of participation and identity were raised at that time, but the actual institutional changes were entirely in the direction of the extension of central governmental power. In 1848 the same pattern was repeated, the introduction of representative institutions being more a means to penetration than an end in itself. The period of unification would seem at first to have been an exception, but while institutional changes affecting identity and participation were involved, Bismarck gave first priority to the Prussian state's capacity to control the new Reich. The first attempts at redistribution of material resources followed the same sequence, Bismarck's massive welfare program being enacted in the name of the defense of the state rather than as a step toward authentic national reconciliation or social equality. In 1918 and 1933 a similar sequence was evident, with the governing elites relying primarily on penetration to deal with the other major problem areas. In Germany's case the history of political development in the modern period is not one sequence, but a repeated series of sequences, revolving around institutional change in the direction of further penetration, raising and agitating the other major problem areas, but always subordinating their resolution to the extension of effective governmental control either as an end in itself or as a means to other goals.

The persistent reliance on the power of the state has often been attributed to the structure of German society, in which authority has remained almost continuously in the hands of the same bureaucratic and military elites since the eighteenth century. But while many of modern Germany's characteristics can be traced back to a heritage of absolutism that placed a well-developed state at the head of a weak, divided society, this static type of explanation is not the only or even the most satisfactory one. When the sequences by which this nation raised and dealt with the challenges of nation-state building are taken into account, then we have a dynamic explanation of its salient features. Other countries entered the nineteenth century with a heritage of absolutism; some had a similar continuity of leadership; but few seemed to be incapable of establishing the bond of state and nation that marked political modernity. As I will argue in this essay, the priority given to penetration during each of the major crisis periods (1806-1819, 1848-1871, 1918-1933) was an essential factor in maintaining a unique dualism between state and nation (or society) in Germany's case, preventing more than a temporary solution in the other four problem areas, particularly the critical questions of identity and legitimacy.

The sequences of political crisis in German history since the eighteenth century tended to favor the capacity of the state at the expense of equality within society and thus of a stable sense of nationhood. Other European countries were able to develop a civic culture that combined high levels of instrumental rationality, efficiency, and effectiveness on the part of the administrative and judicial organs of the state with universalistic standards of civic and political equality among the citizenry. By their standards, the conflict in Germany between *Staat* and *Gesellschaft*, or state and nation, was exceptionally great, with nothing like the English concept of commonweal or the French notion of citizenship bridging the gap. Initially, Germany's vulnerable international position contributed to the defensive character of the country's experiments in nation-state building, which tended to push capacity of the state well ahead of society's ability to absorb political changes. But even when the German Reich under Bismarck had achieved a high level of capacity relative to other European states, her elites continued to react negatively to suggestions that strength and stability required a greater degree of civic equality and differentiation. Under these conditions, political movements advocating reform in that direction were seen by the ruling groups as alien and dangerous elements. It was to be Germany's fate that external threat tended to provoke internal crisis, producing a political dynamic which, instead of progressively creating national consensus, exacerbated conflict and eventually opened up the ultimate question of legitimacy itself.

Crises in German history do not form a neatly ordered sequence in which each major question is settled definitively, each in turn. One can hardly speak of the final resolution of German political problems. If what we mean by development is the creation of a stable nation state on the English or French model, then Germany, still divided socially and geographically, must be termed "underdeveloped." Obviously such a narrow definition of development is untenable however, and for this reason I have focused this essay on the recurrence of crises, attempting thereby to identify the inherent contradictions that time and again have characterized German history. I have tried to avoid the normative assumptions implicit in the notion of "underdevelopment," a concept sometimes applied to the German case. Development, as it is used here, has no single prescribed outcome, but is instead a description of the political history as it actually occurred.

In order to identify the contradictions in the German case, I have chosen to concentrate on three formative periods since the eighteenth century—1806-1819, 1848-1871, 1918-1933. These do not exhaust the possibilities for analysis of crisis defined as significant institutional change; nor do they include all the rapid, violent sets of events that by more conventional criteria would count as crises. Yet, in each of the three crisis periods selected, some important effort at building a nation state on the Western model (though not always with Western means) was involved; in each, the German political elites were confronted by some particular challenge, internal or external, real or imagined, which resulted in significant change. In the Reform Era military survival was at stake; during the period 1848-1871 the challenge was nation building; in 1918 defeat in war and domestic revolution threatened. In 1933 another radical attempt at nation-state construction was attempted.

The urgency, violence, and depth of the challenges faced in each of the three periods differed enormously; naturally, the outcomes also varied. What remained relatively consistent, however, and what allows us to generalize about a distinctive process of German political history, was the manner of decision making and conflict resolution common to all three periods. In each instance it was a "revolution from above" that produced institutional innovation. In the first two periods, the course of change was controlled by the state elites, the bureaucracy, and the military. In the third, insurgent groups, first of the left and then of the right, were involved, though they too were dependent on the state elites to carry through their programs, thus making this also a form of revolution from above. If the outcome of these crises is not strictly comparable to that of her Western neighbors, the process is. It is therefore to this that this essay directs its attention.

Sequence

1806-1819

Penetration came first in time and importance in the priorities established in Germany's Era of Reform. Problems of identity and participation were raised, mainly by groups outside the ruling circles, but it was reforms involving the extension and effectiveness of state control that determined the shape that participation and identity were to take. Crisis in both Prussia and Austria was triggered by the threat posed by a foreign power, namely Napoleonic France. For many educated Germans the right of cultural as well as political self-determination was worth fighting for; though, like their counterparts in Asia or Latin America today, they were to some degree a product of the foreign culture that they now professed to reject. Not only the liberals but also the conservatives among them owed much to the French Revolution, which had caused the German elites to take stock of their own political and cultural resources with an unaccustomed urgency. This was not the first time that they had been made aware of Germany's relative weakness, but it was certainly unprecedented that the consciousness was so widespread and the temper so impatient.

That so much of the anti-French resistance during these years was militantly antirevolutionary has obscured the degree to which even the most conservative Germans were capable of discriminating between that which was specifically French and that which could be adapted to serve their own purposes. On the whole, the response to the French Revolution and Napoleon was conservative but not blindly reactionary. Like the anti-Western politicians in today's developing countries, Germans set no tariffs against their enemy's administrative and military techniques, protecting themselves only from the importation of his civic culture. The practice of selective borrowing was not new. Frederick the Great had used French administrative ideas and personnel in the eighteenth century. Staffed by small elites of high educational standards, both Prussia and Austrian states entered the new century with a strong indigenous tradition of institutional development provided by the thrust of monarchical absolutism. Precedent for reform in the direction of higher levels of penetration already existed.

The Prussian state, which was humiliated at Jena in 1806, and the Hapsburg state, which lost its imperial title that same year, were not victims of backwardness in any absolute sense, but of the decay of highly developed forms of monarchical absolutism that had lost their flexibility and capacity to respond to the demands of the era ushered in by the political revolution in France and the industrial revolution in England.

In Prussia, the military and administrative reforms of Frederick William I and Frederick the Great had created a state which, on paper at least, was a model of enlightened government. The *Allgemeines Landrecht* of 1794 provided a form of written constitution for a political system that provided unitary administrative and judicial institutions, efficient taxation, and allocation of civil duties if not civil rights for all Hohenzollern subjects. As far as the central government was concerned, the Prussian state had been one of the most flexible and adaptable in Europe. To the traditional corporate system of three estates (*Geburtsstände*) had been added a complement of functional estates (*Berufsstände*), thus recognizing the importance of both the army and the civil service. The feudal representative institutions were already moribund by the end of the eighteenth century, but the disenfranchised nobility and *Bürgertum* were offered a form of participation in government through the military and the bureaucracy, institutions that were open to talent to a degree unparalleled in other European states. The French system of purchase of office was virtually unknown in Prussia and birth as a requirement was already giving way to new merit standards, particularly in the civil services. The bureaucracy and, to a lesser extent, the military constituted the most forward-looking elements of a Prussian society that economically was relatively more backward than its central bureaucratic and military institutions. In this respect, Prussia was very much like those developing countries in which capacity at the center initially outdistances economic, social, and cultural levels of development. It is against this background of unbalanced development that the crisis sequence of the period 1806-1819 must be interpreted.

Organization at the very top of the administrative hierarchy had become chaotic after the death of Frederick the Great in 1786, and there was strong pressure for reform long before the military disaster of 1806. Members of the administrative and army elites were growing restless under the inept rule of Frederick's weak successors, and there were signs that monarchical absolutism was ripe for replacement by a form of bureaucratic absolutism. The higher civil service was the major beneficiary of the eighteenth-century reforms, which had created a powerful "aristocracy of service" in a society already sharply divided into corporate as well as territorial units. This was the body that represented modern standards of achievement and utility, the only group to which members of all the traditional estates could give common allegiance and respect. In a country whose economic progress lagged well behind its level of administrative efficiency and effectiveness, the bureaucracy constituted a kind of middle class, different from its English or French counterparts in the way its members measured their prosperity—not by the health of the economy, but by the well-being of the state. The only serious rival for political power was the landed aristocracy, but the agricultural basis of its strength had been seriously undermined, and its members were also becoming dependent for their social and material strength on the services and offices of the state.

Given this dependence of the upper reaches of Prussian society on the central institutions of the state, it is little wonder that the defeat of 1806 precipitated a period of extended debate on the future of the central political institutions. Jena was much more than a military disaster, it was a powerful shock to the self-confidence of the Prussian elites, producing a degree of disorganization and demoralization within the ranks of the civil and military services that seemed to threaten the very existence of the state itself. Prussia's salvation lay in the hands of a generation of army officers and civil officials who were disgusted with the political decay that had taken place since the death of Frederick the Great, and were ready with plans for reform. Defeat at the hands of Napoleon was proof for them not of the inadequacy of absolutism but the failure to realize its full potential. Almost to a man, the reformers of 1806-1819 were professional servants of the state, officials rich with the practical experience of law and administration, or soldiers tested on the field of battle. The most dynamic among them, Stein, Hardenberg, Gneisenau, Yorck, and Clausewitz, were not without appreciation for the institutions of popular participation that in revolutionary France had mobilized such tremendous forces against them, but for the most part it was the administrative and military aspect of Napoleonic France which fascinated them. The gains in social and civil equality had been hailed by them only insofar as they enhanced the potential for extracting political loyalty from a traditionally passive society. In no way blind reactionaries, they were simply reflecting the perspective of the professional soldier or bureaucrat whose major concern was the maximization of the capacity of the state to respond to a threatening international situation.

The challenge as the elites perceived it was one of mobilizing the population in service of the state. There were others who saw it differently, and stressed the need for solution of the problem of German national identity and the creation of a new concept of legitimacy based on a recognition of the sovereignty of the people, but they were in the minority and unable to arouse a German population still politically indifferent. Except for the opposition of feudal traditionalists, the bureaucratic reformers had almost universal support among the old elites for their efforts to increase the capacity of the state. Participation of the population in certain tasks of government, particularly military service aimed at securing a source of disciplined strength, was encouraged. Citizenship was defined in terms of duties rather than rights, and although there were some experiments in municipal self-government, the reformers stopped well short of political suffrage, not even eliminating the corporate divisions inherited from the Old Regime. A higher level of instrumental rationality was obtained by administrative reorganization; greater efficiency was the goal of opening the civil and military careers to talent. Thus, in the sequence of crisis, participation followed penetration and was subordinated to it.

No effort was made to transform the basic civic culture or social structure of Prussia; indeed, Stein tried to revive a feudal sense of responsibility by invoking traditional civic symbols and by restoring corporate representative institutions. The regenerated estates system not only underlined the corporate divisions in Prussian society, but retarded the growth of a modern sense of citizenship based on equal civil and political rights. In all the various institutional changes of this period, both the permanent and the temporary, the goal was primarily to strengthen the hand of the central government. The Reform Era marked no real departure from the course of development codified in 1794, for at the top of the list of priorities was the replacement of an inefficient monarchical absolutism with an effective form of bureaucratic absolutism. For the most part, this emphasis had the support of "enlightened" opinion; and it was not the reforms but the reaction that followed 1819 which drew the criticism of those small intellectual elites who were committed to national unification and popular sovereignty.

The view that the Reform Era constituted a period of national upheaval has therefore little justification, though it was of undoubted cultural importance insofar as the future evolution of the symbols of German nationalism was concerned. The French had made no attempt to overthrow either Prussia or Austria, and the indigenous nationalists were too weak to force the issue of German unity to the forefront of political priorities. What the reformers liked to call their "revolution from above" had worked in two apparently contradictory directions: it had modernized the state, but further "feudalized" society by legitimizing new functional corporate groups, most notably the bureaucracy. A new, more open elite, an aristocracy of service, had replaced the old aristocracy of birth, thus reinforcing the conservative tendencies of the Prussian society without blunting the thrust toward political development at the central executive level.

Defeat had assured political innovation in Prussia; similar events had dissipated what little momentum was left from the efforts of the Hapsburg reformers of the late eighteenth century. The territorial settlement of 1815 forced Prussia to refine its instruments of bureaucratization in order to consolidate its hold on its newly acquired western provinces, but such methods proved inappropriate for governing the new Austrian territories in Italy. While the Hohenzollern monarchy moved toward further centralization, Austria was forced to experiment with looser arrangements. Her strength was increasingly staked on diplomacy rather than on internal political development; and even the ability to win support among other German states through creative forms of federalism could not in the long run make up for the growing capacity of her Prussian rival.

Prior to 1848, however, this weakness was not evident. Metternich's skill in diplomacy, together with his delicate handling of internal affairs, sufficed to maintain an internal and external status quo. The threat posed by the Prussian dominated *Zollverein* had not yet materialized, and during the 1840s Prussia was in something of a period of political decay. Some of Prussia's central political institutions had begun to lose their efficiency and effectiveness, and there was criticism both inside the government and among the general public of the way excessive centralization was stifling constructive participation of groups outside bureaucratic and military circles. In 1806 desire for participation had been satisfied by opening the bureaucracy and army to men of talent. By 1848 such demands could no longer be handled by this device. Indeed, the original reforms had facilitated the emergence of a type of bureaucratic absolutism that now proved extremely resistant to further change. The years between the Reform Era and the Revolution of 1848-1849 had only widened the gap between the interests of the service elites and those of the mass of the population. By the 1840s even the bureaucracy was losing something of the dynamism that the Reform Era had created, for it was becoming castelike and unresponsive to the needs of a society on the brink of industrialization and urbanization.

1848-1871

The period of German unification began with the problems of participation, identity, and to a lesser extent legitimacy being pushed to the fore; but throughout, the imperatives of penetration remained uppermost in the minds of those who directed the course of events. In 1848 there had been a genuine crisis of participation resulting in the establishment of representative institutions, but this had been overshadowed by a simultaneous crisis of penetration, which had virtually nullified the effect of civil and political equality on the society at large by furthering the extension of the powers of the executive at the expense of the legislative branch. Nor did the triumph of the *Kleindeutsch* solution to the identity problem by 1871 really alter the sequence pattern, for unification was another case of "revolution from above," in which civic development of the nation was sacrificed to the enhanced capacity of the Prussian state.

The Revolution of 1848, which initiated this critical period, can only be properly understood in the light of the political decay that preceded it. For a variety of reasons, some foreign but most domestic, the thrust of the Reform Era was played out by the 1840s; and bureaucratic absolutism, burdened by new social and political demands generated by the emerging industrial middle class, was unable to adapt effectively. In some sense, the Prussian state was a victim of its own success, or of what I have chosen to call unbalanced development. The thrust toward strong, centralized bureaucratic government had taken precedence over all other concerns. Popular demands for representative institutions were viewed with suspicion; the contradictions of the corporate legal system, which provided equality of duties but not of rights, were ignored. The educational system was geared toward producing what the bureaucracy required, with the effect that the technical needs of the economy were sacrificed. Broader participation in the affairs of the state was rejected, not because participation as such was opposed, but because according to the mystique of the bureaucratic state the civil service itself fulfilled that function. The achievement of "careers open to talent" was thought to satisfy the aspirations of the educated middle class, even though it stopped well short of true civil and political equality. The bureaucracy, in attaining the status of one of the country's exclusive social elites, had lost some of its original reformist orientation and had become a part of the conservative social structure. The gains in capacity were being endangered by the internal petrification of an "aristocracy of service" which, among its older members at least, was opposed to further equalization of opportunity and jealous of further political change.

The Revolution of 1848 in Germany took the form of political collapse rather than popular upheaval, more the product of the failure of nerve on the part of the elites than a measure of the strength of the forces questioning the legitimacy of the existing governments or demanding national unification. In fact, the opposition was also taken by surprise by events. Though the liberal middle class viewed themselves as representing the interests of society against those of the state, they had never really challenged the legitimacy of the political or social systems as such. The possibility of social revolution by the lower classes frightened them; and they accepted the monarchy's concessions of constitutional civil rights and representative institutions gratefully, believing strong monarchical institutions to be compatible with their social and economic interests. In the course of the revolutionary year, the liberals moved to the side of the state, thus guaranteeing that the legitimacy of the regimes survived intact. Furthermore, the old elites were able to turn the liberal reforms to their own purposes. The Prussian monarchy was the beneficiary of the extended franchise, using aroused local patriotism to oppose more radical programs of national unification. The granting of a constitution that guaranteed both civil equality and participation through modern representative institutions turned out to complement the interests of the traditional elements in the Prussian state, explaining why, even after the complete restoration of order in 1849, the clock was never turned back. From the very beginning, the traditional elites had controlled the direction of events. Universal participation in civil and political rights was granted, but only as part of a program that put administrative and judicial reform near the top of the list of priorities. Released from the last remnants of feudalism, and able to manipulate the new representative institutions, Prussia's executive organs were stronger under the new constitution than they had been under the old corporate legal order.

In 1848 the corporate legal structure was abandoned, and Prussians became citizens in the modern sense of the term for the first time. The old contradiction of equal duties and unequal rights was eliminated by the Constitution of 1850, a document that was to serve as the basic law until 1918. The nondemocratic Three Class Suffrage of 1849 precluded the attainment of equal voting rights in Prussia itself, but did not rule out participation as such, as long as this did not threaten the legitimacy of the central executive or suggest the principle of popular sovereignty. It was the latter, above all else, which the ruling elites tried to discourage during the 1850s and 1860s. Every effort was made to suppress the development of a genuine sense of political community apart from the officially sanctioned representative institutions. The old dualism between state and society was adjusted so that the new representative institutions could serve the purposes of the executive. At first hostile to parliament, the Manteuffel regime of the 1850s gradually learned how to manipulate elections to its advantage, a precedent that was appreciated by later German chancellors. In this sense, representative institutions were coopted to benefit the penetrative capacity of the executive. While parliamentary politics were generally despised by the bureaucratic and military elites, the institutions themselves were viewed as useful instruments for authoritarian goals. This helped discredit parliament still further in the eyes of the general public, leaving it in a stage of institutional limbo from which it never really recovered.

Parliamentary parties were allowed a certain freedom, but extra-parliamentary political organization and education was discouraged. Where the government itself intervened in elections, it relied on the use of state officials to preserve loyal majorities. The individual civil servant, previously allowed considerable latitude, was placed under tight discipline. The nongovernmental parties relied on established local "notables" for vote getting, rarely experimenting in large-scale organization or extensive mobilization of the voters. The parties remained weak and inconsequential, parliamentary groupings without roots in the general population. For its part, the electorate was suspicious of the parties, and thus was difficult to organize except along ideological, religious, or class lines. Under these conditions, society remained as segregated from the parliament as it had previously been from the central government, reached in a mechanical way by the apparatus of the state but sharing little in the way of civic habits and values associated with parliamentary democracy in other European countries.

Austria's experience had been somewhat different from that of Prussia. The Revolution of 1848 had furthered political decay by imposing on an already weak political structure representative institutions that tended to accelerate the centrifugal forces inherent in a multinational empire. There the penetration by the central government did not go far enough to counteract the divisive tendencies promoted by the multiplication of parties and special interests. Whereas in Prussia civil equality and institutional differentiation had been made to serve executive capacity, in Austria these same elements were constantly in contradiction throughout the subsequent life of the empire. The attempts by Schwarzenberg to reassert Austria's position in Germany during the 1850s were to be defeated not only by Prussian guns in 1866, but by the logic of political development of the empire itself. Each successive shock, instead of strengthening the capacity of the state, weakened it, raising by the early twentieth century questions of legitimacy and national identity that would eventually result in its destruction.

It can be argued that already in 1866 Austria was facing multiple problems leading to a crisis of legitimacy. In Prussia, on the other hand, the consequences of unbalanced development were not yet apparent, for there penetration continued to precede and contain other institutional changes which might have threatened the political system. It is well known that Bismarck did not conceive of unification primarily as a final solution to Germany's problem of national identity, but rather as a means of insuring Prussia's existence by placing her at the head of a new configuration of German states. His solution was revolutionary only insofar as in his diplomatic and military methods he rode roughshod over the rights of lesser German states. Though he exploited the liberal nationalists' desire for German unity, he avoided arousing extreme nationalist fervor or suggesting the notion of popular sovereignty. Extreme care was taken not to unduly weaken the defeated Austrians. Both his liberal and conservative critics might denounce him as a Bonapartist, the former for his despotic methods and the latter for his alleged violation of the divine right of kings, but Bismarck viewed his role as that of a traditional Prussian statesman, not a revolutionary nationalist.

The Reich created in 1871 was a triumph of this statesmanship, but it also introduced a repetition of the sequence of political crises that had been characteristic since the eighteenth century. His mastery of the political situation allowed Bismarck to make it appear that unification had been a victory for the liberal-nationalist cause, while in reality it was a successful repetition of the old Prussian tactic of "revolution from above," a process that gave priority to penetration over either participation or identity, and resulted in the extension of the power of the old elites. The Prussian army and civil service became twin pillars of the new Germany, gaining more power and prestige than ever before. For the army in particular, Bismarck's methods were a blessing, but not only did they dissipate the threat of parliamentary control over the military, but they secured for the generals a degree of independence from the civilian executive that even Bismarck was later to regret. From these years can be traced the evolution of the army toward the position of a "state within the state."

The bureaucracy, while it did not enjoy the same degree of autonomy as the army, became ever more effective an instrument of executive power. Its earlier reputation for liberalism had evaporated, and it lost its former capacity to mediate between the interests of the monarchy and those of society. Like the officer corps, the Prussian bureaucracy remained socially segregated from the rest of the nation, open to talent drawn from the emerging industrial middle classes, but still largely resistant to the values of other groups. Having never really absorbed the popular nationalism of the early nineteenth century, Prussian officers and officials tended to adjust to Bismarck's ersatz nation state by developing their own parochial, chauvinistic brand of patriotism. It was aggressive in orientation, elitist rather than democratic, and served to insulate the elites from the forces of democratic nationalism and socialism, while doing little to foster a viable sense of civic cohesion and consensus in the population at large.

The second half of the nineteenth century represented a triumph of conservatism as far as the bureaucracy and army were concerned. The greater burden of mediating between state and the national society now fell to the parliament and the parties. Unfortunately, unification did not diminish the parliament's isolation from either the state (executive authority) or society in general. The fact that the new constitution left authority entirely in the hands of the executive, placed the parties, like the parliament, in a kind of limbo, depriving them of incentive to evolve effective coalitions on the basis of common interests.

The powerlessness of the parties increased their tendency to form around ideologies and to reflect rigid class or religious interests instead of coalescing into an effective opposition to the power of the executive. The fault was not entirely with the system, however. From the beginning of parliamentary politics in 1848, the liberal parties had been willing to accept a position of impotence. Even during the so-called constitutional conflict of the 1860s, they demonstrated no eagerness to raise the ultimate question of legitimacy. Not until the emergence of the socialist parties of the 1870s was there fundamental opposition to the constitutional dualism of the Second Empire; and then it was not really until the eve of World War I that the notion of parliamentary government had the support of a broad front of parties.

The party system in Germany passed from a relatively amateurish stage of representation by local "notables" to a highly bureaucratized, top-heavy political professionalism without mobilizing the support or interest of the mass of the German people. To the old elites, party politics was a vocation beneath the dignity of their social station. Civic duties were traditionally exercised through civil service; civic virtue was embodied in the ethos of the bureaucracy and the army, which in normal times stood above the squabbling of politicians. In its isolation from the executive, a parliamentary career could not attract men of social prestige and real influence. Members of the industrial working class could aspire to move up within the hierarchy of the Social Democratic party, but even this powerfully organized party tended to lose touch with its constituency. Just as with central government, participation was secondary to penetration, and the party's own institutional imperatives were given primary consideration over the sentiments of the voter. Even so, the urban working classes did have representation through the SPD; and Catholics had their Center party. The same cannot be said for the Protestant lower-middle strata, whose political passivity and traditionalism had been encouraged and manipulated by the state, and who only gradually came to have a consciousness of politics *per se* at the very end of the century. The programs that appealed to them stressed private rather than public virtues and exploited a parochial ethnocentric sense of patriotism, extremely hostile to all forms of cosmopolitanism. It was among these unorganized, inarticulate masses that the right-wing extraparliamentary movements of the Wilhelminian period found growing support.

Bismarck is often credited with resolving the problem of German identity, but it is more correct to say that he delayed that resolution.

In effect, he had continued the tradition of Prussian state-building that subordinated all other questions to the necessity of executive power. He had temporarily "solved" the German problem, but without really overcoming the traditional dualism between state and society. Nationhood had been imposed without the preparation of consensus as to the form of national identity or the nature of the political regime. These issues continued to be objects of political manipulation rather than subjects for equitable solution so long as the priorities of the Prussian state were placed at the top of the agenda. The character of Bismarck's nationalism was evident in the *Kleindeutsch* Second Empire. It stopped well short of bringing all German-speaking peoples together in one state. The Hapsburg Germans were excluded for reasons dictated primarily by Prussian *Staatsräson*, both because their inclusion would seriously endanger Prussian hegemony within the new Reich, and because they were needed to man the ramparts of the Austrian Empire, and thus to protect the new Germany's southeastern flank. What Bismarck could not foresee was the relatively rapid disintegration of the Hapsburg Empire, a disintegration that would turn loose the forces of ethnic nationalism not only in the Balkans and Eastern Europe, but within the Second Reich itself. Up to 1871, ethnic nationalism had been more an intellectual preoccupation than a political fact, but with the creation of a *Kleindeutsch* Germany, calling itself a nation but not including all the German-speaking peoples of Europe, the question of identity had a new, more concrete form, not only for millions outside its borders but also for millions within.

Serious questions of the Reich's legitimacy did not emerge as rapidly as those of identity, but they too were to some degree a product of the unification process that gave the penetrative capacity of the Prussian state first priority. Bismarck had used the forces of liberalism and nationalism to strengthen the position of the Prussian monarchy. Although there had been serious initial resistance to Bismarck's methods from the liberals in the Prussian Parliament, this had quickly melted in the face of military victory over Austria. Throughout the 1860s and 1870s the most serious opposition that the chancellor had to face was not from the left but from the right, from those Prussian conservatives and traditionalists in other German states who saw his tactics as a betrayal of the principle of legitimacy. In order to rally their support, Bismarck had found it useful to justify his moves in terms of the defense of the legitimacy of the state. If there was no real, immediate crisis of legitimacy, then one had to be created. First the democrats, then the Catholics, and later the socialists, all were stigmatized as enemies of the state. The perception of danger was heightened by Bismarck's frequent use of diplomatic crises to reinforce the image of a state under constant seige from within and without.

The dualism of *Staat* and *Gesellschaft* served in the short run to strengthen the executive's hand; in the long term, however, prophecy became reality. Those stigmatized as enemies of the state, particularly the socialists, but also some Catholics and left-liberals, began to take their role seriously. Nothing illustrates this process better than the effect of the antisocialist legislation of 1878-1890 on the Social Democratic party. The ban on all socialist organizations had been imposed by Bismarck during one of those periodic internal crises in which he felt compelled to raise the bogey of revolution (that is, the question of legitimacy) in order to rally support for his policies. The ban extended to socialist publications and agitation, but did not cover electioneering. Thus the SPD was forced to concentrate all its energies on this one area of activity, with the result that it developed into Europe's most highly organized political party, strong enough to resist the pressures of its enemies. At the same time, its pariah status strengthened the ideological and class tendencies that were apparent but not entirely dominant when the repression began. In order to maintain itself in the hostile environment of the Second Empire, the SPD developed an inflexible stance based on an ideology of class warfare. Initially a product of the general liberal-nationalistic feeling of the time of unification, the socialist movement gradually assumed a posture of antiliberalism and antinationalism that seemed to justify its outlawry even to its former allies. Yet, at the same time, the SPD attempted to maintain some semblance of legality, thus endowing the party with a commitment to parliamentarism that contrasted strangely with its avowed Marxist principles of class revolution. It became, as one historian has put it, a party of "ambivalent revolutionaries," ideologically opposed to the system in which it continued to have an important emotional as well as political stake. Neither a true revolutionary elite nor a conventional party, the SPD was what J. P. Nettl has chosen to call a "nonparticipating opposition," an obstacle to the effective functioning of parliamentarism in Germany but hardly an immediate threat to the legitimacy of the state.[1] In a sense, the party

[1] J. P. Nettl, "The German Social Democratic Party 1890-1914 as a Political Model," *Past and Present*, 30 (1965), 65-95.

became a reflection of the state that it opposed, concentrating heavily on its own penetrative capacity, building a large bureaucracy, thereby ultimately opening between itself and its constituency the same kind of gulf that characterized the civic culture of the Bismarckian Reich.

Certain right-wing political groups also never completely reconciled themselves to the institutions of the Second Empire. Conservatives had opposed Bismarck at several stages of the unification process, but it was not until later that the depth of conservative disenchantment became fully apparent. During the Wilhelminian period right-wing politics began seriously to endanger the stability of the state. Once again the fact that participation and identity had been subordinated in time and importance to penetration produced troubling results. Like the left-wing radicals, right-wing groups developed in the direction of a nonparticipating opposition. Such groups as the *Bund der Landwirte* and the Pan-Germans employed a combination of antimodernist slogans and political anti-Semitism which, while not entirely new, had never before been so widespread. In its diatribes against the betrayal of traditional landed interests by the industrial-bureaucratic state, the *Bund der Landwirte* appealed to the one yet unmobilized section of the population, namely the Protestant lower middle class. Using a potent mixture of antiparliamentarianism and anti-Semitism, its propagandists played on the atmosphere of fear, uncertainty, and pessimism that characterized the mood not only of the rural population but also a large part of the urban *Mittelstand*. Less susceptible to street-corner demagoguery, but nevertheless also ready to listen to those who blamed Germany's woes on such apparently contradictory phenomena as industrial capitalism and social democracy were some members of the officer corps, the bureaucracy, and the industrial middle class. Serious identity and legitimacy problems lay just beneath the surface of the late empire, but in a political system in which the powers of institutional change lay in the hands of elites isolated from the aspirations of large segments of society, little of this consciousness was translated into constructive reform.

On the eve of World War I, the contradictions of the development process that had placed Prussia at the head of the German nation were glaringly evident. The priority given to penetration, the way the requirements of the Prussian state had shaped or postponed the solution of the identity, participation, and legitimacy crises of the new German nation, had produced results analogous to those created by the Reform Era. Even the Bismarckian social welfare legislation, hailed as a pioneering effort at solving the demand for more equitable distribution of material resources, had been bent to the imperatives of the Prussian state and its service elites. As in the earlier process of institutional innovation, political development after 1871 had resulted in high levels of capacity, equality, and differentiation at the central governmental level, but little in the way of complementary change either in society at large or in those mediating institutions, the parliament and the parties. Instead of growing in effectiveness and capacity, the parliamentary parties remained impotent. Now extraparliamentary movements were introducing into public life elements that seemed diametrically opposed to the previous trend toward rationalization and secularization instituted by the state. Chauvinistic nationalism, frequently accompanied by political anti-Semitism, seemed to signal a decline not only of liberal cosmopolitanism but also of the state's earlier commitment to universalistic standards of citizenship. Antiparliamentary sentiments had never been so strong as during the late Wilhelminian period, indicating a loss of faith in civil and political equality. Up to 1914 the state itself resisted these tendencies, but it now seemed clear that the old tactic of "revolution from above," so successful in a more passive social order, could no longer contain or control the explosive forces of nationalism and socialism evident in German society at large.

1918-1933

The Revolution of 1918 initiated a period of political crisis in much the same way the Revolution of 1848-1849 had, and with some of the same results. This time the revolutionary thrust from below was stronger, but once again power remained substantially in the hands of a civil and military establishment trained to view political development almost entirely as a matter of extending the security and capacity of the central governmental institutions. The socialist, liberal, and Catholic leaders of the former parliamentary opposition proved reluctant revolutionaries and almost immediately turned over to the army and bureaucracy the central instruments of power, thus repeating a pattern that had been set in the previous century. Once again Germany underwent a process of "revolution from above," with results analogous to those of the two previous crisis periods.

The revolutionary movement of the Soldiers' and Workers' Councils was defeated by a combination of foreign and domestic forces, some of which were outside the central government's power of control. The international situation, including the threat of Bolshevism and the consequences of military defeat, drove the moderate German left into an alliance with the old forces of order. The powerful Social Democratic party was split into a moderate wing, which put restoration of political stability before social experimentation, and the radical Independents, who viewed the Soldiers' and Workers' Councils as the vehicles for a social revolution of a democratic, non-Bolshevik character. Even more disastrous for the new Republic was the fact that behind the smoke screen created by the so-called "stab-in-the-back" legend, the army remained not only undefeated on the field of battle, but also virtually unchecked on the domestic front. By 1919 the new Republic had been forced to turn for salvation to the twin pillars of the old Reich: the Prussian military and the civil service, and so sealed its own fate. Once again Germany was a state without true support through consensus at the national societal level.

The fact that the parliamentary Republic was gradually forced to turn to the old elites to consolidate its position should not obscure, however, the degree to which 1918 marked a turning point in German political development, establishing questions of distribution, legitimacy, and identity in new and more urgent forms. The importance of the left wing Soldiers' and Workers' Councils lay not in what they accomplished but in what they revealed about the mood of German society. The same thing can be said for the right-wing Free Corps, insofar as their activities also demonstrated that henceforth formal institutions would no longer dominate or contain political conflict. Effective, stabilizing penetration of society by the central government had reached its limits, and had even been reversed. The real division was no longer between the executive and the legislature but between the state, represented now by both administrative and parliamentary institutions, and society, represented by extraparliamentary, extralegal movements of both the left and the right.

In many ways, the Weimar Republic was like the Second Empire. The Prussian monarchy was gone, but Prussia, by virtue of its size and political traditions, dominated Weimar's politics in much the same way as it had controlled the Second Reich. The new constitution provided for democratic representation and parliamentary government with full ministerial responsibility, but left unsolved the key question of the place of political parties within the political system. The sham constitutionalism of the past was formally abolished, but the attitudes of the electorate and the behavior of the parties reflected that the absence of a tradition of civic participation that could not now be created by republican legislation. In bringing in proportional representation, the new constitution probably widened rather than narrowed the gap between the parties and the electorate. A presidential form of government was superimposed on the parliamentary structure in such a way that it interfered with the full implementation of parliamentary government. Designed to counterbalance the parliament and to provide a symbol of authority to compensate for the loss of the monarchy, the institution of the *Reichspräsident* became instead a source of penetration, interfering with the creation of the kind of participatory institutions that could create stable loyalty to the regime and a sense of cohesion within the nation.

The only tested elements in the Weimar constitution were the army and civil service, both of which were imperfectly subordinated to parliamentary control. The officer corps successfully defended its traditional independence, while the bureaucracy, now nominally subject to parliamentary control, resisted all attempts to alter either its conservative ethos or its elitist composition. Both were now more willing than ever before to use parliamentary means to further their administrative ends. The interference of both the army and the bureaucracy in the politics of the Republic was but another disruptive element. Together with other segments of the upper and middle classes, members of the officer corps and higher civil service tended to drift further to the right during the 1920s, many ending up in the camp of radical groups such as the Nazis, whose *volkisch* ideologies condemned not only the Republic but also many of the features held over from the Second Empire. Somehow the members of the old elites managed to reconcile antirationalist, antimodernist politics with their own highly rational bureaucratic and military functions. Their longing for a return to a purer form of the traditional bureaucratic state was sufficiently compatible with the metapolitical romanticism of the National Socialists to ensure that by 1933 Hitler had a fervent following among a significant minority of the army and civil service.

Not all the weaknesses of the Weimar Republic can be attributed to structural factors, however. The burdens imposed by the Versailles Treaty also increased its difficulties. Foreign and domestic opposition gave the moderate parties of the Republic little choice but to maintain the high level of penetration inherited from the Second Empire, and therefore to limit experimentation in democratization and decentralization. Contrary to the hopes of the revolutionaries of 1918, the hegemony of Prussia was not diminished. The socialists themselves had a vested interest in maintaining the autonomy of that state, whose government they managed to dominate until 1932. In other areas centralization and concentration of power continued. The size of the central bureaucracy grew during the period of the Republic, and there was a tendency for the federal government to use its power of emergency decree at the expense of the *Länder*, as at the time of the Hitler *Putsch* in 1923, and with greater frequency after the beginning of the Depression in 1929. This culminated with the coup against the government of the state of Prussia in July 1932, an act that provided a legal precedent for the Nazi seizure of power in the following year. All this was done in the name of the Republic, but instead of ensuring the stability of the constitutional order, it only called into question the basic legitimacy of the democracy itself.

A similar pattern was evident with respect to identity. Again the Republic was burdened by the unwelcome inheritance of the empire's *Kleindeutsch* solution. Much of the fault for Weimar's inability to satisfy the nationalist aspirations of the German people can be traced to the territorial settlement imposed on it by the Treaty of Versailles and on the stubborn opposition of the Western powers to any attempt by the Republic to reach an economic or political accommodation with the Austrian Germans. It could be argued that this particular problem, because of its international ramifications, was not really a problem of German political development as such; yet there can be little doubt that the internal politics of the Republic played a large part in heightening the tension over national identity. Conflict associated with the national issue tended to feed the trend toward extraparliamentary opposition, thus further weakening the already fragile legitimacy of the Republic.

Had the Republic been of longer duration, it might have overcome some of the contradictions of its participatory institutions. However, it was also burdened by the social and cultural divisions inherited from the Second Empire, aspects of which were much more difficult to alter. The radical left, now represented by the communists, fed on the German workingman's ideological commitment to class conflict, while the right-wing parties cultivated the *volkisch* nationalism previously absorbed by large sections of the rural and urban lower middle classes. Even the socialist, Catholic, and liberal parties had great difficulty adjusting to their unaccustomed role as legitimate participants in the decision-making process. Its earlier role as a "nonparticipating opposition" had not equipped the SPD for these responsibilities, though it must be admitted that this party did not waver in its loyalty to the Republic despite the enormous difficulties the new role heaped upon it. The Catholic Center party did less well in the end, its right wing ultimately deserting the Republic in the critical events of 1933. But it was the liberal parties, with their middle-class constituencies, who were most susceptible to the tendency to slip back into the old role of opposition or to stand by uncommitted while life drained out of Weimar democracy. The elders of these parties, who had grown up in the shadow of the *Kulturkampf* and the Anti-Socialist Laws, had learned that political survival meant disengagement and withdrawal. During the Weimar period they therefore tended to adopt the tactics that had served the Catholics and socialists so well in the earlier period. The idea that the methods appropriate to politics under the old monarchy might not be applicable to the new parliamentary democracy did not occur to them. Though most disavowed any revolutionary intention, their withdrawal of support necessarily raised the question of legitimacy.

Naturally, the extremist parties of the right made the most of the disenchantment of the middle classes. The most successful of these, the Nazi party, managed to forge an alliance of the most unlikely elements, ranging from conservative monarchists to radical socialists, but there is little doubt that it won its greatest support among those small-town Protestant constituencies that had once voted liberal under the Empire. The party's ideology, however logically contradictory it may have been, exploited the issues of participation, legitimacy, identity, and distribution in a way that permitted both socialists and nationalists to see salvation in its programs. Everyone was encouraged to believe that his particular objective would be given highest priority. Conservatives were assured that socialism was only a means to an end; the radicals, on the other hand, were convinced that nationalism was only a temporary expedient, a prelude to social revolution.

In many ways the Nazis were the successors of the SPD, a "nonparticipating opposition" that consciously adopted the role of the outlaw party, though in this case the pariah party was not identified with a pariah class but a pariah nation, thus broadening its base of appeal beyond all social divisions and even beyond the boundaries of the Reich itself. Every effort was made to steer a course between *Staat* and *Gesellschaft*, so that hostility to both could be exploited. Hitler was careful to link his ultimate aspirations with the metapolitical notion of the *Volk*, an identity transcending the *Kleindeutsch* Reich, that satisfied the widespread feeling of disengagement from the state and general ferment within the existing society. Above all else, identification with parliamentarism was avoided; the Nazi styled their organization as a *Kampfbund* or *Bewegung*, thus avoiding association with the conventional political parties. All this was reminiscent not only of the earlier politics of the pre-war SPD but of the Free Corps and other paramilitary organizations that had occupied an ambivalent position in the early days of the Republic.

When it took power in 1918, the Social Democratic party and its allies abruptly dropped the role of nonparticipating opposition, wedding themselves to the state in such a way that they foreclosed their options for further reconciliation with society. Revolutionary by heritage, the Social Democrats quickly became conservative in practice, particularly when it came to tampering with the existing bureaucratic and military structures. By contrast, Hitler came to power by nonrevolutionary means in 1933, but initially avoided the kinds of commitments that had prevented the pursuit of radical solutions to the identity and legitimacy problem by his predecessors. The Nazi movement and the state continued to exist separately, in a flexible arrangement that Ernst Frankel described as the "dual state." The rhetoric and, to a lesser degree, the action of the movement was revolutionary; the action and, to a lesser degree, the rhetoric of the state remained essentially conservative. This coexistence of revolutionary goals and conservative means, the unresolved tension between radical appearances and staid realities, between grandiose expectations and mundane results, represents the most puzzling but fundamental aspects of the Third Reich. According to David Schoenbaum, Hitler's revolution was "at the same time a revolution of means and ends. The revolution of ends was ideology—war against bourgeois and industrial society. The revolution of means was its reciprocal. It was bourgeois and industrial since, in an industrial age, even a war against industrial society must be fought with industrial means and the bourgeois are necessary to fight the bourgeoisie."[2]

If the Weimar Republic can be called a democracy without democrats, then the Third Reich can be termed a revolution without revolutionaries. Despite their radical rhetoric, Hitler and his associates were content to leave the inherited dichotomy between state and so-

[2] David Schoenbaum, *Hitler's Social Revolution: Class and Status in Nazi Germany, 1933-1939* (London, 1966), p. xxiii.

ciety virtually intact. They might attempt to "purify" the *Volk* by first expelling and later destroying those elements that they considered racially alien, but it is difficult to find any evidence of substantial change in either the structure of society or the organization of the state that, apart from the effects of the second world war, were the direct outcome of Nazi programs. Hitler's failure to fulfill the expectations of his more radical supporters was due in part to the fact that to achieve his social and national goals he required the services of the powerful military and administrative machinery of the existing state. In a less highly developed political system something like the tribal *Volksstaat* ideal might have been realizable, but instead of destroying the traditional state apparatus, Hitler was content to play off its elites against his own radical supporters to the benefit of his own personal power. External expansion depended on the services of the army; internal repression necessitated reliance on the bureaucracy. Apart from the SS and the Labor Front, the Nazis were able to generate no institutions outside the existing state that could function as effectively as the professional civil or military services.

Evidence of the "demodernization" which some political scientists claim to detect in the Third Reich is hard to come by, at least as far as the central governmental institutions were concerned. The instrumental rationality of the service elites was not seriously affected by the irrational ideology of the party; the complexity of central government organization and its continued effectiveness are attested to by the fact that, despite the wasteful duplication of functions that sometimes occurred, the state maintained its efficiency. Any demodernization that did occur involved the party organs themselves, where corruption and inefficiency were most common.

The more that is discovered about the actual workings of the Third Reich, the more reason we have to question the assumption that this regime achieved the kind of tight bonds between state and society that we usually associate with stereotyped notions of totalitarianism. The fit between the Nazi state and the German nation was never as exact as Hitler proclaimed it, even when the pressures of terror and propaganda were at their most severe. Ironically, the limits on Hitler's power were a product of the same divisions between *Staat* and *Gesellschaft* that had characterized Germany's earlier political evolution. The very conditions that had permitted Hitler to present himself as the focus of Germans' hopes for national cohesion ultimately prevented him from achieving a permanent, stable nation state. It was no accident that it was those European countries where the gap between state and society was greatest—Germany and Italy—that charismatic leadership had its strongest appeal. These were countries where the intermediary institutions of parliament and party were the weakest, where the desire to achieve the condition of national consensus took on the most desperate extralegal forms, and where coercion was consistently resorted to as an instrument of change. It was precisely this reliance on power that was self-defeating, insofar as each new attempt to impose forms of nation-statehood drove state and society further apart, the Third Reich being no exception to this pattern of political development.

Hitler's attempts to use the powers of the state (penetration) to create a new sense of identity and legitimacy failed. His dictatorial effectiveness was compromised and even moderated by the tendency of the German people, when faced with repression, to withdraw into passive resistance. The so-called "internal emigration" that occurred during the Third Reich had been foreshadowed by the disengagement from politics evident during the Weimar Republic and even as early as the Second Empire. Limits on totalitarianism were also set by the other element of the dualism, the highly developed institutions of the state. Military and administrative institutions did place limits on the arbitrary use of power; and the civil and military elites did remain faithful to the minimum of law and order required of them in their capacity as functionaries. In the end, some were even prepared to move beyond passive to heroic resistance in order to maintain the remnants of their civil and military traditions.

Resort to penetration to solve the accumulating questions of legitimacy and identity explain the origins, form, and fate of the Third Reich. We have already seen how the Nazis played on both the nationalist and revolutionary passions of the Weimar period. Hitler promised the German people a new national identity and a radically new form of government that would solve internal social and economic problems. Like many authoritarian movements in developing states, the Nazis claimed to be able to cure all their country's ills through political means. In theory, the Third Reich was to dissolve the traditional divisions between state and society and heal the wounds of class conflict, but in practice it succeeded in demonstrating the Nazis' incapacity for social and political revolution. In attempting to integrate a highly developed central government and a weakly developed civic culture, Hitler relied heavily on parochial, traditional symbols as a means of political mobilization. He interpreted the political world in the only way that many of his fellow Germans could understand it, but ultimately even his enormous skill in arousing popular hopes and fears was not enough to overcome the effects of a lack of consensus and commitment at the grass roots. In the short run he was able to achieve, largely through propaganda and coercion, a remarkable mobilization of the German people, accompanied by a substantial but temporary change in their sense of national identity along racial lines, and a new consensus of loyalty to the regime itself. For a moment in its history, Germany's dualism of state and society seemed to be overcome under a system in which all authority was placed in the hands of a Führer. Yet to achieve this power Hitler had had to play two powerful elements against one another—the party representing the nation against the bureaucracy and the army, the apparatus of the state. In the long run, dualism of state and party was no more satisfactory in creating political stability than had been the older dualism of the executive and parliament. Like his predecessors, Hitler had capitalized on the gulf between state and society to build a base for his personal power; and, to the extent he relied upon it, he was unable to alter it.

Hitler's actual achievement, one that stopped well short of his real goals, lay in his ability to persuade the German people that they were experiencing a genuine national revolution. He managed to divert their attention to such an extent that they ignored not only the mundane but also the horrific aspects of the Third Reich. He convinced the Germans that he had solved the festering problems of identity and legitimacy, thus bringing to an end the crisis period that had begun in 1918. He did this in part by employing the oldest of political tactics, the use of war to direct attention away from domestic concerns. Bismarck had used international crisis and the lust for imperial glory for similar purposes, but he had never committed himself to extensive overseas expansion, and after 1871 had not given in to the impulse toward war to solve domestic difficulties. It remains debatable whether the German leaders prior to and during World War I really departed from the Bismarckian policy, but it is incontestable that Hitler intended to use the instrument of aggressive expansion to solve the twin problems of identity and legitimacy once and for all. In this sense, 1938 and not 1933 marked the beginning of the real Nazi revolution. With the outbreak of full-scale war in 1939, the revolutionary course was irreversibly set. Defeat in 1945 terminated a crisis period that had begun in 1918, but without solving the central questions of identity and legitimacy.

In the last days of the Third Reich the old questions loomed larger than ever before. The regime that had begun by questioning the legitimacy of its predecessor, ended in an orgy of self-destruction that called into question the principle of legitimacy itself. Nazism had initially rejected the *Kleindeutsch* solution in favor of racial nationalism. In time, even the limits of this identity became blurred until, as the Nazi war machine expanded eastward and westward, this form of nationalism seemed to be absorbed in a new form of supranationalism revolving around the amorphous concept of the Aryan race. Long before 1945, the Third Reich had ceased to resemble anything like a Western nation state. The dynamism of coercion and expansion had even overrun the boundaries of the German ethnic nationality; and like its predecessors, Hitler's regime was still a state without a nation, as far from the solution of the problems of identity and legitimacy as when it had begun. Hitler's will to power had exceeded even the limits of German *Staatsräson*, extending the capacity of the powerful central government to the point of collapse. This time, unlike 1918, defeat would be complete, returning Germany to the status of a divided country and depriving its parts of legitimacy in the eyes of the community of nations.

Once again, although in a very different manner, the German sequence pattern had repeated itself. Like its predecessors, the Third Reich had placed heavy emphasis on penetrative capacity, even subordinating the questions of legitimacy and identity raised by its own supporters to the strengthening of the central organs of the executive, the army, and the bureaucracy. It is true that penetration was not defined as an end in itself but rather a means to the solution of other questions. But whether a goal or an instrument, penetration continued to be placed at the top of the list of priorities, first in time and importance. The old bureaucratic and military elites no longer directed events, but their functional importance was not lessened under either the Weimar Republic or the Third Reich. In both cases, movements that had begun as efforts to dislodge the power of entrenched elites ultimately had the effect of strengthening them. In this sense, Hitler's regime was a continuation of the experience of the Weimar Republic. Both showed that the institutions of the German state could not be used for revolution ostensibly directed against themselves.

Revolution from below could not be combined with a tradition of revolution from above where the gap between the power of the state and the passivity of society was as great as in Germany.

Conclusion

European historians have accustomed us to thinking of the nation state as the norm for political development. The German case, together with examples of contemporary Third-World countries, suggests that a stable association of state with nation may in fact be an exceptional condition. The experience of the vast majority of existing polities confirms Peter Nettl's observation that "stateness" and "nationness" are two different variables, whose combination requires peculiar historical circumstances.[3] Germany was one of those countries for which the combination has never been successfully achieved, and perhaps never will be. The heritage of absolutism had much to do with this, but so did the sequence of institutional change that followed the decline of the Old Regime, particularly the rapidity and authoritarianism with which Germans were forced to deal with the five major problem areas we have been discussing. It seems that the competition with the Western European nation states, together with internal conditions, dictated the emphasis on penetration, thus furthering the attributes of stateness while delaying and even impeding the kind of common societal experience that fosters nationness. Since the early nineteenth century, even the most progressive sectors of German society looked to the central government (and thus to penetration) as the only instrument that could produce that desired unity and consensus which they associated with the ideal of nationhood. They staked their hopes on the kind of "revolution from above" that left the mass of society uninvolved and even disaffected. Prussia created a territorial nation through force of army, but this failed to resolve the dualism between state and society, between stateness and nationness. When parliament and the legally constituted parties also failed to bring about the desired conditions, more radical measures were adopted, but always in the tradition of the "revolution from above." The Third Reich did not deviate from this pattern, ultimately relying on the power of the state in its attempt to carve out a new sense of nationness. Hitler repeated the mistake of his predecessors, attempting to achieve the west-

[3] J. P. Nettl, "The State as a Conceptual Variable," *World Politics*, 20 (1968), 559-592.

ern ideal of the nation state at a price and with means that were actually incompatible with that goal.

If there is a generalization to be drawn from the German experience, it is that the priority given to penetration necessarily leads to faulted nationhood. It demonstrates that while states can be made, nations are the product of a more complicated process in which the application of power at the central level is perhaps more hindrance than help. Those countries whose sense of national identity and political legitimacy were established before the advent of the modern period found it easier to evolve a close fit between state and nation, even when problems of participation and distribution arose. Where priority was assigned to penetration, either as an end in itself or as an expedient means to identity or legitimacy, even the instruments of participation and distribution were insufficient to create the complementary unity and loyalty. At the risk of sounding excessively Whiggish, it does seem that the lesson here points to the limits of state power. Repeated attempts to forge national societal consensus out of bureaucratic rulings and military actions proved in Germany's case unproductive, not only because the latter led ultimately to defeat, but also because the former increased the passivity of the population at large. Today, new nations trying to emulate the Western ideal-type of the nation state encounter many of the same difficulties—civil war, dictatorship, military disaster. Perhaps this is not so much their fault as the fault of the ideal that they pursue. For the stable union of state and nation has been arrived at only in a few cases—England, America, France, and the Scandinavian countries—and it is not necessarily accessible to countries whose timetable is dictated by the pressure of international events or distorted by the necessity of state action. They would do well to consider, as Germany herself must, the possibilities of an arrangement other than the classical nation state.

Some Related Readings

WORKS OF GENERAL INTEREST

Bendix, Reinhard. *Nation-Building and Citizenship*. New York, 1964.

Bracher, Karl D. "Staatsbegriff und Demokratie in Deutschland," *Politische Vierteljahresschrift* (1968), pp. 2-27.

Dahrendorf, Ralf. *Society and Democracy in Germany*. New York, 1967.
Meinecke, Friedrich. *The German Catastrophe*. Boston, 1948.
Neumann, Sigmund. "Germany: Changing Patterns and Lasting Patterns," in Sigmund Neumann, ed., *Modern Political Parties*. Chicago, 1956, pp. 354-90.
Verba, Sidney. "Germany: The Remaking of Political Culture," in L. Pye and S. Verba, eds., *Political Culture and Political Development*. Princeton, 1965, pp. 130-70.

CRISIS PERIOD, 1806-1819

Koselleck, Reinhart. *Preussen zwischen Reform und Revolution: Allgemeines Landrecht, Verwaltung und soziale Bewegung von 1791 bis 1848*. Stuttgart, 1967.
Krieger, Leonard. *The German Idea of Freedom*. Boston, 1957.
Rosenberg, Hans. *Bureaucracy, Aristocracy and Autocracy: The Prussian Experience 1660-1815*. Cambridge, 1958.
Simon, Walter. *The Failure of the Prussian Reform Movement, 1807-1819*. Ithaca, 1956.

CRISIS PERIOD, 1848-1871

Craig, Gordon A. *The Politics of the Prussian Army*. Oxford, 1955.
Gillis, John R. *The Prussian Bureaucracy in Crisis, 1840-1860*. Stanford, 1971.
Hamerow, Theodore. *Restoration, Revolution, Reaction*. Princeton, 1958.
———. *The Social Foundations of German Unification 1858-1871*. Princeton, 1969.
Kehr, Eckart. *Der Primat der Innenpolitik*. Berlin, 1965.
Lidtke, Vernon. *The Outlawed Party: Social Democracy in Germany, 1878-1890*. Princeton, 1966.
Nipperdey, Thomas. *Die Organization der deutschen Parteien vor 1918*. Düsseldorf, 1961.
Pflanze, Otto. *Bismarck and the Development of Germany*. Princeton, 1963.
Roehl, J. C. *Germany without Bismarck*. London, 1968.
Rosenberg, Arthur. *The Birth of the German Republic, 1871-1918*. London, 1931.

Roth, Guenther. *The Social Democrats in Imperial Germany*. Totowa, N.J., 1963.
Schieder, Theodor. *Staat und Gesellschaft im Wandel unserer Zeit*. Munich, 1958.

CRISIS PERIOD, 1918-1933

Allen, William S. *The Nazi Seizure of Power*. London, 1966.
Bracher, Karl D. *Die Auflösung der Weimar Republik*. Villigen, 1964.
Carsten, F. L. *The Reichswehr and Politics, 1918-1933*. Oxford, 1966.
Diehl-Thiele, Peter. *Partei und Staat im Dritten Reich*. Munich, 1969.
Feldman, G. *Army, Industry and Labor in Germany, 1914-18*. London, 1967.
Krausnick, Helmut. *Anatomy of the SS State*. London, 1968.
Maier, Charles S. *Recasting Bourgeois Europe*. Princeton, 1975.
Mason, Timothy W. *Sozialpolitik im Dritten Reich*. Opladen, 1977.
Runge, Wolfgang. *Politik und Beamtentum im Parteienstaat*. Stuttgart, 1965.
Ryder, A. J. *The German Revolution of 1918*. Cambridge, 1967.
Schoenbaum, David. *Hitler's Social Revolution: Class and Status in Nazi Germany, 1933-1939*. London, 1966.

CHAPTER 10

RUSSIA

WALTER M. PINTNER

RUSSIAN HISTORY provides an intermediate case for the study of economic development, and perhaps for the whole process of modernization. In the early nineteenth century, and probably before that, Russians were well aware of the special position that their country occupied in relation to both Western Europe and the rest of the world. In economic development, technology, and the diffusion of education, Russia for centuries followed a Western path although, at times at least, the lag has been great.

Political institutions in Russia have, however, evolved quite differently from those in Western Europe since the middle ages. One could say that the very early appearance of a reasonably effective centralized autocracy in Russia was, in some sense at least, "advanced" in the fifteenth or sixteenth centuries. Advanced or not, it was different; and Russian political institutions, imperial or Soviet, have remained fundamentally different and, on the whole, very successful. Except for brief periods of instability in the early seventeenth and twentieth centuries, they have maintained thoroughgoing political control of a large area and population without effective participation of any substantial element of the society in the operation of the state.

The traditional Russian-liberal and Western interpretation of the nineteenth and twentieth centuries has seen the political development of Russia as the story of the continual thwarting of "natural" tendencies to develop along liberal-constitutional lines. This direction was seen as "natural," if not inevitable, because it was the pattern established in nineteenth-century Western and even Central Europe. If Russia built railroads, expanded literacy, produced great novels, symphonies, and scientists, abolished serfdom, and even established an effective and independent judiciary, what could be more reasonable than to expect that parliamentary government would soon follow, as it had elsewhere. That the revolution of 1917 ended the progression

Crises of Political Development in Europe and the United States
0-691-07598-0/78/000347-35$01.75/1 (cloth)
0-691-02183-X/78/000347-35$01.75/1 (paperback)
For copying information, see copyright page

is seen in the traditional view as either the immediate result of World War I or is blamed on the failure of the imperial government to make adequate and timely political reforms throughout the nineteenth century. Soviet scholars see the course of nineteenth-century development as one of growing contradictions between an "aristocratic-feudal" monarchy and the rapidly developing capitalist economy that produced a revolution through an alliance of workers and peasants.

Both interpretations recognize some of the significant processes that were going on in Russia, but they neglect the importance of the long-established tsarist political institutions. The nature of these institutions helps to explain both the failure of liberal constitutionalism and the character of the political system that emerged from the revolution. A summary examination of Russian political history in terms of the five crises may provide a different and revealing perspective. Although all five types can be identified at various points in Russian political development, it is the relationship between problems of penetration and distribution that has been the crucial element throughout the centuries. The crises have come when the demands made by the state on the population—that is, its ability to redistribute resources through taxation and military recruitment—has exceeded its effective control, that is, administrative penetration, of the countryside. Significant demands for participation in government, problems of identity, and questions about the government's legitimacy have become serious only when the balance between penetration and distribution has been upset.

Crises

IDENTITY

Taken in its simplest terms and applied to the whole Great Russian population (as opposed to Ukrainian or Belorussian peoples), it is difficult to point to any clear crisis of identity in Russian history. Almost from the beginning of recorded history there seems to have been some sort of conception of "Rus," although what exactly it implied is difficult to discern.[1] The early Muscovite state was certainly composed of Orthodox Slavs speaking a common East Slavic language. The expansion of Muscovite territory from the fifteenth through the seventeenth centuries placed some non-Orthodox and non-Slavic peoples within its borders, but in general the identity between Muscovite subject and orthodox Russian remained. Tatars who abandoned Islam,

[1] George Vernadsky, *Kievan Russia* (New Haven, 1948), pp. 175-76, 214-15, 317.

Poles or Lithuanians who renounced Catholicism, were rapidly assimilated into the Orthodox Russian Muscovite state. After the fall of Constantinople to the Ottoman Turks in 1453, Muscovy became the only independent Orthodox state; and it developed a political ideology that identified Moscow as the "Third Rome" and stressed its role as the defender of the true faith. It must be noted that this ideological development followed the substantial political success of Moscow in the mid-fifteenth century, but it undoubtedly served to consolidate and develop a consciousness of the *de facto* situation, that Muscovy was an Orthodox Russian political entity ruled by a well-established dynasty.[2] Certainly the religious element was paramount, but it is difficult to disentangle the two because there were no competing Orthodox political entities. During the early seventeenth-century dynastic crisis, the attempts of claimants to the Muscovite throne identified as Polonophile, and of Polish royalty itself, failed in large measure because of religious-cultural antipathy to what were seen by the Muscovite population as foreign, heretical incursions. A schism in the mid-seventeenth century destroyed the unity of the Orthodox church, but both elements in the split continued to identify themselves with a "Russian" as opposed to a "foreign" image.

Despite the xenophobic attitude of much of Muscovite society in the early seventeenth century, Russia had more and more contacts with Western Europe in the course of the century; and this influence was dramatically accelerated in the first quarter of the eighteenth century, during the reign of Peter I (The Great). Seventeenth- and early eighteenth-century Westernization was, first and foremost, a matter of the successful assimilation of enough Western military organization and technology to survive and to expand, largely at the expense of Sweden, then one of Europe's leading military powers. In the later eighteenth century and in the nineteenth, Russia was able to maintain and strengthen her position as one of the great powers of Europe (first achieved by the defeat of the Swedes at Poltava in 1709).

Peter's modernization effort was fully consistent with the practices of previous centuries; but it was a far more intense effort in his day, and it affected most of the elite of Russian society. For the first time in Russian history the long-established service obligation of the nobility became an onerous full-time requirement rather than an occasional duty that did not interfere excessively with established pat-

[2] Robert Lee Wolff, "The Three Romes: The Migration of an Ideology and the Making of an Autocrat," *Daedalus* (Spring 1959).

terns of life. Most important for the problem of identity was the forcing of Western cultural forms on the traditional Muscovite nobility. To remain an accepted member of the governing class a man had to change his style of dress, shave, and adopt domestic and social patterns of life that were modeled on those of Western Europe. Literacy (in Russian) and some knowledge of arithmetic became increasingly important.[3] For the highest levels of the nobility, particularly those associated with the court, knowledge of a foreign language became important. The extent to which French became the primary language of the Russian nobility, however, has been greatly exaggerated. Only a very small wealthy group could afford the tutors and foreign travel necessary for real mastery of an alien culture.

These changes in cultural forms did not make the Russian nobility into what other Europeans would consider Westerners, but they did destroy the cultural unity that the Muscovite state had enjoyed. No longer were the boyars and the peasants part of one homogeneous culture, dominated by orthodoxy and headed by the tsar. Orthodoxy was not formally abandoned; but it became, in the eighteenth century, an appendage of the state rather than an integral part of it. The full-time service that engaged the nobility in the first half of the eighteenth century, as well as the new cultural patterns, destroyed the ties between the nobles and their estates, the people on them, and even the locality from which they came. The cadet school, the officers' barracks—both Western institutions and much the same throughout the empire—became their home; and service provided their identity as well as their source of material support and social status.

The superficially Westernized Russian noble was cut off from his traditional culture, but could not feel at home in a non-Russian environment. The striving of these men to find their place in world culture by creating their own eventually produced the great works of literature and music of nineteenth-century Russia. Resolution of the identity crisis, at least in cultural matters, was most productive. The intelligentsia that began as alienated eighteenth-century nobility also provided the bulk of the military officers and bureaucrats that ran the Russian state; and, as the nineteenth century progressed, it filled the ranks of the illegal political opposition as it developed.

[3] In practice, this was a gradual development. In the 1760s a great many nobles in the provinces were illiterate, but the *cahiers* sent by provincial nobles to Catherine II show that the desire for education as a prerequisite for a successful career in state service had become well established.

All educated Russians were in some degree involved in the identity problem that had its roots in the seventeenth century. But it is difficult to discern a clear connection of their identity problem with that of political stability until the late nineteenth century. The seventeenth-century boyars did become Westernized in the eighteenth century, and continued their basic role in the social order. Russia's success as a great power in the eighteenth century, culminating in her defeat of Napoleon and her continental primacy in the first half of the nineteenth century, eased the strain of adapting the strong traditional identity to new Western forms. By the second half of the nineteenth century, the substantial achievements of Russia in cultural endeavors could provide the educated class some substitute for the loss of international prestige suffered through unexpected defeat in the Crimean War. There need not have been the direct substitution of novels and symphonies for diplomatic prestige as a source of satisfaction for the same individuals. Before 1856 a large portion of the educated class derived satisfaction from Russian prestige as a great power. After 1856 a portion of the educated public could look with pride at Russian cultural achievements.

The identity crisis was over, at least in its acute form, for most Russians by the latter nineteenth century. As such it never caused a crisis of political order, even though it was a major feature of the development of the radical intelligentsia. When they finally caused serious difficulties for the government, it was no longer the problem of identity that was mainly involved. The major radical and moderate groups, and the state itself, were all "Western" in orientation. The political crisis of the early twentieth century was not one in which the major issue was one of a "Russian" versus a "European" identity. It was a crisis in which the kind of European (that is, modern) state that Russia would be was at issue. Each group saw particular advantages or problems in the institutions that Russia had inherited from past generations, as in the famous debate among both radical and official circles regarding the role of the peasant village communal organization in Russia's future development.

The identity question for both imperial and Soviet Russia involves the matter of non-Russian groups. The first major accretion of non-Russian peoples was in the mid-sixteenth century with the conquest of Kazan and Astrakhan, and by the end of the nineteenth century the Great Russians were only about forty-four percent of the total population.[4] In the Soviet Union today the situation is similar, and the non-Russian population is growing more rapidly than the Russian. The variety of national groups involved is immense: small and primitive tribes in remote areas, non-Western peoples with ancient literary and artistic traditions such as the Uzbeks; large Slavic groups such as the Ukrainians, with close historical, linguistic, and religious ties with the Great Russians; small but highly educated and advanced populations, as in the Baltic States, with cultural traditions far closer to Central Europe or Scandinavia than Moscow; and many, many more. For each of the national groups the question of identity has arisen, mostly in the later nineteenth century, but earlier for some, later for others. Were they to regard themselves as imperial (or Soviet) citizens? What did this mean? Should they try to become more Russian or emphasize their own national tradition? These have been familiar issues for countless millions of people in the nineteenth and twentieth centuries. However, from the point of view of the history of the political development of the imperial Russian and Soviet state, the question of identity for the national minorities never was one of crisis proportions. It has been a significant problem for at least one hundred years, but has always been overshadowed by other issues. Despite crude efforts at Russianization in the late nineteenth century, most of the national groups in the Russian Empire, with the notable exception of the Poles, aspired to nothing more than some sort of cultural autonomy or federal solution of their problems. Poland is best regarded

[4] N. A. Troinitskii, eds., *Pervaia vseobshchaia perepis' naseleniia Rossiiskoi Imperii, 1897 g., Obshchii svod*, II (St. Petersburg, 1905), pp. 1-19, cited in Richard Pipes, *The Formation of the Soviet Union*, revised edition (Cambridge, Mass., 1964), p. 2. With the Ukrainians and Belorussians, the Orthodox Slavs totaled 66.81 percent. The Turkic peoples were 10.82 percent, and the Poles 6.31 percent of the total. No other group exceeded 5 percent. Some non-Russians were probably counted as Russians on the basis of language; and, according to Pipes, the non-Great Russian proportion of the population may have been close to 60 percent.

In the eighteenth and nineteenth centuries the upper levels of Russian military and civil service included a substantial number of non-Russians, particularly Germans from the Baltic provinces of the empire. These men served loyally, not because of a "Russian" identity but because of their devotion to a political order that recognized and supported their privileged social, economic, and cultural position in their home provinces. In the second half of the nineteenth century that special position was somewhat eroded, but by then the numbers of well-educated Russians available for service had increased so greatly that the special advantages that their education had previously given Baltic Germans in government service was largely gone. For a discussion of the available statistics on non-Russians in civil service, see Walter M. Pintner, "The Social Characteristics of the Early Nineteenth-Century Russian Bureaucracy," *Slavic Review*, 29 (September 1970), 436-38; and "The Russian Higher Civil Service on the Eve of the 'Great Reforms,'" *Journal of Social History* (Spring 1975), 65.

as either a satellite or federated state, or a colonial territory, depending on the period in question. There never seems to have been any serious question of the Polish ruling class regarding themselves as Russians, although at times some adopted a pro-Russian policy. The collapse of central political authority in 1917 produced a number of short-lived independent or semi-independent national entities, but with the exception of Finland, the Baltic States (between the wars), and Poland, none survived the civil war.

Soviet policy has granted most national groups limited cultural autonomy but not political autonomy. The slightest hint of autonomous nationalism has brought severe repression. The question is clearly a sensitive one that is viewed as potentially dangerous, but thus far in both the empire and the Soviet Union the dominant position of the Great Russians has not been seriously challenged. Some, perhaps many, Ukrainians, Georgians, and Balts may regard a Soviet identity as a "Russian" identity and reject it for that reason, but there is very little that they can do about it. The Great Russian population is far larger than any other single group, and the cultural differences between Russians and Ukrainians and Belorussians are far less than those between these Orthodox slavic peoples and other important minorities: Georgians, Armenians, the various Muslim Turkic groups, or the Baltic peoples. Within the largest single minority, the Ukrainians, who inhabit a rich agricultural and industrial area, there is some strong separatist sentiment, but also there are very strong pressures tending toward at least partial Russianization. The linguistic and cultural differences are not great (this does not mean that they cannot be very important for many Ukrainians); in urban areas the populations tend to be mixed, and the practical advantages of a "Russian" identity can be substantial in a system where almost all real power is centered in Moscow, and in every field the best jobs are to be found there. The same pressures operate on all the national groups, and their response varies in the light of their own cultural traditions, but all are confronted with the necessity of coming to grips with a reality that offers no easy alternative to the acceptance of the Soviet policy.

In summary, it can be said that the Great Russian people seem to have developed a sense of identity based at first primarily on orthodoxy, but this has coincided with a linguistic and dynastic unit since the fifteenth century. The Tsar was the champion of the true faith in a long series of conflicts with neighboring peoples—Islamic, Catholic, and Lutheran—who also spoke different languages. The "crusading" element in many of these conflicts has certainly been exaggerated after the fact, both in nearly contemporary propaganda efforts and in later historical scholarship. Nevertheless, the religious and linguistic divisions corresponded to the divisions of political power. If you were Orthodox, you spoke Russian and you knew what side you were on.[5] The invasion of Moscow by Polish Catholic forces at the very beginning of the seventeenth century certainly increased the general consciousness of the difference between "us" and "them." Poles did not dress, act, or talk like Orthodox Russians. Acceptance of the need for strong central leadership was undoubtedly facilitated by the incursion of these foreigners in a time of internal political crisis. The increased contact and competition with Western Europe in subsequent centuries has changed the content of the sense of identity, but has not destroyed it. A Russian may not be able to say for certain whether he is a "European," an "Asian," or something totally unique; but he knows he is a Russian, even though it may be hard to define exactly what that means. He may despise his government, but he will almost certainly retain an intense pride in his nation.

LEGITIMACY

We have argued that modern Russian political development has not been marked by any crisis of identity even though certain groups—the critical intelligentsia and the national minorities—have experienced such crises. Very much the same thing can be said in the case of legitimacy. There have been only two periods since the formation of the Muscovite state when there was no widely accepted (if not popular) government: the "Time of Troubles" at the start of the seventeenth century and a few years following the 1917 revolution. In contrast to southwestern Russia (Kiev and areas to the west) and the northwest (Novgorod and Pskov), the political development of northeastern Russia (Vladimir, Suzdal, Tver, Iaroslavl, and later

[5] The only autonomous orthodox political entity (excluding the semi-independent and remote principalities of Moldavia and Wallachia) were the Cossacks of the Ukraine in the late sixteenth and early seventeenth centuries. Their *de facto* independence of the king of Poland, their theoretical ruler, depended on a fragile balance of power involving Ottoman Turkey, Poland, Sweden, and Moscow. Internal problems and the breakdown of this balance in the mid-seventeenth century induced the Cossacks to seek the support of their powerful neighbor, Moscow. Support rapidly came to mean political domination. Despite its political integration with Muscovite Russia, the Ukraine remained a distinct cultural entity, and because of its proximity to Poland was the most important channel through which Western European culture was brought into Muscovite Russia.

Moscow) was characterized by strong princes. In the southwest the great nobles came to have more power, and something closer to Western feudalism developed. In the commercial cities of Novgorod and Pskov a merchant oligarchy dominated political life through the operation of the popular assembly (*veche*). The northeast was largely settled by people fleeing the depredations of nomads in the areas to the southwest. They sought the protection of the local princes, who actively encouraged colonization of the area. Too remote from the main trade routes, their commerce never prospered, towns remained small, and the popular assembly did not become influential, as it did in Novgorod and Pskov.

For centuries there was intense rivalry among the various northeastern princes, but no challenge to their authority within their own territories, from either popular or aristocratic elements. The Mongols, after their conquest in 1240, ruled the northeast indirectly through the Russian princes, and gave the Russians their first experience with autocratic authority that extended over a wide area. After Mongol unity broke down, the princes of Moscow were the victors in a long period of struggle in which rival Russian princes and Mongol khans combined and recombined with little regard for ethnic and religious differences. Muscovite authority was steadily extended, first over the other princes of the northeast, then over the independent cities of Novgorod and Pskov. In the course of subsequent centuries expansion continued to the southeast in areas having a non-Russian population, and to the southwest, where the decentralized feudal monarchy of Poland-Lithuania had incorporated the remnants of Kievan Russia shattered by the Mongol conquest.

The prince in the northeast was accepted as the legitimate political authority in his own small territory. As long as there were a number of competing princes, a noble could shift his loyalty from one prince to another. The "right of departure" was recognized, and it served to inhibit the development of a tradition of independent political rights among the nobility. The more successful a prince was, the greater the material rewards and security he could offer to his supporters. It was a symbiotic relationship, not an antagonistic one. When there was only one prince left, the "right of departure" became meaningless in fact, and was shortly abolished in law. The triumph of Moscow over rival princes and khans meant that it assumed a position of authority somewhat like that of the Great Khan shortly after the conquest. Formal ideological justification for the prince of Moscow's new role was sought, however, in Byzantine models that were more acceptable to the Orthodox church.[6]

Despite the ending of the "right of departure" the mutual interests of the prince (now called "tsar," the Russian for "Caesar") and the nobility remained. For the sovereign, the nobles were his source of military manpower in the constant struggles on the frontiers, as the Muscovite territories grew steadily. The nobility depended on the tsar for grants of land and authority over the peasants who made the land useful. The landlords, particularly the lesser ones, needed the help of the central authority in recovering fugitive peasants, who tended to seek protection from the largest landlords, and it was the central government's need to maintain the labor supply on the estates of the mass of its noble servitors that was the primary cause of the enserfment of the peasantry in the course of the sixteenth and seventeenth centuries.

The important point for our purposes is this: from the earliest times the legitimacy of some sort of autocratic central political authority was established and accepted in Muscovite Russia. As the territory involved expanded, effective central authority became an increasingly important element in the ability of the nobility to retain an adequate labor force on their estates. The mobilization of the nobility for military service thus required their acceptance of central authority as legitimate. Without it their peasants would have been free to move and leave them without economic support. There was an alliance, then, between the central authority and the only other group in society that could conceivably have opposed it effectively.

No political crisis in Russia prior to the twentieth century involved a challenge to the principle of autocratic rule itself. The succession crisis during the "Time of Troubles" of the early seventeenth century, the peasant revolts of Stenka Razin and Pugachev, the palace coups of the late seventeenth and eighteenth centuries all were challenges to the legitimacy of a particular individual's claim to be the legitimate sovereign. The principle of monarchical autocracy itself was not seriously challenged until late in the nineteenth century. Very early, however, the peasant masses came to differentiate between a remote and essentially mythical "good tsar" and the oppressive landlord and officials they knew. In the post-Petrine period certain members of the

[6] This *ex post facto* development included not only the famous doctrine of the "Third Rome," but a whole series of changes in court ritual, the social relationships of the prince and his retainers, a grandiose construction program in the Kremlin, and even the marriage of Ivan III to a Byzantine princess.

nobility developed an analogous attitude toward the more impersonal bureaucratic government of the eighteenth and nineteenth century. The tsar himself remained a popular figure, among the masses at least, until the "Bloody Sunday" riot of 1905, when troops fired on unarmed and orderly workers who wished to present a petition to the tsar. For many peasants and workers the legend of the "Little-Father Tsar" undoubtedly remained alive even down to 1917 or later, though it was not powerful enough to keep the Romanovs on the throne.

Among the educated elite the rejection of autocratic government can be traced back at least to Alexander Radishchev in the late eighteenth century. Throughout the nineteenth century more and more of the increasingly large educated segment of the population came to believe that some other form of government, one more like those being established in Western Europe, or possibly something more radical, should replace the existing system. The striking fact, however, is that after the 1917 revolution another centralized authoritarian system replaced the old one very quickly. Its ideology, its entire public image, was utterly different from imperial Russia. It used some different techniques for gaining support, but it was not effectively challenged by forces that opposed autocratic centralism. When the Constituent Assembly was forcibly dissolved by the Bolsheviks, there was no immediate reaction against them.

There had, indeed, been a legitimacy crisis from 1905 to 1917. The changes embodied in the October (1905) manifesto can be viewed as the regime's attempt to regain legitimacy in the eyes of the middle class. However, the creation of a parliament (Duma) with limited powers and other concessions did not win the whole-hearted support of the middle-class liberals, many of whom expected much more rapid progress in the direction of full fledged parliamentary democracy on the British model. The collapse of the imperial government in March 1917 and the events that followed show clearly, however, that it was not the issue of autocracy versus liberal democracy that was of concern to the masses in the capital or the peasants throughout the countryside. A government's legitimacy was determined by its ability to perform, or seem to perform, certain basic functions. The provision of security or defense meant, in the circumstances of the day, the conclusion of peace with the central powers. The satisfaction of minimal economic demands meant acceding to workers' control of industry, requisitioning grain, and endorsing peasant seizure of landlord's estates. The Bolsheviks' adoption of such a program enabled them to assume power and be accepted as legitimate in the eyes of a portion of the population. In the eyes of many Russians some government was better than none, and the new one at least proposed to solve the problems of distribution that were of central importance to most Russians. The Bolshevik solution was based on Marxist theory, a powerful ideology whose appeal was by no means limited to their faction. A challenge to the new regime based on notions of law (questioning the illegal dissolution of the Constituent Assembly), or its failure to be democratic in its own actions simply could not generate effective support. The government was doing, or promising to do, what masses of people wanted it to do. It was like the "good tsar" that Pugachev said he was. In the end the new government failed to do much of what it promised, but by then it had had time to resolve the crisis of penetration that had helped to bring about the collapse of the imperial regime. With increased penetration (control) the regime could not only dismiss the feeble challenges to its legitimacy on political grounds, but was in a position to mobilize more resources from the population and accede to fewer of its distributive demands.

PARTICIPATION

In Russia the issue of participation has not taken the familiar form of widespread and repeated demands for the extension of suffrage to involve larger and larger segments of the population in the formation of a national government. As Weiner points out, political participation has often been associated with the growth of central authority.[7] Russian centralized political authority is far older than notions of almost any sort of popular political participation. The boyars of the medieval period were indeed intimately involved with their prince in the operation of the "state." But the establishment of the supremacy of the prince of Moscow over the other princes, both Russian and Tatar, reduced the participation of the boyars and of the formerly independent princes to an advisory role in the "Council of Boyars." As the princely power grew, the boyars were consulted less and less; and they resented it. The occasional summoning of a larger "Assembly of the Land" was a device for mobilizing support in times of crisis rather than an institution through which the various elements of the population required to attend could participate in governmental decisions.

[7] Myron Weiner, "Political Participation: Crisis of the Political Process," in L. Binder *et al., Crises and Sequences in Political Development* (Princeton, 1971), p. 173.

In the sixteenth century there may have been conflict between the great nobles and the dynamic Ivan IV (The Terrible). During the confused decades that followed Boris Godunov's death (1605), the boyars were able to install their own candidate (Shuiskii) on the throne for a short time (1606-1610), but he made no significant concessions to them in the area of participation in government. Their prime concern, after the traumatic period of confusion under Ivan IV, was for guarantees against arbitrary arrest and confiscation of property. In any case, Shuiskii was unable to maintain his position for long. The Romanovs were established on the throne in 1613, with the support of the lesser gentry (*pomeshchiki*) who had no interest in special privileges for the old elite. The device of an "Assembly of the Land" was used to select the new sovereign; but as the Romanovs consolidated their power, the assembly was called less frequently, and was abandoned entirely by the later seventeenth century.

Just as peasant revolts or palace coups cannot be considered challenges to the basic legitimacy of the system, they cannot be viewed as demands for participation in government. The supporters of Pugachev and Stenka Razin wanted a "good tsar"; the court intriguers wanted a sovereign who would support the interests of their own clique. When a small group of powerful courtiers tried to impose some limits on Empress Anne as a condition of her accession (1730), she successfully ignored them by appealing to the lesser gentry for support of her absolute sovereignty. The mass of the provincial service gentry saw no reason to prefer the rule of a handful of magnates in the capital to the personal authority of the sovereign that they had long known. The tsar was their source of favor and the magnates were rivals, not allies.

Some sort of representative democracy became one of the aspirations of most of the critical intelligentsia in the nineteenth century, although a few romantic nationalists thought in terms of a mystical or paternalistic relationship between the orthodox Russian people and the sovereign, which would replace the artificial, rational, bureaucratic state that had corrupted an imaginary, pure pre-Petrine Muscovite society. But, as already noted, representative government did not have mass appeal, and the imperial government did not fall in the face of demands for that kind of participation. Worker and peasant protests were, in a formal sense, demands for participation; but in actuality their demands were either for government by their own leaders ("all power to the Soviets") or for no government at all, in the case of most peasants. In the actual event, the revolution produced, almost at once, a new centralized autocracy in which meaningful participation in government was entirely absent. Of course the general population "participates" in many meetings and demonstrations, in "elections," and the Communist party members even more, but these are better understood as part of the regime's technique for mobilizing the population and should not be viewed as either direct or indirect participation in government.

Not only has participation in government by all elements of the population been lacking at the central level throughout Russian history, but it has not been well developed at the local level, either. Central authority, in the fifteenth or sixteenth century, as much as in the Soviet Union today, was loath to see the growth of strong participatory organizations of any kind. Provincial and municipal government have always been instruments of central policy, not bodies actively involving the local population in civil affairs. Private and semi-private organizations have been viewed with distrust and either forbidden or carefully supervised. At various points in Russia's development the central government has attempted to place greater responsibility in the hands of provincial authorities. But whether in the time of Ivan IV, Peter I, Catherine II, Alexander II, or Khrushchev, close examination shows that the motive has been the desire to relieve the central administration of onerous burdens without delegating significant power.

The most important organs of local government that involved participation by the local population were the provincial *zemstvo* organizations created after the emancipation of 1861. They became the focus of the more liberal elements of the provincial nobility. Here for the first time in Russian history, it was felt, was an opportunity for doing worthwhile things (in education, agricultural improvement, public health, collecting statistics, and the like), without being directed by the state bureaucracy. The more radical of the *zemstvo* enthusiasts hoped to develop from these purely provincial organizations into an increasingly broad union that would eventually culminate in some sort of constitutional formation for the whole nation. The imperial regime accordingly regarded the *zemstvos* as a potential threat to the existing political order. The regime wanted its own, centrally controlled agencies to run local affairs. In sharp contrast to the major social, economic, judicial, and military reforms, Alexander II's program left the autocratic political system untouched, and so it remained until 1905. All attempts at expanding *zemstvo* work beyond the local level were thwarted and their work increasingly restricted in the later nineteenth century.

The *zemstvos* were not entirely without impact on Russian political history. Along with various voluntary organizations that developed, despite governmental restrictions and suspicion, in the late nineteenth century, they provided elements of the Russian middle class experience in working in an organized way for common ends. It was from this small but influential group of gentry liberals and, increasingly, urban professionals that the demand for participation in government came.

For the mass of the Russian people, the peasantry, participation in political life was confined to the operation of the village communal organization (often a far cry from the democratic ideal of some populist romantics) and, for some, the cooperative organizations that began to be organized at the close of the nineteenth century. The urban workers were almost completely prevented from forming even the most innocuous types of organization until after 1905. On two occasions, however, once in Moscow and once in St. Petersburg, the Ministry of the Interior attempted to control worker discontent by sponsoring an "official" labor organization, and on each occasion the response of the workers was so enthusiastic that it rapidly got out of control. In St. Petersburg the organization led by Father George Gapon actually touched off the general strike of 1905. The working class, largely composed of peasants only recently departed from their villages, clearly sought some avenue through which to voice their discontents. However, it was not participation in the central government but a redistribution of wealth that was their main concern.

When the more radical of the middle class constitutionalists tried to force extensive political concessions from the government in 1906, through the Vyborg declaration, they received no support from the masses. A portion of the middle class was, in fact, willing to accept modest concessions made by the tsar in the manifesto of October 1905 which promised a semiparliamentary government but left all the vital powers in the hands of the tsar. The modicum of participation through parliamentary representation achieved for all segments of the population through the state Duma did little to strengthen the tsar's claim to legitimate power. Participation was not what concerned most Russians. The basic discontent was distributive, and the final crisis came when the imperial system of penetration and control broke down.

PENETRATION

The basic problem that has confronted all Russian rulers, at least until the late 1930s, has been how to maintain a large military establishment with the meager surplus above subsistence that could be produced by the poor and scattered peasantry. The harsh climate limited the possible returns from agriculture, and the patterns of interregional trade that had favored medieval Kiev were never restored in the Muscovite period. Thus the central concern of the Muscovite state has been with penetration, that is control of the countryside, in order to direct the distribution of resources. For distribution one might better say mobilization or collection. The problem was to take things away from the peasants and put them in the hands of the state's servitors without destroying the productive capacity of the peasant economy and driving peasants into desperate revolt or disorderly flight. The great crises of Russian history have come when the demands of the state for the redistribution of resources (from the population to the state) have exceeded the state's effective penetration of the countryside, its ability to collect without producing chaos. In the Russian case two concepts, penetration and distribution, are closely related and cannot be treated in isolation.

The system that was developed to perform the difficult task of penetration has been called by historians the "service state." In it, a relatively large number of nobles served the state, and in turn the state supported the nobles by tying the peasantry to their lord's estates. In Russia serfdom was not accompanied by feudal political decentralization; it was largely the result of the successful establishment of centralized government. Harsh though it was for all concerned, the system was remarkably successful in terms of political power. Not only did Russia maintain its independence in the face of major foreign enemies, but it was able to expand from a very small principality into a large empire. Prior to 1917, there was only one occasion when the central government was unable to maintain effective control of its territories, during the "Time of Troubles" of the early seventeenth century.

The "Time of Troubles" came after a period of prolonged military effort against Poland and Sweden begun by Ivan IV in his effort to take control of the Baltic coastline. Initially partially successful (Russians held Narva for 23 years), the effort proved to be beyond the ability of the nation to maintain, at least when accompanied by the more excessive of Ivan's internal policies. These domestic measures involved the destruction of many of the established great noble families and the confiscation of their property. The general direction of Ivan's actions was consistent with the development of an increasingly centralized autocratic state and the expansion of the class of service nobility; it was, however, carried out with so much violence and irrationality that the government's ability to mobilize resources was certainly impaired.

The extinction of the house of Ruric with the death of Fedor in 1598 came at this most inopportune time, and was followed by a series of severe famines (1601, 1602, 1603). Thus what was basically a crisis of penetration and distribution, that is the ability of the state to mobilize the resources needed to meet its needs, became one of dynastic legitimacy as well. Various factions struggled to place their candidate firmly on the throne. The period of crisis was lengthy; but once the famines had abated, the foreign invaders were repulsed (that was, in large measure, a matter of balancing off the mutually hostile Poles and Swedes), and the old political system was slowly reestablished without significant change. Processes that had been well under way in the mid-sixteenth century continued. The "service state" continued to develop, favoring the lesser nobles, as opposed to the great landholders. The peasants were put more firmly than ever under the control of landlords, and the law code of 1649 was the final step in the enserfment of the peasantry. In terms of a legitimate dynastic claim to the throne, the Romanovs had no better reason to be the successors to the house of Ruric than did Boris Godunov and his son. But the forces opposing the continued development of the centralized autocracy were exhausted. The rebellious peasants and Cossacks could offer only disorder, the Poles were seen as heretical foreigners by most Russians, the great nobles who supported Shuiskii could muster no support for him outside the capital. The church and the service gentry, the two bodies with the greatest interest in a strong central government, finally rallied; and the new dynasty was established (1613).

The crisis had come about when the state's ability to mobilize resources (penetration) had been unequal to the demands made upon it, and it could not deal with the distributive demands of the population. The new dynasty probably had no more, perhaps even less, ability to mobilize resources than did Ivan IV, but for decades it was careful not to place undue strain on the resources available to it. In that sense we can say that the balance between penetration and distribution was restored, a balance that was preserved until the next major crisis in Russian history, in 1917.

In the later seventeenth century, and particularly in the reign of Peter I (1682-1725), Russia underwent, if not a crisis of penetration, a period of terrible strain in which massive and generally successful efforts were made to mobilize resources on the scale needed to continue competition with her neighbors to the West. Western systems of military organization and technology were adopted. Although cultural change was not the immediate aim, it followed and had a profound effect on the Russian elite, as had already been noted. The basic social and political structure of the state, however, remained unchanged; the service state was simply made more comprehensive, and the men and materials assembled were used in more modern ways. The tax system and the recruitment system were still essentially Muscovite, and they remained so until the mid-nineteenth century. Taxes were assessed on the basis first of household units and, from Peter's time on, on a per capita basis; but they were collected from entire village units, through a village elder and the local landlord. Since each village was responsible for its total assessment, the peasantry came to ignore the per capita principle and divided the village's burden according to the ability of households to pay, and periodically redistributed the land according to the ability of a household to use it productively. The effect was to transform a head tax into a crude form of income tax, but the introduction of technological change in agriculture was rendered impractical. From the state's standpoint, the great virtue of the system was that it made collection of taxes easier. Recruitment of common soldiers was handled in much the same way. Every few years landlords, and in turn village leaders, were given a quota of recruits to supply for lifetime service, and the most unpopular and uninfluential young men of the village were sent off and rarely heard from again.

Both taxation and recruitment were accomplished with the absolute minimum of administrative effort. Direct governmental involvement in the countryside was reserved for the occasional suppression of peasant disturbances with military force. Aside from the establishment of a few small industries geared to specific military needs, the state did virtually nothing to expand the wealth and prosperity of the country. It was content to exact its tribute from the traditional economy. Throughout the eighteenth century and well into the nineteenth, the Russian system of penetration, crude though it was, succeeded in providing the means that supported Russia's role as a major European power and enabled her to achieve continental supremacy after her defeat of Napoleon in 1812.

The emancipation of the serfs in 1862 and the subsequently legal, local governmental, fiscal, and military reforms, were events of such overwhelming implications for Russian society that all of the factors under discussion here were involved in some degree. However, the state's decision actually to undertake the emancipation, which had been discussed in theory for half a century, is best understood as the state's response to a threatening crisis of penetration. It became necessary to devise a new method of control and resource mobilization to replace the serf system that had worked so long. The defeat in the Crimean War had an immense impact on Russia, even though the material losses in the war were small. For the first time since Peter I's disastrous encounter with the Swedes at Narva (1700), the Russian state was confronted with the need to reorganize itself drastically in order to meet a challenge from outside. Just what kind of reorganization was actually needed, and how the need was perceived by those in power (especially Alexander II), is a matter of great and, as yet, unresolved debate by historians.

The ruling elite (a very small group of high officials and the tsar himself, definitely not the "nobility" or the landowning group as a whole) found that the old system could no longer provide the essential resources needed to maintain the military power of Russia, military power that had always been the basic reason for the existence of central authority and was identified with the state interest by the emperor. The need for general economic development in the modern sense was not recognized by Russian statesmen, though there was certainly a well-established belief among educated Russians that serfdom was not "appropriate" in some ways—be it moral, economic, or both—for a great power in the mid-nineteenth century; but it is difficult to show a direct connection between this attitude and state policy. One leading American scholar has argued that a major consideration in spurring the government to act on the question of emancipation was the need to shift from the traditional Russian reliance on a large standing army based on lifetime service to a smaller standing force plus a large trained reserve developed through universal military training.[8] The problem that arose during the Crimean War was that once the standing army was committed, it was nearly impossible to raise ad-

[8] Alfred J. Rieber, ed. and tr., *The Politics of Autocracy: Letters of Alexander II to Prince A. I. Bariatinskii, 1857-1864* (Paris and The Hague, 1966).

ditional forces. To enlarge the standing army in peacetime was financially out of the question, so the shift to the reserve system can be regarded as an attempt to get "more rifles for the ruble." Universal military training was incompatible with serfdom. Not only was the young peasant taken from the village, trained in warfare, and exposed to the outside world, but it was a well-established tradition in Russia that military service ended the serf obligation. Few men survived long enough to be retired under the old system, but those who did were free. Such a system was only possible when only a small portion of the serf population was ever inducted into military service. Thus the need for a more modern military organization to meet external pressures not only required changes in the military organization but a drastic reorganization of the entire system of governmental penetration-mobilization. Simultaneously, it increased the amount of contact between the ordinary citizen (peasant) and the state.

Emancipation changed the basic system through which resources were mobilized and redistributed to support the state, and emancipation demanded the extension of bureaucratic activity to a much lower level throughout the empire than had previously been required. By retaining the principle of collective village responsibility for both taxes and land redemption payments (obligations that arose from the terms of the emancipation), the state attempted to minimize the added administrative effort. It could not, however, continue to use the landlord as the collection agent; and the local organs of the Ministry of Finance and Interior became more important, the one responsible for revenue collection, the other for maintaining public order. The implementation of the emancipation settlement was put in the hands of local noblemen, but they acted as agents of the state and were carefully selected by the central authority. Some responsibilities of a local nature (roads, health, some aspects of education, and so forth) were delegated to newly created representative organizations, the *zemstvos*. The central government did not choose, however, to entrust the essential functions of revenue collection and public order to bodies not directly responsible to it. In 1889 centrally appointed officials, called land captains, were given extensive authority and operated in closer contact with the peasantry than had any central agency in the past. Central governmental operations were greatly improved by the institution of comprehensive planning of the state budget and by modern auditing procedures. For the first time in Russian experience, it was possible to have a reasonable idea about what funds came in and where they were used. It the latter part of the century the growth of the market economy in the countryside enabled the state to rely increasingly on excise taxes, and the importance of the peasant head tax declined to such an extent that it was abolished in 1885. Penetration in this case was achieved by flexible adaptation to changing conditions rather than the actual extension of governmental operations. On the whole, however, the state became increasingly involved with the population in the countryside and also in the cities, with the enactment of meaningful legislation dealing with industrial working conditions (1882, 1885, 1886, 1890). The final, and most important, stage in the development of governmental penetration was the massive program to reorganize the land tenure system that began after the 1905 revolution, to be discussed below.

The state's response to the mid-nineteenth century crisis of penetration was dramatic: emancipation and the series of related measures designed to replace the old system of resource mobilization. But the state's response was also entirely consistent with the traditional pattern of governmental reaction to difficult situations. The aims of the state had always been limited to the traditional primary functions. Changes were those that were felt to be necessary for the state's continued survival and growth. When, for example, Catherine II crushed a major peasant revolt led by Emelian Pugachev, she moved to strengthen provincial government, which had proved to be unable even to warn the center of the impending uprising, much less to contain and suppress it. The empress established smaller units of local government than had previously existed, and she was able to staff them with retired military officers who had elected to return to their estates after compulsory service for all nobles was abandoned in 1763. Her measures greatly stimulated the development of provincial centers both as administrative and social centers, but nothing was done that dealt seriously with the problems of distribution that were involved in the peasants' desperate rebellion. Nevertheless, Catherine's minimal response proved adequate (for the state) for nearly a century.

The solution of the 1860s was less successful. The state could not lessen its demands on the population because it felt compelled to compete as a great power with the rapidly industrializing nations of Western Europe (and Japan). At the same time, the economic position of the peasantry was declining because of rapid population growth and static agricultural technology. Flight to the frontiers, which had been an important safety valve even after it has been made illegal, was no longer adequate—the frontier was now too far away. Even with vigorous official support, migration to Siberia was now entirely inadequate to solve the problem.

The imperial government's greatest effort to deal with the growing crisis of penetration-distribution in rural Russia came after the 1905 revolution. The state, led by an intelligent and energetic conservative, P. I. Stolypin, combined ruthless repression of disorders with an imaginative attempt to restructure Russian rural society. The social program was designed to destroy the repartitional commune, long identified as a brake on agricultural productivity, and to create a substantial class of prosperous peasants who would have a stake in the *status quo*, an entirely new and positive approach to the problem of controlling the countryside. Almost every aspect of this program, its aims, substance, and impact, are matters of current controversy among historians. It was certainly a major attempt at bureaucratic penetration of the villages on a scale hitherto unknown, and at least some aspects were highly successful.

During the years from the revolution of 1917 to collectivization, the Russian peasant was subject to less effective control than he had been for centuries. This relaxation of the traditional pattern of penetration and the new demands by the state brought on a new and acute crisis of penetration-distribution at the end of the 1920s. This last and most decisive crisis of modern Russian history involved, of course, the collectivization of agriculture and the great industrialization drive of the 1930s. In broadest outline it was the reestablishment of effective governmental penetration to solve what had become a severe crisis of distribution in the late 1920s. The Bolsheviks could not hope to control the actions of millions of individual peasant cultivators; but they could control, to some meaningful extent, the activity of thousands of collectivized villages. The collective farm officers and the party organization assumed the functions that had been performed by the gentry landlords before emancipation and, less well from the state's standpoint, by the bureaucracy and the peasant communal organization after it. Each collectivized village was required to sow an assigned area of land with specific crops and to deliver designated quantities from the harvest at low prices fixed by the state. The members of the collective farm were paid in accordance with the number of days they worked throughout the year; however, the amount received for a day's work was not fixed in terms of time worked or items produced, as in the case of an industrial worker. The collective farmer had only a residual claim to his proportionate share of the farm's output after compulsory deliveries to the state, payments for services to the Machine Tractor Station, and so forth. In practice, most peasants survived on what they could grow on their own small garden plot or steal from the collective. Since the death of Stalin, substantial effort has been made to develop meaningful incentives for collective farmers, but the basic structure of the system remains unchanged.

In the course of the 1930s and subsequent decades Russia was transformed into a primarily industrial society, and for the first time in its history the mobilization of resources in the countryside has ceased to be the preeminent problem of central government. Rapid industrialization has been possible because of the reinvestment of a very large proportion of the national product each year, at the expense of the consumer. Centralized planning has not proven to be strikingly efficient, but it has made all enterprises throughout the nation far more dependent on Moscow than would be the case in a market economy. To accomplish the very high degree of control of the population necessary a series of both "positive" and "negative" techniques have been used. The positive devices include such things as the widespread introduction of piece-work and incentive payments in industry and the glorification of workers who overfulfill their quotas. Throughout Soviet society, there is an intense and constant attempt to build up enthusiasm for governmental (party) policy in all forms of the mass media and throughout the educational system. The constant problem in such efforts is the tendency for it to become routine, boring, and to lose its effectiveness in the face of the drab realities of everyday life. Except for a small but vigorous critical intelligentsia, the total saturation of the media with the official viewpoint tends at least to prevent Russians from being aware of alternatives and to produce an unenthusiastic but passive acceptance of state policy in many areas.

The "negative" devices used in governmental penetration include such traditional techniques as internal passports, control of residence, and the like. Most important, however, has been the use of terror, the threat of imprisonment or death, on unprecedented scale. Terror has been used, not simply against those in actual opposition to the government, but widely among party members, the bureaucracy, and the educated segments of society as a whole. The effect, particularly under Stalin, was to produce a situation in which each individual was isolated from all others and to eliminate a wide range of topics from discussion, even among close friends. In contrast to the tsarist regime, when certain things were prohibited (plotting against the state, strikes, slandering the tsar, and so on) with varying degrees of severity, the Soviet regime has attempted, with considerable success, to prevent the expression of anything but positive support for the state. In addition to the normal network of governmental agencies and the various economic enterprises that are all state owned, the Communist party and the secret police provide supplementary and overlapping networks of control, feeding information upward through a hierarchy that converges only at the very top. In any Soviet institution—whether it be a factory, school, or laboratory—there will be party members (usually occupying important positions) and also persons who are connected with the police either as regular employees or merely as informers.

Although the economic and political controls used in the Soviet Union have their drawbacks from the standpoint of the state—low levels of productivity in some areas, lack of initiative, indifference, official propaganda, and so forth—the system survived a severe test in World War II and shows no signs of breakdown or radical change at present. Some intellectuals or members of national minorities may question the legitimacy of the system, or even reject a "Soviet" identity totally, but the degree of penetration now achieved seems to preclude any crisis in the foreseeable future.

DISTRIBUTION

At least until the second half of the twentieth century, Russia must be considered a land of extreme scarcity and poverty, due primarily to a climate that does not favor agriculture—cold, and poor soil in the north, better soils but frequent drought in the south. As already noted, the limited resources available had much to do with the forms of Russian political development. Only a strong central government could have collected enough to support the apparatus of a great power. When the state had taken its share, there was little left for private accumulation. There were few really wealthy nobles, and those who were, were directly indebted to the state. Commercial and industrial fortunes were rare, urban centers few and small, except for the two capitals. Although agriculture was the source of the nation's wealth, it received little serious attention from the state until the late nineteenth century (the Ministry of State Lands did not become the Ministry of Agriculture until 1894). The state simply let the peasants follow their traditional practices and extracted what it could from them. Thus the available income was essentially fixed, although fluctuating annually with the harvests. The state's ability to mobilize resources to meet its needs depended on its success in extracting revenue without producing disorder in the countryside. Crises, or potential crises, of distribution were "solved" by heightened efforts at control or by reducing demands, not by increasing the total wealth available. The need for a more productive economy had long been recognized by some Russians; but official policy remained essentially passive until some years after the emancipation, and then the emphasis turned immediately to industrialization, exacerbating, in the short run, the problems of the peasantry. Famines of varying degrees of severity were frequent occurrences throughout Russian history, and they limited the amount that the government could spend on the military or on internal improvements. However, except when severe famines coincided with other pressures, war or internal political difficulties, they did not produce a crisis of distribution. The early seventeenth century time of troubles was the last time that famine threatened total disruption of government until the 1890s and the great crisis of the first third of the twentieth century.

The first phase of the twentieth-century crisis was the Revolution of 1905, set off in the immediate sense by the Russo-Japanese War, but reflecting the problems of the half-century since the Great Reforms. It was, first and foremost, a crisis of distribution. The urban working class played a major political role for the first time in Russian experience; and once word of the weakness at the center spread throughout the land, peasant disturbances were common. The workers and peasants were demanding a larger share of the pie. For the peasants hard hit by policies that favored industry and by the famines of the 1890s, this meant more land. They had no way of knowing that population growth had actually made mere land redistribution an unsatisfactory solution of the problem.

The active role of the urban workers, the new element in the situation, was the result of a vigorous and successful program of state-sponsored industrial development, most pronounced during the administration of Minister of Finance Count Witte (1892-1903), but substantially underway before his tenure in office began. It was a program of industrialization undertaken at state initiative for state ends, to maintain Russia's position as a great power, which was again in serious question after the humiliating Congress of Berlin. As such, it was fully in accordance with the long-established Russian tradition, but quantitatively far more extensive than any that preceded it. Investment in heavy industry and railroad construction was large and ultimately financed by squeezing the agricultural population even harder than ever. There was substantial foreign capital invested, but it was secured only through the maintenance of a positive balance of trade, made possible by exporting grain at prices determined in the world market. Ultimately the industrialization depended not on low wages for workers (they were, in fact, not particularly low by nineteenth-century standards) but on the ability of the state to maintain order in the countryside, to permit the collection of taxes, rents, and debt payments, and an orderly market in which the peasantry had to sell their grain at prices low enough to meet North American competition in the world market.

The state's attempt to maintain its position as a major power by the rapid development of heavy industry in the late nineteenth century made very substantial progress. Ultimately, industrialization could be seen as a solution of the problem of distributing wealth between the state and the population through a massive increase in the productivity of the economy. However, the penetration of the countryside remained essential. Without effective control of the rural areas, there would be neither grain for export nor for the growing urban centers; and the peasant would not always sell his grain for existing prices unless he was forced to make money payments to the state or to banks and landlords supported by the state's traditional apparatus of administration.

Rapid industrialization, advantageous though it was for Russia's national power, brought with it new problems, notably a large working-class population strategically concentrated in St. Petersburg, Moscow, and a few other centers. Techniques of control developed over the centuries for the peasantry were not entirely effective in dealing with uprooted peasant-workers. The urban working class was the first group, excepting the few disaffected intellectuals, that began to question the legitimacy of the tsar's rule itself, instead of the traditional rejection of the bureaucracy as a distorter of the benevolent tsar's will. Between 1905 and 1917 the state did little to improve the material condition of the workers, and its efforts at exerting more effective control over them were confined to the progressive suppression of the trade unions that had been legalized immediately after 1905. Ultimately the failure of the state to cope effectively with the urban working class was a crucial element in its downfall in 1917.

The dramatic program of rural reorganization forwarded by Stolypin has already been cited as an attempt to put the control of the villages on a more self-sustaining basis, grounded in the self-interest of conservative small-holders. It was also a major attempt to improve the economic efficiency of Russian agriculture by removing the obstacles to agricultural improvement that were inherent in the system of repartitional tenure and scattered holdings. For some peasants the program did solve the land problem. The fundamental problem of Russian agriculture at the beginning of the twentieth century, however, could not be solved by mere redistribution of land and consolidation of holdings, difficult though that was. Very substantial investment was needed to raise productivity; and even with this, migration from the country to the city was unavoidable. The Stolypin program provided some, but certainly not enough, financial support for investment beyond the process of consolidation. It also stimulated the migration to the city of many peasants who were able for the first time to sell their miniscule holdings. This movement was undoubtedly beneficial in an economic sense, but it could only make the problem of social stability in the cities more acute in the short run. World War I suspended the positive features of the reorganization program and exacerbated its effects in the cities.

With the outbreak of World War I, Russia entered the greatest conflict modern Europe had ever known while facing grave internal problems. The legitimacy of imperial authority was seriously questioned by substantial segments of the population, now widely organized for the first time in Russian history into groups on both social-class and national lines. The problem of the distribution of wealth that had worsened in the half-century after 1862 had not been solved and was exacerbated by the rapid but irregular industrial development of recent decades.

World War I made Russia's acute problem of resource mobilization into a crisis. After three years of tremendous strain, the traditional devices of penetration—police control, taxation, and the market economy—proved inadequate to provide the supplies needed to avoid a crisis of distribution. The mass of the population, following the lead of the strategically located St. Petersburg garrison, simply ceased to recognize the legitimacy of imperial authority. As in the seventeenth century "Time of Troubles," the demands upon the state had come to exceed its means of meeting them. Instead of seeking a "good" or "true" tsar, the population sought an alternative symbol of authority, but one that had to perform similar functions of control and distribution in a similar manner.

In an immediate sense, the fall of the imperial regime was caused by the refusal of the peasant soldiers in the St. Petersburg garrison to suppress the rioting workers. Had the soldiers continued to obey orders as they had done in the past, there could have been no revolution. This is not to say that there would have been no social or political change; but if the army had remained loyal, the process of change would clearly have taken a markedly different form, perhaps more like that of 1905. Peasant dissatisfaction arose from the distribution of wealth in the economy, and in that sense the 1917 crisis was the result of the long-standing problems of rural Russia. The state had not resolved these difficulties either by increasing agriculture productivity or by devising a new way to control the rural population that would have permitted a more adequate mobilization of resources (the Stolypin program was moving toward both of these ends). As it was, the state could neither extract enough from the peasants nor satisfy enough of them to maintain stability.

The coincident and inextricably interconnected crises of penetration and distribution produced a fatal crisis of legitimacy for the imperial government, but the continuing crisis that followed the end of the dynasty did not, indeed could not, differ essentially from that which preceded it. The elimination of the tsar and his chief associates could do nothing to substantially affect the distribution of resources. And it simply accelerated the collapse of administrative control of the countryside and even of the cities. There was no widely accepted substitute for the old regime, nothing regarded by most of the population as a legitimate successor. The middle-class parliamentary institutions, the old regime's answer to demands for participation, had little standing with the population as a whole.[9] The various segments of society, both social and national, had never worked together through any system that involved political compromise. What eventually emerged from the confusion of the civil war years was not the product of compromise or the participation of large segments of the population but the triumph of one particular group. It was able, through its organizational ability, ideological fervor, and ruthlessness, gradually to reestablish the apparatus of political control. It asserted a new ideologically based claim to legitimate power that was accepted with enthusiasm by a small but loyal segment of the population. No competing group could do as much.

In its first decade of power, the new Bolshevik regime did not, and

[9] Even the long-awaited Constituent Assembly enjoyed no real popular support; hardly anyone would fight for it after the Bolsheviks closed it down by force.

could not, solve the great problems of distribution that had contributed so much to the imperial collapse. One might say that the Bolsheviks surmounted the crises of penetration and of legitimacy in spite of the severe and continuing problem of distribution in the years from 1917 to 1929. The crisis of legitimacy was overcome, but not in the sense that the regime was accepted by the mass of the population as legitimate and its ideology widely adopted. It was simply tolerated as the least offensive available alternative. The various right-wing groups, foreign powers, and the poorly organized non-Bolshevik left had less to offer and less force at their disposal. In many areas, particularly in the non-Russian regions, and among substantial segments of the population, the Bolshevik government was not regarded as legitimate at all, and was accepted only under the threat of force.

Central control in the urban areas was restored by the effective organization of the urban working class from which the Bolsheviks drew most of their support and by the suppression of opposition from hostile middle-class elements. In the countryside, the crisis of penetration was not solved but avoided by *de facto* withdrawal and a substantial lessening of demands made upon the peasants during the 1920s. Probably never before or since were the Russian peasants subject to so little pressure from the central government. Such a situation could not, and did not, last long. If an urban-based central power bent on rapid industrialization was to survive, increasing demands upon the peasantry were unavoidable; and they produced the final and decisive stage of Russia's twentieth-century crisis, collectivization and the industrialization drive of the 1930s.

The new ideology and the changes of staff in the top jobs in the central government could not alter the fundamental problem of mobilization of resources that had shaped the development of the Russian state and Russian society from the earliest times. During the civil war the urban population, much diminished by flight to the countryside, was able to survive through forced requisitions of food. The urban economy was producing virtually nothing that could be supplied to the peasants in exchange. What little was manufactured went to support the Bolshevik military effort. As a short-term emergency measure, confiscation worked well enough to supply the army and keep the urban population barely alive. However, it caused a catastrophic decline in agricultural output as peasants stopped planting crops that they knew would be confiscated or bought at fixed prices with worthless money.

Lenin, always amazingly sensitive to the requirements of the real situation that confronted him, persuaded his more doctrinaire Bolshevik colleagues to introduce what was called the New Economic Policy (NEP), in essence an admission that the state did not have the coercive power to force the peasants to plant and harvest without hope of return. The NEP recognized the necessity of allowing the peasantry to sell some of what it did not need for its own use at whatever price could be obtained on the open market. The response of the rural population was rapid; and within a few years agricultural production was at, or above, 1913 levels. The cities had at least minimum supplies of food, and many who had fled to the countryside returned to the urban areas. The relaxation of economic policy under the NEP took place while demands for increased participation voiced by the Worker's Opposition and the Kronstadt rebels were ruthlessly suppressed.

The problem of distribution, however, had been solved only from the point of view of the peasantry and possibly only for the more prosperous part of the peasantry. The position of the urban population was perilous, and the central government was in a most difficult position. It was able to levy limited taxes on the peasantry, but by no means as much could be extracted as before 1917. The old imperial bureaucratic and police system of enforcing the collection of taxes, rents, and debts had not been restored. The total share of agricultural income that left the rural sector of the economy was smaller than in the prerevolutionary period.

By the end of the 1920s, the government was faced with a grave crisis. The peasantry was not willing to sell enough of its harvest to provide adequate food for the cities and to permit the investment required for the expansion of industry, a problem that became more and more acute as the restoration of prewar capacity was completed and increased new investment was needed for further rapid growth. To accomplish this in the absence of a substantial influx of foreign capital, the rural population had either to be persuaded or forced to provide the resources for the urban sector. Persuasion would have involved more favorable terms of trade for the peasant, more manufactured goods in exchange for his bushel of grain, and a decline in urban living standards. Increased investment without coercion could only be achieved through voluntary saving by an increasingly prosperous rural population and particularly by the most successful peasants, known as the kulaks. Whether or not such a program was economically practical, with or without substantial foreign investment, was the subject of much debate at the time and has been in subsequent years. From the political standpoint of the Bolshevik government, now dominated by Stalin, such a policy was clearly unacceptable; for it would mean favoring the kulak at the expense of the urban workers, that is, favoring the most hostile group in the population at the expense of the regime's strongest supporters.

To obtain the resources needed for the rapid expansion of industry in a manner politically acceptable to the state, it was essential for the regime to achieve more control of the countryside than had existed in either pre- or postemancipation Russia. In this respect, the collectivization program was successful. By grouping the peasants into large units, by giving them only a residual claim to the production of the collective farm, and by making them dependent on the machine tractor stations for draft power, the Soviet government gained a degree of control that exceeded that exercised by most estate owners in the days of the serf system. The destruction of "peasant power" permitted the diversion of resources to industrial investment that has transformed Russia into a country where slightly more than half of the population is urban and far more than half of the national income is nonagricultural, thereby solving the central problem of Russian historical development, the dependence of the state on the peasantry. All of this is true despite the fact that millions suffered and died in the process of collectivization that was politically, but not economically, necessary, and that as a system of efficient agricultural production collectivization has proved to be, and remains, a colossal failure.

The industrialization of the thirties was sufficient to make a Soviet victory in World War II possible. The human and material losses suffered were immense, unimaginable by Western standards, yet in the postwar years the pattern of resource distribution remained unaltered. A very large proportion of the national income was devoted to investment in heavy industry and defense, while little effort was made to improve the standard of living, despite the desperate needs of the population.

Since the death of Stalin in 1953, somewhat more emphasis has been placed on consumer-goods production and agriculture, with significant but far from spectacular results. Compared to other major industrial nations, the level of consumption in the USSR is low; compared to underdeveloped nations it is, of course, very high. Given the effective system of political control, the slow increase in the standard of living is not likely to cause the state serious trouble.

Sequence

What, in summary, can be said about the problem of the sequence of crises in Russian political development? The problem of identity was resolved very early for the dominant Great Russian population. The content of the Russian's idea of his identity shifted from one that was essentially religious to one more national in character, but this process caused no great difficulty. The relationship of "Russianness" to Western European culture troubled the intelligentsia, but it was not this issue that was the primary stimulant to revolutionary activity in the late nineteenth and early twentieth centuries.

The legitimacy of central government under a prince was also established early, and the gradual triumph of the prince of Moscow over his neighbors merely extended the geographical scope of this authority. Until the late nineteenth century, there was no serious challenge to the principle of monarchic autocracy, although there were challenges to the claims of particular individuals. Demands for parliamentary government were put forward by elements of the intelligentsia in the nineteenth and twentieth centuries, but they enjoyed limited support. The main challenge to monarchical autocracy came from groups that wished to substitute the authority of some other class for that of the imperial government. Some envisioned an institutionally vague socialist utopia, others the authoritarian domination of society by the workers (at times rhetorically joined with the peasants). The latter group succeeded; centralized autocracy was restored after a brief period of anarchy, and as such it has not been seriously challenged. Autocracy is now legitimized in a different way than before 1917; but it is still centralized authoritarian government, and that principle has never been seriously challenged. No political crisis in Russian history has actually centered on the issue of autocracy versus some nonautocratic alternative, even though it was put forward by some groups in 1905 and in 1917.

A demand for participation in government has not been a matter of central concern in Russian political development, except as a slogan of an unsuccessful liberal minority. The Russian people have never participated actively in their government. On the local level, the delegation of tax collection and similar chores by the central authority has become in the Soviet period the forced, but passive, participation in meetings, demonstrations, and elections, that endorse the policy of the party.

The crucial elements in the development of the Russian political system have been penetration and distribution. Limited resources spread over a wide area, and the military pressure, first of the steppe nomads and then of Western Europe, made effective penetration to mobilize resources essential to the survival of the political entity. Crises and periods of strain have come when techniques of penetration have not been sufficient to meet the demands made by the state without creating massive dissatisfaction over problems of distribution. The better the system of penetration, the more that could be extracted without disaster. The two greatest crises, in the early seventeenth and early twentieth century, have been followed not by any immediate solution of the problem of distribution, but by a relaxation of demands, followed by a strengthening of the system of penetration after the initial period of disorder and conflict.

Conclusion

Russian experience is very different from that of Western Europe, and also differs markedly from that of the underdeveloped and former colonial nations. It is a modern industrial power, in aggregate size (if not in overall technological sophistication) the second in the world. Yet its political history diverges strikingly from that of all the other important industrial nations. It alone has had almost no history of even semiparliamentary, constitutional regimes. Even Japan has had far more experience with nonauthoritarian forms of government. Russia is the chief evidence that a nation can successfully modernize, at least in the industrial and technological areas, and yet retain and develop markedly different political institutions.

The early resolution of the question of identity and the establishment of a form of government that was accepted as legitimate for very long periods of time facilitated the successful penetration of the steadily expanding territories to the degree necessary to control the distribution of resources for the support of the state and its further expansion. Of course, the acceptance of princely authority as legitimate and penetration facilitated each other, but acceptance of the prince as a legitimate power within his small territory came first. Early penetration and the continued successful control over distribution of resources through the elaboration of the service state made positive popular participation in government unnecessary and allowed autocracy to maintain its supremacy without major interruption. As already noted, the crises came when demands on the resources of the state exceeded the ability of the system to mobilize them. This could be the result of a combination of poor harvests, external pressure, and dynastic succession problems in the time of troubles; or the failure of the old mobilization system to enable the state to compete with other powers, as in the case of the mid-nineteenth-century crisis. In 1905-1917 widespread economic discontent, combined with increased demands by the state and its inability to increase the effectiveness of its apparatus of control throughout the country, produced the revolutionary crisis. Finally, the renewed distribution crisis of the late 1920s was resolved by the creation of a new, brutal, but effective system of penetration that replaced the one that had broken down in the mid-nineteenth century and had never been satisfactorily replaced.

The present situation in the USSR conforms to what has been the typical pattern throughout most of Russian history. There is no question of national identity, at least in the minds of the dominant nationality; the legitimacy of the system is questioned by only a small and helpless minority; demands for meaningful participation are insignificant; the desire of the state to play the role of a major power in the world leads it to mobilize a very large portion of the national income for state purposes, and to do this a thorough-going system of bureaucratic penetration keeps control of the population.

Some Related Readings

For a good general bibliography of works in Western languages see Paul L. Horecky, ed., *Russia and the Soviet Union, a Bibliographical Guide to Western-Language Publications* (Chicago, 1965). The following includes some general studies that may be useful as an introduction and a selection from some of the more specialized English-language works that have proved of particular help to the author.

Alexander, John T. *Autocratic Politics in a National Crisis: The Imperial Russian Government and Pugachev's Revolt, 1773-1775*. Bloomington, 1969.

Billington, James H. *The Icon and the Axe; an Interpretive History of Russian Culture*. New York, 1966.

Black, Cyril E. *The Transformation of Russian Society; Aspects of Social Change since 1861*. Cambridge, Mass., 1960.

Blum, Jerome. *Lord and Peasant in Russia from the Ninth to the Nineteenth Century*. Princeton, 1961.

Chamberlin, William Henry. *The Russian Revolution 1917-1921.* 2 volumes. New York, 1935.
Crummey, Robert O. *The Old Believers and the World of Antichrist: The Vyg Community and the Russian State, 1694-1855.* Madison, 1970.
Erlich, Alexander. *The Soviet Industrialization Debate.* Cambridge, Mass., 1960.
Fainsod, Merle. *Smolensk under Soviet Rule.* Cambridge, Mass., 1958.
Fedotov, George P. *The Russian Religious Mind.* 2 volumes. Cambridge, Mass., 1946, 1966.
Field, Daniel. *Rebels in the Name of the Tsar.* Boston, 1976.
Fischer, George. *Russian Liberalism from Gentry to Intelligentsia.* Cambridge, Mass., 1958.
Florinsky, Michael T. *The End of the Russian Empire.* New Haven, 1931.
Gerschenkron, Alexander. *Economic Backwardness in Historical Perspective: A Book of Essays.* Cambridge, Mass., 1962.
Haimson, Leopold. "The Problem of Social Stability in Urban Russia," *Slavic Review,* 23 (December 1964) and 24 (March 1965).
Jasny, Naum. *Soviet Industrialization 1928-1952.* Chicago, 1961.
Jones, Robert E. *The Emancipation of the Russian Nobility.* Princeton, 1973.
Kahan, Arcadius. "The Costs of 'Westernization' in Russia: The Gentry and the Economy in the Eighteenth Century," *Slavic Review,* 25 (March 1966).
Karpovich, Michael. *Imperial Russia 1801-1917.* New York, 1932.
Keenan, Edward L., Jr. "Muscovy and Kazan: Some Introductory Remarks on the Patterns of Steppe Diplomacy," *Slavic Review,* 26 (December 1967).
Kirchner, Walther. *Commercial Relations between Russia and Europe, 1400 to 1800: Collected Essays.* Bloomington, 1966.
Kliuchevskii, Vasilii O. *Peter the Great,* translated by Liliana Archibald. New York, 1958.
Kornilov, Aleksandr. *Modern Russian History from the Age of Catherine the Great to the End of the Nineteenth Century.* Translated by Alexander S. Kaun. New York, 1943.
Lewin, Moshe. *Russian Peasants and Soviet Power: A Study of Col-*

lectivization. Translated (from French) by Irene Nove. Evanston, 1968.
McNeill, William H. *Europe's Steppe Frontier, Fifteen Hundred—Eighteen Hundred.* Chicago, 1964.
Pipes, Richard. *The Formation of the Soviet Union: Communism and Nationalism, 1917-1923.* Revised edition, Cambridge, Mass., 1964.
Raeff, Marc. *Origins of the Russian Intelligentsia: the Eighteenth Century Nobility.* New York, 1966.
Ransel, David L. *The Politics of Catherinian Russia: The Panin Party.* New Haven and London, 1975.
Riasanovsky, Nicholas V. *Nicholas I and Official Nationality in Russia 1825-1855.* Berkeley and Los Angeles, 1959.
Riasanovsky, Nicholas V. *Russia and the West in the Teaching of the Slavophiles: A Study of Romantic Ideology.* Cambridge, Mass., 1952.
Rieber, Alfred J., ed. and tr. *The Politics of Autocracy: Letters of Alexander II to Prince A. I. Bariatinskii, 1857-1864.* With an historical essay by the editor. Paris and The Hague, 1966.
Robinson, Geroid T. *Rural Russia under the Old Regime.* New York, 1932.
Rogger, Hans. *National Consciousness in Eighteenth Century Russia.* Cambridge, Mass., 1960.
Schapiro, Leonard. *The Communist Party of the Soviet Union.* New York, 1960.
Seton-Watson, Hugh. *The Decline and Fall of Imperial Russia.* New York, 1956.
Starr, S. Frederick. *Decentralization and Self-Government in Russia, 1830-1870.* Princeton, 1972.
Sumner, Benedict H. *Peter the Great and the Emergence of Russia.* London, 1950.
Wortman, Richard S. *The Development of a Russian Legal Consciousness.* Chicago, 1976.
Yaney, George. *The Systematization of Russian Government.* Urbana, 1972.

CHAPTER 11

POLAND

ROMAN SZPORLUK

FOR WELL over a hundred years Poland experienced its crises of development under rather peculiar circumstances. Just as Poland had begun to modernize and establish a new political system under the Constitution of the Third of May 1791, it was partitioned by its powerful neighbors. The Poles survived as a "nation without a state," and this lack of national statehood seriously influenced the sequence of crises and their outcome in Poland.

The decline and fall of old Poland has been a central theme of Polish historiography for a long time. "Was Poland's destruction caused by the superior force of its neighbors, or were the Poles themselves to blame for the weaknesses of their state and its eventual demise?" The so-called "pessimists," represented by the Cracow historical school, blamed the Poles. Poland's fall had been due, they argued, to a faulty institutional development in the centuries preceding the partitions: weak royal power, excessive forms of political representation, exclusion of the nonnobles from political life. The "optimists" of "the Warsaw school" did not deny that old Poland's institutions weakened the state. They insisted, though, that the country had been on the way to recovery by its own effort precisely at the time when Russia, Prussia, and Austria chose to destroy it. Poland fell not because it refused to reform itself but because its neighbors feared a reformed Poland.

This essay applies the concept of crises to the history of a nation that lacked a state for the larger part of the past two hundred years. And yet, the concept of "crises of development" not only presupposes a national state in whose frame they occur, but also a state that is relatively free from external influence and interference. The experience of Poland seems to confirm the validity of Ranke's *Primat der Aussenpolitik* formula, at least with regard to weaker states. This may be translated to mean that the preservation of sovereignty (or "penetra-

Crises of Political Development in Europe and the United States
0-691-07598-0/78/000383-35$01.75/1 (cloth)
0-691-02183-X/78/000383-35$01.75/1 (paperback)

tion" if it is understood not only as the state's capacity to exercise its power "within" but also to use that power to survive among other sovereign states) is a central concern for a national government. The period of partitions (1772-1795) exposed the weaknesses of their state to the Poles. Between the first and second partition (1772-1793), the Poles attempted to improve the state's capacity to defend itself, and the Constitution of 1791 was a culminating stage in their effort to overhaul the existing order. Adopted when the state's integrity was again threatened, the constitution was a revolution that aimed at producing a new system of penetration, participation, identity, legitimacy, and distribution in Poland.

This early modernizing revolution in Poland was unsuccessful. The liquidation of the Polish state in 1795 was an extreme case of the failure of penetration—or, rather, a proof that Poland failed to resolve successfully its "crisis of sovereignty." From that time on, what had been Poland would undergo the processes of modernization within the frame of three partitioning powers. However, Poland as a distinct entity survived those crises and reemerged as an independent state in 1918. Although they lacked a state of their own, and were thus severely restricted in their capacity to influence their political, economic, and cultural development, the Polish elites did not reconcile themselves with the disappearance of Poland. They remained active as Poles, developed their own program for change and development, and influenced the course and eventual outcome of the development crises as they occurred in Polish lands.

There are several reasons why the Polish case is interesting to a student of the crises of development. The Poles were undergoing the crises of development as subjects of three different states, and one might have assumed that they would eventually emerge from them as Germans, Austrians, or Russians. Though of course some Poles became assimilated, a vast majority did not. The survival of the Poles as a distinct nation was secured by the transformation of the old Polish one-class nation into a modern nation of all classes, and this outcome has to be attributed also to the efforts of the Polish elites themselves. The Polish elites had their own concept of modernization, competing with those that the powers ruling over Poland were advancing; and in the end, the vast majority of their potential constituency, the masses of the peasant population (who had not yet been brought to a conscious political life when Poland ceased to exist) identified with the Polish nation.

Under the old system (that is, until the Constitution of 1791), Poland had a king who was elected for life at an assembly that every adult nobleman had the right to attend. The election took place only during an interregnum to make sure that the king would have no influence on the selection of his successor. National government virtually ceased at those times. As the condition of assuming his office, the king-elect swore to obey the laws of the country and to fulfill various specific obligations negotiated with his electors; should he violate them, his subjects were released from their duty of obedience and could form a "confederation," seek redress even with force, and if necessary depose the king.

The king's power was severely limited. He appointed the officials of the state, but they were irremovable and continued in office from reign to reign. There was little coordination between the various agencies of the state. There were two sets of central officials: one for the "Crown" (that is, Poland proper), the other for Lithuania, only the ruler and the diet (Sejm) were common. Ever fearful of absolutism, the diet was very sparing in appropriating the resources for the operation of government. There was almost no professional bureaucratic apparatus, and the armed forces were deliberately kept very low in number. Those rulers who were ready to support the army out of their private purse were forbidden to do so, lest they attempt to violate the "golden liberty" of the Polish nobility.

Beginning in the fourteenth century, a series of royal privileges divested the king of the right to tax his subjects or to call them to military duty without their consent. The king also agreed not to enact new laws except by consent of his subjects, and to respect the inviolability of their persons and properties.

The decline of the royal power was not accompanied by a corresponding and commensurate growth of representative government. Limited penetration by the king and officials subordinated to him was not supplemented by penetration from a representative government. In its participation in state affairs, the nobility tried to wrest power from the king, but it was not concerned with establishing an equally strong government of its own; it claimed above all to value liberty, which it conceived as liberty *from* government, not a freedom to operate government. The Polish diet consisted of two chambers: the Senate, composed of life members, and the chamber of deputies elected by provincial assemblies of the nobility ("dietines" or *sejmiki*). The deputies were delegates, bound by instructions from and accountable to their electors. In accord with the unanimity principle, one deputy could veto a bill under consideration, and thereby bring the Sejm session to an end, invalidating even those resolutions that had been adopted unanimously earlier during the session. These arrangements made sense when one believed, as the Polish nobility strongly did, that it was not the purpose of representative bodies to initiate change. The existing system was highly satisfactory, and change was more likely than not to be for the worse. For this reason even a single individual—"the one just man"— should have the power to frustrate a reformist majority.

Liberty extended only to the noble class itself (the *szlachta*). Towns were controlled either by the monarch (royal towns) or the nobility. They were not represented in the Sejm. The Jews, who formed a legally distinct group in the urban population, lived under the supervision of the government. The peasantry lived either on royal domains or on the estates of the nobility, where the lord exercised full patrimonial authority.

Only members of the nobility could own land. The land used by the peasants for their own maintenance was legally the noble's; the peasant paid rent in the form of compulsory labor service. In the area of "distribution" the nobility, besides being virtually exempt from taxation and holding the monopoly right of landownership, was exempt from import duties and the salt tax, and held the monopoly of liquor distilling. If one considers the political rights of the nobility (no penetration, exclusive participation, legitimacy divorced from the government), it becomes clear what Rousseau had in mind when he wrote that in Poland the nobles were everything, the bourgeoisie nothing, and the peasants "less than nothing."

Legally, all members of the Polish nobility were equal, without regard to their wealth or position. In fact, a dozen or so magnate families shared real power in the state, even though the entire noble class (about 10 percent of the population) enjoyed the right of suffrage, occupied government posts, and otherwise functioned as the ruling class. Despite this inequality in wealth and power, the Polish *szlachta* as a whole still preserved a high sense of unity based on its clear-cut separation from the rest of society. Style of life, economic and social status (even a landless noble in the employment of a magnate was a master over the serf), culture, Catholic religion, education, political participation in the Sejm, all helped to forge a powerful sense of identity among the Polish "nation of the nobility" (only the noble was a "Pole" in pre-1791 Poland).

Russia, Prussia, and Austria found Poland's political system highly advantageous. They agreed to "guarantee" Polish liberties, that is, to block any internal reform that might strengthen the king's power, make the diet workable, or increase the size of the army. Foreign courts were active in domestic Polish politics from the second half of the sixteenth century, when the "free election" of king was instituted. Russia's influence gave the Polish throne to Augustus III in 1733 and to Stanislaw Poniatowski in 1764. In 1768 the empress of Russia formally became the guarantrix of the Polish constitution, and the Poles thus limited the sovereignty of their state. (In 1775 Prussia and Austria joined in to guarantee the inviolability of the Polish constitution.) Russia, and at times other powers, also intervened in Poland's internal affairs, and the result of one such intervention on behalf of the non-Catholics was the granting of political rights to the "dissident" (non-Catholic) nobles in 1768. Catholic traditionalists resisted this measure with arms by forming a Confederation at Bar. This confederation was "antimodern" insofar as it attempted to prevent the extension of political rights to a religious minority; but as a nationalist revolt against foreign interference, it was also "modern."

The immediate consequence of the revolt and its suppression by the Russians was the partition of Poland in 1772. This was carried out peacefully—there being no army that could possibly have resisted the occupation—and the partition treaties were ratified by the Polish diet in 1773. The partition was a shock, however, and helped awaken a movement for reform. The following two decades saw a struggle between the forces of change and reform, and those of tradition. The divisions between the two sides were not always clearly marked, but the movement for change was gaining in strength. The diet elected in 1788 organized itself as a "confederate" Sejm (that is, one requiring a majority, not unanimity, for its decisions) and was expected to adopt important reforms. It continued for another term after the elections of 1790, when its size was doubled. The patriotic or reform party did not command a majority. The Constitution of May 3, 1791, was adopted by a minority of the Sejm in violation of parliamentary rules. It was a bloodless revolution carried out with the king's connivance and support.

Even before 1791, the Sejm repudiated foreign protection and reasserted Poland's sovereignty. In the constitution it formulated a new principle of legitimacy, which was to emanate from the nation represented in its constitutional bodies; it abolished the right to refuse obedience and the right to resort to insurrection. Although the *szlachta* retained political power, the towns received the right to send nonvoting "plenipotentiaries" to the Sejm. Full representation was still far away, but the political monopoly of the *szlachta* was breached. The language of the constitution, especially its use of the term "nation," indicated that its authors thought the Polish nation would ultimately consist of all social classes; and it is significant that the constitution included an article on the peasants, recognizing their contribution to the country's welfare and promising them the "protection" of the state. The property rights of the nobles and their dominial authority over peasants were left intact, however. Burghers were allowed to buy land, and the nobles to take up "dishonorable" occupations, such as trade or commerce, without losing their class status.

The new concept of identity was also reflected in the constitution's description of deputies as representatives of the nation (and not as spokesmen of particular regional interests). Abolition of the requirement for unanimity made it possible for parliament to work, and the restriction of suffrage to property-owning nobles eliminated those most susceptible to control by the great magnates. These changes were expected to make the diet more responsive to the need for reform. One of the most radical breaks with centuries-old Polish traditions was the adoption of the hereditary principle in place of the "free election" of the king. The executive consisted of the king and a cabinet responsible to the Sejm. The constitution also provided for a thorough reorganization of the government in order to establish an effective army. The bureaucratic apparatus (interior, finance, education, and war departments) would be able to penetrate the society to an extent impossible before.

The constitution was met both with enthusiasm and resistance in the country. In 1792 a "confederation" was promulgated in Targowica (in fact it was organized in St. Petersburg), repudiating the constitution and other reforms that had violated the ancient laws of Poland. First the Russian and then the Prussian army entered Poland. Although the domestic enemies of the constitution were very powerful, foreign intervention was decisive. The powers decided first to partition (1793) and then to eliminate (1795) the Polish state.

Crises

IDENTITY

The disappearance of the Polish state forced those politically aware Poles to question their identity. Were they still Poles? Did Poland perish together with the Polish state? The answers to these questions ranged between two extremes. Some shared the view of the Polish magnate who said that since Poland had perished, as had so many nations in the past, he was now a Russian; and Russia would be his country. Others simply refused to concede that the battle was over. For them the only justification of the foreign occupation was its superior force, which they considered temporary. These Poles were determined to carry on the struggle until the invaders were expelled. As long as there were Poles ready to fight for Poland, she would still exist.

There were not many who were ready to leave their homes and wage an armed struggle for Polish independence whenever an opportunity would arise, but it seems correct to estimate that a majority of Poles sympathized with this position rather than with that of the magnate quoted earlier. True, at various times in the nineteenth century there were some writers who took an assimilationist or nihilistic position, and there were no doubt Poles who abandoned their nationality in favor of a German or Russian identity without writing books or articles about it. But the bulk of men and women in Poland continued to regard themselves as Polish, even if some made peace with and worked with the new regime. It was in their midst that the controversy about the meaning of "Poland" and "Pole" was carried on.

Who was a Pole? In 1772, a Pole was a member of the noble class. The Constitution of 1791 had broadened the concept of "Polishness," and the law correctly reflected a change in social reality: in Warsaw (and other towns) people of nonnoble status—merchants, artisans, teachers, clergymen, writers, journalists, actors—demanded recognition as Poles. What was it that made *them* Polish?

The Polish political nation was in the process of being redefined. Although the actual change accomplished in 1791 was modest, its authors and supporters thought that the third of May was only a beginning. The anti-Russian and anti-Prussian insurrection of 1794 did even more to support the belief that Polish society was beginning to include urban patriotic elements (including Jews) and that the peasants, too, were capable of serving the country and should be rewarded accordingly. It is not so important how many shoemakers, Jews, or peasants participated with distinction in the patriotic war: the historic names of Kiliński, Joselewicz, and Bartosz became symbols of what might happen if only Poland were free again.

Thus, even after the final defeat in 1795, "Polonism" remained as a political program, ideology, and organization. Perhaps it was better that the Constitution of 1791 did not have time to be tested in practice—it could thus become a slogan and a standard under which all those who rejected the rule of Vienna, Berlin, and St. Petersburg could gather. The Polish independence movement was not only a program aimed at reclaiming certain areas ruled from St. Petersburg or Vienna. The reestablishment of a Polish state, as understood by its partisans, would entail profound political changes: a constitutional regime, parliamentary bodies, a responsible ministry, rights of man and citizen, religious and cultural freedom. The Poland to which the patriots looked forward was not the disorganized, backward, and feeble state of the eighteenth century; it was the renovated and reformed state that had almost been established in the short years between 1788 and 1794. The legend thus created enabled various kinds of people, including those of foreign ethnic origins who had settled in Poland, to identify with the Polish nation and its struggle.

Polish nationalism was not restricted to ideas. Throughout the period of partitions, beginning with the suppression of the 1794 insurrection, there were always various organizations of men and women who conducted political struggle (including underground or open military action) at home and abroad for the restoration of Poland. With time the composition and outlook of these people changed and their concerns gradually extended to individuals of quite diverse social, religious, and ethnic backgrounds.

In addition to the new "political nation in the making," a Polish cultural nation functioned largely in the open. Polish culture survived the loss of the Polish state, and the men and women who were creating it hoped that their work would help to restore a political Poland one day. Despite unfavorable political circumstances, Polish culture began to reach the urban class, and later in the nineteenth century, also the peasantry. Art, literature, and history were able to bring various groups together in a national community based on a shared culture and historical memories. A partitioned Poland might have had various capitals politically but, for most of the time, Warsaw was the capital of the Polish *Kulturnation*. During the nineteenth century, Warsaw's population grew from a low of some 60,000 in 1800 (a decline from about 100,000 in the 1780s) to almost a million by 1914, and a Polish cultural "common market" was being formed in defiance of political boundaries, with Warsaw functioning as the chief producer and distributor of cultural wares. Warsaw had Poland's leading theatres, libraries, publishing houses, and periodical press. As old, stable social forms broke down, culture came to acquire importance as a factor of social integration and individual self-orientation; in the ex-Polish territories this culture was to a surprisingly high degree Polish.

The long process of integrating the peasant masses into a Polish nation proceeded at different rates in different parts of the country. It was the fastest and most thorough in the Prussian-ruled section of Poland—where the peasant question, that is, the distribution crisis, had been solved first, producing a farmer class and propertyless workers in the countryside, along with the surviving great landowners. Neither in Russian Poland nor under Austria did the Polish peasants at large identify themselves with such Polish national actions as the revolts of 1830-1831, 1846, 1848, or 1863-1864. In some cases, such as 1846, they in fact struck against the "Poles," that is, patriots, and sided with the Austrians.

The "Polonization" of the Polish rural masses in Galicia and, under different conditions, in Russian Poland, took place during the second half of the nineteenth century and was not quite completed by 1914. It proceeded in two stages: at first, as literacy spread, the peasantry accepted a cultural Polish identity; gradually, political organizations reached the peasants (or were formed by them), and these functioned as Polish political organizations. In a symbolic gesture, shortly before 1914, the Polish peasant deputies in the Vienna Reichsrat joined the "Polish Circle," the parliamentary club of the nobility and the intelligentsia.

Even after Polishness was no longer solely equated with the *szlachta* or "educated strata" but was extended to the masses (whose language and folk culture were Polish), Polish leaders maintained their territorial definition of Poland. Virtually without exception, until the January Insurrection of 1863 at least, they conceived the new Poland to coincide territorially with the old state of 1772. In the earlier decades of the nineteenth century, the Lithuanian, Belorussian, and Ukrainian peasants were thought by many to be ethnically Polish, more or less like the peasants from the provinces of Warsaw, Poznań, or Cracow. Later, the ethnic and cultural diversity of the peoples of the old Commonwealth was more readily recognized, but many still refused to regard this fact as politically relevant: all the inhabitants of old Poland, it was argued, were Polish in a political sense by virtue of the past that they shared with Poland, or they would become Polish in the future, when they would also live in a common state; the community of political rights would provide a firm bond uniting citizens of different ethnic and cultural backgrounds.

The 1863-1864 insurrection against Russia showed that a Polish solution in any form (whether through a total merger with Poland or a political association with Poland without renouncing regional cultural identities) was unacceptable to the peasant masses of old Poland's Eastern regions and to the emerging intelligentsias of the Ukraine and Lithuania. The defeat of the uprising made the Poles realize that the restoration of Poland in the historic boundaries of 1772 was no longer a practicable policy. The emancipation of the peasants (1861 and 1864) coincided in time with the uprising, and its provisions were influenced by the Russian government's desire to deprive the Poles of peasant support. (The peasantry in those areas where Polish landlords prevailed received land on more favorable terms than the peasantry in Russia proper.) The peasant reform abolished the most important vestige of Polish rule in the East: serfdom and the dominial authority of the landlord over his village subjects. After the debacle of 1863-1864, the constituency of Polish politics (both legal and underground) was narrowed to ethnic Poles, primarily but not exclusively in ethnic Poland: what Poland was remained unclear, however, once the last "legitimate" boundary, that of 1772, could no longer be upheld.

Two major concepts of Poland existed in Polish political thought before World War I. One was based on a combination of ethnic and territorial principles, advocated by the National Democratic party led by Roman Dmowski; the other was an "historic" or "federalist" concept of Józef Piłsudski. (The idea that Poland was only where Poles constituted a majority of the population appeared in the peasant movement in the second half of the nineteenth century, but was not endorsed even by it.) Dmowski did not limit the territorial extension of Poland to the land inhabited by Polish-speaking majorities but demanded, by virtue of Poland's superiority as a cultural and civilized nation, the incorporation of some non-Polish parts of Lithuania, Belorussia, and the Ukraine into Poland. The limit that the National

Democrats set for eastward expansion was practical: Poland was to take only as much of non-Polish lands as it could assimilate. In the west, where the historic principle worked against Poland, the National Democrats advanced a combination of an ethnic and a strategic criterion: Poland was to acquire those parts of East Prussia and Silesia where the common people—peasants and workers—spoke Polish dialects (no argument of a *German* cultural ascendancy was admitted here); much emphasis was also put on the necessity to establish Poland firmly on the coast of the Baltic. The "National Democrats" or "Nationalists" defined the Poles by ethnic criteria, as opposed to political ones such as citizenship. They favored the forcible assimilation of Slavic minorities but advocated anti-Jewish measures because they thought the Jews were unassimilable on racial grounds. Although Dmowski and his party remained out of power for most of the interwar years, it was their national ideology rather than that of Piłsudski (who was Poland's *de facto* dictator for almost ten years) that was implemented in Poland after 1918.

Unlike Dmowski, who regarded Poland's western areas as the source of the country's greatest strength, Piłsudski was interested in the east; and he stood for the creation of a Greater Poland that would be the leader of associated and allied peoples. Piłsudski believed that there was nothing the Poles could do to eliminate Germany as a powerful neighbor; in the east, however, he thought that it was possible to bring about a major rearrangement of forces. He thought that Poland ought to support the nationalist movements of Russia's subject peoples, from Finland down through Estonia, Latvia, Lithuania, Belorussia, and the Ukraine, to Armenia and Georgia. Facing Poland's great foreign policy dilemma of "Germany or Russia," Piłsudski chose the anti-Russian policy; but his ultimate aim was to transcend the dilemma by removing Russia as Poland's direct neighbor.

When an opportunity came, in 1919-1920, to realize his design, Poland proved too weak. The hoped-for allies, most notably the Ukrainians, displayed less enthusiasm for a partnership with Poland than had been expected, and Russia proved to be too strong. To the peasant masses of the non-Russian and non-Polish peoples, even as late as 1920, Poland signified the old landlord rule. The treaty of Riga (1921) gave Poland much more land in the east than one could call Polish on the ethnic principle, but not enough to force the Poles to adopt a policy of partnership with the Ukrainians and Belorussians.

The western Polish boundary, established in Versailles, was not entirely satisfactory to the Poles, and quite unacceptable to the Germans. The Poles were disappointed because they did not get Gdańsk (that it had a German majority of something like ninety-eight percent did not weaken their conviction that it was a Polish city). They also thought that in East Prussia and Silesia they had received less than they deserved on the basis of the ethnic criterion. The Germans regarded the Versailles boundary, in particular the "Corridor," as an outrage and were to recognize that it had not been without some virtue only after World War II, when the Corridor had ceased to exist.

When their state was restored after World War I, the Poles accepted its new territorial shape, the "Versailles-Riga" model of Poland. It seemed that the Polish crisis of identity might at last be resolved. This was not the case, however, because the answer to the question "who is a Pole?" was not compatible with the answer to the question "what is Poland?" even if the arrangement was satisfactory to the Poles themselves. About one-third of the population of post-World War I Poland received Polish *citizenship* but was not thought (nor did it generally conceive itself) to be Polish by *nationality*. This conflict of identity, involving conflicting concepts of state and nation, bore directly on the resolution of distribution, legitimacy, participation, and penetration crises.

The restored Polish state survived for a mere twenty years before it was crushed once again. It reappeared not only under a new government, but with a substantially different population and in a new geographic location. The country had almost no national minorities after 1945; it had ceded about one-half of its pre-1939 territory to the Soviet Union, and about one-third of its post-1945 territory had not been Polish since the middle ages. Nation and state became as closely commensurate with each other as was practically possible. The experience of the war and Nazi occupation also brought to completion the process of national self-identification of all ethnic Poles, whose survival was threatened by the Germans. Moreover, the land reform of 1944 totally abolished the landlord class—a living reminder that at one time the Poles had been divided into masters and serfs. It appeared, therefore, that after World War II the crisis of identity was solved in Poland.

PENETRATION

One of the most significant aspects of the crisis of penetration in modern Polish history was the fact that it was resolved mainly by non-Polish administrations from 1795 (in some parts from 1772) until 1918. Since penetration served the interests of foreign states, the more patriotically inclined a Pole was, the greater was his hostility to the government and law of Austria, Prussia, and Russia. No matter what mental reservations or real purposes a man may have had, there was a danger that by acting in accordance with law, "within the system," he was helping to keep Poland unfree, recognizing the legitimacy of foreign rule, and weakening the separate Polish identity.

Not all inhabitants of Poland *were* patriotic Poles, however; the peasantry had reason to welcome the strengthening of the central government, in particular when it extended to noble-peasant relations, serfdom, and landownership. It was the Austrians and Prussians who made the first attempt toward a modern penetration of the peasantry in the areas which they took in 1772. Their reforms concerning urban population also indicated that state authority wanted to treat the whole population according to generally applicable legal norms. The eighteenth century in Europe was the age of enlightened absolutism, and the "police state" in Austria and Prussia contrasted sharply with Poland before its reforms.

Austrians and Prussians put the patrimonial authority of the landlords under the supervision of the bureaucracy. The landlord was required to employ a specially trained official, instead of acting as a judge himself. This was an attempt to rationalize and formalize the landlord's public authority and, equally important, to subject the judicial and administrative process to state control. Both in Austria and in Prussia the peasants received the right to address their complaints against the landlord to the state. The unlimited personal authority of the landlord over his serfs was restricted (peasants could marry, for example, or send their children to town to learn a craft without the lord's permission), and the amount of labor service was regulated. In Austria, protection was extended to peasant holdings by a separation of "rustic" and "dominial" lands. Elementary schools were set up in the villages. In towns, various restrictions concerning Jews were revoked, and they received greater freedom of employment and residence, extending to agriculture. Their children began to attend public schools. All Jews were required to assume German surnames, and they were made subject to military service.

In both Austria and Prussia the government established control over the church, taking over its landed properties, closing down many monasteries, and reorganizing the educational system. Frederick II found that the talents of the *szlachta* could be used for his benefit: he established a (German-language) cadet school for young Polish nobles, and it supplied him with many new Prussian officers (and incidentally also helped to integrate the state's new subjects). After the Austrians discovered that in its eastern part Galicia was inhabited by a Ukrainian population of the Uniate rite, they elevated the Uniate clergy (kept in an inferior position before 1772) to a status of equality with the Latin clergy. They established schools for training Uniate clergy and reorganized the structure of the church itself, thereby winning over the Uniates.

This intensified penetration, besides serving its immediate aims (taxes and conscripts), had the effect of legitimizing the new rule and producing a sense of identification with the monarch of Vienna or Berlin; conversely, it impeded the growth of a Polish identity. (Some peasants in Galicia described themselves, well into the nineteenth century, as "the emperor's people.") The peasant saw the emperor's or king's official as his protector from the landlord. Since landlord and Pole were the same for the peasant, he thought of Poland as a country where the peasant enjoyed no legal protection. In the towns, the Polish Jews were beginning to leave the ghetto and enter the world of *German* law and *German* culture.

Penetration by the Russian imperial government followed a different pattern. The area that Russia took in 1772 became assimilated very easily with the rest of the empire; but in Poland's Lithuanian, Belorussian, and Ukrainian provinces acquired in 1793-1795, no concentrated attempt was made to introduce Russian law, language, institutions, or education. The Poles, or more exactly Polish landlords, constituted the leading social and economic force, and were in fact recognized as a "nation of the state" (somewhat like the German nobility in Russia's Baltic provinces). The entire state school system, topped by the University of Wilno, was Polish. Even the imperial army stationed there formed a separate unit, the so-called "Lithuanian Corps." The central Russian government did not begin to assimilate the area culturally or integrate it administratively until after the 1830 revolt. Since the general quality of Russian law, administration, and justice was inferior to that of Austria or Prussia or the Kingdom of Poland, increased penetration by the Russian state did not improve the status or condition of any group in the population and in some respects it signified a retrogression. The Jews, for example, were subject to new discriminatory laws and brutal treatment (the drafting of children for military service), while the Uniate church was abolished. This was of course also a penetration of sorts, but hardly one to produce modernization if one means by that extension of equality, universal laws, "meritocracy," and so on.

The historical importance of the Duchy of Warsaw (1807-1813) and the Kingdom of Poland (1815-1831, and to some extent also in 1860-1863) was that they helped to bring about the modernization of Poland by the Poles themselves acting as Poles. Although the Duchy of Warsaw existed for only a brief period, its record was impressive. The duchy's constitution, granted by Napoleon, abolished "slavery," that is, in principle it extended personal liberty to the peasants. The *Code Civil*, which became the law of the duchy (and remained in force until 1945), abolished feudal-type relations and made landlords the uncontested owners of the land (including the land that traditionally had been used by the peasants). Nonnobles with property or educational qualifications were admitted to public office, could vote and be elected, rise to officers' rank in the army, and enjoy equality under law. These reforms helped to bring the nobility and the urban population together. However, the duchy retained and in some respects even sharpened discriminatory treatment of the Jews, who not only lacked political rights (participation) but also equal protection of the law (penetration and identity). And serfdom remained, despite the grand-sounding words of the law abolishing slavery.

The "Kingdom of Poland" established at Vienna with the tsar as its king was in many respects a continuation of the duchy. The administrative machine and the army were taken over intact. The government of the kingdom actively promoted modernization and industrialization by means of tariffs, taxes, and loans, and established the Bank of Poland. The government encouraged the immigration of skilled workers and technicians from abroad, granted facilities to foreign entrepreneurs, and promoted technical and professional education. A university, including a school of law and public administration, was organized in Warsaw. A government-funded rabbinical college was also established, but this measure could not be successful in penetrating the Jewish population so long as Jews as a whole remained under discriminatory law (which they did until the 1860s).

The period of reaction in Russia (1825-1855) ended after the Crimean War. The reforms that followed also benefited Russian Poland. Between 1860 and 1862 the central government of the kingdom was largely restored and the highest posts were filled by Poles. The

Polish administration attempted to regulate the status of the peasantry by abolishing compulsory labor and replacing it by rent in money. It also carried out a broad educational reform and finally extended to the Jews the rights enjoyed by the Christian population (such as equality before the law, freedom of residence, property rights, and suffrage).

The political and educational reforms were withdrawn after the 1863 revolt, but the peasant reform was completed by a grant of landed property. The Jews in the Kingdom of Poland continued to enjoy civil rights denied to them in the other parts of the empire (where the Pale of Settlement remained until the revolution). One consequence of the civic emancipation of the Jews by a Polish administration was the emergence of the concept of a "Pole of Mosaic confession": a clear sign that the meaning of "Polishness" was being modernized.

The policies pursued by Austria, Russia, and Prussia with regard to their Polish territories in the second half of the nineteenth and in the early twentieth century were different, and their success in penetrating Polish society was also different. The penetration by Prussia/Germany was probably the most thorough, but its aims and achievements could be valued by Pole and German alike: there was law and order; officials were stern but honest; the state provided various kinds of insurance, old age pensions, a universal school system, vocational training, and sanitary and veterinary services, and so on; the state's tariff policies protected the agricultural interests of the Poles, too. The Poles paid taxes and served in the army, and some of them went to work the mines and steel mills of the Ruhr. Polish dissatisfaction with the state grew and Polish-German relations became tense owing to the intensification of German nationalism and great-power ambitions after 1871. Polish citizens of Germany were being alienated by the increasing restrictions on the use of the Polish language in church and school, by officially supported colonization plans in Poznania, and by the expropriation of Polish landowners. This intensified penetration, instead of promoting the equality of all imperial citizens, was making it clear to Poles that in the eyes of Berlin they were regarded as second-class citizens. For this reason it is a tribute to the high quality of the German administrative machinery (and in the language of crises, of the relatively successful penetration by the German state of its Polish subjects) that after the Poles overthrew German rule in Poznania (December 1918), they chose to keep German civil servants in their jobs for a time rather than admit less well-qualified Polish applicants.

This would have been inconceivable in the Russian part of Poland where there had been less law and order, the welfare functions of the state were more limited, and officials were less competent and more corrupt. At various times the area was either ruled by martial law or at least was under a military administration. Considerable contingents of troops were required to keep internal peace. Admittedly, Russian Poland was difficult to control even when the regime had a partially Polish character. For example, the insurrection of 1863 was provoked by the government's decision to draft young men into the army, whereupon many of the would-be conscripts escaped to the forests and formed guerrilla units under a secret "National Government" that proclaimed a national insurrection. Although it was suppressed, the revolt had the effect of making the operation of government in Poland exclusively a Russian affair, and thus more difficult.

Compared with Russia or Germany, the Austrian state during the constitutional era (1867-1918) made smaller demands on its subjects, and penetration by the state was effectively facilitated by its admission of Poles to the bureaucracy at all levels, without demanding that they cease to regard themselves as Poles. Thus the Polish language was official in Galicia's administration (German and Ukrainian were also recognized, but not so widely used), and schools were under an autonomous school board that made them a tool of patriotic Polish education for the masses. The governor of Galicia, representing imperial authority, was usually a Pole; and the administrative posts subordinate to Vienna were filled by local Poles. Poles also rose to great prominence in Vienna, not only in the civil service but also as ministers: there was a time when the Austro-Hungarian foreign minister, Austrian prime minister, and the ministers of the interior, of finance, and for Galicia were all Polish. All these Poles were loyal Habsburg subjects as long as the Habsburg monarchy functioned, because they felt that their service was compatible with their understanding of Polish national interests. If, as Polish historians agree, of the three powers that ruled Poland, Austria came closest to making the Poles its own citizens in heart, this was largely due to the fact that it had opened to them the ranks of its bureaucracy.

However, even the Austrian system did not succeed in bridging the chasm between the functions of identity and participation on the one hand and those of penetration on the other. Although many government workers were Polish, public authority was viewed with distrust.

One reason was that despite everything it remained Austrian (identity); the other, because even in the constitutional period the bureaucracy, composed in its upper ranks of aristocrats and noblemen, retained a high degree of independence from representative institutions and from the society at large (participation). This lack of coordination between the functions of penetration and participation survived the establishment of the Polish state, with its Polish officials, judges, and police. The English expression "civil servant" sounds absurd in Polish (or German or Russian) and never is literally translated, but is rendered as "official of the state."

The unresolved crisis of identity (and legitimacy) influenced the processes of penetration and participation in post-1918 Poland. In the eyes of many of its minority citizens, the Polish state lacked legitimacy because it was not their national state, and consequently they either used participation for purposes contrary to the interest of the state or else rejected participation as a sham covering the reality of bureaucratic rule. Simultaneously, they denied that the state had a right to rule them. Some Poles, led by Piłsudski, rejected the parliamentary regime and resorted to a revolt which resulted in freeing the executive branch from parliamentary control. Thus, the administration could afford to act without restraint, such as when it employed the army to fight sabotage or imposed preventive detention on "subversive" elements. This, in turn, had an effect on the citizens' perception of the state's legitimacy.

The difficulties with keeping "law and order" were but one part of the penetration crisis that the Polish state underwent. It was also necessary to adjust to the new perceptions of the scope and dimensions of penetration as such. After the war, in many countries of Europe the state was thought responsible for the performance of the national economy. The Polish government was involved in both military and industrial development (the "Central Industrial Region"; the construction of the port and city of Gdynia; railroad construction), and the government frequently appointed army officers to bank and factory directorships.

The Nazi occupation represented a new crisis of penetration: against the official German administrative apparatus a "secret state" functioned underground, and its orders were generally obeyed. There was an underground army, courts, schools, and police.

The scope of penetration was extended after the second world war and the *de facto* civil war between the anticommunist and communist forces. The new regime nationalized virtually all industrial, commercial, financial, and transport enterprises. Nationalization was a crisis of penetration, as well as of distribution. For a time the centrally administered "command" economy served the purposes of the state, but gradually various difficulties evolved. How much power should be left under the direct rule of the state, how much freedom should one grant to local enterprises, regional councils, workers' self-government and, finally, the market? How should economic administration be related to the political core of the party?

In the late 1920s and early 1930s, Soviet leadership had perceived its agricultural problems as a crisis of distribution (abolition of private property, financing industrialization), but it handled these problems as a crisis of penetration (violent suppression of a potentially disloyal class, use of punitive taxes, destruction of property, famine, terror). In an analogous situation twenty years later, the Polish leadership at first began to follow the Soviet model, though without Stalinist excesses. For various reasons this approach proved an immediate failure and, moreover, was recognized as such even by the party leaders. The Polish party wisely decided not to treat its agricultural problems as a political crisis (penetration) that would require the extensive use of police measures. Without abandoning their ultimate aim of a socialized agriculture, they chose instead to achieve it by means of economic and educational measures, such as tax incentives, loans, and agricultural schools.

Similarly, policies toward the church have contrasted sharply with those of the Soviet government. The Polish government appears to have decided early that it could eliminate religious instruction from public schools, influence church appointments and the training of the clergy, and so on, while still allowing the church enough autonomy to keep it from open resistance.

PARTICIPATION

Between 1795 and 1918 there were several rather distinct levels of political participation in Poland. First, there was participation in the regional representative bodies established by the respective partitioning powers; second, participation by Poles in the central political organs of Prussia (1848-1918) and Germany (North German Bund 1867-1871, German Reich 1871-1918), Austria (1848-1849, 1861-1918), and Russia (1906-1916); third, participation in Polish underground and emigré organizations; and finally, participation in formally nonpolitical organizations that in fact performed political functions.

It was important to the political survival of the Polish nation that for something like sixty to eighty years (in the case of Austria and Prussia) and over one hundred years (in that of Russia) Polish lands did not participate in any central parliamentary bodies. There were groups in Poland that might have welcomed an opportunity to participate in such bodies had they existed. When those parliamentary bodies were finally set up, a new, "multiclass" Polish identity already was in an advanced state of formation and the crisis of distribution, potentially disruptive of Polish national identity, had been or was being resolved. It was advantageous to the Poles that both in Prussia and in Russia the peasants were liberated and given land long before they were granted suffrage and thus admitted to political participation in non-Polish bodies. In Austria, these two events coincided in the revolutionary year 1848, which also witnessed a crisis of legitimacy in the empire at large and in its Polish part. This coalescence of crises allowed the imperial Austrian government to form a common front with the peasants (by means of changes in participation and distribution) against the Polish nationalists who sought separation from Austria. The vote in the Austrian *Reichstag* on the crucial issue of compensation of landlords produced a split between the Polish and Ukrainian peasant deputies from Galicia, who voted against compensation (as did the German radicals), and the patriotic Polish nobles, who voted for it. The Austrians did not further exploit the opportunities that the establishment of a representative system might have given them at that time, and the parliament itself was sent home in 1849. When it met again, the Polish nobility was firmly in control of parliamentary and provincial elections in Galicia. Still later, when a peasant political movement arose in Galicia at the turn of the century, it was possible to combine the defence of peasant interests with a Polish patriotic outlook.

The Austrian experience suggests that participation by various ethnic groups in central representative assemblies does not by itself strengthen the unity of the state, unless this participation is accompanied by the development of an all-state identity and is rewarded by benefits in the area of distribution. The sequence in which these particular problems are solved appears to be of decisive importance. When in 1907 universal suffrage was introduced in the Reichsrat elections (the provincial diets retained the "curia" system), it had been hoped in Vienna that deputies elected by the uncorrupted *Volk* would be concerned with social questions in the framework of the whole state, unlike those chauvinistic bourgeois lawyers and journalists chosen by a narrow electorate. Instead, the deputies of the people proved to be as imbued by their particular nationalist outlook as anyone else, except that often they did not even understand or speak German—a dubious gain for those caring about the reinvigoration of the empire. Even Austria's Social Democrats broke down into regional subparties. Galicia had three such parties (Polish, Ukrainian, Jewish). The Polish-Ukrainian electoral reform, adopted in 1913, aimed to resolve the conflict by separating the contestants, not by bringing them together. No one expected that it would foster a sense of "Galician" or "Austrian" identity.

There is a certain ambiguity in the concept of "participation," and the Polish experience brings this out. Participation may be in the nature of pressure-group activity, or it may imply not only petitioning and pleading but also a share in the making and implementing of decisions that are part of penetration. It was in the latter sense that the Poles participated in Austrian politics after 1867. Galicia received an autonomy wider than that enjoyed by any other crownland, and until the end of the monarchy its provincial administration was coordinated with the local diet. The Poles were also influential in the Reichsrat.

The situation under Prussian/German rule was different because there Poles were not participating in decision making on either a local or a central level. The Polish deputies to the Prussian *Landtag* and German *Reichstag* usually acted as a national bloc under the leadership of the landed nobility. The intensification of German national feeling after the establishment of the German Empire in 1871, tended to make the members of the Polish parliamentary club in Berlin feel themselves even more strongly a national minority.

When a Russian quasi parliament was established in 1906, there was no question that the deputies from the kingdom would go there not as Russian parliamentarians but as delegates of Poland. Perhaps things might have been different if a Russian parliament had been set up in 1860 or 1865 and the Polish peasants granted suffrage then.

Participation in the regional legislative assemblies in Poland during the first half of the nineteenth century was restricted to the upper and middle classes, but even so it was more extensive than that available to Russians, Austrians, or Prussians. The urban bourgeoisie and the intelligentsia—but not its Jewish part—participated in the lower house of the Duchy of Warsaw and the Kingdom of Poland, even though the landed nobility still elected a majority of deputies. During the Polish revolt against the tsar in 1830-1831, the kingdom's diet did not feel compelled to recognize the peasants as equal members of the national community or grant them property.

The Diet of Galicia was elected in four curiae, heavily favoring great landed property, the urban business classes, and towns in general. This socio-economic composition also produced a disproportionately large representation of the Polish and a corresponding underrepresentation of the Ukrainian population. The struggle for reform of the system for electing representatives to the Galician Diet assumed crisis proportions in the twentieth century, until a reform was voted in 1913, although, because of the war, it was never implemented.

Extralegal and nonpolitical participation defy easy generalizations, because both were very highly developed, complex, and of lasting influence. Emigré and underground organizations, more or less formally constituted, kept the Polish issue alive in the minds of their less activist compatriots at home and as a subject of concern in the West. In the underground, aside from the obvious importance of the various organizations that prepared and led insurrections, it is necessary to single out the Polish socialist movement that emerged in the 1870s in Galicia and the kingdom. Socialist workers and intellectuals in Poland found a way to reconcile their attachment to and participation in socialism with the struggle for national independence. A vast majority of those politically aware workers gave their support to the PPS (Polish Socialist party), which was both socialist and patriotic, while the SDKPiL (an "internationalist" party whose leaders as late as 1918 regarded Poland's independence as a "utopia") attracted very few. It was from the ranks of the SDKPiL and the left wing of the PPS that the Communist party of Poland was formed in December 1918.

Finally, although Poles participated everywhere in ostensibly nonpolitical activities, the Prussian section of Poland was most advanced in establishing a network of agricultural, industrial, commercial, religious, and cultural associations, which taken together virtually formed "a state within the state." Opportunities under Russia were more restricted, but their importance for modernization may have been even greater inasmuch as the Russian administration lagged far behind the Prussians in sponsoring agricultural improvements, building schools and libraries, providing credit, and so on. At a time when no formal political organizations were allowed, an ostensibly economic agricultural society (established in 1857) functioned as a forum of public debate, and its leaders acted as Polish representatives in their discussions with Russian authorities.

Some of the difficulties of participation in the restored Polish state will be mentioned in the discussion of legitimacy. But lack of national homogeneity was not the only obstacle to the functioning of the democratic parliamentary system established in Poland after 1918 (the Constitution of March 17, 1921). Parliamentary majorities were unstable and governmental crises frequent—and not just because a proportional system favored the proliferation of factional parties. (Czechoslovakia had the same system and more numerous minorities, but coalitions there worked much better.) In 1926 Piłsudski overthrew the government by force, and his action was ratified by the parliament when it elected him president. Piłsudski did not accept election, however, and remained only a *de facto* dictator until his death in 1935. The parliamentary and democratic system, its substance destroyed in 1926, was formally abolished by the "April Constitution" of 1935. The place of parliament as the supreme organ of the state was now taken by the president, who bore responsibility for his actions "before God and History" (Article 2). The Senate, two-thirds of it chosen by a narrow electorate ("the elite": college graduates, army officers, clergymen, holders of state decorations) and one-third appointed by the president, was to enjoy greater power than the lower chamber. The latter was elected by popular vote, but the government controlled the selection of candidates. The elections of 1935 and 1938 were boycotted by all Polish political parties other than the government bloc, and doubts were raised as to the legality of the constitution itself, since it had been adopted in violation of parliamentary rules.

Participation in the People's Republic of Poland is circumscribed by the Communist party's claim to rule by virtue of its alleged insight into the laws of history and society. Simultaneously, the party claims popular support. There exists an elaborate mechanism for formal participation. Do these bodies adequately serve the nation? In 1956, and again in 1970, there emerged independent workers councils, and the crisis of 1976 gave birth to a host of unauthorized associations

(Workers Defense Committee, Movement for Human and Civic Rights) and periodicals. Also the Catholic Church spoke forcefully on national, not just strictly religious, issues.

DISTRIBUTION

Poland was obviously not a modern country so long as peasants, a majority of its population, lived under serfdom. The circumstances under which peasants were transformed into property owners were different in each of the three states under which the Poles lived. The solution of the distribution crisis directly influenced the resolution of the crisis of identity, and was made possible through the penetration of Polish society by foreign powers. The role of those Polish regimes that existed in parts of Polish territory was more limited.

In old Poland, the peasantry's permanent dissatisfaction frequently erupted in revolts, such as the one in the Ukraine in the late 1760s. After enactment of the Constitution of 1791, there were local disturbances when some peasants got the impression that they would no longer have to work for the landlords. During the anti-Russian and anti-Prussian insurrection of 1794 (which closely followed the second partition) its chief, Kościuszko, announced that peasants who joined the army would be freed from compulsory labor, the duties of others would be reduced, and all would be granted personal freedom. Kościuszko's measure, sabotaged by the *szlachta*, was never implemented.

In the meantime, Austria and Prussia in their respective parts of Poland had carried out a number of peasant reforms. The Austrians and Prussians thus politicized the Polish peasants by appearing as their friends and protectors. The peasant question, which was primarily a question of distribution, became a very difficult problem for the Polish national movement. It would have been logical, at least according to "nationalist logic," if the Poles who were fighting for national independence against foreigners and who considered all inhabitants of the old state, including peasants, to be compatriots, had declared that in a future Poland, peasants would enjoy full equality and would receive land free or on convenient terms. This was not done, however, because to do so would have meant the self-liquidation of the *szlachta*, the social class that was the primary force in the struggle for Poland.

The Prussians showed that it was neither necessary to abolish the *szlachta* as a class nor to carry out a revolution. A major redistribution of land and services in Prussia, which resulted in the abolition of compulsory labor and the granting of land to the peasants, began in

1807-1811 and continued through the 1820s. The abolition of serfdom removed the basic source of antagonism between the peasants and the landlords, even if small issues remained, such as the property rights of certain groups of peasants. This became apparent in Poznan during the 1848 Revolution, when Polish national unity was not broken by class conflict.

Unlike Prussia, the Duchy of Warsaw and the Kingdom of Poland did not feel compelled to carry out the emancipation of the peasantry. Even the kingdom's war for its life (1830-1831) did not induce the Polish diet to abolish compulsory labor and grant land to the peasants who were being asked to fight for their country's freedom. The peasants were taken for granted until the Galician massacre of 1846 fully disclosed the abyss that separated the patriotic *szlachta* and the intelligentsia from the peasant masses. The importance of 1846 was not lost on the Austrian and Russian governments. Later in 1846, Nicholas I issued a decree guaranteeing the peasants tenure of their land holdings in the kingdom; and during the Revolution of 1848, the Austrians took care to abolish serfdom in Galicia rather than let Polish leaders enact such a measure themselves. The 1848 decree did not specify the terms on which land would be transferred to the peasants, and that decision was left to the imperial Parliament to which both landlords and peasants could elect deputies. Over the protests of peasant deputies, the parliament decided to indemnify the landlords.

Reflection on the failure of their insurrections, especially on the experience of 1846-1848, persuaded Polish leaders to look again at the order of priorities in their struggle for independence. Until 1846, they regarded the recovery of independence as their immediate and primary task. The uprisings then taught Polish leaders that they were not strong enough to fight their oppressors, especially when a majority of Poles neither felt themselves to be nor acted as Poles.

While the recovery of national sovereignty remained the chief aim of the Polish struggle, the organizers of the anti-Russian insurrection in the early 1860s were determined to avoid the mistakes of the past. Simultaneously with the inauguration of armed struggle in January 1863, the underground "National Provisional Government" issued a decree granting the peasants ownership of all land they had been using. It also decreed that veterans of the national war (or their heirs) would receive free land after the war was over. The success of such a distribution policy depended on the degree of penetration that the revolutionary government could achieve. However, the insurgents did not convince the peasants that they were a real government; and the peasants did not rise against the Tsar, whom they regarded as their legitimate authority. The landlords, on the other hand, were not eager to implement decrees that deprived them of their property, and the insurgents were neither able nor always willing to coerce them. Throughout the revolt the Russians retained control over all the towns in Poland and gradually reasserted their authority in the countryside. St. Petersburg decided to beat the Poles with their own weapons: a sweeping decree issued under the name of the tsar granted land to the Polish peasants. The government also radically revised in favor of the peasants the terms of the 1861 emancipation, which had been carried out in the Russian Empire proper (in what the Poles regarded as their "eastern provinces"). This crisis of distribution in Poland was thus solved by the tsarist government and not by the Poles.

The reforms of 1864 did not abolish the landlord class, however, which remained an economic but also a social and cultural power in the countryside. In time noble-peasant relations became less hostile, and forcible Russification (the introduction of Russian as the official language in all offices and the abolition of all Polish schools) showed peasants and landlords alike their common interest in the defense of Polish identity.

In the long run, the 1864 reform did not satisfy the peasantry, and they sought further land redistribution. It might have seemed that their opportunity to win all the land came in 1920, when the "Red Army of Workers and Peasants" entered Poland with a Polish revolutionary committee promising the land to those who worked it. However, by then most Poles agreed that the preservation of independence was the first task, and that neither participation nor distribution should be neglected. A "Government of National Defence" was formed, headed by a politician who was a genuine peasant; his deputy was a socialist; the commander-in-chief, a former socialist; and parliament enacted in time a land reform that provided for the transfer of land to the peasants. This was also a period of wide-ranging social legislation. After the war, the land reform began to be implemented, though many felt that it was being done too slowly. In fact the "land hunger" of the peasantry could not be quenched by any land reform—an expansion of industrial jobs was needed. Thus when the communist regime announced final abolition of the landlord class in 1944, the measure had more symbolic than practical significance. By completely abolishing the landlord class, the communists removed the last surviving element of the old "nobles' Poland." The authors of the 1944 measure could claim to have completed the process, started in 1791-1794, of redistribution of land and integration of the peasantry into the nation.

The post-1945 nationalization of industry and private business in general (except peasant farming) was not felt as a major distribution crisis because the large industrial enterprises had in any case been taken over by the Germans during the war. Nazi annihilation of Jews not only radically changed the ethnic composition of Poland, but also substantially weakened the middle class. Since the early 1950s, virtually the entire economy in Poland except the farming sector has been state owned, and any tensions that have arisen have involved the state, on one hand, and the employees and consumers at large, on the other. The Polish crisis of 1953-1956, which culminated in the Poznań strike of June 1956 and the political upheaval of October 1956, although it had its origins in the distribution sphere, contained elements of other crises: it challenged the Soviet-style political regime, with its unfree elections and police terror (participation, penetration), and its cultural policies that distorted history, repressed literature and art, and isolated Poland from the West (identity).

Under socialism, where the state runs the economy, distribution is inseparable from penetration and participation and may even reflect on legitimacy. This seems to be the lesson of the events of 1970 and 1976, when sweeping price increases decreed by the government were met by mass strikes and demonstrations. An economic issue thus produced a crisis of penetration and revealed the malfunctioning of participation. (Those increases had been endorsed by parliament and official trade unions.) Fearful of a possible challenge to its legitimacy, which might in turn probe the limits of Poland's sovereignty (Czechoslovakia in 1968 was not forgotten), the regime backed down both times.

LEGITIMACY

The first modern crisis of legitimacy broke out in Poland right after the revolution of 1791. Since the institutions abolished were precisely those that had been the condition of the government's legitimacy, how was one to justify a demand for obedience made by the government that had just overthrown them? The Confederation of Targowica was illegal under the regime of the Third of May. But the regime of the Third of May was illegal under the Polish law invoked by Targowica, while measures like the Confederation were perfectly legal. The supreme political principle that the organizers of the 1791 constitution adhered to was Polish independence. Those who appealed for help to St. Petersburg regarded the old system as a supreme value, even if it had to be restored with foreign help.

Those Poles who were politically active in the nineteenth century regarded the national character of the government as the primary condition of its legitimacy. The more Polish a given regime was, the more it could expect to be accepted as legitimate, that is, entitled to claim the loyalty and obedience of its subjects. By contrast, a regime lacking Polish national character was certain to face a revolt whenever its survival was at stake. Thus the Poles in Poznań revolted against the Prussians in 1806 (during Napoleon's war with Prussia), and again in 1809 in Galicia against the Austrians. When Napoleon next attacked Russia in 1812, he expected that the Poles living under that power, mainly in Lithuania, would revolt, too, and join his forces. The response of the Lithuanian Poles was disappointing, however. Economically, they were quite comfortable in the Russian Empire, and they enjoyed broad national self-government under Russia. Napoleon was not very specific about the degree of independence and the territorial extension of the Poland he was supposed to be restoring. Only very definite commitments on this could possibly have led to a break with Alexander, who, moreover, also was said to favor a restoration of Poland under *his* scepter.

The Vienna settlement of 1815 once again redistributed Polish lands, in a manner defying summary here. Compared with the partitions of 1772-1795, there was something new in the Vienna solution of the Polish question. The powers formally agreed to respect the national character of their Polish provinces by granting them appropriate institutions, and they even undertook to maintain an economic unity of the old Commonwealth by means of special tariff and customs provisions. These provisions were unenforceable and largely remained on paper, but their importance was great nonetheless. Thus, the legitimacy of the settlement that the Poles were asked to accept rested to a high degree on recognition by the powers of Polish national rights.

These rights were most extensive in the "Kingdom of Poland" (by and large the old Duchy of Warsaw), which was attached to the Russian Empire. It was internally an independent state; only its foreign policy was conducted by the St. Petersburg government. The kingdom had its ruler (who was separately crowned in Warsaw), parliament, government, law (the *Code Civil* was retained), and army. In post-1815 Europe, its constitution was among the most liberal on the Continent. Its electorate was larger than France's, although in population France far exceeded the kingdom. Why did the Poles revolt in 1830?

The revolt had many causes, of course, but one of the more important ones was probably the dissatisfaction Poles felt with the separation of their kingdom from what they regarded as Polish lands in the east. The crisis of 1830-1831 was a crisis of legitimacy in that Poles objected to their increasing dependence on Russia, but it was intensified because they refused to accept two separate Polands under the same ruler. Perhaps a Kingdom of Poland extending to the Dnieper would have been more acceptable. Yet, one hesitates to stress too much the aspect of legitimacy in the insurrection of 1830. It is frequently overlooked that the revolt initially did not command much support. It was started by a group of young army conspirators, and the established national leadership joined in very reluctantly. A number of Polish generals and other officers simply refused to join the revolt and were killed by their young subordinates during the night of November 29, 1830. These officers had not been Muscovite collaborators but veterans of Polish national wars since the late eighteenth century. For them a revolt against the tsar-king was illegitimate. If in January 1831, the Polish parliament thought it proper formally to dethrone Nicholas and the house of Romanov, there must have been people in Poland who even after November 1830 had continued to think of Nicholas as a legitimate king.

The Poles again revolted against Russia in 1863, and as before, the actual outbreak of the insurrection was brought about by diverse causes. The continued separation of the kingdom from "the east" probably explained the general sense of discontent with the reform policies pursued by Alexander II, which were restricted to the kingdom. Despite its moderation and reforms, the regime against which the Poles rose in 1863 was much less legitimate in their eyes than that of the pre-1830 period. Even unsuccessful insurrections, such as that of 1830-1831, are useful to a nationalist movement when they force the state to adopt harsh policies (as between 1831-1856) and thus to behave as an oppressor.

Poles also unsuccessfully attempted to start an armed revolt in 1846 in Cracow (it was to spread to Austrian Galicia), and they actively participated in the revolutions of 1848 in Prussia and Austria. No doubt the Polish nationalists regarded the governments against which they rebelled as illegitimate. However, not all Poles were nationalists. As noted before, in the eyes of Polish peasants the Austrian emperor or Russian tsar was a legitimate ruler. Only after they had become free proprietors of land did the country people in Poland begin to display an interest in Polish politics and gradually find a common language and a sense of shared identity with the other classes of the nation. Many years of patient patriotic work by the Polish intelligentsia brought about a gradual integration of the "upper" and "lower" classes into a national community. If the Russian Empire provided the impetus and framework for social and economic transformation, the Poles managed to assimilate the "mobilized" masses culturally and to implant in them their conception of legitimacy. Until this happened, these masses were, at best, potentially Polish.

Legitimacy was also an internal Polish problem. The insurrection of 1863 was condemned by moderate and conservative groups in Poland. The effectiveness and usefulness of insurrectionary struggle was questioned. More relevantly from the point of view of the crisis of legitimacy, opponents asked if those who had started the latest insurrection (or those earlier ones) had in fact had the right to commit their nation to such action. Recalling the prepartition Polish custom of "liberum veto," they characterized the insurrectionist policy as its continuation in the form of "liberum conspiro." The issue was serious indeed: who was to exercise national leadership when the nation was divided between several states, some allowing legal political representation and others not? Second, what was to be the relationship between official Polish spokesmen, such as parliamentary deputies in Vienna, Berlin, or (later) in St. Petersburg, and the conspirators in the underground or in exile? Everybody felt he owed allegiance to Poland, of course, but in practice conflicts were inevitable. Thus, until Poland was restored in 1918, all Poles were subject to conflicting demands of loyalty. They had faced this dilemma in various ways, including denial of the legitimacy of foreign rule; the restoration of the state resolved the crisis of legitimacy by identifying legitimacy with the constitution and the constitutional government of the Polish Republic. After 1918 it was no longer conceivable that any segment of the Polish people would accept as legitimate a government other than that of a formally sovereign Polish state. However, Poles were prepared to question the legitimacy of their political system if they happened not to approve of its functioning. In 1922, a right-wing nationalist assassinated the first president of Poland several days after he was elected in accordance with the constitution. The killer—and many other people—regarded the president as illegitimate because he had been elected by a majority in the National Assembly that included non-Poles, while a majority of ethnic Poles in the assembly had voted for another man. The constitution said that all Polish *citizens* were equal; it did not say that a majority of ethnic Poles was to determine the election of the president. This was how some felt, however, and one of them decided to express his "liberum veto," in defiance of the constitutional process. Perhaps Piłsudski's *coup d'état* of 1926, which he justified as an attempt to "heal" a Republic that had been ill-served by a government and parliament of dishonest and incompetent men, can best be understood as the last of Polish "Confederations," an insurrection against the government in the name of a higher, extralegal principle of commonweal.

These problems of legitimacy (made even more difficult by the 1935 constitution) were still unresolved when Poland faced an unprecedented threat to its existence from the Nazis. The Poles reacted to this threat by forming a network of military and political organizations, and a vast majority of them recognized the authority of the Polish government-in-exile that had been formed in accordance with the 1935 constitution after the German conquest. Under the conditions of war, all Polish parties agreed to recognize this constitution, thus preserving the continuity of the Polish state and its identity.

Communism in Poland had traditionally been regarded by its opponents as an antinational force. Its opposition to Polish independence before and in 1918, its support of the Russians in the Polish-Soviet war of 1920, and its ties with the Third International, seemed to confirm this opinion. The Communist party of Poland functioned in the underground throughout the interwar period until 1938, when it was dissolved by the Comintern. Under Nazi occupation, it was reconstituted in 1942 as the *Polish* Workers Party (PPR). The party said that it disapproved of the old party's national nihilism, and that it favored Poland's independence. Soon thereafter the PPR organized a "provisional parliament" in the underground, an armed force separate from the regular underground army under the authority of London, and, finally, when the Soviet army entered Poland in 1944, a government. All this amounted to a revolution against the London regime carried out while the country was occupied by Germany. Both sides were getting ready to assume power in the country. The London regime had a complete administrative apparatus waiting to come out into the open as soon as the Germans left, while the communists enjoyed Soviet support. A virtual civil war raged between 1944 and 1947; and when armed resistance to the new regime ceased, it was not certain that its legitimacy had been recognized by all.

The new government at first justified its power by nationalistic arguments, not those of class: it was the only government, its spokesmen said, that had been capable of winning for Poland the western provinces (the Soviet Union would not have supported a noncommunist Poland in this matter), while those in the east would have been lost in any case. The government also appealed to all to join in reconstruction, arguing that as the survival of all Poles had been threatened in war so all, without regard to their politics, should join in the restoration of their country. It firmly proclaimed that Poland would remain independent and would never become a "Soviet republic."

It is possible that this regime, calling itself a new or people's democracy, would eventually have won acceptance as a legitimately Polish government, somewhat along the lines of the Yugoslav communist regime. However, it was forced in 1948 to denounce "nationalism" and accept a satellite status, thus reviving the argument that communism in Poland had to mean a loss of political independence to Russia. In the Polish crisis of 1953-1956 the resentment of political dependence on the Soviet Union was one of the main issues. The Poles could not accept as legitimate a government that was controlled by foreigners. Only a regime with a measure of independence from Moscow could pass the test of legitimacy in Poland, and the government after 1956 did so to some degree. Poland's participation in the Czechoslovak crisis of 1968, however, raised doubt again about the locus of the country's sovereignty, and accordingly about its government's legitimacy. The principle that Czechoslovakia's internal affairs are a matter of concern to all socialist states, and that not only the Czechs and Slovaks as a whole but even their Communist party are not allowed to run affairs as they think fit must also apply to Poland. When, following the example of Czechoslovakia and the GDR, the regime proposed in 1975-1976 to insert in the constitution an article affirming Poland's permanent alliance with the USSR, this step was perceived as legalizing the country's limited sovereignty. Public protests resulted in the adoption of a less offensive language.

Sequence

It may sound paradoxical to claim that it took the Poles about one hundred and fifty years to resolve their crisis of identity: surely the Poles, if anyone, know who they are. And yet, if one takes the resolution of the Polish identity crisis to mean the establishment of practical compatibility between the concept of Pole and that of Poland, and the formation of a state (citizenship) roughly coterminous with the nation, then the Polish crisis was not solved until after World War II.

The absence of a state for such a long period of time was the principal and obvious reason why there occurred a protracted crisis of identity in Poland. The transition from the old *szlachta* identity to an "all-class" Polish identity took place apart from (and often in conflict with) the operation of the state, that is, the processes of participation and penetration. But participation and penetration originated from foreign centers and had they proved successful the Poles would have been integrated into the states that ruled them, and would thus have lost their separate political identity.

Separation and antagonism between identity and participation/penetration prevented the development of a political definition of the Pole as a citizen of the state. It also prolonged the retention of two clearly premodern elements of Polishness (landlords as Poles, Catholics as Poles) in the modern Polish conception of nationality based on cultural or language unity. It thus became difficult, and at times impossible, for certain inhabitants of Poland to become (or be accepted as) Polish.

The separation between the (Polish) nation and (alien) state also produced a crisis of legitimacy that could not be properly resolved until after the state was restored and became virtually all Polish in population. Though both penetration and participation were conceived as a threat to Polish identity, they were not thought equally dangerous. Participation in institutions established by the foreign powers facilitated a reconciliation with foreign rule, but it also offered Poles opportunities to defend their interests. In this respect participation sometimes conflicted with penetration, the greater of the dangers to Polish nationality.

The emancipation of the peasantry was the most serious of the problems of distribution in Poland, and in all parts of the country it was solved by non-Polish governments. This helped to produce a protracted crisis of identity and legitimacy. The early (though limited) penetration of the peasant masses by the Austrians and Prussians (which preceded the distribution crisis) had brought the peasants into direct relations with non-Polish governments and weakened their dependence on the Polish landlords. The Austrians and Prussians, later also Russians, thus for a while found an effective way to counteract the force of Polish nationalism.

It seems best to view Polish developments in terms of an identity crisis being resolved while the solution of the crisis of distribution (and to a smaller degree the crises of penetration and participation) depended upon non-Polish forces. A conclusion that emerges from this survey, then, is that it is fallacious to assume that only centralizers and unifiers are the modernizers, while those who resist *Gleichschaltung* and advocate separation from larger entities and national independence are *ipso facto* reactionary, traditionalist, and isolationist.

Conclusion

Nationalist Poles wanted first to restore Polish sovereignty, thus settling the issues of legitimacy and identity. The crises of participation and penetration were to be resolved by the Poles themselves, and the solution to the distribution crisis was to become a product of the political process in a Polish state. The foreign powers (partly because they attempted to frustrate the Poles, partly because of the sequence of crises *their* states were going through) were primarily concerned with securing penetration of their Polish lands and with carrying out those changes in distribution (land grants to peasants, abolition of compulsory labor) which, among other effects, tended to legitimize their rule, in the eyes of some Poles at least. These powers did not successfully solve the crisis of participation and failed to win the Polish masses to a non-Polish political identity. The Polish people accepted Polish cultural and political identity, and participated in the political processes of Austria, Germany, and Russia *as Poles.* Consequently, their sense of the legitimacy of those states became subverted.

The prolonged incompatibility between identity, legitimacy, participation, and penetration has had a profound influence on Polish political culture. Polish writers of all persuasions agree that foreign rule (and then the German occupation in 1939-1945) reinforced the traditional Polish suspicion of the state and government. While distrustful of penetration, the Poles have always believed in meaningful political participation. And yet, the Soviet political model, adopted with modifications in 1945, treated all public institutions as the party's tools, its "conveyor belts" to "the masses"; in brief, it made participation a function of penetration. By nationalizing industry, trade, and transport, socialism expanded the functions of government and thereby further increased an imbalance between penetration and participation. In the 1970s, participation emerged as the most critical issue in Poland—just as penetration had been in the 1780s-1790s. As then, so in the 1970s, Poland's freedom to deal with its internal crisis was defined by its external ties.

Some Related Readings

Backus, Oswald P., III. "The Problem of Unity in the Polish-Lithuanian State," in Donald W. Treadgold, ed. *The Development of the USSR: An Exchange of Views*. Seattle, 1964, pp. 275-95. See also, *ibid.*, pp. 296-313, the comments by Oscar Halecki and Joseph Jakstas.

Beneš, V. L., and N.J.G. Pounds. *Poland*. New York, 1970.

Brock, Peter. *Nationalism and Populism in Partitioned Poland*. London, 1973.

Bromke, Adam. *Poland's Politics: Idealism versus Realism*. Cambridge, 1967.

Buell, Raymond L. *Poland: Key to Europe*. New York, 1939.

The Cambridge History of Poland, edited by W. F. Reddaway *et al.* 2 volumes. Cambridge, 1931 and 1950.

Dmowski, Roman. *La question polonaise*. Paris, 1909.

Dziewanowski, M. K. *The Communist Party of Poland*. 2nd revised edition, Cambridge, 1976.

———. *Poland in the Twentieth Century*. New York, 1977.

Feldman, Wilhelm. *Dzieje polskiej myśli politycznej 1864-1914*. 2nd edition, Warsaw, 1933. German translation: *Geschichte der politischen Ideen in Polen seit dessen Teilungen (1795-1914)*. Munich, 1917.

Gieysztor, Aleksander *et al. History of Poland*. Warsaw, 1968.

Halecki, Oscar. *A History of Poland*. Chicago, 1966.

Horecky, Paul L., ed. *East Central Europe: A Guide to Basic Publications*. Chicago, 1969. See part V for the literature on Polish history, the state, economy, and so on.

Kieniewicz, Stefan. *The Emancipation of the Polish Peasantry*. Chicago, 1969.

Komarnicki, Titus. *The Rebirth of the Polish Republic: A Study in the Diplomatic History of Europe, 1914-1920.* London, 1957.

Kukiel, Marian. *Dzieje Polski porozbiorowe, 1795-1921.* London, 1961.

Lepkowski, Tadeusz. *Polska narodziny nowoczesnego narodu, 1764-1870.* Warsaw, 1967.

Leslie, R. F. *Polish Politics and the Revolution of November, 1830.* London, 1956.

———. *Reform and Insurrection in Russian Poland, 1856-1865.* London, 1963.

Morrison, James F. *The Polish People's Republic.* Baltimore, 1968.

Pobóg-Malinowski, Władyslaw. *Najnowsza historia polityczna Polski, 1864-1945.* 3 volumes. Paris, 1953; and London, 1956-1960.

Polonsky, Anthony. *Politics in Independent Poland, 1921-1939.* Oxford, 1972.

Polska Akademia Nauk, Instytut Historii. *Historia Polski.* Warsaw, 1958. This is a multivolume synthesis of Polish history, some parts of which have already gone through several editions, while others are yet to be written.

Rose, William J. *The Rise of Polish Democracy.* London, 1944.

Roos, Hans. *A History of Modern Poland from the Foundation of the State in the First World War to the Present Day.* New York, 1966.

Rothschild, Joseph. *East Central Europe between the Two World Wars.* Seattle, 1974.

Serejski, Marian Henryk. *Historycy o historii.* 2 volumes. Warsaw, 1963 and 1966.

Szczepanski, Jan. *Polish Society.* New York, 1970.

Thomas, William I., and Florian Znaniecki. *The Polish Peasant in Europe and America.* 2 volumes. New York, 1958 (first ed., 1918).

Wandycz, Piotr S. *The Lands of Partitioned Poland, 1795-1918.* Seattle and London, 1974.

———. *Soviet-Polish Relations, 1917-1921.* Cambridge, 1969.

Wereszycki, Henryk. *Historia polityczna Polski w dobie popowstaniowej (1864-1918).* Warsaw, 1948.

———. "The Poles as an Integrating and Disintegrating Factor," *Austrian History Yearbook,* 3:2(1967), 287-313.

Ziffer, Bernard. *Poland: History and Historians. Three Bibliographical Essays.* New York, 1952.

CONTRIBUTORS

DAVID D. BIEN, born in Baltimore, Maryland, in 1930, is Professor of History at the University of Michigan. He received his A.B. from Washington and Lee in 1951 and his Ph.D. from Harvard in 1958. He has taught at Wesleyan, Princeton, and the Ecole des Hautes Etudes en Sciences Sociales; and has held research fellowships from the Guggenheim Foundation, ACLS, NEH, SSRC, the American Philosophical Society, and the Institute for Advanced Study. His publications include *The Calas Affair: Persecution, Toleration, and Heresy in Eighteenth-Century Toulouse* (Princeton, 1960), and "La Reaction Aristocratique avant 1789," *Annales ESC* (Nos. 1 and 2, 1974).

FOLKE DOVRING, born December 1916 in Sweden, is Professor of Land Economics at the University of Illinois in Urbana-Champaign. He was Associate Professor of Economic History at Lund University (Lund, Sweden) from 1947 to 1953 and Economist with the United Nations' Food and Agriculture Organization in Rome from 1954 to 1960. He has held a Rockefeller fellowship, 1953-54, been a consultant to several international organizations, and to the Department of Energy in Washington, D.C. His publications include three books on Swedish economic history as well as *Land and Labor in Europe* (1956, third revised edition 1965); *History as a Social Science* (1960, Japanese translation 1972); *The Optional Society* (1972); a text edition of Grotius' *Inleidinge tot de Hollandsche rechts-geleerdheid* (1952 and later editions—from text by Grotius discovered by Dovring); and numerous articles published in both scholarly journals and periodicals for the general reader in the United States and in many foreign countries.

JOHN GILLIS, born in Plainfield, New Jersey, in 1939, is Professor of History at Livingston College of Rutgers University. He is a graduate of Amherst College and Stanford University, and has taught at Stanford and Princeton. He considers himself a "generalist," having done research in both German and British history. His publications include: *The Prussian Bureaucracy in Crisis, 1840-1860; Youth and History*; and *The Development of European*

Society, 1770-1870. He is currently working on a history of marriage in nineteenth- and twentieth-century England.

RAYMOND GREW, born in San Jose, California, in 1930, is Professor of History at the University of Michigan, Director of the Center for Western European Studies there, and co-editor of the international quarterly, *Comparative Studies in Society and History*. He did his undergraduate and graduate work at Harvard; has taught at Brandeis, Princeton, and the Ecole des Hautes Etudes en Sciences Sociales, and has held Fulbright and Guggenheim Fellowships. His book, *A Sterner Plan for Italian Unity* (Princeton 1963) won the Unità d'Italia Prize, and his most recent publications include *The Western Experience*, written with others (New York, 1974; revised edition, 1978) and "Modernization and its Discontents," *American Behavioral Scientist* (1977).

J. ROGERS HOLLINGSWORTH, born in Anniston, Alabama, in 1932, is Professor of History and Chairperson of the Program in Comparative World History at the University of Wisconsin (Madison). He presently teaches and does research on comparative public policy, and he has done research and/or taught in Europe, Africa, and Asia. He has held postdoctoral fellowships from the American Council of Learned Societies, the German Marshall Fund, the National Endowment for the Humanities, the Commonwealth Fund, the Woodrow Wilson Center for International Scholars, and the American-Scandinavian Foundation. His publications include *The Whirligig of Politics; The Politics of Nation and State Building in America* (editor); *The Integration of History and the Social Sciences: Perspectives on American Cities*; and *Social Theory and Social Policy* (editor).

STANLEY G. PAYNE, born in Denton, Texas, in 1934, is Professor of History at the University of Wisconsin (Madison). He received his Ph.D. from Columbia and has taught there and at the Universities of Minnesota and of California at Los Angeles. He has held fellowships from the Guggenheim Foundation, the Social Science Research Council, and the American Philosophical Society. His most recent books include, *A History of Spain and Portugal* (Madison, 1973); *Basque Nationalism* (Reno, 1975); and *Politics and Society in Twentieth Century Spain*, which he edited (New York, 1976).

WALTER McKENZIE PINTNER, born in Yonkers, New York, in 1931, is Associate Professor of Russian History at Cornell University. He received his B.A. and M.A. from the University of Chicago, and an M.A. and Ph.D. from Harvard. He has served as an Intelligence Research Specialist for the Department of State and been an Exchange Scholar at Leningrad State University on three occasions, a Fellow at the Kennan Institute for Advanced Russian Studies, Woodrow Wilson International Center for Scholars, Smithsonian Institution. He is the author of *Russian Economic Policy under Nicholas I* (Ithaca, 1967); "The Social Characteristics of the Nineteenth-Century Russian Bureaucracy," *The Slavic Review* (1970); "The Russian Higher Civil Service on the Eve of the 'Great Reforms,' " *Journal of Social History* (1975).

ROMAN SZPORLUK, born in Grzymalow, Tarnopol, Poland (now Ukrainian SSR), in 1933, is Professor of History at the University of Michigan. He received his college education in Lublin, Poland, and did his graduate work at Oxford and Stanford. He is the editor of *Russia in World History: Selected Essays* (by M. N. Pokrovskii, 1970) and of *The Influence of East Europe and the Soviet West on the USSR* (1975). He has contributed chapters in *Handbook of Major Soviet Nationalities* (edited by Zev Katz, 1975); *Ukraine in the Seventies* (edited by Peter J. Potichnyj, 1975); and *Poland and Ukraine: Past and Present* (forthcoming); and has published articles in *The Slavic Review*, *Survey*, *Journal of International Affairs*, and other periodicals.

KEITH THOMAS, born at Wick, Glamorgan, in 1933, is Fellow and Tutor of St. John's College and Reader in Modern History in the University of Oxford. He was Visiting Professor at Louisiana State University in 1970 and Visiting Fellow at Princeton University in 1978. He has published many essays on the social and intellectual history of early modern England, and is the author of *Religion and the Decline of Magic* (1971).

ARISTIDE R. ZOLBERG, born in Brussels in 1931, is Professor of Political Science and in the College at the University of Chicago.

He received his A.B. degree at Columbia University, his M.A. at Boston University, and his Ph.D. at the University of Chicago. The holder of a Ford Foreign Area Fellowship, he worked initially on contemporary Africa, and his publications include *One-Party Government in the Ivory Coast* (Princeton, 1964 and 1969) and *Creating Political Order: The Party-States of West Africa* (Rand McNally, 1966). He subsequently shifted the focus of his research to the political transformations of Western Europe in the nineteenth and twentieth centuries. He is currently working on the comparative study of international migration policies and of ethnic regionalisms in Europe and North America.

INDEX

LIBRARY OF CONGRESS CATALOGING IN PUBLICATION DATA
Main entry under title:

Crises of political development in Europe and the United States.

(Studies in political development ; 9)
Includes index.
1. Comparative government—Addresses, essays, lectures.
2. Europe—Politics and government—Addresses, essays, lectures. 3. United States—Politics and government—Addresses, essays, lectures. I. Grew, Raymond.
II. Bien, David D. III. Series.
JF51.C67 320.3'094 78-51166
ISBN 0 691 07598 0
ISBN 0-691-02183-X pbk.